Escape From Sobibor

Richard Rashke

Escape From Sobibor

With a New Afterword

University of Illinois Press

Urbana and Chicago

The author is grateful for permission to quote from "No Time for Tears" by Thomas Blatt, which appeared in *Santa Barbara News and Review,* December 1977; *The Song of the Murdered Jewish People* by Yitzhak Katznelson, translated by Noah H. Rosenbloom and published in Israel by Beit Lohamei Haghetaot, 1980; *Story of a Secret State* by Jan Karski, published by Houghton Mifflin Company, 1944; and *Inferno Em Sobibor: A Traagédia de um Adolescente Juden* by Stanislaw Szmajzner, published in Brazil by Edições Bloch, 1968.

Maps by Paula Kaufmann

Manufactured in the United States of America
P 9 8 7 6 5

This book is printed on acid-free paper.

Library of Congress Cataloging-in-Publication Data
Rashke, Richard L.
Escape from Sobibor / Richard Rashke.
p.   cm.
Previously published: Boston : Houghton Mifflin, 1982. With a new afterword.
Includes bibliographical references.
ISBN 0-252-06479-8 (pbk.)
1. Sobibor (Poland : Concentration camp) 2. Holocaust, Jewish (1939-1945)—Poland. I. Title.
D805.P7R33   1995
940.53'1503924—dc20   94-47590
                                              CIP

Contents

Illustrations follow page 182

for
the more than two hundred and fifty thousand
who did not escape from Sobibor

to
Guy

Introduction

ALMOST EVERYONE knows of Auschwitz and Dachau. But few people have ever heard about Sobibor, although the biggest prisoner escape of World War II took place there, on October 14, 1943. Why history has been so silent is no mystery.

In 1945, the Allies captured a mountain of German documents, bequeathing to historians an incomparable war library. Among those millions of pages, however, were only three short documents about Sobibor, part of Heinrich Himmler's Operation Reinhard, the code name for three top secret death camps in eastern Poland.

The death camps — Sobibor, Belzec, and Treblinka — were quite different from Dachau, a prison, and Auschwitz, a concentration camp with gas chambers for those too weak to work. They were giant death machines. Every Jew sent there was to be gassed within twenty-four hours, with the exception of between a hundred and six hundred Jews chosen to maintain the camp. They, too, were destined to be killed when Operation Reinhard was completed, if they lasted that long.

The Polish Central Commission for German War Crimes estimated that the Nazis gassed a minimum of 1.65 million Jews — about one quarter of all those killed in the Holocaust — in these three death camps. Sobibor, where more than two hundred and fifty thousand died, was the smallest, and Himmler's best-kept secret.

If the Germans did not leave enough documents about Sobibor to satisfy historians, they did leave living records — some thirty survivors scattered around the world. I interviewed eighteen of them in the United States, the Soviet Union, Brazil, Poland, and Israel. On one level, most were reluctant to talk about Sobibor because of the pain that comes from reliving a personal hell. But on another, most were eager to have a professional writer tell their story "for their grandchildren." I was somewhat surprised, for I am not Jewish, and I thought that fact might create an atmosphere of distrust, discouraging openness and honesty. On the contrary, I got the distinct impression that I was welcomed as a writer precisely because I was not a Jew.

Most of the survivors I interviewed vividly remembered aspects of the Sobibor story, almost as if they could still see, hear, and feel it. Although they all contributed something to this book, three emerged as extremely important. Alexander (Sasha) Pechersky was co-leader of the escape from Sobibor. He wrote a short account of the revolt soon after the war. I found and interviewed him in the Soviet Union. Stanislaw (Shlomo) Szmajzner, a key planner in the escape, lived in Sobibor almost from the day it opened to the day of the escape. He wrote a book in Portuguese about his experiences in the camp. I found and interviewed him in Goiania, Brazil. Thomas (Toivi) Blatt, who spent six months in Sobibor, made it a point to know everything he could about the camp while he was a prisoner and after he escaped. He wrote a diary, parts of which have been published as articles. I found and interviewed him in Santa Barbara.

The research and writing of *Escape From Sobibor* presented two predictable problems. As everyone knows, eyewitness accounts of almost anything vary. Some are even contradictory. Sobibor was no exception. The basic story of the camp, the uprising, and the escape emerged with a great deal of freshness. But there were some contradictions because survivors either embellished details over the years, and then accepted the exaggerations as facts, or confused rumors with reality. As a researcher, I sifted through the stories, discarding what I felt were embellishments, and I analyzed the differing versions of an incident, deciding for myself which was more or most accurate. I explain my important choices in the notes at the end of the book.

Dialogue posed the second problem. The reader will note that some portions of the book are rich in dialogue and others are not. The reason for the unevenness is that for some sections I was able to draw on books, articles, diaries, and interviews with people who had excellent memories; for others, either I was unable to find eyewitnesses to the events I was describing, or those I found had poor recall. The end notes list my sources by chapter.

It stands to reason that much of this book and its dialogue is a memoir — a compilation of recollections of incidents and conversations as people remembered them happening almost forty years before. The dialogue, therefore, is as accurate as their memories. Furthermore, all of the dialogue came to me through the filter of translation. Eyewitnesses heard or spoke the original in one language and gave it to me in another, often through an interpreter. Most of the time, the oral translations were rough and grammatically incorrect, as interpreters arbitrarily switched from direct to indirect quotations. I handled these problems as best I could, using my judgment and rendering the dialogue into colloquial English.

In sum, I am certain that the dialogue in this book accurately describes who said what to whom, and that it is reasonably faithful to the words that were spoken.

I owe a debt of gratitude to Thomas Blatt, the first survivor I contacted when I began to work on *Escape From Sobibor*. He did more than break the ice for me. During the sixteen months I researched and wrote the book, I interviewed him for more than ten days. He shared his diary with me, served as my Yiddish interpreter in Brazil, Russian interpreter in the Soviet Union, and Polish interpreter in Poland. He guided me through the Sobibor campsite, and reviewed for accuracy the first draft of this book. I can only imagine the emotional pain and fatigue he suffered as I dug and picked and probed, not always with gentleness and sensitivity.

Mr. Blatt is one of a handful of Jewish survivors from Izbica, Poland, which once had a thriving Jewish *shtetl* of four thousand. He dedicates his work on *Escape From Sobibor* to his mother, father, and brother, who were murdered there, and to the Jews of Izbica who, unlike him, did not escape.

Washington, D.C.
March 1982

ix

Sobibor, Poland
October 14–19, 1943

SS SERGEANT KARL FRENZEL waited until most of the shooting was over, then tried to call Security Police headquarters in Lublin, twenty-five miles away. But the phones were dead, and the officer in charge of Sobibor was missing.

Frenzel walked through the main gate, crossed the tracks to the small public railway station, and handed a message to the Polish telegraph operator: JEWS REVOLTED . . . SOME ESCAPED . . . SOME SS OFFICERS, NON-COMS, FOREIGN GUARDS DEAD . . . SOME JEWS STILL INSIDE THE CAMP . . . SEND HELP.

The Security Police dispatched SS and police task forces to Sobibor to round up the Jews still trapped behind the fences; they also ordered the army to chase those who had escaped and the Luftwaffe to buzz the pine forests. The next day, October 15, the Security Police sent the following report to Berlin:

On October 14, 1943, at about 5:00 P.M., a revolt of Jews in the SS camp Sobibor, twenty-five miles north of Chelm. They overpowered the guards, seized the armory, and, after an exchange of shots with the camp garrison, fled in unknown directions. Nine SS men murdered, one SS man missing, two foreign guards shot to death.

Approximately 300 Jews escaped. The remainder were shot to death or are now in camp. Military police and armed forces were notified immediately and

1

took over security of the camp at about 1:00 A.M. The area south and southwest of Sobibor is now being searched by police and armed forces.

The SS ferreted out the 159 Jews still inside Sobibor. A few had pistols and fought back; the others hid wherever they could. When the Jews were executed in the woods and buried, the SS dismantled the gas chambers, razed the buildings they didn't want to move, and planted pine saplings where the barracks had once stood.

The Nazis left Sobibor — the forest of the owls — as they had found it. In the center of what had been the camp stood the foresters' tower, reaching a hundred feet above the pines. And across the tracks from the public train station sat the old post office, where the Sobibor Kommandant had lived.

On October 19 — five days after the Jews of Sobibor had escaped — SS chief Heinrich Himmler halted Operation Reinhard. The Red Army was less than three hundred miles from Sobibor, and the evidence had to be destroyed before they found it. Besides, Operation Reinhard had been a complete success. In twenty months, it alone had killed almost two million Jews. (Not even the Nazis knew the exact number; they did not keep records.) And there were no more Jews left to murder in the ghettos of eastern Poland, Latvia, Estonia, Lithuania, White Russia, and the Ukraine.

But Himmler couldn't destroy all the evidence. When the Russians crossed the Bug River into Poland and pushed past Sobibor, a few miles away, the evidence, hidden in the barns and fields, or fighting with the partisans, was among the first to hug them.

The Prisoners

Chapter 1

Spring 1942

STRETCHING to look taller than he was, the boy stood next to the men in the open field surrounded by a barbed-wire fence, seven feet high. It was a sunny May afternoon, and after the ride in a boxcar smelling from urine and death, the air was a perfume of spring and pine. Painted over the gate in foot-high black letters was SS SONDERKOMMANDO, and the sign perched on white stilts in front of the railway shack across the tracks said SOBIBOR. The boy had never heard of Sobibor, nor had he any idea of what kind of special SS camp it was. He looked around.

Carved out of the thick pine forest along the main railway line, Sobibor looked peaceful and quiet. Although the German and Ukrainian guards were carrying leather whips, pistols, and rifles, the boy tried to convince himself that Sobibor was just another work camp for Jews. In the middle of the camp, a foresters' watchtower rose a hundred feet into the clear spring sky, and across the tracks, behind the wooden station, sat a half-dozen woodcutters' cottages.

The boy was only fifteen years old, barely five feet tall, thin as an alley cat, and just as wary. Afraid to turn his head, he looked as far to the left as he could and saw the women and children scramble into a column, four abreast, and march through a huge gate, braided with pine branches so that no one could see in or out. The sign next to the gate read SHOWERS. He tried to catch a glimpse of his mother and older sister, but they were lost among the shuffling thousands. The gate swung closed,

5

and the Nazis turned to the men and the boys who tried to pass as men.

"Line up," shouted a tall SS officer with lanky arms that hung almost to his knees. "Four across."

The boy gave a last furtive look around for his father, from whom he had been separated after the Ukrainians drove them out of the boxcar with whips, but he couldn't see him as the men pushed and shoved into the semblance of a formation. He grabbed the hands of his brother, nephew, and cousin, lest he lose them, too, and have to face alone the thatched gate and whatever was behind it. Hand in hand, the boy and his family formed a row in the long column.

"Stay together, no matter what," he whispered to them. "Promise."

They nodded in fright.

The tall Nazi walked down the line, peering at faces as if he were searching for someone he knew. To the boy, he looked like a black giant, dressed as he was in a black uniform perfectly pressed, a black cap with a silver skull — the Death's Head, the SS called it — shiny, knee-high black leather boots, and a black whip curled in his hand like a snake.

"Tailors, shoemakers, painters," the tall Nazi called. "Forward."

The boy began to panic. What should he do? Who would get better treatment? Those who stepped forward or those who stayed in line? What would happen if he lied and said he was a tailor? As the Nazi approached him, the boy fought his fear, as he had done so often during the past three years, and heeded the feeling churning inside him, making him say and do things for reasons he didn't understand.

"I'm a goldsmith," he shouted above the other voices. "Do you need a goldsmith?"

Before the SS officer could say a word, the boy reached into the knapsack at his feet, and whipped out a wallet with a monogram of gold on it. "See?"

He offered the Nazi the wallet. "I made this."

The boy's initials gleamed in the late afternoon sun, finely crafted and smooth as ice on the lake.

"You? This?"

"Yes," the boy snapped back, afraid to allow a second to slip between the question and his answer. "These are my tools." He dipped back into his sack and fished out a kerosene burner, charcoal, pliers, and chisels.

"Out, then," the Nazi said. "Over there. We'll see."

"I have three brothers who are goldsmiths, too," the boy lied. He was surprised at his own boldness, for his brother, cousin, and nephew hardly

6

knew the difference between gold and brass. The Nazi quickly looked over the three youngsters and nodded to them to join the boy.

"My father," the boy asked. "What about my father?"

"Don't worry." There was a note of kindness in the Nazi's voice. "Tomorrow . . . Sit. I'll be back."

The boy hugged his tools. They had saved his life before, and if he had made the right decision today, they would help him again. He had learned to spot the glimmer of greed in a Nazi's eye; the tall SS man had that glint.

The huge gate swung open, and the column of men and boys marched through, as the women and children had done. Then it slammed closed. A Ukrainian in a drab gray-green uniform and black soldier's cap stood guard, rifle pinned across his chest. The boy wasn't sure whether the "Blackie," as the Jews called every Ukrainian auxiliary, was there to keep people in or out.

While the "goldsmiths" waited for the tall Nazi, another lad sat down beside them, and the boy became nervous. It was important to obey the Nazis exactly, or they could turn on you like German shepherds.

"Beat it," he told the newcomer. "*We* were told to sit here. Alone!"

"No," the newcomer said. "I paint signs, and the big Nazi told me to sit here, too."

The boy accepted the sign painter reluctantly; he would be just one more risk, one more person to say a wrong word, to do something to anger the tall SS man. But the boy had no choice, so he sat as straight as he could and waited. Within an hour, some Ukrainian guards came back to the field and marched a group of shoemakers and tailors to another part of the camp, but the tall Nazi did not return. The boy waited, his fear pushing his imagination to see behind that huge gate. Finally, as darkness began to paint the forest black, the big gate swung open and the tall Nazi walked through. He was alone. Before he closed the gate, the boy caught a glimpse of a long corridor that seemed to go nowhere, a tube lined with barbed-wire fences thatched with pine branches.

"Come," the tall SS man said. He led them to a pine barracks with a tarpaper roof, slanted slightly for the heavy winter snow, and pushed the door open with his boot. "Inside. Stay! No one else in." He slammed the wooden door behind him and left.

Except for a patch of dusk streaming through the narrow, high window, it was as dark as a tunnel. A shadow moved in the corner of the long building.

7

"Who is it?" The boy tried to scream, but only a hoarse whisper came from deep inside his dry throat. "Who's there?"

The shadow moved again. "I'm a Jew, too," said a timid voice that quivered like tin. "I'm a sign painter. Who are you?"

They sat in the dark on the bare wooden floor — the two young sign painters, the boy, and his brother, cousin, and nephew. They were tired, thirsty, and hungry, but their tension and fear drove away the fatigue, hunger, and thirst. They told one another where they had come from, what had happened to them on the way to Sobibor, how they had been chosen from the long line of men. But no matter where they began their whisperings, huddled in the corner as far from the door as they could crawl, they always came back to the gate with the sign SHOWERS and the corridor behind it leading nowhere.

The sign painter with the timid voice said he had been sitting in the barracks for a whole day. He described how a crew of Jews had come back through that gate with brooms, rakes, and carts, and how they had cleaned from the field the toys, caps, and scraps of paper that littered it, even raking up the footprints in the sandy soil. It must be some kind of trick, he said. The Nazis must want each trainload to think it is the first. But why? The question hung over them, and they dared not speak an answer.

The tall Nazi with long arms kicked open the door. "Goldsmith," he ordered. "Take a bucket. Follow me."

The boy crossed the yard with the Nazi, half-running like a child at its father's heels to keep up with his huge strides. They entered a storeroom piled almost to the ceiling with cheeses, salamis, canned sardines, and tins of milk.

"Whatever you want," the Nazi said.

The boy had never seen so much food before in all of his fifteen years. The musty smell of cheddar and garlic was enough to drive him mad, but he fought the urge to dive into the pile and tear at a piece of soft cheese. He suspected that the Nazi, who barked out words, rather than sentences, with a thick Austrian accent, was trying to trick him.

"No, thank you," the boy said. "I'm not hungry."

"Better eat." The Nazi laughed. "A lot of work tomorrow."

Sensing a veiled threat in the Nazi's voice that tomorrow he would be on trial and that he had better be a good goldsmith, the boy picked the longest salami he could see. The Nazi took him into the kitchen next to the storeroom, where a cook filled his bucket with coffee and gave him a loaf of fresh bread.

As best they could in the dark, the boy and his friends divided the bread

8

and salami. If they had had a scale, they would have weighed the portions to make sure each got equal shares. The bread, they devoured; the salami, they chewed very slowly, as if they were eating a bony fish. But no one could drink the coffee. Someone had used the bucket to clean paintbrushes, and the coffee tasted of turpentine.

They talked late into the night, and when the others finally had drifted into a restless sleep filled with dreams of boxcars, train rides, and tall Nazis, the boy lay on the wooden floor and stared into the patch of moonlit darkness framed by the window. Next to him the second sign painter, who had arrived the day before, lay shaking.

Questions rolled in the boy's mind like marbles, and the faces of his mother, sister, and father flashed before his eyes.

What was behind that gate?

What did "showers" mean?

Where were they — his family?

Would the tall Nazi march him through the gate in the morning?

When dawn filtered through the window, the boy had no answers.

Chapter 2

Spring 1942

THE BARRACKS was seventy feet long and forty feet wide, with beams running along the ceiling like the ribs of a wooden whale. It was empty. The boy, Shlomo Szmajzner, crept to the door and looked through the cracks, then cautiously peeked out the window. The soft spring morning was fenced in by barbed wire and ringed with watchtowers — tiny pine huts on stilts twenty feet from the ground, with Ukrainian guards inside holding Mausers. With their ladders gently sloping to the yard below and their slanted tarpapered roofs, the watchtowers looked like clubhouses where little boys puffed cigarettes and talked about little girls. The fence, guarded by Ukrainians, was seven feet high, and its pine posts were so perfectly spaced, they looked as if an architect had placed them.

Two hundred yards straight ahead from the barracks where Shlomo watched, the railway tracks cut a ribbon through the pine forest. A switching track broke from the main line, and from the switching track a spur, long enough to hold ten boxcars, jutted into the camp. Inside Sobibor, next to the spur and the main gate, stood a pretty two-story woodcutter's cottage, surrounded by May flowers and neatly trimmed shrubs. Shlomo could see some Germans with Finnish submachine guns entering and leaving the house.

Standing alone in what looked like the center of the camp were several sheds, a camouflaged fence, and the gate through which his mother, sister, and father had walked. The boy strained, half-expecting to hear his mother's

10

call, "Shlomo, Shlomo," or his sister's laugh drift across the yard on the thin spring air. But there wasn't a sound, and if the yard had not been covered with litter, no one would ever know that two thousand Jews had passed through the gate just the day before. How could so many Jews be so quiet, Shlomo wondered.

Three pine-boarded barracks identical with his stood close by, like new barns waiting for the cows. Other than Ukrainians tramping across the yards and an occasional German with a guard dog, the camp seemed empty and still.

The reality of Sobibor grabbed Shlomo with pincers of steel. He had ridden into a barbed-wire trap, and with the fences, the Mausers, the dogs, and submachine guns, there was no way out for a fifteen-year-old goldsmith with a kerosene lamp and charcoal, pliers and chisels. Despair glued him to the windows.

As he watched, without a whistle or a warning the huge camouflaged gate creaked open, and fifty to sixty men and boys shuffled out and began to clean the yard. Shlomo's heart pounded when he recognized a tall, thin boy. Shlomo stared at his friend, Avi, hoping his intensity would draw the boy's eyes up to the window. Avi bent over his rake like a robot, but when his Ukrainian guard wasn't looking, he stole a glance at the barracks as if he knew Shlomo would be there. Avi nodded almost imperceptibly, then went back to raking litter. When the yard was clean and the footprints smoothed away with brooms of pine branches, Avi disappeared into the tube leading nowhere.

Taking turns spying through the window, the boys waited for the tall Nazi. The sight of the Jews cleaning the yard had given them a sense of hope, because if there were fifty or sixty, there must be more. But where were they all working? Why was it so quiet? Why didn't more Jews cross the yard?

At noon, the Nazi with the long arms kicked open the door of the hut. The boys leaped to their feet like German soldiers.

"What do you need to work?" the Nazi asked the goldsmith.

"Just tables and chairs," Shlomo said. The painters nodded, too frightened to open their mouths. The six boys followed the Nazi into one of the sheds packed with tables and chairs, clothes, linens, and blankets tossed into careless piles. Shlomo struggled to make one decision at a time, to focus all his energy on this one situation, for he hadn't yet figured out how he would hide from the SS the fact that his brother, Moses, his nephew, Jankus, and his cousin, Nojeth, were not goldsmiths. He selected a table and chair for himself and one for each of them.

11

"Our clothes are filthy," Shlomo told the SS man. "And we don't have beds."

"All the blankets and clothes you need," the Nazi said. "No beds. Not even for us."

They carried their loot back to the barracks. "Stay inside," the tall Nazi warned them. "If a Ukrainian calls, don't go. Understand? Stay away from the fences. Understand?" He left them without an explanation.

In the clean pants and shirts and new high leather boots, the boys felt better than they had for a long time. Perhaps the Sobibor Nazis were different. Maybe they weren't so bad after all.

Within an hour, the Nazi returned with another German in a white jacket. "The Kommandant," the tall Nazi said. He eased the door closed behind him.

His name was Captain Franz Stangl, he said. He pulled up a chair and ordered Shlomo to sit across the table from him.

Captain Stangl was impeccably dressed. His white coat was buttoned from top to bottom, his gray slacks pressed and creased, and above a film of yard dust, the top of his boots gleamed. He was thirty years old, thin and wiry. From under the silver skull on his SS cap, light brown hair brushed the tops of his ears and there was the hint of a dimple under his lower lip. In his right hand, he carried a pair of cloud-white gloves. He spoke in soft, passionless tones and smiled easily. To Shlomo, he had the polished elegance of a university professor torn from his classroom by the war and planted in the sandy soil of eastern Poland.

Captain Stangl explained that, as Kommandant, he had unquestioned authority and that in his hand he held the power of life and death. He asked the boy how he could possibly make jewelry without a workshop, and how someone so young could already be an artisan. His questions were friendly, even courteous, and Shlomo forgot for a moment that Captain Stangl was a Nazi.

Shlomo spread his tools on the table. To melt the gold, he explained, he used a small kerosene burner and a piece of charcoal. The burner looked like Aladdin's lamp, with a wick poking out its long nose. Holding the kerosene lamp in one hand, the charcoal in the other, and a glass tube in his mouth, he blew the top of the charcoal into a glowing ember. Then, Shlomo explained, he put the gold in a hole in the center of the charcoal. When it melted, he poured it into the mold he had made. Sometimes, he said, if he was not in a hurry and he had some lime, he would cover his hand with it so that he could work more comfortably. But it wasn't necessary, since his hand was used to the heat of the charcoal and molten gold.

12

Shlomo showed Captain Stangl how he made the mold out of wire, and how he placed it on one piece of waxed sheet metal, and then covered it with another. After screwing the two pieces tightly together, he poured the gold into the mold. Once the basic design had set, he carved the jewelry with chisels.

"It's very simple," he told the Kommandant with pride, "but it works."

Captain Stangl was fascinated; he questioned Shlomo about each tool, almost as if he were giving the boy an exam. But the little goldsmith answered every question with great detail and authority, all the while hoping the Nazi would not toss a question at his "brothers." When he seemed satisfied, Captain Stangl told Shlomo he wanted a gold monogram. And using the tabletop as a blackboard, he traced with his delicate finger the design he wanted.

Shlomo had hidden some gold in his knapsack, but hardly enough to make the large monogram Captain Stangl wanted. He had been saving the gold for an emergency, perhaps even to buy his life. He sensed that this was an emergency.

"I have *some* gold," he said. "But not — "

"I'll send over whatever you need," Captain Stangl said.

The German seemed so friendly and gentle that Shlomo decided to press his luck. Ever since he had seen the women and children walk through the huge gate, he had been thinking of little else but his mother, father, and sister. He felt a vague stab of pain as he tried to convince himself that they were well. But now, in the presence of the kind German, he had a foreboding that seemed out of place, a doubt that nagged with the stubbornness of a deer fly.

"My parents and sister came here with me," he told the captain. "I miss them. Can I see them?"

The Kommandant listened to Shlomo with his head down, as if he didn't want to look the boy in the eye. "Don't worry." The Nazi's voice was fatherly. "They're fine. Don't be afraid or upset. They just went to take a shower. They got new clothes and are working in the fields, happy and well. But they do have to work harder than you do . . ." He paused. "You boys will have everything you need. Tools, material, plenty of good food, beds. And I promise on my word as an officer, soon you'll join your parents."

Captain Stangl so tranquilized the boy that a sense of relief washed over him. Maybe Sobibor wasn't such a bad place, he tried to convince himself. The Nazis were humane, and he had clothes and food. He would work in relative comfort. There were promises. Soon he'd be with his father and

13

mother and Ryka. Hadn't Captain Stangl promised that on his word as an officer? Shlomo didn't doubt him, for the Kommandant was sincere and compassionate, and the boy wanted to believe him.

Captain Stangl sent Shlomo a handful of scarred gold rings, some so precious they looked like heirlooms, and the tall Nazi brought him a slightly used, but more complete, set of goldsmith tools. Shlomo didn't dare ask himself where the gold and chisels came from. He concentrated on embossing *F. S.* on an intricate gold setting.

Shlomo stationed Moses, Jankus, and Nojeth at their tables, gave them the tools he wasn't using, and told them to pretend to be busy. It will be a life or death performance, he warned. There's no telling what the tall Nazi would do if he knew they weren't smiths.

Shlomo worked on the Kommandant's monogram with more zeal than on any piece of jewelry he had ever crafted. He sensed that to survive here, as in the ghetto, he'd have to make himself indispensable — such a valuable little Jew that the Germans would not be tempted to trade him in for an older, more experienced artist. He hammered until dark that second day at Sobibor, numb from the work, the pressure, and the emotion.

After a huge meal — as much bread, cheese, salami, milk, coffee, and sardines as he could eat — Shlomo slipped into a heavy sleep, clutching Stangl's promise. By dawn, he was back at work in the other end of the barracks. Like a musician, he performed all day long for a stream of Nazis who dropped in to watch the little Jewish goldsmith. And whenever there was an audience, Shlomo slowed down to make his work look more demanding than it actually was, so that the Nazis would forget the other boys, scraping and banging at their tables.

Late the next morning, his third day in Sobibor, Shlomo sent word to Captain Stangl that the monogram was finished. The Kommandant rushed to the barracks, and when he saw the gold *F. S.* carved on the intricate setting, just as he had ordered it, he acted like a greedy child. "Magnificent! Magnificent!" he said as he turned the piece in his hand. "Just beautiful."

Shlomo beamed. Not only was he proud of his work and pleased that he had executed the Kommandant's design to perfection, but he had passed the test. No Nazi at Sobibor would ever doubt again that he, Shlomo Szmajzner, was a master goldsmith.

The tall Nazi was the next SS man to order a gold monogram — *G. W.*, for Gustav Wagner. And the other Germans who had watched Shlomo work dropped in to congratulate him and to ask for rings and bracelets for wives and sweethearts, for monograms and good luck charms.

The boys savored their first performance. They were now working for

Sobibor's top brass. All they had to do was please every Nazi as they had Captain Stangl, and their lives would get even better. There would be a steady flow of work, for when it came to gold, they knew, there would be no end to greed, no end to wives and sweethearts, brothers and sisters, no end to children and friends, each of whom would be delighted with a piece of jewelry made by a little Jew with a kerosene burner and charcoal.

Maybe he would even see his father, mother, and sister soon, Shlomo thought. Maybe some Sabbath, Captain Stangl would allow him to go for a walk in the village. Maybe soon he'd be free. Maybe . . .

But first, there was a delicate problem. Whose jewelry should he make next? It was obvious that he'd have to satisfy Sobibor's most powerful Nazi after the Kommandant, but who was that? And what would happen if he made a wrong choice?

Deep down, Shlomo knew that he'd make the right choice. He was a survivor. And he had lived this long while others died precisely because he had made the right choice over and over again.

Chapter 3

Spring 1942

SHLOMO WAS BORN in Pulawy-on-the-Vistula, fifty miles west of Sobibor. The story of his family was not unique.

Shlomo's shtetl was isolated from the Polish Catholic community that surrounded it. The Jews spoke Yiddish better than they did Polish. The men wore beards and caftans; the women kept their heads covered. Jews married Jews, sold their bread and meat mostly to other Jews; their children played with Jewish children, attended schools run by the Jewish community or went to both the town school and Hebrew school.

But lessons bored Shlomo; it was goldsmithing that fired his imagination. Whenever he could sneak away from his father, he sat in the shop of Herzl, the master goldsmith of Pulawy, watching for hours the artist at his bench. At ten, Shlomo made a deal. If his father would permit him to serve as an apprentice to Herzl, he'd work extra hard in school. By the time he was twelve, Shlomo was a qualified goldsmith.

When the Germans invaded Poland in September 1939 and occupied Pulawy, Shlomo begged his parents to flee to Russia, where, he had heard, the Jews suffered less. But his parents refused to go. What about the house? Who would watch it for them? And the family business — how could they just give it up?

Over the pleading of his parents, Shlomo stuffed his clothes and tools into a knapsack and boarded a train east. He was thirteen years old.

Shlomo tried to pass as an Aryan, because in 1939 the Germans had

16

forbidden Jews to travel without a special permit. But the Poles on the train denounced him, and the Germans forced him off. After weeks of hitchhiking and riding trains, Shlomo reached the Bug River — the border between Poland and Russia — and sneaked across. A Jewish jeweler gave him a job, and the boy had plenty to eat. He was free.

Before the winter was out, Shlomo was homesick for his mother and father, brother and sister. The Russians caught him trying to cross the Bug into Poland. After questioning him for hours, they let him go home. If the crazy little Jew wanted to live under the Germans, they said, that was his problem. Once across the river, he hitched a wagon ride to the nearest train station, trying to look as Polish as he could. But no sooner had the train lurched to a start, than a Pole pointed at him. "A Jew!" he shouted. "A Jew!"

The Germans dragged him off to the nearest Gestapo station. "Are you?" the agent asked.

"Yes," Shlomo said. He couldn't deny his heritage, and he didn't know that while he was in Russia, the Germans had issued a decree requiring all Jews to wear a Star of David.

"Take off your boots." The German pushed Shlomo out the door. "Stand here until I come back." Then, checking his watch, the Nazi went inside.

Shlomo knew he'd get frostbite, possibly lose his legs, if he just stood in the snow and the freezing wind, so he began to run in place, as if he were warming up for a soccer game. Soon the sweat was dripping into his eyes. The Gestapo agent came back in a half-hour, blew his whistle, and let him go, with a stiff warning to wear the Star of David in the future.

A Jewish tailor carried Shlomo to his home, bathed his feet in cold water, rubbed them with alcohol, and fed him. Shlomo stayed a week, until he was rested and could walk again. He had heard that the Nazis had driven the Jews of Pulawy from their homes — "resettlement," they called it — and that his family was living in Wolwonice.

As he approached the edge of the Jewish ghetto the Germans had carved in Wolwonice, Shlomo saw his mother, hanging out the wash in front of an old shack. Almost as if she could hear his footsteps in the snow, she turned. She seemed puzzled as she stared at the boy, then shocked. "My son!" she screamed. The tears streamed down her face. "My son."

Shlomo was so happy to be home that he couldn't stop touching everyone, hugging and kissing his mother and sister. They had thought they would never see him again, and as the times got worse, they used to say, "At least Shlomo is free." Now, they couldn't believe that he would give up his freedom for a ten-by-ten hovel with paper stuffed in cracks, a leaky roof, no water, and a clay oven to warm the family if they managed to scrounge wood or sawdust.

Shlomo told them that he had thought of nothing but them in Russia, that his love had driven him back, and that he would never desert them again, never. Not even if it meant death.

Before the winter of 1940–1941 was out, food had become so scarce in Wolwonice that Shlomo and his father cut off their Stars of David and crept out of the ghetto to beg for food from relatives nearby. But a Pole turned them in for a kilo of sugar, and the Gestapo tossed them into jail. Shlomo and his father argued most of the night away. Shlomo had heard stories about the Nazis killing Jews who traveled without papers or the Star of David. He told his father that if they didn't escape, they'd be murdered. "Maybe not tomorrow. But the next day or the next," he said.

At first, his father couldn't believe the Nazis would be so brutal. "They'll just keep us for a few days to scare us," he argued. "Then they'll let us go."

"I've seen more of the Germans than you have, Father," Shlomo said. "We can't take the chance. We have the family to think about."

In the end, his father agreed to make a break. The next day, after lunch, as the prisoners lined up for work and the Germans changed the guard, Shlomo and his father edged to the rear of the column. When the German guarding them turned his back, they ran.

Back in Wolwonice, Shlomo helped feed his family by silver- and gold-smithing for German soldiers — rings out of forks, bracelets from gold rings. Somehow, Shlomo and his family survived, feeding on the hope that things would get better.

Then, without warning, the Germans cut the ghetto in half, squeezing the four hundred Jewish families of Wolwonice into a tiny closed ghetto around the synagogue. Within weeks, the ghetto was a shanty town without water, crawling with lice, and smelling like a sewer. At night or early in the morning, the Germans raided workers from the ghetto, marching them to nearby farms or factories or building projects. Every day, a few more failed to return.

Shlomo's family, living in the synagogue, were so desperate for food that Shlomo slipped away one day from his work detail and went to beg for food and money from relatives in western Poland. (By the fall of 1941, the Germans decreed that any Jew traveling without a Star of David and a permit could be executed.) An aunt fattened him up and pleaded with him to stay with her, where, for the time being, it was safer, but Shlomo told her he had promised never to desert his family again. One cold autumn night, he crept back into the ghetto with a few gold coins in his pocket and some bread under his shirt.

When the money and the food ran out, Shlomo's father cut off his Star of David, slung a bag over his shoulder, and walked from village to village, door to door, begging food from Catholics in the name of Jesus. Posing as a Christian made the proud Jew feel so ashamed and guilty that he used to sit in the corner of the synagogue at night and cry, unable to eat the cabbage leaves and stale bread he brought home on the best of days.

One day the Judenrat — the Jewish Council set up by the Nazis to carry out its decrees in the ghetto — assigned Shlomo and nineteen others to pick the last of the fall beets and potatoes on a farm nearby. Shlomo sniffed an opportunity. The old German sergeant who walked with a cane seemed like a fair man. At least, he never beat anyone, let the Jews rest from time to time, and made certain they ate reasonably well. Shlomo told him that he was a goldsmith and that he would be pleased to make something for him — a ring, maybe, or a bracelet for his wife — but that he'd have to go back home to get his tools. The old soldier didn't believe that a fourteen-year-old boy could be a goldsmith; he assumed that Shlomo was lying in order to escape. But Shlomo kept pestering, and eventually the old German sent him home, under guard, to get his tools.

The German, who wanted a ring with his unit insignia, set Shlomo up in a cozy room in the farmhouse. As the sergeant watched Shlomo for hours on end, he began to call the boy by his first name. Shlomo sensed that the old soldier didn't understand what the Nazis were doing to the Polish Jews, so he told him about his home in Pulawy, his parents, the filth and lice, the hunger. "While potatoes and beets are rotting in the fields," Shlomo complained, "we are starving in ghettos."

The old German listened in silence. One day, he said, "I'm going to give you a wagonload of potatoes."

Shlomo couldn't believe the German. A kilo, yes. But a ton?

"You get the wagon," the German said. "You can have all it carries."

It wasn't easy to smuggle a wagon of potatoes into Wolwonice without creating a stampede, but Shlomo managed to do it under the cloak of night. He and his family hid enough potatoes to tide them over for two weeks. Then, taking turns guarding the wagon outside the synagogue, they distributed the rest among the other Jews, according to need.

19

Shlomo continued to make jewelry for the old German until the first winter snow, when, because there was no more work in the fields, the Judenrat called him back to the ghetto.

Given the lice, fleas, and lack of sanitation, it was inevitable that typhus would strike Wolwonice. When it did, the Nazis stuffed all the Jews into the synagogue in an attempt to control the epidemic. Two Jewish doctors worked around the clock while the fever spread from family to family and while the Judenrat collected money to buy black-market medicine from the Germans and the Poles. Old Jews were the first to succumb to the diarrhea and fever. Most died. Shlomo, his sister, Ryka, Moses, and Jankus all caught it, and for twelve to fourteen days, they tossed on their mats in delirium. But, young and resilient, and driven by a determination to live, they got well.

Hardly had the tiny ghetto recovered from typhus, in the spring of 1942, when the Nazis swooped. The German officer in charge of selecting non-Jewish Poles to work in factories in the west had been assassinated, and the Nazis blamed the Jews. In retaliation, they shot the whole Judenrat in the town square and ordered the rest of the Jews to assemble for "resettlement." It was the first time most Wolwonice Jews, Shlomo included, had seen the Nazis murder people in cold blood; the shock sent a shiver of fear through the four hundred families. There was no logic to the action: it was unlikely that a Jew would assassinate a Nazi who rounded up Aryans for German factories, so why had the Germans killed the Judenrat? And what did "resettlement" mean?

To a person, the Jews of Wolwonice refused to go to the square, but with no guns, little strength, and no place to hide, they were no match for the Nazis, who routed them from the synagogue and the few houses left in the ghetto, herded them into the square, and marched them all night to Opole, thirty miles away.

Compared to Opole, Wolwonice was a kindergarten. The ghetto was a sealed tomb of four thousand Jews. They huddled in parks, schools, and synagogues — anyplace they could find a spot to sit or lie. And shocking to Shlomo, who thought he had seen all of life in his fourteen years, was the moral degradation into which the war and poverty, fear and hatred had driven some Jews. Besides the Judenrat in Opole, the Nazis had created a Jewish Ghetto Police. Both groups had become corrupt, trading gold and girls for food and work papers. The corrupted Jews were few in number, but they had the Opole ghetto by the throat.

With few exceptions, it was now everyone for himself or herself, as Jews fought to stay alive for just one more day, telling themselves that Opole was the bottom, that nothing could be worse, that if they could survive Opole, they could take anything. Like dogs, hundreds died of hunger in the streets. Their corpses were stripped, piled on carts, and buried in mass graves outside the ghetto.

It didn't take Shlomo long to learn how to save himself and his family. After a few days in Opole, he was making badges for the Ghetto Police and rings for them to trade with the SS for food and privileges. He even threatened a Jewish dentist into allowing him to use his laboratory so that he could melt gold faster, make more rings, gain more friends, more favors, more food.

One month after Shlomo was resettled in Opole, the Nazis raided the ghetto. During the first week of May 1942, they rounded up half the Jews. Rumors spread like typhus, for no one knew what the sly Germans were up to. Some Jews argued that resettlement anywhere was better than living in Opole; others, like Shlomo, smelled a trick. Hadn't each move the Nazis forced him to make been for the worse? Shlomo persuaded his family to hide. When an SS officer dug them out, Shlomo bribed him with a gold ring to pass them by.

The Nazis marched the first two thousand Jews out of Opole. For days, Shlomo waited in the sealed ghetto for news. There was nothing, not even a rumor. Then, on May 10, the Nazis pounced again, this time trapping the rest of the Jews, including Shlomo and his family. The Germans herded everyone into the town square, piled the old, the sick, and the children into carts, and ordered the others into a column of four abreast. As the half-starved Jews began to march northeast, they heard the shots of the Nazis executing the Judenrat and the Jewish Ghetto Police.

Shlomo walked close to the front of the column with Moses, Jankus, and Nojeth. The Nazis, in cars, on horseback, or on motorbikes, kept the column moving — a silent cortège marching to the rhythm of hoofbeats and motors, the shrill cries of whistles, and orders shouted in Polish and German. Occasionally, as the column passed farm after farm tinted green with promise, a gunshot would shatter the peace of the spring morning. Whispers floated up and down the line: "They're shooting stragglers. Keep moving."

An older Jew a few rows ahead of Shlomo began to slow, first swaying slightly in the sun, then missing a step here and there, at last faltering. A Nazi on a motorbike raced up and jerked the man to the ground. Pulling his pistol, he shot the Jew in the neck and remounted his bike as if he had just killed a lame horse. Instinctively, Shlomo straightened up and put more bounce into his step.

At noon, a German blew his whistle and shouted, "Halt!" The Nazis lunched while the Jews stood in the sun. After a rest, the Germans began to play games. They took into the woods several wagons filled with children and the old and sick. There were screams and shots. Then silence. Terror gripped the column of Jews. What was going on? Where were they going? Why the shooting? Those in the remaining wagons sobbed or looked into space, eyes glazed with fear or madness. But the Nazis weren't finished. They walked up and down the column, yanking out the best-dressed men and women. At the side of the road, they shot them and auctioned off their clothes to the Poles. The highest bidders stripped the Jews, leaving their corpses to rot in the sun.

After lunch, another whistle, and the cortège continued northeast. Along the way, Shlomo saw hundreds of Poles in wagons or resting on hoes in the fields, watching with curiosity, some even smiling. By nightfall, the exhausted column from Opole had marched into a barbed-wire pen next to the train station in Naleczow.

People frantically searched for members of their families, hugging, kissing, or crying as they found a father and a mother, or learned that a son and a sister had been murdered on the way. Shlomo was lucky; his entire family had survived the day. The Poles of Naleczow came to the pen to sell bottles of water for gold and jewelry, and the barbed wires vibrated like cello strings with the rumble of Jews reciting Kaddish, the prayer for the dead.

It was the worst day Shlomo had ever had. It must get better, he argued with himself. He would probably ride the rest of the way to wherever he was going. A work camp, probably. That was why the old, the sick, the children, and those who couldn't keep up were shot. It made terrible sense. The Germans wanted only those who could work. He and his family were still strong. They would survive. He was sure of it. He huddled near them on the ground, for the comfort of closeness, and waited for morning.

Before dawn broke, the Nazis stuffed and locked the Jews of Opole into railroad cattle cars, and terror spread as people fought for space and air. Surrounded by hundreds of legs, the children who couldn't clutch a mother's hand or skirt were smothered to death; the old and the sick who fell to the floor were trampled; the feet of others caught in the crush of bodies never touched the boxcar floor.

After the two thousand Jews were packed and sealed, the locomotive tooted as if it were the last call for a holiday trip to the Baltic seashore. As the cargo swayed to the rhythm of the train like water in a barrel, people relieved themselves out of need or fear wherever they stood. Those closest to the door and walls clawed at locks and boards, and the Ukrainians riding on the boxcar roofs tried to shoot off hands and fingers and noses. Shlomo and his family had fought for a corner, and together, as a family, they guarded their turf. If they could just remain standing, Shlomo reasoned, they would survive the trip. To the rhythm of the train, he recited over and over: "Stay standing . . . stay together . . . never leave again."

Twice along the way the train stopped — at Lublin and Chelm — and the Jews waited, hoping the doors would slide open with a gust of air, yet fearing what waited outside. They prayed, they raved, they retreated into catatonic silence. But the locomotive tooted again, and the wheels began to grind them eastward.

Late in the afternoon, the transport halted on a switching track. Instead of sitting on the rail as it had done twice before, it backed up slowly, then jerked to a stop. It was as quiet as a snowfall, except for the whimpering of a child and the "hush, hush" of a mother. Shlomo strained to hear a voice or the bark of village dogs or orders in German. The tension almost broke them, and all eyes fixed on the door.

They heard the lock click and saw the door slide. Spring air rushed in like a wave of sweet perfume. Shlomo gulped as his eyes tried to adjust to the sunlight. Outside stood a dozen SS officers and just as many Ukrainians armed with Walther and Nagan pistols, whips, and billy clubs.

"*Raus!*" they began to shout. "*Raus, schnell!*"

Shooting into the air from a platform, while supervising the organized chaos, was a Nazi in creased gray slacks and a white jacket. He seemed oddly out of place, almost as if he had interrupted his dinner to greet the Jews and was eager to get back to it before it turned cold.

Shlomo had arrived in Sobibor. As he stood in line, looking for his mother and sister and father, he thought that nothing could be worse than that train ride. Absolutely nothing.

Chapter 4

Spring 1942

Sᴇʀɢᴇᴀɴᴛ Gᴜsᴛᴀᴠ Wᴀɢɴᴇʀ, weighing 240 pounds and standing six feet, four inches tall, seemed a giant to Shlomo. He had blond hair, an expressionless, handsome face that looked as if it had been carved from a huge piece of soap, and intense blue-green eyes that pierced the boy. Unlike Captain Stangl, he was not polite, polished, or fatherly. True, he had never been cruel to Shlomo, but the boy sensed that behind his controlled face was an anger that could erupt at any moment. Shlomo decided to work on his monogram first.

It was a good decision; the thirty-one-year-old Wagner, an Austrian, was close to Stangl, also an Austrian. As the Kommandant's whip, Wagner supervised the processing of the transports. He selected* some, like Shlomo, for special jobs, and he was responsible for their work.

No sooner had Shlomo begun Wagner's monogram than SS Sergeant Kurt Bolander dropped in to watch Shlomo work. He was a tall, slim man with a neatly trimmed goatee, and at his side stood Barry, a tame, black and white spotted mongrel with the pug face and floppy ears of a Saint Bernard.

"Make something for me," Bolander demanded. "Something for the handle of my whip."

---

* In concentration camps and in work camps with gas chambers, like Maidanek and Auschwitz, "selected" meant chosen for death. Sobibor survivors define the word as chosen for life. I use "selected" as they do.

The Nazi threw a fistful of gold on the table, enough to gold-plate the whole whip. Then, as an afterthought, he said, "I also want a gold coin in the end of my handle. Send one of your helpers to get it tomorrow. Same time . . . I'll be near the gate to the showers."

For the rest of that day and late into the night under the flickering yellow of a kerosene lantern, Shlomo shaped the *G. W.*, afraid he'd make a mistake because he was so tired, yet afraid to quit, sensing that somehow he might get caught between Wagner and Bolander.

The next day — his fourth at Sobibor — a large transport from Zamosc, thirty miles south of Sobibor, arrived with five thousand men, women, and children. Shlomo glanced out the window a few times to watch the long lines of prisoners march through the huge gate while the locomotive pulled ten empty boxcars out of the camp and pushed ten more, crammed with Jews, into the camp. But the little goldsmith was in such a hurry to finish Wagner's monogram that he had no time to think of them. Occasionally, a pistol shot or scream would break his concentration, and he'd flinch or think of his mother and his sister, Ryka.

Early that afternoon, Shlomo sent his thirteen-year-old nephew, Jankus, to get Bolander's gold coin. While the boy was away, Shlomo finished Wagner's monogram and began to design an insignia for Bolander's whip handle. When Jankus didn't return after half an hour, Shlomo became worried. Maybe he hadn't been able to find the Nazi, he thought. Or maybe Bolander was busy and had made Jankus wait. Or maybe the Nazi told him to clean the yard.

The barracks door creaked open indecisively, as if a gust of wind began to push it and then changed its mind. Jankus stood there, trembling, his eyes darting in panic and terror. He was limp, and he couldn't talk.

"What's wrong!" Shlomo shouted at him. "What happened? What took you so long? Did someone beat you? Did you find Bolander? Did you see something? What? What did you hear?"

The boy tried to speak, but only gurgles came from his throat. Shlomo and Nojeth, the oldest of the family, led Jankus to his bed. Deep into the night, they talked to him gently, bathed his brow, told him to rest, not to worry, that they were there to love and protect him, that they would be there when he woke, always, that they would never leave him. They rocked him into a sleep broken by a cry or a sob, while Moses, Shlomo's thirteen-year-old brother, sat nearby, too terrified to speak or sleep. The next morning, Jankus was calm enough to talk, and Shlomo pulled the story from him in pieces, broken still more by fits of sobbing and trembling:

All the Germans and Ukrainians seemed to be near the boxcars and in the field in front of the mysterious gate, so Jankus walked into the field, looking for Sergeant Bolander. A long line of men stood waiting for the gate to open. There were no women or children in sight. Jankus didn't see Bolander in the field, so he opened the gate and entered the long corridor with the camouflaged walls. At the end of the corridor stood a Ukrainian armed with a Mauser. He guarded a door that led into a corral of boards so tightly fitted that one could not see through them. At first, Jankus heard weak cries and screams, but as he approached the Ukrainian, they grew louder. Jankus began to panic. What should he do? Turn around and go back? Or ask the Ukrainian where Sergeant Bolander was?

"Herr Oberscharführer Bolander ordered me to come," Jankus told the Ukrainian. "He said he'd be waiting."

The Ukrainian grinned, as if he were enjoying a private joke, opened the door, and pushed the boy inside. Jankus fell on his face. When he got to his knees, he froze in terror. There were three hundred to four hundred women and children in the corral, most already naked, the others stripping. The Ukrainians and Nazis tore off the clothes of those who resisted, or beat them with whips and rifle butts, or shot them. The women wailed, screamed, pleaded, "No . . . No, please . . . My baby! My baby!" The Nazis and Ukrainians shouted, "Quick! Undress! Quick!"

Nazis pried away the children who clung to their mothers, grabbed them by the feet, smashed them against the wall, and left them in a heap. In the midst of the scene from hell stood Sergeant Bolander, tall and handsome, barking orders and lashing his whip as if he were in a fever.

Luckily, Bolander saw Jankus before someone else did, and ordered him to come over. Jankus had an overpowering urge to shut his eyes and cover his ears, but he obeyed the Nazi.

"Here!" Bolander handed Jankus a twenty-dollar American gold piece. "Don't you ever come to this part of the camp when there's a transport here! Do you understand? Never! And make sure you don't tell anyone what you saw. Clear?"

Jankus was too frightened even to nod.

"Take him out of here," Bolander shouted.

Shlomo didn't believe Jankus' story at first. Yes, he thought, his nephew must have seen something to shake him up. After that, his imagination must have run wild. But when Jankus stopped crying and trembling, and when he refused to change any detail of his story as Shlomo probed this part or that, hoping to catch an inconsistency, the little goldsmith knew that Jankus was telling the truth.

Shlomo finally admitted to himself that he had been holding on to the thread of hope to keep his sanity, that he had deluded himself because his desire to live, to survive, to see one more sunrise, another hour, was so strong that it had buried the truth under lies. He had believed Stangl's soothing words — "work camp . . . showers . . . don't worry . . . you'll join them soon" — because he needed to, wanted to. But Jankus jerked him back to reality, burning him with a question as hot as a branding iron. Why would the Nazis bash babies against a fence?

Shlomo didn't have an answer, but he did have a conclusion. He was a fly in some demonic web spun of Nazi lies. He knew only half the truth, and not knowing the other half — what happened after the women and children left the corral for the showers — seemed more frightening than the full truth, no matter how terrible.

Wagner gave the little goldsmith no time to sort his feelings. The Nazi bulled into the barracks, took his monogram without a word of praise or criticism. "Never again! No job without my approval!" he screamed at Shlomo. "Your chief. *Me.* No one else. Obey me or regret it."

Shlomo was so frightened by the giant that he could barely speak. In his mind, he could still see Nazis whipping naked women and smashing heads with rifle butts. "The others will beat me if — "

"Tell them 'Wagner!' That's all." He spun around, his monogram in his clenched fist, and kicked his way through the door.

Shlomo's worst fears had come true. He was trapped in a Nazi power struggle he didn't understand. Until he did, he was in great danger, because if he refused to make rings and trinkets for the Nazis who had already placed orders, there was no telling what they would do. Beat him, maybe? Kill him? And if he did work for them, Sergeant Wagner would make him "regret" it. Shlomo believed the giant, and he felt as if Wagner had set him down in the middle of a minefield. He couldn't just stand still, but he wasn't sure whether to turn right or left. All he had were his instincts to guide him and luck to smile on him . . . maybe.

Minutes after Wagner stormed out, Kurt Bolander pranced in to get his whip. He gushed all over Shlomo, confusing the boy even more. "Wonderful, wonderful!" the Nazi said as he fingered the gold emblem on the handle and tested the twenty-dollar gold piece to make sure Shlomo had set it tightly. "You're an artist. This should be in an exhibition."

The next day, Wagner solved the goldsmith's dilemma. The giant was cheerful. "Talked to the Kommandant," he said. "A ring for each SS officer." He sat at the table across from the goldsmith and explained precisely what Captain Stangl wanted.

The rings were to be made of silver with a gold *Totenrune* on them —

two *Y*'s, the normal one representing life and the upside-down one representing death. The officers would come for measurements, and later in the day he, Wagner, would bring all the silver and gold Shlomo needed.

Shlomo made a board with twenty nails, one for each SS officer whose finger he measured. On the nails, he hung the wires with ring sizes, and on the tablet next to the board, he wrote down names. Shlomo was happy; he knew he would survive at least until he finished the twenty rings, and he would get to know each SS officer personally. That was a break, for if he was going to survive, it would be important to know the enemy well.

One day, while Shlomo was working on the SS rings, Wagner barged into the barracks demanding from the two painters, Herszel and Moniek, the signs he had ordered. They told Wagner that the signs weren't ready, that he had not given them a deadline or said that he was in a hurry, that they were taking special care to do them well.

Wagner exploded with a punch that knocked out two of Herszel's teeth and sent him flying to the floor. The boy lay half-conscious. Next, the giant, his handsome face twisted with hatred, began beating Moniek. When he, too, collapsed, Wagner picked up both boys by the collars, one in each hand, and began shaking them like rag dolls until he saw that they were out cold. Then he tossed them through the door into the yard.

Shlomo watched the brutal beatings, but didn't dare say a word. After Wagner left, Shlomo, Moses, Jankus, and Nojeth carried the sign painters to their beds and bathed them with cold compresses. Their eyes and mouths were swollen shut, but no bones had been broken. The next morning, they forced slits in their eyes, big enough to see their brushes, and continued painting signs with a fervor Shlomo had never seen before. The beatings, which had taken less than three minutes, had confirmed Shlomo's feelings about Wagner. Underneath his stone-rigid face was a rage that could explode at any moment, for any reason. Wagner was as unpredictable as Shlomo had feared. That made him all the more dangerous.

Life during the second week at Sobibor pulsed with a steady rhythm that Shlomo found comforting. He worked on the SS rings; the Nazis continued to demand extra bracelets and jewelry; and when Shlomo repeated that he couldn't make them without Sergeant Wagner's permission, they muttered, cursed, and threatened. And the transports kept arriving — sometimes two or three a day. Women to the left; men to the right. Women and children through the gate first; the crew to clean up the traces the Jews had left in the yard; another transport.

More and more questions tumbled around in Shlomo's mind. Where did the Nazis get all the clean clothes for the thousands who went to the showers? Why did only Jews come to Sobibor to work? Why did the Nazis whip and beat women if they were saving them for work? Why would the Nazis send all these Jews to the forest of the owls, a stone's throw from the Bug River and the Russian border, when Germany occupied the whole of Poland? Why couldn't he see his mother, father, and sister?

Shlomo asked Captain Stangl about them a second time during one of the Kommandant's daily visits, and the captain again told him: "They are in a much better place. They have everything they need. You'll join them soon. I promise."

Shlomo tried to push aside the questions, to concentrate on his work, to think only of pleasing the Nazis, for he knew that if he let them, those questions would drive him mad or sap his hope or lead him to a mistake.

At the end of May, Shlomo met his first Ukrainian guard, a young man of about twenty who seemed to have had some education and who spoke German well. He was a Volksdeutscher, a Ukrainian of German ancestry. When the Germans invaded Russia in June 1941, they recruited a quarter of a million Estonians, Latvians, Lithuanians, and Ukrainians. Since the Nazis didn't trust them completely (most were Ukrainians), they gave them nonmilitary police jobs. Guarding the camps under the SS was one. Most Ukrainians hated the Germans, and the Nazis knew it. But they had no love for the Poles, who had taken a big bite out of the Ukraine after World War I, or for the Russians, who had starved and beaten them into submission after the Red Revolution, or for the Jews, whom they had persecuted since the Middle Ages. And the Nazis knew that, too. So the Ukrainians — poor, uneducated farmers, for the most part — volunteered to help the Nazis. The camps were a safe place to sit out the war.

The young Blackie at the door of the barracks was nervous, almost as if he had orders to stay away from the goldsmith but had decided to risk a visit anyway. "I have a message from your friend Avi." He offered Shlomo a piece of paper.

The boy was wary. Was it a trick? Hadn't Wagner warned him about the Ukrainians?

The Blackie sensed the goldsmith's confusion and, as if to put him at ease, said, "My name is Klat. Avi already gave me gold. But I want more."

Believing the Ukrainian's greed and stung by intense curiosity, Shlomo accepted the note. "I'll have your gold tomorrow," he said.

The message burned in his pocket, but he wouldn't read it during the day, when Wagner or Stangl or Bolander could pop in at any moment.

Every now and then, he'd touch the note, and the crinkle of the paper would remind him that it was real, that there were Jews behind that gate. Maybe Avi had news about his parents and Ryka. Maybe they had asked him to write the note.

Late that night, while Moses, Jankus, and Nojeth kept a lookout at the window and door, Shlomo hunched over the kerosene lantern, trying to study the hastily written note. As hard as he tried to decipher the scribble, he could make out only two phrases: "No one lives . . . say Kaddish."

Shlomo was too stunned to cry as he tried to explain away the note. For whom should he say the prayer of mourning? For his mother? For his father? For Ryka? What about the rest of the Jews from Opole? For them, too, the Kaddish? In his mind, Avi kept shouting, "No one lives . . . no one lives . . . no one lives."

While Nojeth recited Kaddish, Shlomo repeated to himself, over and over, the first line: "Exalted and hallowed is the name of God . . ." Wrapped in the prayer shawl of despair, the two young men faced east — toward the Holy City — and intoned the ancient words, searching for meaning, fighting to hang on to a shred of hope, pleading for understanding.

Moses and Jankus lay on their beds, sobbing. Nojeth and the two sign painters were silent. And Shlomo's emotions were locked in a struggle. Tears began to form, but couldn't flow; screams from deep inside died before they were heard. Hatred tugged at him and slowly overpowered him, strangling all feelings of sorrow or pain or love. In their place, hatred left a gulf of emptiness.

By the time the morning light dappled his workbench, something indefinable had died inside the boy. A passion to live, to survive, to avenge his parents and Ryka, yes, even to kill, was born. He couldn't understand or explain his strange, new feeling. Only one thing was clear — he had to pretend to be calm, not let the Nazis suspect that he knew the terrible secret of Sobibor.

Chapter 5

Spring 1942

WHEN KLAT came to the barracks for his gold the next morning, Shlomo handed him a note for Avi: "Should I say Kaddish for my parents only or for all the Jews?" Shlomo asked. "What happens to the Jews assigned to your part of the camp?" If his mother, father, and sister were really dead, Shlomo had to know how they had died. Had they suffered? Been beaten? Shot? For, ever since Jankus had described the scene in the corral, he had visions of Nazis ripping the clothes off his mother and sister, whipping them as they fought for their last shred of human dignity.

No sooner had Klat left than SS Sergeant Poul staggered in, tipsy. Shlomo was certain that Poul had seen Klat leave, but if he had, the Nazi didn't seem to care. He emptied a pocketful of gold rings onto the table and slurred, "Make me a r-r-ring."

"I can't," Shlomo objected. "Not unless Herr Oberscharführer Wagner or Herr Kommandant Stangl tells me to. Besides, I haven't finished the other — "

"I don't want to hear about any orders from Wagner or Stangl." Poul's face was red. "I want a ring. In three days."

"But I — "

Poul punched the goldsmith in the eye, and when Shlomo staggered backward, he slugged him in the mouth. Luckily, Poul was so unsteady that his punches were somewhat weak. The sight of the swelling eye and the blood trickling from Shlomo's split lip seemed to calm the Nazi. He cursed, then weaved out the door.

In spite of his pain, Shlomo didn't cry. Hatred held back his tears, and as the day wore on, he became more used to the new feeling, until he wore it like an old shoe.

"Who did it?" Wagner asked that afternoon. Shlomo didn't answer; he was afraid that Sergeant Poul would come back to beat him again. But Wagner insisted, and there was the hint of a threat.

"Herr Oberscharführer Poul," Shlomo said at last.

The goldsmith half-expected Wagner to tell him not to worry, that he was working for him and no one else, that he'd talk to Poul, that Shlomo should concentrate on the Totenrune rings, and that no one else would ever bother him again. Instead, Wagner chuckled in delight at Shlomo's beating.

As confused as he was, Shlomo still thought Wagner was his best protection. "I'm trapped," he told the Nazi. "You told me not to work for anyone without your permission. I obeyed you, and look what happened. How can I work if the others beat me up? How will I finish all these rings for the Herr Kommandant? I can't win. What should I do?"

Shlomo picked the right thing to say, for Wagner softened. "Work on those rings. Leave the rest to me," he said.

Wagner and Poul returned later in the day. They were both smiling, and they whispered as they watched Shlomo carve and chisel the silver rings with the gold symbol of life and death. "After these," Wagner said finally, "do the ring for my friend."

To make sure that Sergeant Wagner didn't suspect that he knew about Sobibor, Shlomo asked about his parents. It was a tough question, and he thought his voice was going to crack with emotion, but his hatred kept it steady and firm. When Wagner told Shlomo not to worry, that he would soon join them, the goldsmith didn't have the courage to look up from his work.

Stangl had not lied to him after all, Shlomo thought. His mother, father, and sister *were* well; they really *had* all their needs taken care of; they *were* in a better place; and he was sure he'd join them as soon as Stangl and Wagner no longer needed him. Hadn't Captain Stangl promised that on his word as an officer? Well, Shlomo would make the Nazi break that word, for he would never go through that gate. He'd survive, somehow.

Before the day was out, Klat returned with a long letter from Avi. He'd be back the next morning for more gold, the Ukrainian said. Shlomo waited for the cover of night to open the letter, dreading what he knew it must say.

Shlomo read aloud.

Dear Brother, I asked you to say Kaddish not only for your parents, but for everyone. Of all the crowds of people who come here, almost no one lives. Of all the transports so far, only a small group is kept to work. Miraculously, I am part of that group.

When the Jews enter the gate, they walk down a long corridor. At the end, they strip and leave all their things and enter a large barracks under the pretext that they will take a shower. Hundreds are stuffed into the barracks at a time. When the place is full, the door is sealed. A large engine is started, and the exhaust goes into a hole in the wall. Everyone inside chokes to death. While this is happening, huge trenches are dug, and we, chosen from the same transport you came on, pull out the bodies and drag them into the trenches. Sometimes the dirt moves over the mass of bodies underneath. Then the Nazis come and shoot.

I tell you this because if someday you escape, you will tell the world what is happening here, as I don't expect you to see me again. Whoever comes to this part of the camp never leaves.

I cannot begin to describe the scene, because you'd never believe what happens in this horrible place. It is inconceivable for the human mind to grasp. I wish you'd see how the Nazi sadists act. They are delirious with pleasure, as if they were watching an opera.

Avi went on to tell Shlomo that there was so much digging and burying to do, there was hardly time to rest. Many of the Jews, he said, couldn't even eat their rations. And it didn't matter to the Nazis whether the workers were strong or weak, sane or crazy; the routine never varied. They would shoot those who couldn't work and replace them with fresh Jews.

With this note [Avi wrote in conclusion],

you will know everything. I cannot hold back any longer; my end is near and I know it. I will be dead like the others. I already have one foot in the grave, close to my brother Jews who have gone forever. I write this letter to you without any trace of fear, because I don't care whether they catch me or not. I am in the hands of criminals, and I expect nothing but death. But you run a grave risk if you are caught with this note. I decided to put you to that risk, in the hope that you may escape from Sobibor someday. Unfortunately, I am not so lucky . . . If you can, *escape!* Your friend, Avraham.

There was a deep silence in the barracks. Avi's letter fell on the boys like an ax, cutting hopes already frayed by suspicion. Jankus was the first

33

to speak. The gas chamber had swallowed his mother and grandmother, and the news of their grisly deaths, fresh on the shock of seeing Nazis beat women and kill babies, was too much for the thirteen-year-old boy. He broke down and rolled on his bed, screaming in hysteria, "Mama, Mama, Mama."

Jankus distracted Shlomo and Nojeth from their private world of grief and shock as they fought with him, pinning him to the bed and covering his mouth with their hands lest the Germans hear his cries in the night. They talked to him as if he were a frightened baby. Nojeth, in particular, had a soothing effect on him and the morphine of his gentle voice sent Jankus into a restless sleep, punctuated by the sobs and screams of a real nightmare.

Nojeth took the news of his family's death as word of God's will. He was a Hasid, a member of the mystical sect founded in Poland about two hundred years before Sobibor, when pogroms threatened to destroy the identity of the Jewish people. At home, Nojeth had maintained the traditional appearance of the Hasidic men: his earlocks hung in curls on either side of his face; he wore the wide-brimmed flat black hat and long black frock coat the Hasidim had long ago adopted. A deeply religious man, he held God at the center of his life.

Shlomo, on the other hand, was not an observant Jew, although his parents had been devout. Besides, he was six years younger than Nojeth and had not examined his faith; he had accepted his religious values as part of his heritage, his family life, his shtetl. Now, he was without a heritage, his family had been killed, his shtetl had been destroyed. God was the last thing on his mind.

"What should we do? What should we do?" Shlomo asked.

"We should think of God," Nojeth said, "for everything He does is good, and we should never fight against Him."

Shlomo was irritated that God would even enter the conversation, much less be part of plans for the future. "God? Where is your God who permits my parents to be killed?" he demanded. "How can He be so good and do nothing for the Jews, allow them to be butchered? Where is He that He doesn't come to help them? Do you want me to pray to your God and thank Him for the way my mother and father were killed? No, Nojeth. Absolutely not! My only desire is to kill. To murder these criminals. Not to pray to your God, who collaborated with them."

Shlomo himself was surprised at the anger in his words. He had never dared speak them before, but they tumbled from his lips with clarity, as if they had been written in his heart a long time ago and were waiting to be read. As he continued to lecture Nojeth, his voice became more heated, his feelings more bitter.

"Could it be, Nojeth, that you've forgotten how we Jews were mistreated before the war, when you and I were still little? Have you forgotten how we went to our religious services to the jeers of the Poles who stoned and spit on us? Is your memory so weak, Nojeth? You *must* remember how they shouted at us, 'Jews, go to Palestine. That's your country.'

"I remember coming home, bruised, clothes torn, all because I defended your God, Nojeth . . . No, a thousand times no! If you Jews had been more radical, maybe all of this would not have happened. At least we would have resisted and killed. We would die, but we would *kill.*

"We were treated as cowards because Jews like you were comfortable on the benches of the synagogues. You forgot about the Maccabees, who were religious and still became legends of courage and bravery.

"Be certain of one thing, Nojeth. If any of us survives, he will tell the world about Sobibor. Then you will no longer see the humble lambs of today, but the many, many Maccabees of tomorrow.

"Think about what the Nazis are doing in the name of God. Remember what is inscribed on their belts — '*Gott mit uns.*' Answer me! Which God? The one who is on our side, or the one on theirs?"

Nojeth accepted the tirade calmly, without shock or anger. "We Jews are paying for our sins," he said. "You are paying, too."

"And the children? The ones the Nazis are murdering, have they sinned, too? Answer me!"

The question thundered in the barracks, and Nojeth could not answer. Shlomo retreated into himself, shocked by his hatred for God, for the Jewish elders who taught patience, for the Nazis. He no longer felt like a boy of fifteen, innocent, naïve, and trusting. He had been transformed into a man, without love or trust, a man filled with a hatred that made him capable of the same brutality he saw around him. To him, the whole world seemed perverted and hypocritical. A world where the strong survived, the end justified the means, and only evil conquered evil.

Nojeth finally broke the silence. "Pray, Shlomo, pray," he said. "We must always pray."

The goldsmith lost all control, pouring out an answer that made Moses cower in the corner. "Stop it!" he shouted at Nojeth. "Stop it! We must *only* think about what to do tomorrow. We should not waste our time calling on your God, who will do nothing to help us anyway."

The blast silenced Nojeth, and for the next few hours they talked about life and survival, pushing away grief and pain and thoughts of death in a sealed gas chamber. They developed a simple strategy — to continue to make rings and jewelry as beautifully as they could, for once Wagner and Stangl felt they were dispensable, they were dead; and to continue to ask about their parents so that Wagner and Stangl would never suspect they knew the secret of Sobibor.

By daybreak, Shlomo had written a short letter to Avi, and when Klat came to collect his gold, he gave the Ukrainian the note:

My friend Avraham [it began]. Your frightening letter did not take me completely by surprise. I suspected it all along. Now that I know the truth, a strength has grown inside me that I cannot explain. With a sixth sense, I know deep down that the Nazis will not kill me, that I will live. If I do, I will take revenge — not for everyone, for that is impossible, but for my family and friends. I promise you on their ashes, I will avenge. One way or another.

Write to me only when necessary, and don't take any chances. Make every effort to live a few more days, or even a few more hours. Luck may smile on you, and you may still escape from this hell.

*

Sergeant Poul came to the barracks, drunk as always. "My ring," he demanded. "I want it."

Shlomo told him that he hadn't begun to work on it yet because he was still making the Totenrune rings for Captain Stangl. He reminded Poul what Wagner had said to both of them: finish the SS rings first, then do his friend's.

"I didn't have time to do yours yet," he said. "If I work on it, Herr Oberscharführer Wagner will punish me."

"I'll be back tomorrow for my ring," the SS man said, tossing a small package on the table.

Shlomo opened the bag when the Nazi left. Inside were gold teeth with blood, gums, and bone still on them. A wave of nausea washed over him. A new transport had arrived that morning, and the Nazis had not wasted any time.

Shlomo worked on Sergeant Poul's ring most of the night, and the barracks reeked with a sweet, nauseating odor of melting flesh. Filled with guilt at using the teeth of the dead to stay alive, Shlomo hated himself that night. But Poul was delighted with the ring, and he rewarded Shlomo with half a bottle of vodka. "Drink," he said. His glazed eyes seemed so mean that the boy took a swallow.

"More," Poul said. "More . . . more . . . more . . . more."

As the boy retched and the alcohol dripped down his chin, Poul laughed wildly. When Shlomo had drained the bottle, he was so drunk that he couldn't stand. Nojeth put him to bed, and he slept the rest of the afternoon and the entire night. It was a gift, that sleep, without tears and nightmares, without fears and hatred.

Poul and Wagner came to the workshop the next morning, yanked open the door, but did not enter.

"Out," Poul ordered Shlomo. "Come on, out."

Shlomo hurried into the yard.

"Pull down your pants and bend over. You're getting ten on the ass. Count."

Shlomo had no idea what he had done wrong, but he knew that to plead or argue could make the drunk even more angry. He bent over and dropped his breeches.

The Nazi uncoiled his black leather whip. The first lash cut like a hot knife, and Shlomo screamed the first thing that came to mind: "Mother! Mother!" Her name gave him strength, and with teeth clenched in hatred, he counted, "Two, my mother . . . Three, my mother." After the tenth belt, he collapsed in the yard. Poul and Wagner walked away, laughing.

Eventually the purple welts that crisscrossed his legs, buttocks, and back stopped pulsing, and Shlomo's thirst for revenge grew. In many ways, it was a hopeless emotion, because everywhere Shlomo looked he saw fences, guards, dogs, and guns. Survival first, he thought; to live is the best revenge.

Chapter 6

Spring 1942

W<small>AGNER</small> needed shoemakers, so he selected Itzhak and his friend Szol. Itzhak came from Zolkiewka, sixty miles from Sobibor. The shtetl was made up of three thousand Jews, mostly merchants and craftsmen, who lived in thatched houses. Itzhak, his father, and brothers were shoemakers; on market day, they sold boots from their stall to the Catholics. There was little open anti-Semitism in Zolkiewka, a lot of Zionism, and ripples of Communism among the younger Jews. When the Germans occupied the town for the first time, in 1939, they left the Jews alone. The Russians came in 1940, and many younger Jews joined the Communist militia. When the Germans declared war on the Soviet Union in 1941, the fleeing Red Army agreed to take along any Jew who wanted to live in the Soviet Union. Few did. Why leave homes, trades, and businesses? Zolkiewka had always been a peace-loving town, and the Germans weren't so bad.

Hardly had the Russians deserted when the terror began. First, the Nazis robbed and shot the rich Jews for furs and gold. Then they murdered the Communists and those young Jews who had been friendly with the Russians. Eventually, the rest of the shtetl population — including Itzhak, his wife and five-year-old son, mother and father, four brothers and a sister — were sealed into boxcars for Sobibor. They had heard stories of mass murder at Belzec, but war always spawns rumors, so they didn't believe them. Still . . .

When the train headed north, away from the town of Belzec, Itzhak hugged his wife and child. They were on their way to a work camp, he told them. They would stick together and, when the war was over, return home. It wouldn't be so bad, he said.

Whenever the train slowed or stopped along the way, Poles would shout at the boxcars, "Hey, you Jews. You're going to burn . . . Throw away your things . . . You're never coming back . . . Don't let the Germans get them."

As the boxcar slid open inside Sobibor, Itzhak froze with fear and held his son tightly. A Ukrainian reached into the car and pulled them out. Itzhak's wife scooped the child into her arms. Before Itzhak could run to them, a Blackie marched him and five other men at gun point to the kitchen. Ordering each Jew to pick up a bucket of soup, he led them through the gate to the door at the end of the thatched corridor. "Put them down here," he said.

From behind the wooden door, Itzhak heard screams, and on the way back, he met a group of naked women and children. He thought he recognized his wife and son in the crowd. Waving and shouting at them, he tried to run through the mass of naked bodies, but the Ukrainian cracked him on the head with his rifle. Itzhak was stunned so badly that he hardly knew where he was.

When he came to his senses, Itzhak was standing next to his father and brothers. Wagner was walking down the line, calling for tailors.

"Push yourself forward," Itzhak's father whispered. Still stunned by the blow, Itzhak stood silent.

"Here's a cobbler," his father said, nudging his son forward.

Wagner stopped. "A cobbler? Samples of your work?" Wagner knew that the Jews would say anything to save their necks, and he didn't have time for "cobblers" who couldn't make shoes.

"Yes," Itzhak lied, sobered by the tall Nazi standing in front of him. He grabbed his friend Szol by the arm. "He's a very good shoemaker, too."

Wagner told both to step out of line.

"My father and brothers are shoemakers, too," Itzhak said. He figured that making shoes would be easier and safer for his father and brothers than digging ditches or potatoes. "They — "

"Enough shoemakers," Wagner said. "Tailors. Any tailors?"

"My wife is an excellent seamstress," Itzhak said before Wagner could move down the line.

"Her name?" Wagner stopped. "I'll look for her."

Wagner walked through the gate to the "showers" and came back a few minutes later. "She's gone," he told Itzhak. "Tailors . . . Any tailors?"

A Ukrainian led Itzhak and Szol, who really was a shoemaker, to the barracks next to Shlomo's. Scattered in the corner of the empty shed were pieces of leather, and on the only table sat chunks of dried bread and two cups. It looked as if someone suddenly had run out of the wooden building because of a fire. Itzhak and Szol divided the bread and ate it slowly, wondering how any Jew could leave food. What had happened to the shoemakers before them, they wondered. Transferred to another camp?

Wagner dropped by later that day. "A pair of boots for the Kommandant," he ordered. He gave Itzhak the measurements. "Better be good."

Itzhak and Szol took pains to make the knee-high black leather boots perfectly, and Wagner was pleased. "You'll stay to the end," he told them.

The end? Itzhak thought. The end of what? He didn't dare ask Wagner, who had just ordered two pairs of boots and a pair of slippers for each SS officer in Sobibor. Before long, the Nazis were demanding shoes and slippers for wives and girl friends.

Itzhak found work a blessing, since it buried for a time his fear for his wife and child, and his intense loneliness. Where were they? Would he be taken to their work camp soon? The questions always ended in his mind with screams and naked women and children walking in terror down that thatched corridor. One day, Itzhak met Shlomo in the yard. The goldsmith was gentle but truthful with the older man. He told him about Sobibor.

Itzhak wouldn't — couldn't — accept the truth. Not his wife and son, his mother and father, his four brothers, his sister. Not his whole family. All dead? It couldn't be. Why? Who could be so cruel? Shlomo's friend Avi must have been mistaken. Besides, Jews *live* behind the door at the end of the corridor; Itzhak had seen Jews carrying pails of soup there every day, as he had done. Why food if no one lives?

One day, when Klat was looking for eight men to carry the soup buckets, Itzhak volunteered. He wasn't sure why. Maybe he hoped to catch a glimpse of his wife and son, or to learn something about them. It was a hope thinner than his shoe thread, but it was all he had. When he reached the wooden door, he bent down to peek through a crack. He thought he saw a woman and child undressing, and he couldn't pull himself away. His wife, his child, naked, going to their deaths like those two, no one to protect them, helpless, alone, afraid. The thoughts pounded him like hail, and he didn't see Klat raise his rifle butt. The other Jews had to lead Itzhak back to the barracks; if he hadn't been such a good shoemaker, Wagner would have sent him through that door.

Shlomo was still young and had tasted little of life beyond hunger, murder, and hatred, but Itzhak was a man in his mid-twenties. Not only had he known the comfort of the love of a mother and father in the bosom of a simple, hard-working family; he had felt the love of a wife and child for whom he was responsible. He had had hopes and plans and dreams for them. He had more to lose than Shlomo, and his grief was so profound that Szol doubted he would ever recover. But he did, and when the shock wore off, he, like Shlomo, fought to stay alive — to survive for just one more day — out of hatred, out of desire for revenge, out of love for his wife and child, out of an overpowering need to tell the world what had happened to his family and to the Jews of Zolkiewka. Surely, if the world only knew, he thought, it would stop the Nazis.

*

While Shlomo continued to make rings and Itzhak shoes, the trains, trucks, and horse-drawn wagons rolled into Sobibor without interruption from ghettos throughout eastern Poland — from those in Rejowiec, Zamosc, Komarow, Demblin, Ryki, Jozefow, Baranow, Konskowola, Markuszow, Michow, Turobin, Gorzkow, Krasnystaw, Izbica, Siedlce, Chelm, Wlodawa, Hrubieszow, Dubienka, Grabowiec, Uchanie, Biala-Podlaska, Krasniczyn. Whole communities died in one day.

Then one steamy July morning, Wagner announced that the next day all workers would be confined to their workshops and barracks because a delegation of SS officers from Berlin was coming to inspect the camp. The prisoners were not completely surprised; the day before, Wagner had commandeered special crews to scrub the officers' quarters, hide the eiderdown quilts, polish boots, and make hors d'oeuvres. Wagner warned the prisoners to shine their barracks like gold in case the Berliners wanted to inspect them, too.

At eleven o'clock the next morning, the locomotive pulling the luxury cars from Berlin puffed onto the switching track outside the main gate. Kommandant Stangl and his whip, Wagner, saluted the six SS officers and three civilians who stepped off the train. Shlomo, Itzhak, and the other worker Jews peeped through windows and cracks.

The delegation immediately walked through the gate to the gas chambers, then returned to the open field in front of the gate. Captain Stangl stood among the visitors, pointing here and there, as if he were giving a stationary tour of Sobibor. He seemed to be talking mainly to a slim, rather tall SS officer, who, in turn, began gesturing, as though he were giving Stangl instructions.

As suddenly as it had come, the delegation left Sobibor. Stangl and Wagner were disappointed, for the Berliners hadn't stayed for cognac. As if to blame the Jews for his chagrin, Wagner sent to the gas chambers the boys who had prepared the food.

But Stangl and Wagner were proud and pleased, too. Heinrich Himmler, chief of the SS, had just paid them his first visit.

Chapter 7

Summer 1942

In 1929, when Heinrich Himmler took over Hitler's bodyguard — the Schutzstaffel, or SS — it had only 280 members. By the time he visited Sobibor in the summer of 1942, he had shaped the SS into a corps of two hundred fifty thousand.

A nonpracticing Catholic, Himmler had always been intrigued by the Company of Jesus (Jesuits), founded by a one-time Spanish army officer, Ignatius Loyola. Bound by oath to the Pope, the Jesuits — his private army — were men of superior minds and character, screened during a rigorous novitiate, united under a vow of strict obedience, and imbued with a fierce loyalty. They were a religious elite and, within the structure of the Roman Catholic Church, a power within a power. Himmler modeled his SS so closely on the Jesuits that even Hitler called him "my Ignatius Loyola."

From the start, Himmler selected what he considered to be "racially pure" and physically strong recruits — aristocrats, intellectuals, scions of the wealthy middle class. He tested them during a nine-month training period, during which he fired them with an esprit d'corps built on SS principles: elitism, racial superiority, anti-Semitism, and obedience. Every year on Hitler's birthday, April 20, the SS cadets took a vow of obedience during a candlelight ceremony, often in the presence of the Führer himself. "I swear to thee, Adolf Hitler, as Führer and chancellor of the German Reich, loyalty and bravery," thousands of voices would thunder in unison. "I vow to thee, and the superiors whom thou shalt appoint, obedience unto death, so help me God."

After his vow, the new recruit, in uniform but without shoulder patches, was further tested for five months. One of his tasks was to memorize the questions and answers to the SS catechism, in form and style identical with the Catholic catechism learned by schoolchildren the world over.

Q: Whom must we primarily serve?

A: Our people and our Führer, Adolf Hitler.

Q: Why do we obey?

A: From inner conviction; from belief in Germany, in the Führer, in the movement, and in the SS; and from loyalty.

As the Jesuit Superior General (the "black pope") had four assistants, so Himmler surrounded himself with assistant generals, who ran the SS branches. And to keep his men identified with the SS after training, he dressed them in striking black jackets and caps with the silver insignia of a skull, taught them an SS song, gave them their own magazine (*The Black Corps*), and rewarded them with silver rings and daggers.

When Germany invaded Poland in September 1939, it was only natural that Hitler would ask his trusted black pope to execute his overall plan: to render Poland harmless by killing its leadership, to Germanicize western Poland and incorporate it into the Reich, to turn eastern Poland into a vast pool of slave labor, and to isolate Poland's three million Jews until he, Hitler, could figure out exactly what to do with them.

Himmler was good at his job. He uprooted over one million Poles from western Poland and dumped them into eastern Poland — renamed the General Government — or sent them to labor camps, giving their homes, farms, and businesses to the Germans whom the Reich relocated there. He also kidnaped more than two hundred thousand Aryan-looking Polish children and gave them up for adoption to German families.

Next, Himmler and his right-hand man, Reinhard Heydrich, created five task forces of elite SS troops, independent of the German army, to round up and execute Polish leadership — the aristocracy, the cultural elite (teachers, writers, artists, doctors), the political leaders (anti-German Polish Nationalists, Socialists, Communists), and the priests and nuns who were leaders in the independent Poland movement. The task forces murdered between one and two million Polish civilians.

Finally, Himmler tagged Poland's Jews and isolated them in ghettos, where they could be used as cheap labor while he waited for Hitler's decision about their future. To the Polish Jews who lived in the General Government,

Himmler added almost a million more Jews, uprooted from western Poland, Austria, Germany, and Czechoslovakia.

When Germany invaded Russia in June 1941, it was only natural that Hitler entrust to Himmler his plan to assassinate all Communist leaders, partisans, Gypsies, and Jews. Russia's five million Jews were sitting ducks. Nine out of ten lived in the crowded cities of Lithuania, Estonia, Latvia, White Russia, and the Ukraine. For the most part, they suspected nothing. Some even welcomed the Germans as their liberators from the Red yoke.

Building on his experience in Poland, Himmler dispatched four Einsatz-gruppen — each a task force of three thousand hand-picked SS men assisted by Ukrainian, Latvian, Estonian, and Lithuanian volunteers — to follow the Wehrmacht as it pushed east toward Moscow. The Einsatzgruppen, and the more permanent squads they left behind in each major city the army conquered, killed one million Jews and seven million Russian civilians.

When Hitler decided on his Final Solution — the murder of all Europe's Jews — it was only natural that he leave the implementation up to his trusted and by now experienced black pope. Himmler selected eastern Poland as his first slaughterhouse for several reasons: one third of Europe's Jews lived there; it had an excellent railway system, with webs into isolated towns; it was cut off from the rest of Europe by the Wehrmacht, language, and culture; and the eastern Poles were among the most anti-Semitic people in Europe.

In a top secret program named after Heydrich — Operation Reinhard — Himmler added three death camps to the more than three hundred labor and concentration camps already in Poland. He tested Operation Reinhard on an old estate at Chelmno in the woods of western Poland, forty miles northwest of Lodz. There were still one hundred thousand Jews in the Lodz ghetto, and Himmler reasoned that it would be easier to kill them close to home than to shuttle them around Poland. Chelmno opened in December 1941, and its system was indeed primitive. The Jews were carried from Lodz to Chelmno by train, and from the station to the mansion by truck or cart. At the estate, they were ordered to undress for a shower, then were loaded into one of four sealed vans. While the vans drove to mass graves in the thick woods, the Jews choked from the carbon monoxide. Those who were still alive when the vans reached the gravesite were shot. The Einsatzgruppen in Russia had tested the gas van technique, and although it was primitive, it was more efficient than shooting.

But the vans were small. So, drawing on the Chelmno experiment, Himmler installed gas chambers in his three death camps: Belzec, southeast of the large Lublin ghetto, opened in March 1942; Sobibor, northeast of Lublin, in April; and Treblinka, northeast of Warsaw, in June, a month before Himmler visited Sobibor.

To run all his camps, Himmler created a special SS corps, made up of the Totenkopfverbände, or Death's Head Units. He formed the first unit six years before the war and trained it at Dachau, a camp for political prisoners. The SS training officers drilled the Death's Head recruits with relentless Prussian discipline, until they were ready to explode with anger. Then they were turned loose on the prisoners. Those who distinguished themselves in brutality were promoted; the soft-hearted were dismissed or publicly stripped of rank and given twenty-five lashes. Sometimes their heads were shaven. The new officers selected for special responsibilities in the Nazi camp system received further training at Dachau.

But by 1942, Himmler had expanded the camps so quickly — sixteen large concentration camps and fifty smaller ones, three death camps, and hundreds of work camps — that there was no time to be picky. The twenty-five thousand Death's Head officers were no longer six-foot-tall Teutonic braves. They were predominantly uneducated, unsuccessful, unemployed, and socially maladjusted. There were older men, soldiers who limped, men with criminal records, and the mentally slow.

And to run the three death camps — Sobibor, Belzec, and Treblinka — Himmler selected ninety-six special SS men who had had experience with gas chambers, for they had all worked in Hitler's euthanasia program. They averaged eight years of schooling and, before they joined the SS, had been policemen, farmers, bakers, salesmen, weavers, butlers, and truck drivers.

As inspector of the three death camps, Himmler appointed SS officer Christian Wirth, a former policeman who supervised the first gassing of mentally ill Germans in 1939. From then until mid-1940, he was roving inspector and head executioner of the six "hospitals" where the mentally and physically handicapped were gassed, as well as the eleven special hospitals where sick children were killed by lethal injections. His Nazi co-workers called Wirth the "savage Christian," because he was so crude and callous.

Himmler appointed Franz Stangl — a former master weaver, Austrian police investigator, and a Catholic who went to Mass on Christmas and Easter — as Sobibor's Kommandant. Like Wirth, Stangl was a graduate of the euthanasia program, which murdered between sixty thousand and eighty thousand German and Austrian "sick" before the churches pressured Hitler to stop. By that time, the job was already done.

When Stangl arrived in Sobibor in March or April of 1942, the gas chambers were still under construction; they were in a wooden house containing three stone rooms, each ten feet square. The false shower heads in the ceiling led to an eight-cylinder Russian tank motor. Each chamber could hold eighty to one hundred people. In mid-April, Wirth came to Sobibor to test the chambers. His chemist installed a meter inside, and while he, Wirth, and Stangl watched through a peephole, the SS drove thirty to forty naked girls into the chambers. Within ten minutes, the writhing bodies ceased to move, and the chemist gave the order to stop the motor. He checked the meter, called the experiment a success, and officially declared Sobibor open for business. By the time Himmler arrived to inspect the death camp two months later, Stangl had gassed more than fifty thousand Jews.

Himmler was so impressed, he ordered Stangl to expand Sobibor, and when he got back to Berlin on July 19, the SS chief issued a new order: "I command that the resettlement of the entire Jewish population of the General Government shall have been carried out and completed by December 31, 1942." Then he sent Lieutenant Kurt Gerstein, head of the SS Technical Disinfection Services, on a top secret mission with 572 pounds of potassium cyanide pellets. When mixed with acid, the pellets released deadly hydrogen cyanide, or prussic acid (used to kill, among other things, lice and bedbugs).

Unlike Himmler, Gerstein looked like the perfect SS man — six feet, one inch tall, slim, with blond hair and finely chiseled Nordic features. But in reality, Gerstein was neither a committed SS man nor a Nazi. A trained chemist, he had joined the disinfection squad to find out what had happened to a dear relative taken to a euthanasia "hospital." Twice he had been interrogated by the Gestapo for alleged activities unsympathetic to the SS and to the party, but the Gestapo couldn't make the charges stick, so they released him.

Gerstein suspected that the poison — manufactured under the trade name Zyklon B — would be used to murder people; he had heard rumors about killing squads and death camps. He decided to accept the assignment to see whether he could sabotage the plan. But he took no chances. Under the stone in his signet ring, he carefully placed a cyanide capsule to swallow in case he was caught.

Gerstein, the Zyklon B, and SS Lieutenant Colonel Pfannenstiel, a professor of chemistry, had orders to see General Odilo Globocnik, chief of Operation Reinhard, in Lublin. General Globocnik told Gerstein about the gassings at Sobibor, Belzec, and Treblinka. "This is one of our highly secret matters," he warned. "You might even say the most secret. Anyone who talks about it will be shot. Yesterday, two men who couldn't keep their mouths shut were executed."

The first purpose of the visit to the camps, Globocnik explained, was to disinfect the mountain of lice-covered clothes taken from the Jews. The second was to improve the gas chambers. "What we need is a more toxic gas that works faster," he said. "Like prussic acid."

General Globocnik assigned his camp inspector, Christian Wirth, to show Gerstein how the system worked. They began at Belzec, the camp closest to Lublin. Since the gassing in Belzec was at its peak in the summer of 1942, forty-five boxcars of Jews were waiting for them. One third of the six thousand people packed inside were already dead.

On the way to the gas chambers, dubbed the Heckenholt Institute after the noncommissioned officer responsible for turning on the gas, Wirth explained that the death rooms in Sobibor and Treblinka were identical with those at Belzec. "There are not ten people alive," he said, "who have seen or will see as much as you."

As men, women, children, and babies filed by Gerstein, an SS man with a booming voice like a priest in a pulpit called out, "Nothing terrible is going to happen to you. All you have to do is breathe deeply. That strengthens the lungs. Inhaling prevents infectious disease from spreading."

By the time the Jews reached the door to the gas chamber building, most suspected they were going to die, but there was no place to run inside the narrow tube, with hundreds of people pressing from behind, naked and unarmed. The children did not suspect. Gerstein saw a five-year-old girl drop her coral necklace, but she had no time to retrieve it. A moment later, a three-year-old boy saw the beads shining in the sun and scooped them up. Smiling, he walked into the gas chamber, delighted with his new toy.

There were four chambers inside the Heckenholt Institute, which had a huge yellow Star of David painted over the door. "Fill them tightly," Christian Wirth ordered, stopping long enough to whip a woman who was shouting, "Murderers, murderers!"

When each chamber was stuffed and the six doors sealed, Wirth turned off the lights. A wail of terror echoed from inside. SS Sergeant Heckenholt started the tank engine. It wouldn't turn over, and Wirth was embarrassed in front of his important visitors. To this point, everything had gone as smoothly as a well-greased machine.

Gerstein took out his stopwatch while Dr. Pfannenstiel peered through a window. "The Jews inside are weeping and praying," he said, "as in a synagogue." An hour passed. Sergeant Heckenholt still couldn't start the motor. Like a mad Xerxes beating the sea that sank his ships, Wirth began to whip the SS man's assistant. After two hours and forty-six minutes, the diesel coughed and kicked and caught.

Wirth waited twenty-five minutes, flicked on the lights, and looked inside. More than half the Jews were lifeless. He waited another three minutes and looked in again. Only a few still moved. After thirty-two minutes, the chambers were still, and Wirth ordered Heckenholt to cut the motor.

Jewish workers opened the doors. Inside, the bodies were standing like chunks of blue marble, mothers still clutching children to their breasts, their hands over the children's eyes.

As a short Austrian Jew played a violin, the workers pulled out the corpses, to be searched for diamonds and gold before burial in pits. One team of Jews pried open mouths with hooks to look under tongues; another checked vaginas and anuses. Dentists hammered out gold teeth.

Fascinated and proud, Christian Wirth walked among the corpses with a can full of teeth. "Just look at how much gold there is," he told Gerstein, whose mouth was as dry as wood chips. "And we collected just as much yesterday and the day before. You can't imagine what we find every day — dollars, diamonds, gold. You'll see."

The next day, Wirth took Gerstein to Treblinka, by-passing Sobibor, where the transports had stopped while Captain Stangl expanded the camp. Gassing at Treblinka, like Belzec, was at its peak, for the Nazis were liquidating the Warsaw ghetto as fast as they could round up Jews. After inspecting Treblinka's eight gas chambers, which worked flawlessly, Gerstein attended a banquet in his honor. Dr. Pfannenstiel gave a little pep talk. "The work you are doing is a great work and a duty so useful and so necessary," he told the Death's Head Unit. "A blessing and a humanitarian assignment . . . When one sees the bodies of these Jews, one understands the greatness of the work you are doing."

Christian Wirth had been nervous from the moment he had heard that Gerstein was coming. Wirth had built a kingdom for himself in eastern Poland; he had a certain reputation to uphold, an image. If Berlin made him convert his gas chambers from carbon monoxide to Zyklon B, it would look as though he didn't know what he was doing. How could he gain respect?

Don't recommend the prussic acid for Sobibor, Belzec, and Treblinka, he begged Gerstein. The system here works well. Why change now?

Gerstein was relieved. He had planned to tell Wirth that the small canisters of blue Zyklon B pellets had begun to disintegrate, losing most of their strength. They could be used only to disinfect clothes. But Wirth had made it easy for Gerstein. So with Wirth's approval, he supervised the burial of the 572 pounds of pellets. He told Wirth he would report to Berlin that because the pellets were already decomposing and extremely dangerous, he had buried them immediately.

On the train from Warsaw to Berlin, Gerstein met Baron von Otter, secretary to the Swedish legation in Berlin. Since neither had made advance reservations, they had to spend the night standing in a corridor. Gerstein seemed very edgy, as if he had something to say but wasn't sure whether he should say it. Von Otter offered him a cigarette to calm his nerves.

"May I tell you a grim story?" Gerstein asked the diplomat.

He talked most of the night, spilling out the details etched on his psyche. He sobbed; his voice grew loud; he hid his face in his hands. A tortured man, wrestling with his conscience, not sure what he should or could do. Only one thing was clear in his mind — he had to tell the world about Sobibor, Belzec, and Treblinka.

News of the extermination of the Jews must reach neutral countries like Sweden, Gerstein told von Otter. He reasoned that once the Germans learned that the Nazis were murdering Jews, they would not tolerate Hitler and his party for another day.

As though to prove he was sane, Gerstein showed the Swede the SS order for the 572 pounds of potassium cyanide, and gave as a reference Dr. Otto Dibelius, a leader of the Protestant Church's opposition to Nazism, who would confirm Gerstein's own anti-Nazism.

When von Otter arrived in Berlin, he checked Gerstein's reliability with Dr. Dibelius and, satisfied that the SS lieutenant was trustworthy, sent Stockholm a detailed report about Sobibor, Belzec, and Treblinka. But, seeking to avoid further tension with Nazi Germany, the Swedish government buried the cable.

Chapter 8

Summer 1942

WHILE THE SWEDISH GOVERNMENT sat on von Otter's report, trains hauled prefab houses and barracks and building materials to Sobibor, and the Nazis expanded the camp into a little city with four boroughs.

In the Officers' Compound next to the main gate and parallel to the railroad, the Germans threw up living quarters for thirty-five SS men and barracks for two hundred guards, a laundry and barbershop, kitchen, bakery, canteen, garage and armory, and a jail for Ukrainians.

On the south side of Sobibor, far from the main gate, the Nazis built Camp I, where all the Jews slept and some worked. A Ukrainian guarded the only gate into Camp I, in the northeast corner, and it was shut at night with a padlock and chain. To make Camp I even more escape-proof, the Nazis erected two more barbed-wire fences around it.

On the edges of Camp I sat buildings of all sizes: a mechanic and blacksmith barracks, two tailor shops and shoe shops — one for the SS and one for the Ukrainians — a kitchen, a paint and carpenter shop where Jews built furniture for the new German and Ukrainian quarters, and barracks for the Jews to sleep in.

To make the "processing" of new Jews even more efficient, the Germans expanded Camp II, at the center of Sobibor. Wooden barracks in which to store clothes, linens, shoes, and household goods they stole from the Jews; open sheds in which to sort and bundle them; a barracks for ironing clothes; an Administration Building with a room for the diamonds, gold, and silver they took, and vegetable gardens, stables, pigsties, chicken coops, and rabbit pens.

In the northwest corner of Sobibor, Camp III, the Nazis doubled the gas chambers, to six. They could hold between five hundred and six hundred Jews at a time, enabling the Nazis to process a large transport in a few hours. To clean out the gas chambers and bury the corpses, the Nazis kept a work force of a hundred Jews, who, like Shlomo's friend Avi, slept in the barracks next to the "showers" and the shed where Jewish dentists chiseled gold from teeth.

To make Sobibor run still more smoothly, the Nazis built a high-powered generator that provided enough light so that they could gas Jews at night, and a small train with dump cars like those used to haul coal in the mines south of Krakow. The train tracks began at the unloading platform in front of the Officers' Compound, stretched into Camp II past the warehouses where the sorted clothes were stored, along the sorting sheds, parallel with the tube leading to Camp III, to the rear of the gas chambers, and then to the mass graves. The miners' train toted suitcases from the boxcars to the sorting sheds, bundles of clothes from the warehouses to the empty cars sitting on the spur inside the camp, wood to Camp III, and corpses from the gas chambers to the burial pits.

SS Sergeant Fallaster was in charge of the Jews who laid the tracks, and he built his railroad with blood. Short, squat, homely, and slightly hard of hearing, he whipped his crew to a frenzy so that his train would be ready for the first transports to squeak into the "new" Sobibor. If a Jew wasn't working fast enough, or if he angered Fallaster, the Nazi would beat him with a sledgehammer. Sergeant Fallaster smashed dozens to death that summer. Those who escaped with broken bones were taken to Camp III and shot.

Up to late summer, the bodies of the gassed Jews were buried in mass graves two hundred feet long, thirty to forty-five feet wide, and fifteen to twenty feet deep. Covered with lime, the corpses would swell six to ten feet in the sun like mounds of dough. Once the gas from decomposition was released, they would sink back down, and the Jews would cover them with dirt. The Nazis found that burying the corpses caused three major problems.

The summer of 1942 was one of the hottest on record, and the stench of the more than fifty thousand Jews rotting in Sobibor was overpowering. Like a pestilence, the smell spread over the sweet-scented pine forest and seemed to penetrate everything, including SS uniforms. Furthermore, the water table at Sobibor, only a few miles from the Bug River, was high.

After the snow melted in the spring, the southern tip of the camp just outside the fences turned into a swamp. The Germans were concerned that their drinking water would become contaminated and that typhoid would break out. They were also worried that someone someday might stumble on the mass graves, and Sobibor would no longer be a secret.

So the Nazis dragged in a steam shovel and forced the Camp III Jews to dig up and burn all the corpses. The Jews stacked them like sacks of rotten potatoes on train tracks resting on concrete pillars. Then they sloshed the mounds with gasoline or kerosene and set fire to the wood piled underneath. They worked in crews around the clock. By night, the sky was bright with an orange glow. By day, black smoke curled in the windless sky as if the forest of the owls were on fire.

With the expansion of the camp came a change in administration. Captain Stangl was promoted to Kommandant of Treblinka, the larger death camp just beginning to exterminate the Jews from the Warsaw ghetto. Captain Franz Reichleitner, Stangl's Austrian friend from the old euthanasia program days, replaced him. Reichleitner was a tall, heavyset soldier who walked with a grace one did not expect from a large man. He was stricter than Stangl, but much more friendly and accessible to the Germans and Ukrainians. The Jews rarely saw him, and when they did, it was only to hear him shout, "Idiot, hurry up . . . Idiot, faster . . . Idiot, not that way, this way." The Jews nicknamed him "the Idiot." His office assistant was Johann Niemann, a slim, withdrawn man who kept to himself and liked to ride around the camp on horseback. The Jews rarely saw him, either. They nicknamed him "Johnny."

Under the new system, Gustav Wagner became a roving supervisor responsible for the overall performance of the worker Jews; SS Sergeant Karl Frenzel was placed in charge of Camp I and took over Wagner's duties when the Austrian was on leave; SS Sergeant Hubert Gomerski supervised the forest brigade, which cut the firewood for heating the SS quarters and burning the dead Jews; and SS Sergeant Erich Bauer was in charge of the gas chamber. The Jews called him the *Badmeister*, "the Bathmaster."

Transports halted during most of August and September while the Nazis rebuilt Sobibor. And with no trains, there was little food to steal. Most prisoners had to survive on the bread and mush the Nazis dished up — hot water with some cabbage, barley, or potatoes and, if they were lucky, scraps of horsemeat. Poor food and hard work weakened dozens. They were simply shot. Jews like Shlomo managed to trade with Ukrainians like Klat — gold for kielbasa and chicken. Others wheedled extra bread from SS Sergeant Joseph Kliehr, a baker before the war and supervisor of

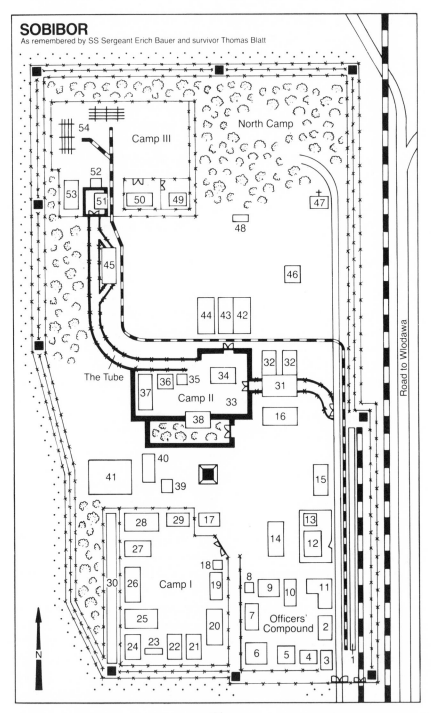

SOBIBOR
As remembered by SS Sergeant Erich Bauer and survivor Thomas Blatt

North Camp

Camp III

54

53

52

51

50

49

47

48

45

46

44 43 42

The Tube

37

36 35

34

Camp II

33

38

32 32

31

16

40

41

39

30 26

28

27

Camp I

18

19

17

29

20

14

13

12

15

8

9 10

11

7

Officers'
Compound

2

24

23

22 21

25

6

5

4

3

1

N

Road to Wlodawa

54

Officers' Compound

1. Unloading platform
2. Dentist office for SS and jail for Ukrainian guards
3. Guard house
4. SS clothing storeroom
5. SS quarters — the Swallow's Nest
6. SS quarters
7. Laundry
8. Well
9. Showers and barbershop for SS
10. Garage
11. SS kitchen and canteen
12. Kommandant's headquarters — the Merry Flea
13. Armory
14. Barracks for Ukrainian guards
15. Barracks for Ukrainian guards
16. Barracks for Ukrainian guards
17. Bakery

Camp I

18. Dispensary
19. Tailor shop for SS
20. Shoemaker and saddler shop for SS
21. Mechanic shop
22. Carpenter shop
23. Latrine
24. Painters' shop
25. Barracks for male prisoners
26. Barracks for male prisoners
27. Prisoners' kitchen
28. Barracks for female prisoners
29. Shoemaker shop for Ukrainian guards
30. Water ditch

Camp II

31. Barracks where new arrivals deposited hand luggage
32. Barracks where hand luggage was sorted
33. Undressing yard

34. Food warehouse and porch from which SS gave welcoming speech
35. Kiosk where SS collected money and jewels
36. Electrical generator
37. Stable and barns
38. Administration building and storeroom for valuables
39. SS ironing room
40. Shoe warehouse
41. Garden
42. Barracks for sorting clothes and suitcases
43. Barracks for sorting clothes and suitcases
44. Warehouse for sorted clothes
45. Barracks where women's hair was cut
46. Incinerator
47. "Hospital" (former chapel) where the sick were shot
48. Latrine

Camp III

49. Barracks for Camp III worker Jews
50. Barracks for Camp III worker Jews, kitchen, and "dentist" workshop
51. Gas chambers
52. Engine room for gas chambers
53. Fenced yard
54. Outdoor crematoria

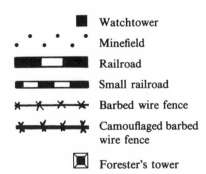

■ Watchtower
• • • • Minefield
Railroad
Small railroad
✳—✳—✳—✳ Barbed wire fence
✳—✳—✳—✳ Camouflaged barbed wire fence
◧ Forester's tower

the Sobibor bakery. He was a decent sort of Nazi, neither mean nor sadistic.

With the expansion came a new wave of Germanic discipline. The Jews were divided into work brigades supervised by Kapos — Jews with whips and the authority to use them. Whistles and bugles called them to get up, work, eat, and sleep.

The Nazis took advantage of the long summer evenings to have fun. They drilled the Jews like SS recruits, teaching them to march around the Camp I yard in columns: "One . . . two . . . left . . . right . . . about-face . . . halt." They taught them marching songs and *Hofbrauhaus* songs, and drilled them until they were fit for a parade.

And they forced them to do calisthenics: "Up . . . down . . . double time . . . duck-walk." The old and the weak couldn't keep up, exhausted as they were from the ghettos, the transports, lack of food and rest, and the hard work. When they slowed, the Nazis yanked them from the lines, forced them to duck-walk until they toppled, or do situps until they vomited. Then they whipped them as if they were tired, stubborn mules. Most were sent to Camp III.

Work in Camp III was maddening. Jews committed suicide there or, unable to eat or sleep, wore themselves out. Most just gave up and died. To make matters even worse, Kapo Franz, appointed by the Nazis to supervise the Camp III workers, went quite mad. He was only eighteen, and both Avi and Shlomo had known him from Opole. The fatigue, horror, and the responsibility had gotten to Franz, and he began to think of himself as an SS man and Jews as termites to be exterminated. Like an SS officer, he wore shiny black boots, polished by some tired Jew, and pranced around with his whip, arrogant and vain. His delusions had reached such a state that he became even crueler than the Nazis and Ukrainians.

One day Franz and Avi, led by Sergeant Bolander, came into the mechanic shop, where Shlomo was now working, to get some nails. The goldsmith could barely recognize his friend. Dressed in rags, stooped, Avi was as gaunt as an old man. Despair haunted his dark eyes, as if they had seen all the horror in the world and there was nothing left to dream or imagine.

Kapo Franz strutted around the shop, watching the Jews pounding, shaping, and welding. He walked by Shlomo without so much as a flicker of recognition. "Hey, good-for-nothing," he began to shout at the workers as Bolander stood smiling. "You live like princes in paradise. You belong in Camp III . . . with *me*. I'd teach you what work means."

Shlomo tried to catch Avi's attention, but the boy avoided his eyes. Then, just before he left, Avi glanced at his friend with great sadness, shook his head slightly, and left with the nails.

Out of sheer desperation, the Camp III Jews began digging a tunnel. When the Nazis found out about it, shortly after Avi's visit to the mechanic shop, they selected every second Jew — including Avi — and lined them up. While the other fifty were ordered to sing a melancholy German ballad, they shot the Jews two at a time.

Shlomo, Itzhak, and the others in Camp I learned about the murders from Klat, who walked into the kitchen, boots covered with blood, bragging about the massacre. "Just make enough for fifty," the Blackie told the cook.

Shlomo and the others were devastated. They weren't sure whether the Camp III Jews had actually tried to dig a tunnel or whether the Nazis simply told them that. But two things were clear. Half of the Jews in Camp III had been murdered, and the Nazis were sending a warning: "If you try to escape, that's what will happen to you."

Chapter 9

Fall 1942

In THE FALL of 1942, the death trains pulled into Sobibor without end, sometimes two or three a day. They came from the smaller ghettos of eastern Poland and from the west — Austria, Germany, Bohemia, and Slovakia. The Nazis had told the western Jews that they were going to a work camp in the Ukraine, and they believed them. There was no reason not to, for Operation Reinhard was still a secret outside Poland and the Soviet Union. And the Nazis were able to deceive them right up to the very end.

They came to Sobibor in passenger trains, not boxcars, some traveling in the comfort of roomettes and sleepers. When they spilled from the trains, dressed in their finest furs and silks and toting the last of their riches — gold and diamonds, linens and leather, heirlooms and herring — smiling Ukrainians greeted them. The *Bahnhofkommando* — a train brigade of Sobibor prisoners sporting smart blue coveralls and caps with *BK* — helped them from the cars, took their luggage, and gave them baggage claim checks. The western Jews swallowed the bait so completely that some asked the train brigade whether they had arrived in the Ukraine, or how far it was to the next station, or when the next train would leave. Some even offered their porters tips. Like sad actors, the train brigade played their roles, because the Nazis had ordered them under pain of death to guard the secret of Sobibor, and SS Sergeant Karl Frenzel stood nearby to make sure they did.

Dressed in a white jacket like a doctor, Sergeant Hubert Gomerski weeded out the weak. "Are you sick?" he'd ask as he looked over the new Jews. "Having trouble walking? Over here, then — on the little train. I'll take you to the hospital for a checkup." When the miners' train chugged into the "hospital" — a prewar chapel deep inside Camp II — SS Sergeant Paul Bredov and his Ukrainian helpers shot them.

Back in the arrival square, SS Sergeant Hermann Michel officially welcomed the new Jews from the west. He was a tall, graceful man with delicate features and a pleasant voice. He had worked in the euthanasia program with Captain Stangl as head nurse at Schloss Hartheim. The Sobibor Jews called him "the Preacher."

"Welcome to Sobibor," he'd say. "You will be sent to a work camp. Families will stay together. Those of you who work hard will be rewarded. There is nothing to be afraid of here. We are concerned, however, about disease and epidemic. So we'll ask you to take a shower. Men to the right. Women and children under six to the left."

Sometimes, more as a joke than to deceive, he'd say, "You'll all be going to the Ukraine as soon as it can be arranged. There the Reich will establish an independent Jewish state for you." Some of the German or Austrian Jews would cheer while Michel tried to keep a straight face.

To the new Jews, Sobibor looked like a Tyrolean village behind barbed wire. As they walked down the sandy road from the unloading platform to Camp II to undress and have their hair cut, they passed the neat rows of SS officers' houses and barracks with sunflowers and geraniums and names like the Swallow's Nest and the Merry Flea. Signs painted by the two boys who lived with Shlomo pointed to the CANTEEN, the SHOWERS, the ROAD TO HEAVEN. If anyone along the way asked Shlomo, Itzhak, or the other Jews about Sobibor, they were ordered to say "This is a work camp. The food is good and the work easy. There's nothing to worry about."

They obeyed, torn between wanting to scream the truth through the fences and wanting the new Jews to go to their death in peace. Secretly, they were happy the transports were from the west, filled with rich Jews who brought hundreds of pounds of cheese, salami, sardines, and chocolate, rather than from Poland, where the Jews had long since been stripped of everything. Without food to steal, the Sobibor Jews were doomed to grow weak or get sick. They'd end up in Camp III before the fall was out.

Once, Itzhak tried to warn the Jews from the west with Yiddish notes, reading, "This is a death camp. Revolt!" But most believed the German lie so completely that they refused to open the notes for fear of getting caught and being punished. Those who did read them, especially the older German Jews, tore them up or shouted, "Don't! It's a trick."

At the entrance to the thatched corridor — ROAD TO HEAVEN — that led to Camp III, the Nazis collected all the gold and money they could wheedle from the Jews, entering names and amounts in a large ledger. Small boys passed out pieces of string, shouting, "Tie your shoes together so that you can find them later." The Nazis passed out postcards to some Jews, asking them to write back to Vienna or Berlin that they had arrived safely at a work camp near Wlodawa. (The Nazis mailed them later.) Prisoners collected passports, identity cards, and personal papers. (They were burned later.) And Wagner or Frenzel walked up and down the lines, calling for shoemakers or carpenters or tinsmiths.

When the women and children walked through the gate alone, the western men did not object strongly. Naturally, it would be immodest to take showers with the women and girls, they reasoned. The Nazis were at least that decent. Some men tipped their hats when a Nazi passed, as they had been ordered to do in Hamburg or Frankfurt. And when they stripped, they folded and piled their clothes neatly, just as they did back home before they bathed.

The women and girls had their hair shorn in a barracks. Then they ran naked to the gas chambers, where Erich Bauer and Kurt Bolander waited for them.

If the Jews from Germany and Austria came to Sobibor like virgins to a brothel, the Polish Jews did not. By the fall of 1942, most had heard of Belzec and Treblinka. More than fifty thousand of them — whole families — had fled to the forests of eastern Poland rather than go there. The Parczew Forest, a few miles west of Sobibor, was one of the best hiding places in the east. It was a two-thousand-square-mile expanse of thick woods filled with lakes and marshes and wagon ruts for roads. More than two thousand Jews earmarked for Sobibor and Belzec, like Elias Liberman and Michael Knopfmacher, had fled there.

On his way to Sobibor, Elias pried loose a few boxcar boards with the knife he had hidden in his boot. He and five other young men squeezed through. Three died in the fall; Elias and two others were only bruised.

Michael escaped from the Wlodawa ghetto in 1941 and hid in the Parczew until the winter. But without food and clothes, he was driven back to Wlodawa. Two Nazis stopped him. "Are you a Jew?" they asked.

"No, I'm a Polack."

A Pole passing by overheard him. "Don't believe him," the Pole had said. "He's a Jew."

The Nazis stuffed Michael in the next train to Sobibor. He and another young man ripped off the window bars and barbed wire and jumped. They lay close to the tracks while the Germans on patrol hunted and shot others who had jumped. The Germans somehow missed Michael, and he fled to the Parczew.

Those who didn't escape because they were afraid, or who decided to take a chance on being sent to a work camp, or who could not abandon their children and wives, aged mothers and fathers, came to Sobibor. When they saw the smoke in the sky and smelled the sweet, fetid air, they suspected the worst. The Nazis took no chances with them. Using fear and panic, the Germans stampeded them from the boxcars to the gas chambers.

To keep the Polish Jews disoriented when the sunlight flooded into the dark boxcars once the doors slid open, the Nazis and Ukrainians shot pistols into the air, shoved, dragged, and whipped, separating children from mothers and husbands from wives. The unloading platform became a scene from hell, with screams and shouts rising in a giant crescendo. The Nazis whipped and beat resisters or shot them inside the cars and along the tracks. They tossed the old, sick, and weak into the miners' train, along with the dead.

Once, the Nazis took three hundred Polish men from a transport and, after the train brigade had cleaned and disinfected the cars, forced the three hundred to reload the train with the clothes, shoes, and toys stored in the warehouses. The men were weak from starvation and exhausted from the long trip to Sobibor, but the Nazis worked them at breakneck speed, beating them with whips. When anyone faltered or fell, they'd yank them from the lines and string them up on a tree, their bodies twisting in the breeze for all to see. Now and then, instead of hanging a tired Jew, the Nazis would force-feed him sand or bottles of pills and medicine taken from the transports until he collapsed in convulsions and died. Somehow the train was filled, and those who had survived the torture were forced to pile the dead into the miners' wagons, and then march to Camp III.

Another time, a transport of mentally sick arrived. They were a wretched lot, totally disoriented, mumbling to themselves, weeping, walking in circles, and shouting in confusion. Because they posed no threat and seemed an interesting group, the Nazis decided to have a little fun before they sent them to the gas chambers. They organized the sick into units and made them do calisthenics, laughing as the sick stumbled, fell, tried to duck-walk or do knee bends like an army of drunken recruits. When they tired of the game, the Nazis led them away.

The Polish Jews resisted. Sometimes all the men, women, and children in a transport arrived at Sobibor naked. Some had tried to escape on the way, so the Nazis made them all strip, figuring that no one would try to run into the woods without clothes.

Another time, a whole group of women, many holding children, attacked the Ukrainians and Nazis in the tube to Camp III. Realizing that they weren't going to a shower, and fearing the worst, they clawed, scratched, bit, and cursed. The SS sprayed them with machine guns. Those they missed were stuffed into the gas chambers.

Then there was the old Jew whom Sergeant Frenzel pushed into the miners' train. Using all his strength to crawl out again, he scooped up a handful of sand. "Do you see how I'm scattering this slowly, grain by grain?" he asked Frenzel. "That's what will happen to your great Reich. It will vanish like flying dust and passing smoke."

The old man joined the long line reciting, "Hear, O Israel." The prayer of faith gave him strength, and when he reached the words "The Lord is One," he quickly slapped Frenzel in the face. Kommandant Franz Reichleitner, who was standing nearby, enjoyed the performance so much that when Frenzel raised his rifle to smash the old man, Reichleitner stopped him.

"Let me," the Kommandant said. "Go on with your job." He pulled the old man aside and shot him on the spot.

Day after day, Abraham Margulies and the train brigade had to watch the western Jews walk innocently to their deaths and the Polish Jews be driven there. It was the most sickening job in Sobibor.

Abraham and his brother had come to Sobibor in May, shortly after Shlomo. Gustav Wagner sent him to clean out the boxcars, and his brother to the gas chambers. When Wagner organized the blue-uniformed train brigade, he kept Abraham on it.

Abraham dragged the dead and sick Poles from the boxcars, cleaned the vomit, blood, and feces from the floors, piled the luggage onto the miners' train, and helped reload transports with clothes and goods destined for Lublin. His supervisor was SS Sergeant Paul Groth — tall, lean, handsome, and vain. When any member of the brigade couldn't keep up the pace Groth had set — some were just fourteen and fifteen years old — he would ask: "Oh, poor fellow, you feel tired? Let's go to the hospital."

Behind the "hospital" was a long, deep ditch. Ordering the tired Jew to stand in it with a tin can on his head, Sergeant Groth would keep picking it off with his pistol or rifle until he missed. Then he'd go back to the unloading platform, looking for more laggards.

Even worse, Groth used to patrol the train brigade with Barry, who was trained to attack on the command: "Man, go get that dog." When the mongrel Saint Bernard attacked, he reached the buttocks and hip of an average man. Groth would watch in fascination as Barry tore off genitals or pieces of buttocks or mauled the Jews who fell down from fear and fatigue. When Sergeant Groth called off Barry, the dog obeyed immediately, becoming a tame pet once again. Those whom Barry had maimed so badly that they could no longer work Groth took immediately to the "hospital." The others loaded clothes or cleaned cars until evening or the next morning, when Wagner or Frenzel noticed a limp or some blood. The wounded were sent to Camp III.

Week after week, Abraham stood by helplessly, while the Nazis beat the newly arrived Poles and tricked the German and Austrian Jews, until he almost lost his sanity. He walked in an unreal zone between reality and dream, not even sure if he himself were alive or dead. And just as he thought he had finally become hardened to screams and gunshots and death, he reached into a car to help a young mother with a baby. When the child saw Abraham's outstretched arms, it smiled and gurgled in delight. Abraham wept. They were tears that he thought he no longer had. They flowed for his parents, his brothers, the baby and its mother, for all Jews. He cried so deeply and so completely from his soul that he knew he would never again cry in Sobibor.

One day in the fall of 1942, a shiver of hope ran through Sobibor like a spasm. Abraham and the rest of the train brigade were loading clothes into empty cars while Sergeant Groth paraded up and down with Barry, shouting his usual "Faster, faster!" He sicked the dog on one of the Jews who wasn't moving quickly enough. Luckily for the prisoner, Barry tore into his buttocks without knocking him over. Groth called the dog off, and the Jew went back to work, knowing full well he'd be shot that night or the next morning.

"Hide me in one of the cars," he told Abraham. "It's my only hope. If I die there, then I die."

"Under one condition," Abraham said.

"What?"

"That you promise to tell everyone you meet about what's going on here."

The Jew agreed, so Abraham and several others hid him under packages of clothes inside a boxcar, careful not to cover up the small window. At the end of the day, the Germans pulled the filled cars onto the switching track and backed in a chain of empty ones.

The next morning, Sergeant Frenzel called the train brigade. He was furious. He had noticed some boards torn off one of the boxcar windows. When he opened the door, he saw that there were clothes strewn on top of a bundle and that the car had not been loaded to the roof, as he had ordered.

"Why wasn't the car filled?" he screamed at the train brigade. "Who broke the package of clothes? Who tore the boards off the window?"

No one answered, so Frenzel ordered fifty lashes for each member of the brigade. For Abraham, there was pleasure mixed with the pain. A Jew had finally escaped. The world would soon know about Sobibor.

Word spread quickly through the camp that night, and in the weeks ahead Abraham heard rumors from the new Jews selected to work at Sobibor that an escaped prisoner was going from ghetto to ghetto, warning Jews about Sobibor. He waited for the partisans to attack the camp or for the Allies to bomb the rails. But the transports of Jews kept rolling in.

Chapter 10

Fall 1942

WHEN THE NAZIS swept Piaski for the last time, they caught Josel, a Czech Jew from Moravia. In the spring of 1942, the Nazis had raided Boskovice and sent him, his father, mother, and sister to Terezin (the Germans called it Theresienstadt), an old Bohemian fortress about twenty miles from Prague. As soon as the Nazis had enough Jews to fill a transport for eastern Poland, they loaded Josel and his family into the boxcars and dumped them in the Piaski ghetto, near Lublin.

Josel was a short, strong, curly-haired man in his mid-twenties. The Judenrat in Piaski assigned him to work on a farm outside the town, and he returned to the ghetto only on weekends. One day in the middle of the week, he and the other Jews working outside the ghetto were ordered to return. It was a bad sign. The Polish farmer Josel worked for offered to hide him until times got better for Jews, but Josel turned him down. He had friends in the ghetto, he said. And although times were bad, they were not that bad.

On the way back to Piaski, Josel met a drunken Pole weaving down the road on a bicycle. "Jew, don't go back," he slurred. "They'll kill you." Josel didn't believe him and joined his friends at an apartment in the building owned by Mordechai Goldfarb's family.

One night soon after his return to Piaski, Josel went to visit some friends on the other side of the ghetto. About two o'clock in the morning, a Jew rapped on the door. "The saddle-maker was called back," he said. The

65

saddler was the last Jew the Nazis allowed to work outside the ghetto. His having been called back signaled another roundup for "relocation."

Like most other Polish Jews in late 1942, the Jews of Piaski knew about Belzec, for they had paid a Catholic to follow the first transport there. All the Jews were taken to a camp in the woods and never heard from again, the Christian told them.

Josel's friends encouraged him to stay with them for the night, because it was past curfew and the gate between the two parts of the ghetto would be locked. But Josel decided to return. He found a hole that a dog had dug and slithered under the fence.

Josel, Mordechai Goldfarb, and a dozen other Jews crept into the Goldfarbs' cellar, scraped sand off a wooden cover on the floor next to the back brick wall, and crawled into a tunnel that led them under the wall and up into a small, damp room. They had agreed to exclude a family with a baby, for fear that the infant might cry and give them all away.

At six o'clock that morning, the SS broke into the basement, shouting. "Out! Everyone out of the hiding place. We're clearing all Jews out of Piaski!"

No one behind the wall dared even breathe.

But the SS went straight to the hide-out entrance and kicked off the cover under the sand. *"Raus! Raus!"* they ordered.

One by one, the Jews filed out. The SS picked Mordechai and his brother, as if they knew it was their cellar, beat them almost senseless, and tied their hands together. Then, with the two brothers at the head of the column, the Nazis marched the Jews six miles to the train station in Trawniki, where they joined a transport from Izbica. The Nazis planted explosives in the half of the ghetto where Josel's friends were hiding. They died under the rubble.

As Josel stood near the unloading platform in Sobibor, Sergeant Michel, the Preacher, called out, "Some heartless mother left her baby in the train. Isn't there one mother here with a big enough heart to take it so that it won't die?"

The Jews understood. Some mother had left her child either because she thought she'd stand a better chance without it, or because she hoped the train would take it out of Sobibor.

"God spared me so far, Josel," a woman next to the Czech Jew said. "I'll take the child." She went over to the boxcar and took the two-year-old into her arms.

The lines divided, men to the right, women and children to the left. As they all waited for something to happen, Kommandant Franz Reichleitner walked down the line of men, calling, "Textile workers? Textilers?" Sobibor needed more Jews to sort clothes, and he thought that men experienced in textiles would do a better job.

Josel knew nothing about textiles, but his instincts told him that he'd probably get an easier job if he volunteered.

"Over here," he shouted. "I'm a textile expert."

"Where are you from?" Captain Reichleitner asked in German thick with a Viennese accent. He was wearing the brown uniform of the SD Security Police.

Josel, who spoke perfect German, knew that the Nazi had never heard of Boskovice. So he lied. "I'm from Brno," he said. Brno was the capital of Moravia and the nation's textile center.

"Over there," Reichleitner said.

Josel glanced at the woman holding the baby. She shrugged at him as if to ask "What's happening? Why did he pull you from the line?" Josel shook his head: "I don't know." And the line of women and children marched through the gate.

A Ukrainian took Josel to Camp II, where he met a girl he had known in Piaski. "Consider yourself lucky," she said, hinting that something was going on in Camp III nearby. "The others are in for a bad time." Josel peered through the camouflaged fence, but a Kapo pulled him away and ordered him to sort clothes.

Josel's father, mother, and sister had already been "resettled." Just hours before the Nazis dragged him away, Josel's father had borrowed his son's new overcoat. Josel found it hanging on a rack in the new clothes barracks of Camp II. And before the day was out, he learned the secret of Sobibor. He wrestled with the truth for three days, using every trick his mind could create to explain it away. In the end, he accepted it and settled down to the business at hand — survival.

Josel noticed there were two categories of Jews at Sobibor: the emaciated and the relatively healthy. He knew that somehow the strong got extra food, and it didn't take him long to figure out one way to do it.

Sergeant Frenzel assigned Josel to sort the odds and ends, found in the pockets and handbags of the Jews, in a ten-foot-square shed near the stables. There were mounds of small items — fountain pens, razors, spectacles, pocket knives, combs, hairbrushes. Since Josel's father used to hide money in the hollow top of his hairbrush, Josel shook and tapped each brush, prying off the top if he suspected something was underneath. Before long, he had a steady flow of gold pieces, marks, and rubles.

A Ukrainian guard who worked nearby used to come to the shed looking for anything he could sell to Polish farmers. Josel offered the greedy Ukrainian a deal — gold for food. The business thrived. Every other day, the guard would bring kielbasa and vodka under his coat and walk away with money in his pocket. Josel ate the sausage and gave away the vodka. Before long, he was one of the healthy Jews.

*

Wagner yanked Mordechai Goldfarb and his brother, still tied together, from the boxcar. "Cut," he ordered a Ukrainian.

The Nazi noticed some papers sticking out of Mordechai's pocket, and his curiosity got the best of him. "What?" he demanded.

"A work permit," Mordechai said as his brother joined the line of men for Camp III.

"For what?" Wagner said.

"I'm a painter."

"Your family here?"

"My brother is with me."

"He's a painter, too? And your mother? A paintress." Wagner's voice dripped sarcasm.

"No, my mother isn't," Mordechai said. "But my brother is a professional. Better than me."

"His name?"

Mordechai told him.

"Wait!"

Mordechai stood for what seemed like hours. The line of women and children disappeared, then the men. The train brigade, under the direction of Sergeant Frenzel, began to toss luggage onto the miners' train and to clean out the boxcars. Just when Mordechai had given up hope of ever seeing his brother again, Wagner walked through the gate with the boy, who was wearing someone else's clothes.

Wagner took Mordechai and his brother to Camp I, gave them something to eat, and then ordered them to clean the sandy road of all traces of their transport, for a train filled with Jews from Germany was sitting on the switching rail outside the camp.

Wagner set Mordechai up in the ironing room in Camp II near the stables and assigned his brother to sort clothes. He gave the artist paints, canvases, and brushes taken from other transports — and a postcard.

"Copy it," Wagner ordered. "I'll be back."

Wagner needed pictures to decorate the officers' quarters, the offices, and the canteen. To copy the postcard was an easy job for Mordechai, even though his profession was sign-painting. Wagner was pleased. He brought more postcards, one of a stormy sky with billowing black clouds and sunlight pushing through.

"For me," Wagner told Mordechai. The scene suited the brooding Nazi. Mordechai selected a 28-by-20-inch canvas, and when the oil painting was finished, Wagner was delighted. He lived near the main gate in the cottage called the Swallow's Nest with Frenzel, Bolander, and Gomerski, so he ordered Mordechai to design a swallow logo and, after he approved it, to paint it on every piece of furniture in the house.

Before winter hit Sobibor, Mordechai caught typhus. He was so weak and delirious with fever, he couldn't paint. He suspected that if Wagner found out, he'd send him to Camp III, because labor was so cheap that fall that the Nazis were killing Jews at the smallest sign of a weakness — even a bandaged finger.

While Mordechai rested in the corner, the ironers kept a lookout for Wagner. "He's coming," they'd whisper, and Mordechai would crawl back to his work table and hold his brushes until the Nazi left. But Wagner was as silent as a black ghost, sometimes hiding between barracks or in corners to catch hapless Jews breaking rules. One day he slipped into Mordechai's shop unseen. The artist waited for the whip to fall.

"Sick?" Wagner asked.

"Yes," Mordechai admitted. He was afraid to lie; the Nazi had guessed the truth.

Wagner walked out. Mordechai waited for him to return with two Ukrainians to drag him to Camp III. Instead, Wagner picked some Jews to clean out an old chicken coop near the ironing barracks and to help Mordechai inside. Wagner liked the artist's work and didn't want to lose him. Furthermore, Mordechai's was the first case of typhus at Sobibor, and Wagner wanted to isolate the artist so that he couldn't spread it to the Germans.

Wagner cared for Mordechai as if he were a prize cock. He looked in, brought food, and told him to rest. Then one day Mordechai learned through the grapevine that Wagner was going home on leave. Work at the camps was considered exceptionally hard duty, and the Nazis got two weeks' leave for every six weeks at Sobibor. Frenzel took Wagner's place. As he wasn't sure what Frenzel would do, Mordechai crawled to roll call. The Jews to the left and right held him up.

One by one, the Kapos counted noses and reported to Frenzel, who tallied the figures. After the first count, Frenzel had one more Jew than he was supposed to. He ordered another count, ready to beat the Kapo who had made the mistake. Still, one Jew too many.

"Who is it?" Frenzel asked Moishe, the head Kapo.

"The painter. He was sick."

"Get him."

They helped Mordechai over to Frenzel.

"Well, painter! Do you want to live or die?" Frenzel asked.

"Live."

"Then get back to bed."

Unable to believe his luck, Mordechai thought Frenzel was going to play a new game with him. But the next day, Frenzel came to the chicken coop at noon while Mordechai was drinking his watery soup.

"You still hungry? Do you want more food?" Frenzel asked.

Mordechai nodded. A few minutes later, the Nazi returned with a plate of eggs and potatoes, and left. Mordechai gobbled the food, unable to believe his fortune. About half an hour later, Frenzel returned again with Klat.

"Still hungry?" the Nazi asked.

"Yes," Mordechai said. Even if he wasn't hungry, he'd eat more.

"Get him something," Frenzel ordered Klat. The Blackie brought a bowl of thick potato-vegetable soup from the Ukrainian kitchen. Mordechai ate as Frenzel watched, his thin smile stretching to a grin.

All the while Wagner was on leave, Frenzel pampered Mordechai. He brought a bed into the old chicken coop and so much food that Mordechai, afraid to turn it down, still thought the Nazi might be playing a game. But Frenzel was sincere. He really wanted the artist to recover, and as soon as Mordechai could sit up, the Nazi brought him his table, canvases, brushes, and paints. Soon Mordechai had five new assistants, including his younger brother. (The two sign painters who had lived with Shlomo had angered Wagner again, and he had sent them to Camp III.) They painted signs while Mordechai copied portraits of Hitler and landscapes from postcards.

One day, when a large transport arrived, Frenzel called Mordechai and his assistants to the unloading platform to help the train brigade move the new Jews more quickly and to clean up after them. Mordechai stood next to a Polish couple. The man hugged the woman and kissed her good-by with all the despair a last kiss can have. A Ukrainian saw them. "Hey, you, come on!" He moved toward them in huge strides. "Let's go."

When the pair clung to each other, refusing to be separated, the guard tripped the man to the ground and stomped on his skull with his boots before the woman's eyes.

"Toss him on the train," the guard ordered Mordechai. But the artist was so shocked, he couldn't bend down to drag the man to the miners' train.

The Ukrainian laughed. "Get out of here," he told Mordechai. "Go on back to your paints and brushes. You're good for nothing over here."

The Nazis never again ordered Mordechai to join the train brigade; it was almost as if they were afraid that the shock might freeze his brushes.

Chapter 11

Fall 1942

Witold walked into a bombed-out house in the suburbs of Warsaw. It was twilight, and the scarred mansion, not far from the walls of the ghetto, stood as a symbol of the German occupation of Poland — not destroyed, but not whole; divided, but not conquered.

Two Jews were waiting for Witold, a courier for the Polish underground. One was Leon Feiner, leader of the Jewish Socialist Alliance, called the Bund; the other was Adolf Berman, leader of the Zionists. Witold was on the eve of his fourth trip west and had volunteered to be a courier for the Jewish underground as well.

Jan Kozielewski, alias Jan Karski, code-named Witold, was a twenty-seven-year-old Catholic. When the Nazis invaded Poland in September 1939, Karski was captured by the Soviets, who had agreed not to block the Germans in exchange for eastern Poland. They returned Karski, a lieutenant in the artillery, to the Germans, but he escaped through a boxcar window and joined the underground. Because he knew and understood the west — he had studied in western Europe for three years — and because of his excellent memory, the underground trained him as a courier.

Karski's job was demanding and dangerous. Without bias or interpretation, he was to explain to the Polish government-in-exile — first in Angers, France, then in London — the conditions inside Poland and the plans and organization of the underground. His route west was complex — across the Carpathian Mountains on Poland's southern border into Slovakia and

72

then to Budapest; on the Orient Express from Budapest to Paris via Milan, under an assumed name and with forged papers.

Karski's first two trips were successful. But on the third, the Nazis caught him in Preshov, Slovakia. They knew he was a courier because they found film on him.

When Karski refused to talk, the Gestapo beat him behind the ears with rubber truncheons, a torture that caused intense pain without loss of consciousness. When he still didn't talk, they beat him with fists and clubs until he passed out, then left him in his cell for three days.

The Gestapo questioned Karski a second time. Again he refused to talk, and again they beat him senseless, knocking out several front teeth. Realizing he couldn't hold out much longer, he cut his wrists with a razor blade concealed in his shoe.

Karski woke up in a hospital, tied to his bed. Almost immediately, the Gestapo demanded that the hospital turn Karski over to them, but the doctors — members of the underground — convinced them that the courier would die if they questioned him so soon. With the help of doctors and hospital nuns, an underground woman, dressed as a man, visited Karski. He would be rescued at midnight, she told him. He was to walk out of his room — the Nazi guard had been bribed — look for a window with a rose on the sill, and jump. She left him a cyanide pill just in case things didn't work out.

That night, naked and with the poison in his hand, Karski jumped. The underground caught him, carried him to a canoe hidden in the rushes, and paddled him across the river to an empty barn. Three days later, buried under hay and cabbages, he rode in a cart to a Polish estate, where he posed as a long-lost cousin from Krakow who was an expert gardener. After he recuperated, he rejoined the underground in Warsaw.

In the fall of 1942, the underground prepared to send Karski west for the fourth time. He would carry over a thousand pages of documents on microfilm sealed inside the handle of his razor. "Witold leaving soon," the underground warned the Polish government-in-exile in a coded short-wave message. "Goes through Germany, Belgium, France, Spain. Two weeks stay in France; two weeks in Spain. Inform all 'transfer cells' in France, also all Allied representatives in Spain. Password: 'Coming to see Aunt Sophie.' Announce him as Karski."

Before Karski left, his superior asked him to help the Jews. "They heard you're going," he said. "They want you to represent them, too. You don't have to. But I would appreciate it if you did. It's the least I can do for them."

Karski wasn't sure what to expect when he walked into the bombed-out mansion. Feiner greeted him. For security, no names were used. With silvery hair and whiskers, and rosy cheeks, the Jew stood tall, like a Polish nobleman. Before the war, he had been a superb criminal lawyer; now he lived outside the ghetto, passing as a Polish businessman. Berman was younger than Feiner and more hotheaded. He, too, passed as a Pole on the Aryan side of Warsaw.

"We do not agree on much," Feiner began. "But we do agree on what is happening to the Jews and what has to be done."

The Bund and the Zionists were at opposite ends of the Jewish political spectrum. The Bundists wanted to rebuild Poland on socialist principles; the Zionists wanted to leave Poland and create a democratic state in Palestine.

"You other Poles are fortunate," Berman said, his eyes filled with intense despair. "Many of you will die, but at least your nation goes on living . . . Your cities will be rebuilt and your wounds will slowly heal . . . Your country will emerge again. But the Polish Jews will no longer exist. We will be dead."

The two Jews told Karski about the death camps. They described the ghetto — the starvation, the waiting, the hiding, the roundups, the murders. They explained that the Nazis were systematically liquidating the Warsaw ghetto, as they had the ghettos in Opole and Piaski. Since July, they told him, three hundred thousand Warsaw Jews had been dragged off to Treblinka. The Nazis were quickly rounding up the one hundred thousand who were left. Soon it would all be over.

Karski sat in an old armchair, listening to the two Jews. They shouted; they whispered; they paced in the candlelight, casting grotesque shadows on the wall. The courier was stunned. He knew the Jews were being persecuted, but he had no idea the Nazis were insanely exterminating the whole race.

"What's the good of talking," Berman said, head in his hands, weeping like a child. "What reason do I have to go on living? I ought to go to the Germans and tell them who I am. If all the Jews are killed, they won't need any leaders . . . But it's no use telling *you* all this. No one in the outside world can possibly understand. You don't understand. Even I don't. My people are dying, and I am alive."

"I'll be in London soon," Karski told them, "in a position to get audiences with the Allied authorities."

"Will you really?" Berman sounded hopeful. "Do you think you'll get to see Roosevelt? And Churchill?"

"Perhaps." Karski was cautious. "What do you want me to say?"

Their demands were well organized, almost as if they had rehearsed them. First of all, they said, in the name of all Polish Jews warn the Polish government and the Allies that Polish Jews are helpless. The underground and the Polish people cannot save them; they have no independent voice in the Allied Council in London; and they have no country of their own to rescue them. Therefore, they said, Polish Jews demand that the Polish government and the Allies take extraordinary measures to end the extermination. If they fail to act, Polish Jews fix the full responsibility for the genocide on *them.*

Karski agreed to pass on the demand, and Berman became more specific.

"Germany can be impressed only by power and violence," the Zionist said. "The cities of Germany ought to be bombed mercilessly. With every bombing, leaflets should be dropped, informing the Germans fully of the fate of the Polish Jews.

"Such a warning, backed by force, may frighten the German people into putting enough pressure on their leaders to make them change. Nothing else will."

Leaflets and radio messages, Berman explained, must be specific about Nazi crimes against the Jews — names, places, crimes, dates, methods. The Allies must warn the German people that if the extermination continues, the full responsibility for the murder of millions rests on their civilian shoulders.

"We demand still more," Berman continued. "Hitler is conducting ,a total war against civilization. His avowed purpose is to destroy the Jews completely. It is an unprecedented situation in history and can be dealt with only by unprecedented methods. Let the Allied governments, wherever their hands can reach — America, England, Africa — begin public execution of Germans. Any they can get hold of. *That* is what we demand."

Those to be executed in retaliation, Feiner explained, should be German POWs and civilians who are avowed Nazis.

"But that's utterly fantastic," Karski objected. "A demand like that will only confuse and horrify those who are sympathetic."

"Of course!" Berman shouted. "Do you think I don't know that? We ask because it is the only rebuttal. We do not dream of its being fulfilled, but we demand it so that people will know how we feel about what is being done. How helpless we are. How desperate our plight is. How little we stand to gain from an Allied victory as things are now."

Berman and Feiner paced the floor. They whispered, pleaded, raised their fists in anger. To Karski, they were earthquakes — cracking, tearing, ripping themselves apart.

If American and British citizens can be saved, they raged, why can't the evacuation of even the Jewish children be arranged on a large scale? Or Jewish women, or the sick, the old? Offer the Germans an exchange. Offer them money. Why can't the lives of a few thousand Polish Jews be bought by the Allies?

"How?" Karski was shaken. "It is opposed to all war strategy. Can we give our enemies money? Can we give them back their soldiers to use against us in the front lines?"

"Everybody tells us, 'This is contrary to the strategy of this war,'" the two Jews argued. "But strategy can change. Let's adjust it to include a fraction of the unhappy Jewish people. Why does the world let us all die? Haven't we contributed our share to culture? To civilization? Haven't we worked and fought and bled? Why do they fight for all the others?".

Karski stood up. The implications of their demands hit him like a grenade. "What do you want me to suggest to the Jewish leaders in England and America?" he asked. "They have something to say about the course of this war. They can act for you."

Feiner grabbed the courier's arm so tightly, it hurt. Karski was shaken by the deep, unbearable pain in the Jew's eyes.

"Tell them to go to all the important English and American offices and agencies," Feiner said. "Tell them not to leave until they have obtained guarantees that a way has been decided to save the Jews. Let them accept no food or drink! Let them die a slow death while the world is looking on. Let them die! This may shake the conscience of the world."

Karski sank back into his armchair, his temples pulsing and his body shivering from the intensity of their despair.

"We do not demand such sacrifices out of cruelty," Berman explained. "We expect to make them ourselves. The Warsaw ghetto is going up in flames. We are not going to die in slow torment, but fighting. We will *declare war* on Germany . . . the most hopeless declaration of war that has ever been made."

Words trickled like drops from a melting icicle. "We are organizing a defense of the ghetto," Feiner whispered as if the Gestapo were listening, "not because we think it can be defended, but to let the world see the hopelessness of our battle. As a demonstration and a reproach."

Feiner explained that the Jewish underground had asked the Polish Home Army for guns, but that its request had been denied. He told Karski to demand from General Wladyslaw Sikorski, prime minister of the Polish government-in-exile and the commander-in-chief of all Polish forces, that he order the Home Army to give guns to the Jews in the Warsaw ghetto.

The two Jews made other demands:

• The Allied Council must announce publicly that preventing the extermination of Jews is now part of the *war strategy*.

• The Polish government-in-exile must ask the Vatican to excommunicate publicly those Catholics involved in exterminating Jews.

• The president must order the Polish underground to punish or execute Poles who blackmail, denounce, or murder Jews.

• The Allied governments must send blank passports for those Jews who can still be smuggled out of Poland.

"I know Anglo-Saxons," Feiner said. "It would be helpful if you were an eyewitness." He invited Karski to visit the Warsaw ghetto and a death camp. It would not be dangerous to sneak in and out of the ghetto, the Jew warned. But to visit a death camp was risky.

Karski agreed to inspect both, for he knew that if he didn't see for himself, he could not speak with conviction about the condition of the Polish Jews.

*

The courier walked through a ghetto cellar door into hell. All the Jews in Warsaw seemed to be in the streets. The dead and dying lay in the rubble and mud; the living shuffled, stood, lay with glassy eyes staring into space, or they flitted like shadows, moving aimlessly, wandering, searching. Even the cobblestones smelled of death.

Karski passed a park of nearly leafless trees poking out of a patch of grass that seemed out of place. Mothers sat there on benches nursing withered babies at withered breasts. Children swarmed like ants, skeletons inside taut, silklike skin.

"They play before they die," Feiner explained.

A group of about a hundred men marched in formation down the center of the street, carrying ragged bundles with bread and vegetable tops sticking out. To Karski, they seemed stronger than the others, but just as miserable. Their clothes were torn and filthy, their eyes blank, the muscles of their faces frozen in fatigue. And they all looked alike.

Feiner anticipated Karski's question. "The Germans still find them useful," he said. "They can work at repairing roads and tracks. They are protected as long as their hands last and their muscles move. Everyone envies them. We supply as many people as we can with forged documents proving that they hold similar jobs. Otherwise, they would be murdered. We have saved thousands of lives this way. But this cannot work much longer."

Karski pointed to the corpses in the street. "Why are they lying there naked?"

"When a Jew dies," Feiner said, "his family removes his clothes and throws his body in the street. If they don't do that, they have to pay the Germans to have the body buried. They've instituted a burial tax, which practically no one here can afford. Besides, this saves clothing. Every rag counts here."

Then, without a word of warning, Feiner pushed Karski into a doorway and up a flight of stairs. "Hurry, hurry, you have to see this," the Jew said. Karski heard a shot from somewhere as Feiner knocked on a door. "Do you have windows facing the street?" he asked an emaciated face.

"No! The courtyard."

Feiner rushed to the other side of the corridor and pounded. Pushing aside the youngster who cracked the door, Feiner tugged Karski to the window. "Now you will see something," the Jew warned, as he yanked down the shade.

Karski peeped through the crack between the shade and the window. On the street below stood two German boys dressed in the uniform of the Hitlerjugend, rosy-cheeked, blue-eyed, their hair golden in the sun. They were bent over in laughter. The younger boy pulled out his pistol, his eyes roaming the doorways and windows. The ghetto street was deserted.

Suddenly the boy stopped. Like a hunter, he raised his pistol and fired. A window shattered, and a man cried in pain like an animal in the forest.

As the boy shouted in glee, his companion slapped him on the shoulder. They smiled at each other and stood silently in the street for a moment, as if waiting for applause from an invisible audience. Then, arm in arm, they walked to the ghetto gate, their uniforms neat, their boots polished. Two heroes, returning from battle.

Karski couldn't tear his face from the window crack. Voice gone, feet frozen, he was afraid that if he moved, the boys would come back, shoot into another window, and smile again.

"You came to see us," said a woman who was the color of chalk. "It won't do any good. Go back. Run away. Don't torture yourself."

Feiner sat on what used to be a couch, his face in his hands as if to hide his pain from the world. "Take me out of here," Karski told him. "I'm very tired. I must go immediately. I will come back some other time . . . "

When they reached the street, Feiner could barely keep up with the Catholic courier as he ran down the street, through the cellar door, and into the Aryan courtyard on the other side of the ghetto. Karski knew that to run was foolish; any German who saw them would become suspicious. But all he could think of was to escape from that hell.

Two days later, Karski returned, walked the ghetto streets, searing into his memory the sights, the sounds, the smells as he turned his mind into a camera for the west. Then, he went to a death camp.

*

Feiner and Berman decided it would be easier to smuggle Karski into Belzec, which was chaotic and corrupt, than into Sobibor or Treblinka, where Captains Reichleitner and Stangl ruled like Bismarcks. The Jews bribed a Polish-speaking civilian, who worked at Belzec, to lead Karski into and out of the camp disguised as an Estonian guard.

In the kitchen behind the Belzec grocery store run by the Polish underground, Karski donned a guard's uniform — trousers, high black boots, belt, and necktie. He had to stuff the cap with paper to make it fit. Then, as he began to walk the mile from the village to the camp, the civilian guide put his mind at ease. Don't worry, he said. Belzec is completely disorganized. Walk anywhere. Germans guard the east gate. They never demand papers. But stay away from the Estonians.

When they neared the camp, Karski heard an almost inhuman wail and some gunshots. "They're bringing in a batch today," the guide said.

"What are the chances of anyone's escaping?"

"None, once they get this far."

"You mean there isn't a single chance?" Karski asked.

"Not alone. With my help, it can be done. But it's a terrible risk. The Jew and I could both get killed. Of course, if the Jew pays well — very well — it can be done."

"How can they pay? They don't have money with them, do they?"

"We don't try to get money out of *them*. We ain't so dumb. We get paid in advance. Strictly a cash proposition. We don't even deal with those in the camp." The guide spoke with contempt as he gestured toward the screams. "We do business with people on the outside, like you. If somebody comes to me and tells me that such-and-such a Jew is going to arrive and that he wants him 'cheated out' . . . Well, if he's willing to fork out plenty in advance, then I do what I can."

"Have you saved many Jews so far?" Karski asked.

"Not as many as I'd like, but a few."

"Are there many more good men like you willing to save the Jews?"

"Save them?" The guide was bewildered. "Who wants to save them? But if they pay — that's a different story. We can all use some money."

Karski looked at the guide's good-natured face and calloused hands. He must have been a farmer before the war, an average man, Karski thought. Neither good nor bad, probably a family man, perhaps religious.

The guide became suspicious. "What are you here for?"

"Well, I'd like to save some Jews, too," Karski said slyly. "With your help, of course. That's why I've come to the camp. To see how everything works."

"Well, don't go trying anything without us." The thought of competition seemed to upset the guide.

"Don't be silly," Karski reassured him. "Why should I work without you? We both want to make money."

The guide became intrigued. "How will your people pay you? A flat rate or for each Jew?"

"Which pays more in the long run?"

The guide paused. "If I were you, I'd make my rates per Jew. You lose too many opportunities of making a haul if you work on a flat rate. You see, each Jew is different. If you get hold of someone who's very anxious to get someone out, and if he looks as though he can pay well, you can get a lot out of him if you use your head."

"You're perfectly right."

"You'll be better off," the guide added. "But remember — fifty-fifty. Don't try any tricks."

As they approached the edge of the camp, the shouts, cries, and gunshots killed all conversation. Oblivious of it all, the guide hummed a folk tune. They broke through a grove of ragged trees and bumped into the fences of Belzec, a pen surrounded by guards standing fifteen feet apart with fixed bayonets. The pen was filled with a throbbing mass of crazed Jews, who shouted, squabbled, and waved their hands in a macabre dance of death. The Nazis had left them in the raw autumn air for three days without food and water because the Heckenholt Institute wasn't working again.

Creating a path through the bodies with rifle butts were the Germans and the guards, silent, like bored pig farmers checking their stock before loading them for market. On the tracks outside the fence a dusty train waited.

Karski and his guide saluted two German noncoms at the east gate and entered Belzec. "Follow me," the guide said. "I'll take you to a good spot."

Half-suffocating from the stink of urine-soaked straw, Karski picked his way through the dehumanized forms. Every now and then, he'd step on a hand or arm. Someone would yelp like a puppy, and Karski would fight back his vomit. Nothing seemed to bother the guide, who made his way through the yard like a goat, surefooted and swift. Every now and then he'd shout over his shoulder, "Come on! Hurry!"

Karski followed the guide across the three-hundred-yard pen to a spot along the west fence where a heavy gate guarded a barbed-wire corridor leading to two boxcars. Usually the Jews arrived in the cars and were driven down the corridor into the yard. But today, they would be driven into the cars and taken to Sobibor.

"Stand here," Karski's guide said. "Stay away from the Estonians. And don't forget. If there's any trouble, you don't know me and I don't know you."

A hefty SS officer impatiently barked an order. Two Germans swung open the clumsy gate and dashed down the barbed-wire corridor to the open boxcars. The SS officer turned to the Jews, feet apart, hands on his hips. "Quiet! Quiet!" he bellowed above the din. The mob stilled. "All Jews will board this train to be taken to a place where work is waiting," he announced. "Keep order. Do not push. Anyone who attempts to resist or create a panic will be shot."

He belly-laughed, pulled out his pistol, and punctuated his command with three random shots into the crowd.

"*Alle Juden, raus — raus!*" he screamed, stuffing his pistol back into his polished black holster.

The Jews nearest the SS officer tried to fight their way to the rear, but a volley of shots from behind stampeded the whole herd forward. Shots from the sides funneled the herd into the corridor.

The two Germans at the end of the corridor fired into the screaming faces to slow down the stampede, and the SS officer shouted, "*Ordnung! Ordnung!*"

"Order! Order!" the two Germans echoed.

Karski couldn't believe his eyes. Feiner had warned him that if he lived to be a hundred, he would never forget Belzec. He knew that Feiner was right.

German military rules specified that freight cars may carry forty soldiers. The Nazis stuffed 120 to 130 men, women, and children into each boxcar. As the Jews in the rear pushed forward, those nearest the train were pressed into the cars like grapes in a barrel. The floors were covered with quicklime to prevent an epidemic. When the cars were full, crazed Jews climbed on top of the heads of those already inside, clutching at hair and clothes, trampling on faces and necks, and shouting in an insane fury.

It took three hours to fill the forty-eight cars, two by two. From the locomotive to the last wagon, the train quivered and rocked, sobbed and wailed. Inside the camp, the yard was littered with a few score dead and dying. The Germans and the guards waded through the filth, shooting at anything that moved. Then the howling train moved out of the station toward Sobibor. Belzec became as silent as a city hit by a plague.

Karski riveted his eyes to the track long after the death train disappeared into the green pines. He felt a rough hand on his shoulder.

"Don't stand there with your mouth open," the guide scolded. "Come on! Hurry, or we'll both get caught."

In a daze, Karski followed the guide back through the east gate. They separated after a short hike, and Karski ran and walked and ran back to the store. Breathless, he assured the underground agent that everything had gone well. Then he rushed into the kitchen behind the store, locked the door, and tried to wash Belzec from his creeping skin.

When the sunlight stirred him the next morning, a wave of nausea seized him. Through the rest of that day and the next night, he vomited and retched Belzec from his stomach, then drank two large glasses of whiskey. He slept between nightmares and fits of feverish tossing. The next morning, the grocer stood over him with bread and milk. Weak, but feeling stronger, the courier hopped a train back to Warsaw.

*

When the train from Belzec pulled into Sobibor, Sergeant Wagner, Abraham, and the train brigade were waiting. Wagner broke the seal on a boxcar and opened it. He turned away as if he were about to be sick. He ordered the Blackies to pass out cigarettes to Abraham and the rest of the train brigade. The Nazis and the Ukrainians stood at a distance, faces covered with handkerchiefs. Abraham and the others unloaded the Belzec bodies into the miners' train. Only a few still breathed or twitched. And they weren't human anymore. Most bodies were already bluish-green, and the quicklime had eaten away the flesh of those who had stood or lain in it.

82

Chapter 12

Winter 1942

J AN KARSKI traveled for twenty-one days with viaticum around his neck in a leather pouch. An underground priest had granted him that privilege so that if the Gestapo caught him again, he would at least die with Holy Communion. It was a harrowing trip. Over the Carpathians on foot and by train to Lyons; to the foothills of the Pyrenees by bicycle and across the mountains with a Spanish guide; three days in the belly of a fishing boat to a contact in a Barcelona butcher shop; to Madrid and Algeciras with the American OSS; a fishing boat to a British motor-boat on the high seas, and Gibralter to London on an American Liberator bomber.

The Polish government-in-exile received Karski as a hero and sent a summary of his report about Sobibor, Belzec, Treblinka, and the Warsaw ghetto to the British Foreign Office and the U.S. State Department. Over one million Polish Jews have already been murdered, the summary said. And the extermination continues. For example, the Nazis printed a hundred and twenty thousand ration cards for the Warsaw Jews for September, but only forty thousand for October.

The summary did not mince words. "The people are packed so tightly that those who die of suffocation remain in the crowd side by side with the still living and with those slowly dying from the fumes of lime and chlorine, for lack of air, water, and food," it said about the transports. "Whenever trains arrive, half the people arrive dead. Those surviving are sent to special camps at Treblinka, Belzec, and Sobibor. Once there, they . . . are mass-murdered."

Karski's report did not surprise leaders in London, Washington, and New York; they had already received three important reports on the extermination of the Jews months before the Liberator flew Karski to London.

Feiner and the Polish Bund had smuggled an accurate report west in May, just about the time that Shlomo, Itzhak, and Abraham entered Sobibor. The Bund report spoke of mass assassinations by the Einsatzgruppen in Russia, gassing vans at Chelmno in western Poland, and Jews in sealed boxcars who disappeared into the forests of eastern Poland without a trace.

While the Nazis were expanding Sobibor in the summer, the Polish government confirmed the Bund report and added details to it. In an information bulletin, it spoke of Jews being sent to "Sobibor, near Wlodawa, where they were all murdered with gas, machine guns, and even being bayoneted . . ." The Polish underground agent in the Sobibor train station asked to be transferred, the bulletin reported, because he couldn't stand the smell.

The BBC broadcast the Bund report in English and Yiddish in the summer of 1942, and the *Daily Telegraph* ran a two-part article under the headlines GERMANS MURDER SEVEN HUNDRED THOUSAND JEWS IN POLAND . . . TRAVELLING GAS CHAMBERS. The *New York Times* picked up the *Telegraph* articles. But apparently torn between disbelief and the fear of missing an important story, the *Times* buried the item deep inside the newspaper. American Jews demonstrated at Madison Square Garden, protesting Nazi atrocities, and President Franklin Delano Roosevelt promised that when the war was over, the Nazi criminals would be "called to account."

The *second* important report to reach London and Washington was a cable sent from Geneva by Gerhard Riegner, a member of the World Jewish Congress, founded to fight the persecution of Jews. Riegner learned from a German industrialist close to Nazi leaders that Hitler had issued an order to exterminate systematically all European Jews — not just Polish Jews.

Riegner was shocked. He knew, of course, about the Bund report and the gassings at Chelmno, about Sobibor, Belzec, and Treblinka, the liquidation of the Warsaw ghetto, the Jews in France who had been sent east, and the trains from Belgium. He had heard isolated reports that those who went east were never heard of again. From the German industrialist, he learned that what the Nazis were doing to the Polish Jews, they were doing to the rest of Europe's Jews. Deportation east meant a trip to Sobibor, Belzec, or Treblinka.

Unaware that the Final Solution was already underway, Riegner wired Jewish leaders in London and New York, transmitting the message through the British and American consuls in Geneva so that the Nazis would not intercept it:

RECEIVED ALARMING REPORT THAT IN FUEHRER'S HEADQUARTERS PLAN DIS-
CUSSED AND UNDER CONSIDERATION ACCORDING TO WHICH ALL JEWS IN
COUNTRIES OCCUPIED OR CONTROLLED BY GERMANY, NUMBERING 3.5–4 MIL-
LIONS SHOULD, AFTER DEPORTATION AND CONCENTRATION IN EAST, BE EX-
TERMINATED AT ONE BLOW TO RESOLVE ONCE FOR ALL JEWISH QUESTION
IN EUROPE . . . THE ACTION REPORTED PLANNED FOR AUTUMN . . . METHODS
UNDER DISCUSSION INCLUDING PRUSSIC ACID . . . WE TRANSMIT INFORMA-
TION WITH ALL RESERVATION AS EXACTITUDE CANNOT BE CONFIRMED . . .
INFORMANT STATED TO HAVE CLOSE CONNECTIONS WITH HIGHEST GERMAN
AUTHORITIES AND HIS REPORTS GENERALLY RELIABLE.

Although the British Foreign Office was skeptical, it gave the cable (as Riegner had requested) to Sidney Silverman, a member of Parliament and a leader in the World Jewish Congress. The Foreign Office told Silverman that it could not confirm Riegner's "wild" story and therefore would not publicize it. If the World Jewish Congress wanted to alert the press, the Foreign Office cautioned, it should be aware that publicity could "annoy the Germans," make matters worse for European Jews, and blow the cover of Riegner's German source. Silverman sat on the cable until it could be confirmed.

Washington was even more skeptical than London. Calling the cable "utterly fantastic," the State Department refused to send Rabbi Stephen Wise a copy, as Riegner had requested, until it could confirm the report. But two weeks after the State Department received the message from Geneva, Wise, a leader of the American Jewish Congress, got a copy from Silverman in London. It shattered the rabbi, who had no doubts whatsoever about the cable's accuracy.

Wise's first reaction was to publish the cable, but after discussing it with other Jewish leaders, he concluded that the news of the Final Solution would demoralize those western European Jews not yet deported to Poland. He returned to the State Department for advice. Like those in the Foreign Office, Under Secretary of State Sumner Welles asked the rabbi not to publicize the cable until the State Department confirmed it.

Wise agreed.

The *third* important report to reach London and Washington came from Richard Lichtheim, a Zionist leader in Geneva. While Riegner was delivering his cables to the British and American consuls, Lichtheim was dictating a report to Rabbi Wise based on the accounts of two eyewitnesses fresh from Poland. One was a very reliable, well-known non-Jew. Lichtheim sat on his own report for two weeks, because, as he told Wise in a covering letter, the contents were "so terrible that I had some doubts if I should forward it or not."

The State Department intercepted Lichtheim's report, which verified the Riegner cable with eyewitness accounts. State withheld the report from Wise, sent a copy to the White House, and asked the U.S. consul in Berne to meet with both Riegner and Lichtheim.

The two Jews were armed with reports when they walked into Leland Harrison's office in October 1942, while Karski was making his way to London. They handed the consul a folio bulging with eyewitness accounts supporting their cables, and a three-page covering memo that summarized Hitler's Final Solution to date, country by country:

• Almost three million Polish Jews have already been murdered.

• Only four thousand of the hundred thousand Latvian Jews are still alive.

• All the Jews from Serbia have disappeared without a trace and are most certainly dead.

• More than seventy thousand of the ninety thousand Slovak Jews have been deported and have been most certainly murdered.

• More than sixty thousand of the hundred and eighty thousand Dutch Jews have already been deported to Poland and are most certainly dead.

• More than fifty thousand French Jews have been deported as well, and are most certainly dead.

• Since there are no more reports coming from Lithuania, one can assume that the hundred and fifty thousand Jews there have been killed.

London and Washington were finally convinced. "We have little doubt that a policy of gradual extermination of all Jews, except highly skilled workers, is being carried out by the German authorities," the Foreign Office cabled the British ambassador in Washington. And Under Secretary Welles summoned Rabbi Wise to the capital. "I regret to tell you, Dr. Wise, that these [folios] confirm and justify your deepest fears," Welles said. He released the rabbi from his promise not to publicize Hitler's extermination plan.

But both the State Department and the Foreign Office were disturbed. There was a war on, and they feared that the news of the Final Solution would distract the Allies into wasting "a disproportionate amount of time dealing with wailing Jews."

*

Thus, Karski and the demands he carried from Feiner and Berman were not welcome in London. The courier, however, delivered them exactly as Feiner and Berman had requested:

Reprisal Bombings. The two Warsaw Jews demanded that the Allies bomb German cities as a reprisal for the continued extermination of the Jews, and drop leaflets telling the Germans why the bombings were taking place. As they had requested, the Polish government presented that demand to the British, but its urgent memorandum to Prime Minister Winston Churchill was not exactly what Feiner and Berman had in mind.

First, the memo said the Polish government was making a *suggestion;* it did not say the Polish Jews were issuing a demand. Next, the memo suggested that the Allies bomb targets in Poland, not in Germany. And finally, it requested air support for those Poles resisting deportation to German work camps in the west, but said nothing about air support for Jews resisting deportation to death camps in the east.

Although Churchill supported reprisal bombings, Sir Charles Portal, chief of the Air Staff, disagreed on principal. Air attacks are military operations against military and industrial targets, he argued. Reprisals would be an admission that the Allies were bombing civilians, and the Germans might retaliate on captured Allied airmen. Furthermore, the suggested reprisals would strengthen Hitler's argument that the Jews started the war to exterminate Germany. The British chiefs of staff and the Allied Council rejected the Polish proposals.

Acceptance of Jewish Refugees. Feiner and Berman also demanded that the Allied and neutral nations, like Switzerland, harbor the Jews who escaped the Nazi net. British Foreign Secretary Anthony Eden objected. "We already have a hundred thousand refugees and not enough food," he told Karski. "There is no room for Jews here. But I will do my best to find a place for them."

Eden didn't, because he had long opposed accepting more Jewish refugees into Great Britain, and he had done his best to keep them out of Palestine, as well. "Unfortunately," Eden's personal secretary wrote in his diary, "A.E. is immovable on the subject of Palestine. He loves Arabs and hates Jews."

Just months before the war, the British Parliament, buckling under Arab pressure and dismissing the protests of Winston Churchill, passed a law restricting future immigration to Palestine to seventy-five thousand Jews — no more than ten thousand in any given year. In effect, Britain slammed the door on eastern European Jews just before Hitler began exterminating them.

Eastern European Jews ignored the quota policy and sailed the Black and Aegean seas in tugs. Most never made it to Palestine. In December 1940, for example, more than two hundred Jews drowned when the *Salvador* sank at sea. A year later, neutral Turkey stopped the *Sturma* with 750

Rumanian Jews, including seventy children, from sailing through Turkish waters unless Palestine agreed to accept them. The British had refused the Rumanian Jews visas (even though there were forty thousand still unused) because Rumania was a German ally.

Fearing that acceptance of the *Sturma* Jews would encourage other Jews to head for Palestine, and arguing that there might be Nazi agents aboard, the British told the Turks they would not accept the ship. Turkey towed the *Sturma* back into the Black Sea, where it blew up the next morning. There was one survivor.

Even while Karski was presenting the Feiner and Berman demands to Anthony Eden, Britain was refusing to accept forty-five hundred Bulgarian Jews — mostly women and children — arguing that welcoming them to Palestine would be "opening the floodgate." There was a sense of urgency, for Bulgarian King Boris was stalling the Nazis. He had already agreed to deport to Poland twelve thousand Jews from Macedonia and Thrace, which Bulgaria had just gobbled, and the Nazis were pressing him to deport the fifty thousand Jews from Bulgaria itself. No one knew how long he would hold out.

If Eden was adamant about Palestine, he was just as tough about not accepting more Jews into England. In the summer, while the Nazis were expanding Sobibor, the Swiss slammed their frontiers on "illegal aliens" and pushed more than a thousand Jews back into France, even though the Swiss press had reported that French Jews were being sent to an almost certain death in Poland. The Swiss government argued that it had already accepted twelve thousand Jews and had no room for more.

Jewish leaders asked Great Britain to take the French Jews, but Home Secretary Herbert Morrison refused. In a secret memo to the Cabinet, he argued that if England took more Jews, they might "stir up an unpleasant degree of anti-Semitism — of which there is a fair amount just below the surface — and that would be bad for the country and the Jewish community."

Parliament joined the debate. Cosmo Gordon Lang, Archbishop of Canterbury, moved in the House of Lords that Great Britain immediately give temporary asylum to any Jew who escaped Hitler. Skillful use of the wireless could win over the sympathy of the English, he argued, especially if most Jews were children.

Lord Samuel agreed. "So small is the number that it seems monstrous to refer to difficulties of food supply . . . or employment," he argued, "when we know that here, also, there is a shortage of labor . . . While governments prepare memoranda and exchange notes and hold conferences week after week, month after month, the Nazis go on killing men, women, and children."

But the British government didn't budge. "The only truly effective means of succoring the tortured Jewish and, I might add, the other suffering peoples of Europe," Eden said in response, "lies in an Allied victory."

Application of Sanctions. Feiner and Berman demanded that the Poles who were blackmailing, denouncing, and murdering Jews be punished. "Executions included," Karski told General Wladyslaw Sikorski, commander-in-chief of the Polish forces and prime minister of the government-in-exile. "The identity of the guilty ones and the nature of their crimes should be publicized in the underground press."

Five months later, when 90 percent of the Polish Jews were already dead, the Polish government issued the following decree: "Some individuals, devoid of honor and conscience and recruited from the criminal world, have now discovered a new, impious source of profit in blackmailing the Poles who shelter Jews and the Jews themselves . . . Every instance of such blackmail will be recorded and prosecuted with all the severity of the law."

The decree was printed in the underground press and read over the underground radio. Eleven Poles were eventually tried and shot for persecuting Jews. No one knows how many were executed without a civil trial.

Weapons for the Warsaw Ghetto. Feiner and Berman also asked Karski to tell General Sikorski that a new Jewish military organization was planning an uprising in the Warsaw ghetto. "They asked the Home Army for guns," Karski told General Sikorski. "Those weapons were denied."

Karski said he had discussed the request for guns with General Stefan Rowecki, commander-in-chief of the Home Army, who had told him: "I am the *military* commander. I must keep arms for *military* strategies. I have the highest respect for what the Jews intend to do. But it has no *military* significance . . . I will do what I can. Other than that, I need specific instructions from London."

General Sikorski listened in silence to Karski's report and the demand from the Jews. Finally, he said: "Lieutenant, measures will be taken." The Home Army eventually gave the Warsaw Jews twenty guns for their "Jewish war against the Third Reich."

Ransom for Jews. Feiner and Berman demanded that the Allies press Berlin to release Jews, even if that meant buying their freedom. Karski presented the demand to Lord Selborne, the British War Office's head of underground resistance. He flatly rejected the suggestion, hinting that the atrocity stories from Europe were more Jewish propaganda and dismissing the fact that Karski was a Catholic eyewitness. Selborne argued that no prime minister or Cabinet would ever approve a plan to buy Jews from Hitler, even if they were women and children, lest the government be accused of helping Hitler kill more British soldiers and of prolonging the war.

The British Refugee Committee also "repudiated any question of trying to do business with Hitler," and the Allied Council rejected any suggestion of negotiating directly with the Germans.

Excommunication. Feiner and Berman told Karski to ask Polish President Wladyslaw Raczkiewcz to lean on Pope Pius XII. "The Polish and other European Jews sent to Poland feel entitled, on humanitarian and spiritual grounds, to expect the protection of the Vatican," Karski told President Raczkiewcz, as instructed. "Religious sanctions, publicly proclaimed, may have an impact on the German people. They may even force Hitler, a baptized Catholic, to reflect."

Shortly after Karski met with President Raczkiewcz, the Polish ambassador to the Holy See sent the Vatican secretary of state a note stressing that "the Germans are liquidating the entire Jewish population of Poland." President Raczkiewcz followed the note with a personal letter to Pope Pius XII. "In this tragic moment, my people are struggling not only for their existence, but for all that they hold holy," he told the Holy Father. "They do not want revenge, but justice. They are not asking for material and diplomatic help; for they know such help could only reach them in very small measure. But they beg for a voice that points to the evil clearly and strongly, and condemns those who are at the center of this evil."

The request did not surprise Pius XII; diplomatic representatives from the United States, England, Brazil, Uruguay, Cuba, Peru, and eight occupied countries had been asking him to condemn the Nazi atrocities. And the fact that the Germans were slaughtering Polish Jews was not news, either. No one was better informed on the condition of European Jews than the Holy See, because through its diplomatic corps of nuncios and apostolic delegates, the Vatican had listening posts in all major occupied, Allied, and neutral cities — Athens, Berlin, Bucharest, Budapest, Bratislava, Berne, Istanbul, Lisbon, London, Madrid, Paris, Sophia, Vichy, and Washington. Berne and London were especially important, since Switzerland was a neutral haven in the middle of Europe, and England was the home of the governments-in-exile.

• In March 1942, nine months before Karski reached London, the papal nuncio to Bratislava, Slovakia, warned the Vatican that eighty thousand Jews were about to be deported to Poland. "Amounts to condemning a large portion of them to certain death," the nuncio wrote the Vatican.

The Pope made no public condemnation; instead, the Vatican tried to intervene privately with pro-Nazi president Dr. Josef Tiso, a Catholic priest. It managed only to delay the deportations for several weeks. In the end, seventy thousand Slovak Jews were gassed in Poland, one third of them in Sobibor.

• While the papal nuncio in Bratislava was sending reports to the Vatican, the nuncio in Berne met with Riegner. The Jewish leader gave the priest a detailed, written report about the murder of European Jews in general, and about the plight of the Slovak Jews in particular. He asked the Vatican to intervene. The nuncio told Riegner that he had already reported to Rome the unfortunate situation of the Jews, and promised to do so again.

• In August, three months before Karski arrived in London, the papal nuncio to France reported to the Vatican that the French did not believe that the Jews being deported to Poland were going to work camps, as the Germans and the Laval government kept saying, because many of the Jews were either small children or sick and aged.

• Also in August, Archbishop Szeptyckyj of Leopol, in Ruthenia, personally wrote to Pius XII to say that two hundred thousand Jews and even more Christians already had been murdered in his small diocese alone.

• In September, while Karski was visiting Belzec, Myron Taylor, President Roosevelt's personal emissary to the Holy See, had shown the Riegner and Lichtheim cables to the Vatican, asking for confirmation and additional information. The Vatican told him, after a long delay, that it could not confirm the reports. But a Vatican source later submitted a report to the State Department that said, in part: "The mass execution of Jews continues . . . They are killed by poison gas in chambers especially prepared for that purpose . . . and by machine-gun fire, following which the dead and the dying are both covered with earth . . . Convoys of Jews being led to their death are seen everywhere."

Pope Pius XII studiously avoided any public statement, promising that he would take a stand in his Christmas Eve message to the world.

Chapter 13

Winter 1942–1943

KOMMANDANT REICHLEITNER had made it clear to the Sobibor staff that he would not tolerate the stealing of gold from the transports. The money belonged to the Reich, he said.

To get around Reichleitner's order, Wagner appointed Shlomo chief of the mechanic shop for cover, and ordered him to continue to make jewelry for him — and him alone — at night. Since Wagner had suspected all along that Moses, Jankus, and Nojeth were frauds, he took Jankus and Nojeth away. "Not goldsmiths" was all the Austrian told Shlomo.

Shlomo once again plunged into despair. He still had his brother Moses, but he was certain that Wagner had taken to Camp III his nephew and cousin, for whom he felt responsible. Above the din of the tinsmiths and blacksmiths, Shlomo strained to hear gunshots.

When the workers returned from Camp II at the end of the day, Nojeth and Jankus were in the column, grinning as if they had just eaten pickled herring. Wagner had given both of them cushy jobs. Jankus he made his valet — he was to draw the sergeant's bath, shine his shoes, clean his room. Nojeth he assigned to hunt for gold. There were piles of toys, kitchen utensils, and small wooden boxes in Camp II. Nojeth had to check each for false compartments or bottoms, and then to collect all the gold, jewels, and money he could find.

Shlomo used his job as shop chief to his best advantage. He assigned himself to clean and inspect the wood stoves and pipes throughout the camp.

That gave him a chance to hide and rest for hours. Then he gave himself the job of cleaning the Ukrainians' rifles. That gave him the chance to memorize every detail about guns (for he intended to escape someday) and to talk to the guards. Soon he was trading again, using the gold that Nojeth smuggled back at the end of the day to barter for sausage, chicken, and vodka. Shlomo had learned to drink as well as any Ukrainian, and the vodka helped him forget for a few hours his fear, his anger, and his hatred.

Because Shlomo wasn't really a mechanic, Wagner protected him by sending him welders, blacksmiths, tinsmiths, and electricians — Polish Jews, Germans, Austrians, French. One mechanic built a child's bike from an old wagon and tricycle wheels. Wagner was delighted, and soon Shlomo's crew had orders for a dozen. The Germans wanted to take them home for their children. A blacksmith built a flue and forge out of old bike parts and taught Shlomo how to weld. Wagner began to call him *Spengler* — the Welder — further to fool Kommandant Reichleitner. At night, Shlomo worked on rings and bracelets for Wagner. One day, a new Nazi — a fat man in his forties, with a face like a chubby tomato — came to the machine shop. The Jews called him the Red Dumpling. He had heard that Shlomo made jewelry on the sly, and he ordered a very large gold ring.

"In three days," he said.

"I can't," Shlomo objected. "Not unless Herr Oberscharführer Wagner tells me to."

"I'm going on leave in four days," the Red Dumpling said. "My ring in three." He set a half-bottle of vodka on the table as if to offer a bribe. Preferring to cross the Red Dumpling, whom he didn't know, rather than Wagner, whom he did, Shlomo decided not to make the ring.

"Is it ready?" the Red Dumpling asked on the third day. Barry, the mongrel Saint Bernard, stood at his side.

"No, I — "

The Red Dumpling left calmly, without waiting for Shlomo to finish the sentence caught in his throat. Barry tagged along. Standing in the middle of the yard like a shell-shocked soldier, the Nazi began to blow his whistle and shout: "Out! Everyone! Lazy Jew dogs! Out!"

Jews streamed from the workshops of Camp I and lined up as if it were a roll call. They were scared, because the Nazis did not break camp routine lightly. "Calisthenics," the Red Dumpling ordered. And the Jews did push-ups, ran and stopped, crawled, duck-walked. As they puffed and wheezed, the Nazi shot at them randomly, to scare rather than kill them. He whistled them to a stop, walked over to Shlomo, and gave him a hard boot in the pants.

"Run!" he ordered. "Run!"

Before Shlomo got ten yards from the Red Dumpling, Barry jumped him from behind, knocking him to the ground. Shlomo fought the dog as best he could while Barry tore into his legs. Shlomo knew it was the end. He was on the ground, Barry was hungry, the other prisoners were helpless, and the Red Dumpling was laughing.

Before Barry could tear Shlomo to pieces, Wagner strode through the gate. He called Barry off, and the dog left Shlomo lying in the sand. "Back to work!" Wagner ordered, giving the Red Dumpling a bear hug. Arm in arm, the two Germans walked through the gate as if nothing had happened. The Red Dumpling was transferred soon after that. He had gone too far. He might have killed the valuable goldsmith.

Shlomo's brush with death taught him a lesson: he would work for everybody but tell no one what he was doing for whom. Unfortunately, he made one mistake. Wagner had ordered a medallion. Before Shlomo could finish it, the tall Austrian barged into the shop, trembling with rage. "Out!" he ordered. Without a word, he pushed Shlomo through the door, then through the gate and toward Camp III. Shlomo searched his memory for what he might have done wrong. In spite of his fear, he managed to ask, "What? What did I do?"

"My medallion," Wagner said through clenched teeth.

A few steps from the gate to Camp III, Shlomo threw himself on the ground and hung on to Wagner's leg like an ankle iron. Through his tears, Shlomo pleaded: "Please! Don't take me there! I was one of the first Jews you chose. You won't get your medallion if you send me there."

Wagner stood motionless, as if he were surprised at what he was doing. He looked Shlomo over from head to foot for a moment, then kicked him.

"Run," he said. "Back."

Afraid that Wagner would change his mind, Shlomo ran back to his shop as fast as he could. Moses was crying when he burst through the door. The boy thought he'd never see his brother again, and he threw himself into Shlomo's arms.

Although Shlomo was happy to be alive, a feeling of stark terror gripped him. Why? What did he do wrong? If he couldn't figure that out, he would make the same mistake again, and the next time Wagner would show no mercy.

Slowly it dawned on the goldsmith, and he relaxed. He had broken his own rule of secrecy and had shown the medallion to Itzhak's friend, Szol, chief of the shoemakers, who worked in the shop next door. Szol inadvertently had told Wagner that the medallion Spengler was making was beautiful. Wagner was worried that Reichleitner would find out.

That brush with death made Shlomo all the more determined to escape from Sobibor. In fact, all winter the Jews in the mechanic shop had been whispering about an escape. It began with a French Jew and a Polish Jew whom Wagner had selected to help Shlomo. The French Jew, an older man, had fought in the Spanish Civil War against the Fascists. He still carried a bullet in his leg, and on damp days he limped around the shop in pain. The Polish Jew had escaped to the Parczew Forest, but the Nazis had caught him and sent him to Sobibor.

"Escape!" they kept urging Shlomo. "Escape."

"How?" he'd say. "In the snow? Let's wait until spring."

"Yellow," they'd say. "Weak."

"Without a plan?" he'd argue. "Not yet. They'll kill us all."

The Polish Jew was especially angry. For weeks after he had arrived, he threatened to bash to death the next Nazi who walked through the door. Shlomo and the Frenchman managed to talk him out of it. In the end, the three of them agreed to wait for spring, and to be careful what they said in the shop. Polish Jews, like Shlomo, didn't trust the German and Austrian Jews. Not that they had specific reason to distrust them. They just did.

Shlomo told Nojeth to bury as much gold as he could safely steal so that when they escaped, they'd be able to buy food from the Poles. Then he turned his mind to another escape . . . women.

*

To the hundred or so men at Sobibor, the Nazis added twenty women to knit, sew, cook, wash, iron, and sort clothes. They slept in two separate barracks. Among them were Esther and Hella, Eda and Bajle.

Esther Terner had lived in Chelm before the war. Soon after they invaded Poland, the Germans nabbed her father and brother Idel. Her father, they shot; Idel escaped with a bullet in his foot. When the Nazis turned Chelm into a ghetto, Esther and her family moved in with relatives in Siedlce nearby. It was safer there, but not for long. In the fall of 1942, the Nazis liquidated Siedlce, sending the strong to a work camp in Staw, and the rest to Sobibor. Esther's mother hid for days, but with her husband dead, her children dragged away, and her friends in Sobibor, the hiding in cellars and attics got to her. One day, she walked out of the ghetto to the cemetery, where the Nazis shot her.

Esther was a beautiful, slender young woman of seventeen, with long chestnut hair in braids, brown eyes, and a bold smile. But starvation, fatigue, and fear had given her face a pale — almost yellow — look, so the Nazis at Staw rejected her. It was a bad omen, and Esther knew it.

Before the Germans could send her to Sobibor, she saw a Catholic schoolmate from Chelm chatting outside the Staw camp with her boy friend. "Look what they did to me," Esther called. She was so scared, she couldn't think of anything to say or to do to save herself.

"Come on," her friend said. "Take off your babushka." She led Esther to the end of the line of strong, young workers, smoothed Esther's hair, and dabbed her cheeks with rouge. "There. Look strong and healthy."

She did, and the Nazis accepted her. She worked in the fields by day and slept in the old mill prison at night. Her brother Idel escaped one night. When she didn't hear from him — it was not that difficult to pass messages along the grapevine — she assumed the Nazis had shot him, as they had her mother and father.

The reprieve in Staw was short; the Nazis liquidated the work camp in the winter to make eastern Poland Judenrein ("Jew-free") by the end of 1942, as Himmler had ordered. They loaded Esther, Hella, and eight hundred other Jews into carts pulled by horses. Ukrainians with rifles guarded the wagons; Nazis with machine guns rode alongside on horseback.

Hella Felenbaum was a tiny girl of sixteen, with blond hair and brown eyes. She could easily pass for a Pole. Her parents had already gone to Sobibor. In a cart with her were her two brothers. As the wagon train passed a woods, her eighteen-year-old brother nodded good-by and jumped; her eleven-year-old brother followed. The Nazis mowed down the youngster before he reached the woods. The elder brother ducked into the trees, but the Nazis caught him later and shot him.

Wagner met the wagon train in Sobibor. "Six girls to knit," he called as he walked up and down the line of women. Mira stepped forward. She was born on the Polish-German border and spoke perfect German. That impressed Wagner. "Pick six more," he told her.

Mira selected Hella, but for some reason passed Esther by. Esther knew she was doomed if she didn't do something.

"What about me?" she piped up. "I'm good."

"Her, too," Wagner ordered.

Wagner gave the knitters a barracks to themselves, brought them wool taken from the transports, and told them to knit knee-high socks — one sock per woman per day — and pullover sweaters. To make sure that the

Nazis wouldn't get lice under their arms, Wagner made the women work and sleep in the same room, away from the other lousy prisoners, and gave them all the laundered clothes, soap, and water they needed to stay clean. Then he appointed as chaperone Mrs. Shapiro, an older Viennese woman. Esther and Hella spent the winter clicking needles.

Eda and Bajle lived in another barracks with ten other women who cooked, washed, and ironed. They would scrub the Nazis' underwear and socks on boards, boil them in big black pots on a wood stove, and rinse the clothes in cold water they drew from the well in the center of the Officers' Compound. When the clothes were dry, they'd press them — as well as uniforms — with irons stuffed with hot coals. It was a demanding job.

Eda was in her mid-twenties, newly wed and widowed almost on the same day. The Nazis had shot her husband before she came to Sobibor. When Wagner walked up to her as she was standing in line in front of the gate to Camp III, she was still lost and lonely.

"Profession?" he asked.

"Kindergarten teacher," she said.

The Austrian guffawed. "To the laundry!" He sent Bajle and another woman with her.

Bajle was the same age as Eda and just as naïve. Her husband and son had walked through the gate to Camp III, and she was worried about them. Shlomo was the first Jew she met in Sobibor, and he told her the secret over the next several days — gently, piece by piece.

This is a work camp, he said on the first day. The Nazis are mean and crude, but the work isn't bad. Bajle seemed relieved, even calmed. After she adjusted to the shock of being torn from her husband and child, Shlomo told her to expect the worst, and not to be surprised by anything she might see or hear. When doubt and fear showed in her melancholy eyes, he told her the whole truth.

Bajle was a strong woman, and gradually, as she accepted the reality, her sense of calm returned. Unlike Shlomo, she wasn't driven by bitterness, anger, and revenge. She retreated into a cocoon of sadness and apathy.

The women's barracks were unhappy places. The women didn't talk of escape and revenge as the men did. They wallowed in stories of parents, husbands, children, fiancés, and the more they talked, the worse they felt. Or they'd dream of the future in a romantic sort of way — rescue by daring partisans, who would blow up the tracks and fences, kill the Nazis and Ukrainians, and carry them off to freedom in the forest; Germans running from the Russians, deserting the watchtowers of Sobibor and leaving the main gate open; the Third Reich collapsing as Allied planes bombed Hitler and Berlin. Illusions, all.

"Don't worry," Esther's close friend, Zelda, used to say. "We'll all end up in the frying pan sooner or later."

But Esther never believed for a moment that she'd end up in the frying pan, as the women called the gas chamber. A friend in Staw had once told her, "Esther, I have a feeling you're going to survive. When you do, knock on my tombstone. Then I'll know that the Germans lost the war."

Esther believed him, and clung to her hope and her God. She came from a religious family, and every time the nagging question arose in her mind — how could God allow children to die — she'd push it away. For Esther, believing meant not doubting or questioning God's wisdom and mercy.

Religious or not, Esther still hated the Nazis for their cruelty. One day a transport pulled into Sobibor while she was dusting the Merry Flea officers' cottage next to the tracks. Hiding behind a drapery to watch the Nazis and Ukrainians, she saw Frenzel pick up a baby by the feet, smash its head against a boxcar, and then toss it into the miners' train like a dead rat. The scene haunted her. How could human beings do that? she'd ask over and over. Don't they ever think of their own children and wives? What kind of monsters are they? The more the murder played before her mind like a grisly movie, the more her hatred grew.

To survive, Esther followed two basic rules. Try not to be noticed, and don't fall in love. Emotional involvement was a risk; she'd have to worry about two people. If she was to survive, she knew, she'd have enough trouble taking care of herself. So she made friends with a small group of Polish Jews but kept emotionally distant.

Wagner appointed Eda the chaperone of the second barracks, where Bajle and the other cooks and laundresses slept. Eda ran a tight ship, but not tight enough to keep out romance. She fell in love with Itzhak, the shoemaker. They were both tentative and shy. She had just lost a husband; he, a wife and son. Their love grew slowly. They would steal food for each other, eat together, and chat in the courtyard of Camp I. Itzhak became protective, and before long he would check in the laundry or ironing barracks to see whether Eda was all right, almost as if she were his wife. One day, he caught a Ukrainian beating her.

The guard had brought Eda a uniform to be washed and pressed by five o'clock the next evening. Eda told him she couldn't finish it by then. Just as the Blackie began to slap her around, Itzhak walked in. He grabbed the Ukrainian's arm. "Aren't you ashamed to beat a woman?" he asked. "She works very hard for you."

Itzhak waited for the whip to fall, but the Ukrainian, who was usually a decent sort of fellow, calmed down and left, more embarrassed than angry.

Itzhak and Eda's love was an open secret at Sobibor. But they never slept together, because they were shy and still emotionally raw.

Shlomo wasn't so bashful. He became infatuated with Bajle and was determined to have her. They became close friends, and he stopped frequently in the kitchen to chat and tease. He liked her gentleness and sensuousness. She enjoyed his attentions and admired his directness and camp savvy. She told him she had no illusions about the future, that she would die in Camp III like her husband and child, that she didn't care anymore. There was no one and nothing left for her in life, she said. It was all meaningless.

Shlomo thought about Bajle constantly. He was too young for her, he told himself. Too inexperienced. How could he declare his love and ask her to become his lover? She was teetering on the brink of total apathy. Hadn't she just lost a husband? Why should she accept him? Or maybe Shlomo the goldsmith was just what she needed to live again.

It wasn't easy for Shlomo to grow into a man under the heel of the Nazis. Ghettos, hunger, terror, death, survival were all he had known since he was twelve. The drive to have a woman was part of that survival, for somehow the constant threat of death made sex all the more important for him.

Shlomo had lost his virginity on the potato farm outside Wolwonice. Zelde cooked for the work gang in the farmhouse kitchen next to the room where he made jewelry for the old German soldier. She was just sixteen, with blue eyes and long black hair. She used to sit close to him, chatting while he worked. At night, she snuggled next to him on the straw-covered floor above the kitchen, where she and twenty men slept. She would put her back to the wall, her breasts tightly against him, and cover both of them with a blanket she had begged from the old German. All night, they would lie like two spoons in a crowded drawer.

Shlomo could feel her softness, the warmth of her breath on his neck, and a strange stirring, but his inexperience and shyness wouldn't let him explore. By the time he mustered the courage to do anything, she was fast asleep. On one of the last nights at the farm, Zelde and Shlomo whispered a little before they fell asleep. Zelde held him tightly.

"Did you ever have a girl?" she asked him finally.

"No," he said.

"I want to be the first."

She rolled Shlomo over to face her. He could feel her heart pounding against his chest, and for the first time in his unhappy life, he felt a surge of desire and emotion that began to pull him out of himself. Her nails dug into his back. The warmth of her breath and the heat of her body excited him beyond anything he had ever known.

They stopped whispering, and his body began to tingle as they made love in the hay. For a brief moment, Shlomo lost himself in her. There were no more Nazis, no more war. No hunger, no hatred, no death. Just him and her and their bodies as one.

When the final shiver of pleasure passed, reality hit him with a force he had never known before. He wanted to whisper to her, caress her in a thousand tender ways, let the torrent of his feelings wash over her in giant waves, but the sounds and smells of nineteen sleeping men, the crack of moonlight creeping through the window like a thief, the reality of tomorrow, killed everything. An irresistible tiredness swept over him, and he fell into a deep sleep. The memory of her last kiss on his cold lips warmed his dreams.

Shlomo wanted to capture those moments of abandon and forgetting again; to escape, if only for a few minutes, the fear and hatred that seemed to strangle every other emotion trying to be born. He had to escape from Sobibor or he would go mad.

One day, he found Bajle alone in the kitchen. "Where are the others?" he asked.

"Bathing," she said.

He kissed her on the cheek and blurted out that he wanted her.

Bajle smiled in her sad, melancholy way. "You're much too young. Why not ask one of the girls?"

Shlomo was flustered, but he recovered quickly. "I like *you*," he said.

Bajle seemed flattered, and before she could object a second time, Shlomo said, "If I'd never eaten an apple before, I sure wouldn't want to try a green one."

Bajle blushed. "I'm married. You better stay away from me. They killed him — my husband."

Shlomo felt her wavering. "They'll kill us all before they're finished," he said.

They lay together in the corner of his shop on a bed of blankets. Over the winter months, they became lovers. He protected her. She washed his clothes and brought him food. And while the other women talked about families and husbands, and the men about escape and revenge, Bajle and Shlomo tried to forget.

100

Chapter 14

Winter 1942–1943

THE TRANSPORTS trickled into Sobibor in the winter of 1942 like water from half-frozen pipes. Most of the Polish Jews were already dead, and the Nazis needed the trains to ship soldiers and supplies to the eastern front, where the Wehrmacht was fighting for its life. The long gaps between transports, and the isolation in the almost snowbound camp, made the Nazis edgy and bored. They took it out on the Jews.

Sergeant Paul Groth made up little games. He'd order four Jews to carry him around the yard like a king while he'd drop burning paper on their heads. Or he'd make prisoners jump from roofs with umbrellas, or scale roof beams until they fell to the floor. Those who sprained ankles and broke legs were shot in Camp III. Or he'd organize a flogging party, forcing Jews to run the gauntlet past Ukrainians with whips. Or he'd order a thin prisoner to gulp vodka and eat two pounds of sausage within minutes. Then he'd force open the Jew's mouth and urinate in it, roaring with laughter as the prisoner retched in the snow.

Groth softened briefly. Three beautiful girls came to Sobibor on a transport from Vienna. Groth took Ruth as his servant and mistress. Sergeant Poul, the drunk, smuggled the other two into the Merry Flea. Groth fell in love with the dark-eyed teen-ager and, almost as a favor to her, or so it seemed, stopped beating the other Jews. But the truce was short-lived. It was against SS regulations to molest Jewesses — an insult to the master race. Himmler was quite adamant on that point. So while Groth and Poul were on leave,

Kommandant Reichleitner transferred both of them. Groth ended up at Belzec.

The Sobibor Jews were delighted to see the two Nazis go, but Groth and Poul were easily replaced, and life went on as usual. The empty winter days also got to Kurt Bolander and Erich Bauer. Because there was little to do in Camp III without Jews to gas, Bauer turned to vodka. He kept a private bar in his room in the Swallow's Nest, and there Jews would come to mix drinks or make eggnog. The short Nazi — he was under five feet six inches — would sit in his armchair, facing a photograph of his wife and children and a portrait of the Führer painted by Mordechai, and drink himself into oblivion. If a prisoner spilled any liquor or broke a bottle, the former street-car conductor would make him wipe the floor with his tongue.

Bolander took out his frustration on the ten Jews who carried the swill buckets from Camp I to the gate to Camp III. Bolander would make them run, and if, as sometimes happened, the Jews in Camp III opened the gate before the Jews from Camp I had left, Bolander would shoot the swill carriers. Somehow, the Nazis had deluded themselves into believing that the Camp I Jews didn't know what went on in Camp III. And they wanted to keep it that way.

The Nazis played other games that winter. They would tie the bottom of the pants legs of a Jew and drop a rat into the trousers. If the prisoner moved, they'd shoot him. They would shave one side of a man's head, half of his mustache, and one eyebrow for laughs. They'd make some skinny, tired Jew push a wheelbarrow filled with sand until he collapsed, or make two Jews cross their arms behind their backs and fight each other like cocks.

One favorite SS game was to gather a group of Jews around a coffin in which the Nazis would lay out a prisoner dressed like a Hasid. Then the Germans would sing, "I am a Jew with a long nose." The prisoner would pop up from the dead, salute, and repeat the phrase. Next, the Nazis would chant:

> *O God, we pray to Thee,*
> *Listen to our plea.*
> *To the Jews put an end.*
> *To the rest, peace send.*

The other Jews had to fall on their knees and cry, "Amen, Amen."

The cooks were so desperate, they concocted a zany escape plan that was doomed from the start. There were seventeen of them — two in the

SS kitchen, two in the Ukrainians' and thirteen in the prisoners'. One of the cooks, Hershel Zukerman, got close to Koszewardski, the Ukrainian who supervised the cooks and who hated Nazis. "I have some friends in the Russian partisans," the Ukrainian told Zukerman. "I have a plan to free us all. There's a doctor in Chelm working with the underground."

The plan was to get poison from the doctor. Then, three to four hours before the partisans approached the camp, the cooks would poison the food of the Germans and the Ukrainians. When the Russians broke out of the woods, the Jews would walk out of Sobibor and join them.

Everything went wrong. First, Kommandant Reichleitner got an order from Lublin to remove all Jews from SS and Ukrainian kitchens. Apparently, prisoners at another camp had tried to poison their jailers. Then, Koszewardski skipped Sobibor with all the money the Jews had given him to buy the poison and pay off the Russians. Zukerman and the others in on the "plan" suspected it had never been more than a get-rich scheme for the Ukrainian.

The torture, the hopelessness, and the moment-to-moment terror of not knowing what would happen, when death would come, why or how, drove many older Jews to the brink of madness. At least ten of the hundred male prisoners committed suicide that winter, most by hanging themselves from the barracks' rafters. Others, who believed that suicide was immoral or who didn't have the courage to kill themselves, begged the Nazis to take them to Camp III, or played sick, hoping to be shot.

The terror reached a peak around Christmas. Not only did the Nazis, snowbound in Sobibor for the holidays, feel sorry for themselves, but the war had been taking a steadily bad turn for Germany since September. In Africa, General B. L. Montgomery defeated Field Marshal Erwin Rommel at El Alamein, and then began chasing his Panzers across the desert. In Russia, the Reds held firm in Leningrad, stopped the Germans before they reached Moscow, and surrounded Hitler's Sixth Army at Stalingrad.

When things were really bad, the Nazis would eat and drink in the canteen deep into the night, and, half-drunk, call the Jews out in the snow for calisthenics.

Christmas Eve was a particularly bad night. While the Germans and the Polish Blue Police swept the Parczew Forest looking for Jews, and while the Nazis in Sobibor were drinking themselves under the canteen tables and the prisoners were doing pushups in snow, Pope Pius XII delivered his long-awaited moral condemnation of war crimes. Forty-five minutes into a sleepy sermon to the world, the Holy Father spoke vaguely about a vow that humanity owed "to the hundreds of thousands of people who, through no fault of their own, sometimes only owing to nationality of descent, are doomed to death or to slow decline."

That was it. And although 2.5 million Jews had already been "deported," according to an official SS report, Pius XII did not even mention "Jew" in his five-thousand-word Christmas address. The Allied, neutral, and occupied countries that had been awaiting his moral condemnation were shocked. He had led them to believe that his statement would be clear, strong, and specific. It was muddled and weak. So they gave the Pope another chance.

Succumbing to pressure from Parliament, the churches, and the Jewish community, Great Britain suggested that the Allies sign a joint declaration condemning Nazi crimes against the Jews. Washington politicians balked. Some in the State Department argued that Hitler's so-called extermination plan was at best an unconfirmed rumor. A joint declaration could stir American Jews to demand actions that would hurt or prolong the war. Others argued that if the extermination plan were a *fact,* and the United States did nothing, the government would be severely criticized at a time when it needed the nation united. So the State Department compromised. It agreed to sign, if the declaration was weakened.

Twelve governments and governments-in-exile approved the declaration, which made the front page of the *New York Times* in mid-January 1943.

German authorities, not content with denying to persons of Jewish race in all the territories over which their barbarous rule has been extended the most elementary human rights, are now carrying into effect Hitler's oft-repeated intention to exterminate the Jewish people in Europe.

From all the occupied countries Jews are being transported in conditions of appalling horror and brutality to eastern Europe. In Poland, which has been made the principal Nazi slaughterhouse, the ghettos established by the German invader are being systematically emptied of all workers required for war industries. None of those taken away are ever heard of again. The able-bodied are slowly worked to death in labor camps. The infirm are left to die of exposure and starvation or are deliberately massacred in mass executions. The number of victims of these bloody cruelties is reckoned in many hundreds of thousands of entirely innocent men, women, and children.

Removed from the original draft at the insistence of the United States were the phrases "which leave no room for doubt that the Germans are systematically killing Jews" and "irrespective of age and sex."

On instructions from the Foreign Office and the State Department, both British and United States envoys to the Holy See tried to convince Pius XII to sign the declaration, too. He refused. Then, even after they had announced the declaration, the Allies continued to appeal to him to support it publicly. But the Holy Father told the British minister to the Vatican that his Christmas Eve message was "clear and comprehensive in its condemnation of the heartrending treatment of the Poles, Jews in occupied countries, and hostages." The Pope emphasized that he had satisfied "all the demands recently made upon him to speak out."

Three weeks after the Allied declaration, Heinrich Himmler came to Sobibor a second time. The Nazis were cleaning the Jews out of the Netherlands, and Himmler wanted to see whether Sobibor was ready for them. If the declaration had shaken him, he didn't show it.

When his light plane landed on the field between the camp fence and the pine forest, Sobibor had a treat waiting. Kommandant Reichleitner had imported two hundred Jewish girls from a nearby work camp — the prettiest he could find. They had arrived the night before Himmler did, and slept in an empty barracks in Camp II.

When Himmler asked to inspect the gas chambers, the Nazis marched the naked girls down the Road to Heaven. Badmeister Bauer was waiting for them on his usual perch, the roof of the "showers," where he had peepholes into the chambers. The Berliner usually wore coveralls like a mechanic when he supervised the gassings, but in honor of Himmler, he donned his best SS uniform.

While Himmler was watching the girls die, Moshe Bahir was preparing hors d'oeuvres and eggnog in the canteen. He was a fifteen-year-old boy who had come to Sobibor about the same time as Shlomo. An excited Nazi burst into the canteen, shouting, "He's coming! He's coming! He's staying for lunch!"

Moshe ducked out of the canteen as fast as he could, for he knew that if he got caught there when the guests arrived, he'd be shot. Heart racing, he ran through the Officers' Compound to Camp I. There were no Jews in sight, because Wagner had ordered them to stay inside. When Moshe got to the gate to Camp I, it was locked. In the distance, he could see Himmler and the other visitors inspecting the buildings. Fortunately for the boy, the Ukrainian guard at the gate let him in. Just before he scampered into a barracks, praying that Wagner had not seen him, Moshe caught a glimpse of Himmler.

After Himmler left Sobibor, the Nazis changed their policies toward the prisoners. They no longer killed the worker Jews so indiscriminately, since they had a death machine to keep oiled and ready for the Dutch, who would be coming to Sobibor soon. So they did everything they could, within reason, to protect the skilled labor. They even gave the sick three days to recover before sending them to Camp III, and they appointed a medic to look after them. Josel got the job.

There were three Jewish doctors in Sobibor, but for some reason that defied logic, the Nazis would not permit them to practice even on the skilled Jews. Through the Ukrainian grapevine, the doctors learned that Sergeant Frenzel was about to appoint a Jew to care for the sick, and they urged Josel to volunteer. He was smart, they said. He had already had typhus and therefore was immune. And they'd give him all the advice they could. Maybe he could save a few lives.

When Frenzel asked for a volunteer "nurse" during roll call, Josel's hand shot up. Frenzel gave him the job and an infirmary in Camp I, close to the gate. It was a tiny house that the Nazis had stolen from a ghetto somewhere. It even had a tiled Dutch stove, but without a chimney.

Prisoners would go to Josel with everything from broken arms to gangrene. The minor cuts and sores Josel would wash, disinfect, and bandage. The major infections, such as those caused by the bedbugs and lice that burrowed into the raw whip lashes, were incurable, for though the Nazis permitted Josel to go to Camp II every other day to scrounge for medical supplies, they allowed him to take only cotton, bandages, and disinfectants like iodine. From time to time, he'd smuggle contraband, especially anesthetics.

Others would come to Josel with broken bones. Wagner, in particular, loved bone-crunching. One day, he stood by a woodpile while the Jews carried clinkers in buckets from the railway tracks to the road inside the camp. There, other Jews would spread the ashes with rakes and shovels so that the jeeps wouldn't mire in the mud. Wagner tossed fenceposts at any Jew who wasn't running fast enough. But before he'd sail a post, he'd ask, "Profession?" If the Jew was unskilled, Wagner would hurl the javelin. Nine men came to see Josel with broken bones that day alone. Eventually, all were sent to Camp III.

Josel also visited the sick in the barracks every day. Most had typhus, and about the only thing Josel could do for them was to bathe them in order to bring down their temperatures (the Nazis allowed him to carry a thermometer) and to feed them stolen food. To protect the sick, at the risk of his own life, Josel devised a system. He'd write down the names of the sick on index cards and the date the prisoner took ill. Then he'd record the Jew's temperature daily. If the prisoner was not well after three days, Josel would rip up the card and write a new one. The system gave the sick Jew a chance to recover before he or she went back to the front lines, and it protected Josel. If Frenzel asked him at roll call who was

106

sick and for how long, Josel could whip out his cards. The system worked so well that two Jews with frostbitten feet spent the whole winter inside the barracks without getting caught.

Josel had a contact in Camp II who ferreted out contraband medicine and food, then buried it in Josel's cotton. One day, when the nurse came for his bandages and iodine, his contact whispered, "There's a can of sardines in the cotton box."

On the way back to Camp I, Josel began to think, as he always did when he was carrying contraband, what he would do if Wagner caught him. The nurse didn't have to wait for an answer. Just before he reached the gate to Camp I, Wagner strode up behind him.

"What?" The Nazi poked Josel's satchel with a long iron rod.

"Bandages." Josel kept walking, thinking that if he could only get into Camp I he'd be safe.

"And?"

"Iodine." Josel tried to act innocent.

"And?"

"Cotton."

"And?"

"Nothing!"

Wagner followed Josel through the gate into the yard, up to a table with benches resting on concrete posts. Wagner pointed his steel stick.

"Dump!" he ordered.

This is it, Josel thought as he emptied the satchel onto the tabletop. Wagner didn't touch a thing. He just poked the boxes and the bandages with the steel rod. When he didn't find contraband, he pounded the table with the rod. The bandages bounced to the sand.

"You had hog," Wagner said and stormed out of the yard. It was the Austrian's pet saying for "Jew, you were lucky this time."

Josel knew he was, even though he had just shit in his pants.

Chapter 15

Spring 1943

THE PASSENGER TRAINS from the Netherlands began to back into Sobibor every Friday. On each transport, there were between one thousand and three thousand Jews, and by midsummer there would be nineteen trains full.

The Dutch had no idea of where they were or what lay ahead. Even though Sobibor was one year old, the British and American strategy not to publicize the death camps had worked, Jan Karski notwithstanding. The Dutch Jews never doubted that they were going to a work camp, as the Nazis had told them. Most had never seen a German kill a Jew, nor personally experienced real Nazi brutality. The Germans had simply rounded them up for Westerbork, a transit camp in Holland, and then onto eastbound trains. Westerbork wasn't exactly home. But it was clean, there was food, families stayed together, and there were no daily whippings or "games" to cause suspicion and panic. It was all part of Himmler's master plan to keep western Jews submissive and quiet until they were inside Camp III, naked and shorn. A few Dutch Jews had been in a concentration camp at Vught, a kindergarten compared to Sobibor.

The Dutch bounced off the trains in furs and silk dresses or woolen suits, carrying their valuables. Unlike the Polish Jews, they were, for the most part, middle to upper class, well educated, not Orthodox, and totally western — a soft bunch, unused to cutting hay and felling trees or to the stark terror of Nazi brutality.

With the arrival of the Dutch like the crocuses of spring, the Nazis expanded the work force to keep up with the sorting of clothes piling up in the sheds. The Dutch selected to sort, cook, wash and iron clothes, or to work in the vegetable garden were mostly young, naïve, rosy-cheeked men and women. On their first day in camp, they would sing Dutch songs, the girls and women swaying their hips or dancing to the rhythm, as if they were on a picnic in the Polish forest, happy that the long, tiring train ride was finally over. The fire that brightened the night sky and the strange sweet smell that filled the air did not arouse their suspicions.

But once they learned the truth, few survived the shock. They gave up or grew weak and sick or made fatal mistakes through carelessness or indifference. The Nazis liked to pick on them, perhaps because of the traditional rivalry between Germany and the Netherlands, or perhaps because the Dutch were weak and educated. They had not been prepared for Sobibor by ghettos, typhus, starvation, fear and hatred, slow death, bullets, whips, gas chambers, the murder of mothers and fathers, sisters and lovers. Most of them died within two weeks of their selection, only to be replaced on the following Friday. Max Van Dam and Selma Wijnberg were two exceptions.

Van Dam was a well-known Dutch artist from Amsterdam, and the Germans gave him and two other artists a studio in Camp I to paint their portraits; Mordechai and his helpers continued to paint signs and landscapes. One by one, the SS — clerks, bakers, street-car conductors, butlers — sat for Van Dam like barons hoping to be immortalized on canvas. Wagner and Frenzel loved to beat the thirty-two-year-old artist, but only enough to taunt and tease, never enough to blur his vision or cripple his brush hand.

With three older brothers and no sisters, Selma had been a tomboy most of her life. At twenty-one, she was tall, big-boned, fleshy and sensuous, with a broad smile that crinkled her gray eyes in an impish sort of way. Even though she had come from a well-to-do family, she was more emotionally prepared for Sobibor than the other Dutch Jews, for she had been in and out of jails for almost seven months.

Selma's father had owned a small hotel in Zwolle, close to the cattle market. Every Thursday evening, Dutch farmers in wooden shoes would come to town to buy and sell. In one of the many hotels that surrounded the market square, they would eat and drink with friends, and spend the night. It was a good business. Selma's father rented out the large hotel hall for meetings, weddings, and dinners, and her brother, who had studied dancing, gave lessons there. Selma was his partner.

Her father died before the Germans began rounding up Jews for the east. When soldiers seized the hotel for a barracks, Selma, her mother, and two unmarried brothers moved. A Catholic priest found Selma a hiding place in the home of a high school English teacher. One night, while she was visiting a Jewish family hiding next door, the Gestapo broke in. Before Selma could sneak out the back door, they caught her. First they sent her to a police station in Utrecht, then transferred her to a jail in Amsterdam, where she bunked with eight women, one of whom was a prostitute. Selma had come to Amsterdam innocent; she left wise. From the jail, the Nazis sent Selma and Ulla, a German Jewess whose family had fled the Nazis into the Netherlands, to Vught, a spanking new concentration camp for Jews. There, Selma learned that one of her brothers was still in hiding but that the Nazis had sent her mother and two other brothers to a work camp in the east.

The ride to Sobibor took three days, and Selma was looking forward to seeing her mother and brothers again. Together, she thought, they would wait out this awful war and then return home, to Holland, to the hotel, to dancing. But the train ride to Poland confused and frightened her. She could hear shooting outside the train, and screams. Once, as the train slowed through a German town, bystanders pretended to slit their throats with their hands. It never really dawned on Selma that they were trying to tell her she was riding to her death. When she finally stepped off the train in Sobibor, tired, dirty, and frightened, the train brigade, dressed in blue coveralls and caps, and Sergeant Frenzel were there to greet her.

"Are you married?" Frenzel asked Selma and the young women with her.

"No," they said.

"Come! Stand over here." Frenzel smiled at Selma.

Selma, Ulla, and about eighteen others, who tried to act older than they were, stepped out. Selma was certain the Nazis were going to rape her; she had heard a lot of stories about German soldiers from the prostitute in Amsterdam.

"Don't worry," Selma whispered to the others, attempting to sound brave. "One bang and it's all over." She tried to smile, but her lips were dry.

When Frenzel sent Selma to Camp II to sort, she couldn't believe what she saw. Piles of cheese, tins of milk, cans of sardines, chocolates and cigarettes, silk stockings and underwear. Where did it all come from? Where was it all going?

That evening after roll call, the Nazis made the Jews sing and dance in the yard of Camp I. For Selma, it was almost like old times, except that there were fences and she was in Poland. Although the fiddle, bugle, and accordion made happy sounds, the Polish Jews were not smiling. One of them, a twenty-eight-year-old man, couldn't take his eyes off Selma as she lightly stepped to the music, hips swaying. He asked her to dance. And for the rest of the evening he guarded her as if she were a piece of fresh butter.

His name was Chaim, he told her, and he had been in Sobibor for seven months. They polkaed and waltzed in the yard. She was light on her feet and gracefully followed his lead. Somehow she felt less afraid with the music and with his hand on her waist, even though she didn't especially like him. Oh, he was handsome, all right, with brown eyes and curly brown hair and a confident swagger. But in his flat hat and leather breeches, he looked like a cross between an American cowboy and a Polish farmer.

After the Germans got tired of watching the Jews dance, they locked the gate between Camp I and Camp II and left. A boy whom Selma had known from Zwolle came up to her. She had seen him earlier that day. "Hi," she had called as she waved. He had lowered his eyes. "Hi. It's me, Selma, from Zwolle." He just kept on walking.

Now he seemed to recognize her. "You know what that is?" He pointed to the north where the orange sky silhouetted the tips of the pine trees on the horizon.

"No. What?"

He told her, and she felt as though someone had jumped on her stomach as she lay in the spring grass watching the stars.

Selma walked to her bunk in a daze. She couldn't talk, not even to Ulla. And as she lay in the dark and looked for the hint of fire shadows dancing on the ceiling, and breathed the sickly sweet smell that penetrated the pine boards and tarpaper, she began to imagine what no one in Sobibor had ever seen. The images fought with each other for space, and as soon as one faded, another took its place. Then she began to weep, first one tear at a time, then a quiet flood, late into her first night in Sobibor.

The next morning, after roll call, Frenzel picked Selma out of the line, smiled, and assigned her to Camp II. Chaim fell in line next to her as they marched four abreast through the gate to the storehouses and sorting tables. He could see she knew. It was in her face. He had seen it happen over and over again to the Dutch — smiles and laughter, the truth, then shock, depression, despair, death. Would this one be different? Selma seemed to have spunk. Maybe she would fight for her sanity. Maybe she would *want* to live. Chaim would watch her closely.

"Follow me," he said when they got to Camp II. "Walk as if you know exactly where you are going. Don't hesitate." Before a Nazi or Kapo could assign her to some other barracks, Selma followed Chaim into the shed stacked with clothes.

The Nazi Economic and Administrative Main Office had designated twenty-eight categories of recoverable items, which it disposed of as follows:

• Reichmarks, foreign currency, gold and silver, jewelry, and precious stones went into a Reichsbank SS account under the name of Max Heiliger — Max the Saint.

• Watches and clocks, pens, razors, knives, scissors, flashlights, wallets, and men's clothing and boots were cleaned, priced, and sold to the troops.

• Sold directly to civilians were women's and children's clothes, underwear, and shoes; scarves, umbrellas, canes, thermos bottles, earmuffs, baby carriages, combs, handbags, belts, pipes, sunglasses, mirrors, cutlery; knapsacks and suitcases; bed linens, sheets, handkerchiefs, washcloths, tablecloths, eiderdown quilts, and blankets.

• Eyeglasses were sold by the Public Health Office.

• Expensive furs were sold by the Economic and Administrative Main Office itself. Cheap furs were sent to the clothing works of the Waffen SS (armed SS) for boot linings.

Chaim explained to Selma the sorting system at Sobibor so that she wouldn't make a mistake and get beaten or worse.

First, sort by quality: no good, good, and new. The Nazis will burn the "no good" and take first pick of the new. Then, sort by item: shirts, tablecloths, sheets, underwear.

Cut off any Stars of David or armbands you find, and search all pockets and linings for gold, money, or jewels. Whatever you find, toss into the large wooden box on the ground. The Nazis will collect it and sort it in the Administration Building in the middle of Camp II.

Put the small items like lipsticks and pens on the blankets spread on the floor. Someone else will sort them. After sorting, stack the clothes into piles of ten to twelve items and tie them with string. They'll be stored in bins until there are enough to fill a train for Lublin. The longest train of goods so far had twenty-three cars stacked to the roof.

The work is light, easy, and relatively safe. Our Kapo is Josef, the camp electrician. He isn't mean, but like the other Kapos, he won't hesitate to give twenty-five lashes if the Nazis order him to do so. If he doesn't, they'll beat him. Two Nazi brothers, the Wolfs, usually check on us. Joseph isn't very bright, and he's slow on his feet. If you run away from him, he won't even bother to chase you. Franz is mean, but not very crafty. He'll beat or kill you if he catches you stealing food, taking money, or not working.

Sergeant Joseph Kliehr, the baker, is in charge of the shoe barracks.

He's harmless and will give you a new pair of shoes any time you need them. He'll even wait on you. But be very careful of the tall Austrian, Gustav Wagner. He kills for the fun of it, and he's the sneakiest and shrewdest of all the Nazis. We warn each other when he's coming with the password "*vayikra*" (the Hebrew name for the third book of the Bible, which means "call").

Chaim explained to Selma his survival system. Don't let anyone know who you are. Be invisible. Don't be pushy. The less the Germans know about you or see you, the better. Then you have a chance.

Chaim had followed his own advice for seven months, and it had worked. He was still alive and intended to stay that way. But he did take a few chances — calculated, to be sure, but still risky. Like most Jews who worked in Camp II, he smuggled food and pocketed the paper money, gold, and jewelry he found sewn into the linings of the clothes he sorted. These he would bring to a friend who burned junk in Camp II. The friend would bury the valuables under old papers, where the Nazis would be least likely to look. And Chaim always wore his leather breeches under his pants just in case he caught the eye of some Nazi or Ukrainian or Kapo with a whip.

Selma took Chaim's advice, but only to a point. It angered her to see the Germans shipping all those clothes back home. They were not only cowards and murderers, but thieves as well. She kept a knife hidden under the pile of clothes she sorted, and every time she found a beautiful shirt or a linen in perfect condition, she slashed it with her knife and tossed it into the "no good" pile.

Chaim warned her. "Invisible," he said. "Remember." But Selma didn't care. "At least I'm doing something," she told him. "Maybe it isn't much. But it's something."

Chaim knew all the signs of life and death at Sobibor, and Selma's knifing clothes as if they were Germans was a sign of life. It meant she hadn't given up, that the spark of the tomboy defiance he had spotted in her the first night was not dead. After a while, he stopped warning her and, instead, listened and watched for her so that she would not get caught.

Selma learned quickly how to cope with the terror and death around her. Like the other Sobibor Jews, she began to live minute by minute, to suck what pleasure she could from the inhuman world she lived in, to hope, to dream of Zwolle and flowers and music.

Soon, she too was smuggling food to share with Ulla, her cousin Minnie, and Chaim. Then she began to look for clothes for herself — silk stockings, pretty dresses, boots, fine underwear. And most of the time she followed

Chaim's advice not to stare at the brutality and torture that filled her days.

"It won't do you any good," he lectured her every time he saw her gaping at another beating or murder. "You can't help anyone. You might see something you're not supposed to. And you'll just get sick thinking about it at night."

It was good advice, but it did not always work. Once, as Selma was about to step out of the sorting shed, she saw Wagner split a boy's head open like a ripe melon. She darted back inside lest he decide to kill her for watching. Another time, Wagner caught a man opening a can of sardines. He called everyone from inside the barracks to watch him beat the man with a shovel until his head, face, and torso were a bloody pulp. Then he drew his pistol and shot him. Selma watched.

But for Selma, the worst were the naked Dutch women and girls. She could hear them through the barracks window, and she knew she shouldn't look. If the Germans saw her, they'd kill her without a thought. But there was a sad, strange fascination that drew her eyes up to the window every time she heard the shouts.

"We're going to take a shower," they'd call to each other as if they were on some Polish holiday. "It's so hot. Come on. Hurry!"

Sometimes she'd recognize a girl from Zwolle, hair unevenly cut as if she were a boy, and Selma would never get used to the sight, torn between wanting to yell "You fools! You fools! You're going to die. This is no game," and wanting them not to know the truth, to be playful right until the Badmeister opened the door for their last "shower."

When Selma wasn't sorting clothes, Frenzel gave her other jobs. She trimmed the flowers and pulled weeds along the train tracks and the outer fence facing the tracks so that everything would look neat for the next Dutch transport. She picked blueberries in the woods for the Nazis' dessert, and at the end of the day a Ukrainian or Nazi would check her tongue and teeth. A touch of blue was certain death. She'd pick mushrooms in the woods, and when her guard wasn't looking, stuff a few in her bra or panties. She was a large young woman, and the Nazis would never notice a few extra bulges. Besides, if she were searched, the Sobibor Germans would never pat her down intimately. In the evening, she and her friends would simmer the mushrooms and savor them.

Once, Sergeant Hubert Gomerski, a former boxer who played doctor when the new transports arrived, drafted Selma to work in the woods. Chaim was worried to death, for the chance of survival under Gomerski was close to zero. At first, Selma just followed the woodcutters and cleaned up and piled branches with which to camouflage the fences. But one day,

Gomerski ordered her to carry a pine trunk into the camp. Gomerski knew the Dutch were not as strong as the tough Polish farmers, and he liked to watch them stumble, grow weak, and give up. Fortunately, Frenzel walked by and saw her grunting under the weight of the tree. He called Gomerski aside, then smiled at Selma. The next day, she was back to pulling weeds.

Frenzel's concern for her, his brazen smiles whenever he saw her, were a constant source of embarrassment to Selma. It wasn't that he ever made a pass at her. None of the Germans or Ukrainians pestered the Sobibor women. Other than Groth and Poul, no SS man had raped a Jewess that anyone could recall. Besides, the Nazis kept a dozen Russian women in forced prostitution. When the women got too tired or the Nazis too bored, they'd kill them and bring a new batch to the house in the Officers' Compound. The Blackies kept women in the huts behind the public train station across the tracks.

Even though Frenzel had saved her life and she had a maddening sense of gratitude, Selma loathed him and would have slit his throat with her sorting knife like a new sheet if she had had the chance. His sick, toothy attention did not go by unnoticed, and Selma had to take some razzing from her Dutch friends. The Polish Jews began to distrust her even more.

Selma and Chaim became so inseparable that Frenzel began to call them "bride and groom." They stood side by side at roll call, worked next to each other, walked in the yard hand in hand. In the evenings, before bed, they'd sit in the women's barracks and flirt and court. Selma grew to love Chaim. At first, she was flattered that the popular and handsome man had singled her out. Then she was grateful that he was taking care of her. He taught her the rules of survival, he nursed her back to mental health, he brought her vodka and pork fat on her birthday (she didn't drink and had never eaten pork before), he scolded her into drinking the daily swill when food supplies in Camp II were scarce, and he always reached for her hand. Chaim became her only safe spot in a life of constant brutality and terror. He kept her heart from growing hard, her emotions from growing dry.

Selma knew she loved Chaim when she saw him walking arm in arm with one of the few Polish Jews who still trusted him. She was jealous and angry.

"He's a homosexual," she told Ulla. That night, she refused to talk to him or sit with him or hold hands. Chaim moped around the camp as if he had typhus.

"See what you've done to him?" Ulla finally told her. "He's not a homosexual. That's just how the Polish men act."

Selma forgave him.

They didn't sleep together, and even if they had wanted to, they would never have found privacy. Privileged Jews like Shlomo used their shops for trysts, where they improvised beds and kept caches of vodka and sausages. The others, like Chaim and Selma, had to be content with sitting in the barracks or outside in the yard.

Chaim paid a price to love Selma. The Polish Jews, who were in the majority, didn't trust the Dutch. Their uneasiness was based on cultural differences: the Dutch were often more socially sophisticated, less Orthodox, and, most important, few spoke Yiddish. There were always stoolies at Sobibor, men and women who buckled under the pressure, and since the Polish Jews didn't understand the Dutch, they avoided them as much as they could. Some of that mistrust spilled onto Chaim. He managed to keep a few close friends, but most of the Polish Jews shunned him or treated him to fewer confidences. They assumed that whatever they'd tell him, he'd tell Selma. And they didn't trust her. Wasn't she Dutch? Didn't Frenzel always smile at her?

Chapter 16

Spring 1943

Toivi had a life decision to make. The Nazi with the round face, the build of a butcher, and the thin smile was shouting, "Women and children to the left. Men to the right." Although he was fifteen years old, Toivi was so small and delicate-looking, with a face as smooth as a marble and wide, frightened eyes, that he could pass as a child or as a young boy. What should he do? Stay with his mother, as he had done so far? Or join his father?

Toivi had known for almost nine months that the Nazis were murdering the Jews they dragged off to Belzec; like the Piaski Jews, those in Izbica had paid a Catholic to find out what happened at the camp. So when the SS caught him after a Catholic schoolmate had turned him in, Toivi thought he was going to Belzec. The Jews of Izbica didn't know that the gas chambers at Belzec had been dismantled months ago while a crew of Jews dug up and burned corpses. Sobibor was now the major slaughterhouse for Jews south of Warsaw.

When Toivi saw the smoke spreading over the sky to the north like ink into a blotter, and smelled the sweetness in the air, he knew Jews were gassed and burned at Sobibor just as they were at Belzec. He knew it as certainly as he knew his name was Toivi and that Izbica was his home. But he couldn't believe it. Whatever the Nazis had in store for him, he reasoned, he'd stand a better chance with his father. So he whispered to his mother and jumped lines.

117

Sergeant Karl Frenzel was walking down the column, inspecting the new Jews. Whenever someone caught his eye — someone strong, interesting, clean, bright-looking, rosy-cheeked — he'd stop and ask, "You! What do you do? What's your trade?" The Nazis were still expanding Sobibor, so they were in the market for good workers. Toivi could hear the Jews down the line shouting: "Shoemaker . . . Carpenter . . . I'm a tailor." He wasn't sure what the beefy Nazi was looking for. The Jews behind him broke rank and pushed in panic to get closer to Sergeant Frenzel. But Toivi held his ground. What if the Nazi didn't even see him? He was so short and thin. What should he say if the Nazi did?

Toivi had no profession. His father had owned a liquor store in Izbica, and his mother had been a schoolteacher. But even though he had no useful skill, Toivi knew the Nazi would notice him; he believed he had a special power inside him. So when Frenzel walked toward him, he locked his eyes on the German's, concentrating all his inner energy on that cold, indifferent face, which always seemed to smile, pouring his whole soul into his eyes. "Pick me," he thought, shouting a silent message. "Pick *me!*"

"You," Frenzel said to him. "What are *you?*"

Toivi did not answer, but kept staring into the Nazi's face, calm and confident.

"Come," Frenzel said. "You'll be my *Putzer* — my shoeshine boy."

As Toivi watched his mother, then his father and brother, shuffle through the huge gate, there were no tears, no anger, no joy at being selected. Just a numbness underneath the realization that, once again, something lucky had happened to him.

Like Shlomo, who was one year older, Toivi had run away from home to escape the Nazis. In the fall of 1942, while Jan Karski was telling London about Sobibor, Toivi was on his way to Hungary as Vlademar Ptaszek. On the way, Toivi passed Belzec. Poles on the train slammed their windows to keep out the stench. Toivi saw flames dancing on the pine tops. He knew.

The Ukrainians on the train caught him three miles from the Hungarian border, pushed him into the railway security office, and ordered him to drop his pants. When they saw he was circumcised, they tossed him in jail to await the next train for Sobibor.

Toivi had learned that Jewish prisoners with typhus were sent to a hospital across the yard from the prison, so he forced a thermometer up to 104°F. and pinched his hairless chest to make red spots, symptoms of typhus. The medic sent him to the hospital, where nineteen prisoners tossed with fever. Before long, Toivi had real red spots on his chest.

118

One day when Toivi was near delirium, the Gestapo ordered all the sick out into the snow-covered courtyard. Sensing that something evil was about to happen, Toivi hid under a bed. He heard the gunshots from the yard.

When one of the doctors found Toivi, he sneaked him from the prison ward to the "free" ward. Soon, the delirium passed, and Toivi grew strong again. He pinned a swastika on his lapel and jumped the express train reserved for Germans. Like Shlomo, Toivi was homesick, and he went back to Izbica. Three weeks later, he was riding the boxcar to Sobibor.

A friend from Izbica, the son of one of Sobibor's three Jewish doctors, took Toivi under his wing. He explained the layout of the camp, the rules, the whippings, whom to watch out for. He brought him bread and sausage until Toivi could steal for himself. He introduced him to his girl friend, and the three of them would sit for hours after work behind the barracks. And ever so gently, he told Toivi what had happened to his mother, father, and brother — the stripping, the gas chambers, the burning — and of the inevitable fact that they would all end up in Camp III, if not today, then tomorrow, if not by Nazi whim, then by design.

When he saw that Toivi understood, the boy from Izbica pushed him out of the nest like a good parent, forcing him to fly on his own. It was his only chance for survival. Everyone at Sobibor knew that. Friends could support you if they had the emotional strength; maybe they could help you if it wasn't their life against yours. But in the end, it was you against the Nazis and the Ukrainians. No one could survive for you.

In spite of his friend's jeremiad, Toivi never doubted that he would survive; he could not picture himself dead. "I'm here," he told himself. "If this is what happens at Sobibor, then I must do what I have to — to live."

In spite of what he had seen and experienced under four years of German terror, Toivi, a naturally shy lad, was naïve, and he found it difficult to adjust to life in Sobibor. He ran whenever he heard prisoners like Shlomo curse or swear. And he was just into puberty. He had never had a girl. True, he had had a girl friend back home. Once he even touched her under the table while they were playing chess in the kitchen after dinner, but he was too timid to go any further.

At Sobibor, Toivi felt isolated and lonely. Although he missed his family, his mind would not allow him to dwell on his father, mother, or brother, whom he had idolized, so deeply buried was the pain of his loss. But he found no community in Sobibor to replace his family, and he was too timid to form one. He hungered for love and friendship, but both were nearly impossible in a camp where fear and staying alive smothered most other emotions. Eventually, he found two Dutch twins his age with whom he used to sit in the spring evenings, chatting about Amsterdam and Izbica; he wished he could kiss one of them.

Toivi may have been bashful and lonely, but he was far from stupid. In a way, Sobibor was safer than Izbica. If the Nazis hadn't caught him, he would have been alone in the deserted ghetto. How would he have survived? The Poles would have killed him or turned him over to the Germans. If he had escaped to the woods, unarmed, he wouldn't have lasted a week. In Sobibor, he was not alone. He knew exactly who his enemies were. And he couldn't believe that there was no chance of survival.

It didn't take Toivi long to puzzle out the best way to stay alive. He noticed three classes of prisoners. The drones carried the brunt of hard, sometimes grueling labor under constant supervision of Germans, Ukrainians, and Kapos. They were dispensable and doomed. They couldn't steal food; day by day they grew weaker. And the weaker they became, the greater their risk of displeasing the Nazis or of making a mistake.

Then there were the Jews with special jobs, like Josel. They nursed prisoners, weeded gardens, fed the geese, groomed the horses. They were dispensable, too. But with more freedom and less supervision, they had more opportunities to steal food and to rest.

Finally, there were the privileged, like Shlomo and Itzhak, who provided services essential to the Nazi machine. They had their own shops, commanded the respect of other prisoners, always seemed to have food, good clothes, and girl friends.

Toivi didn't have any special skills, so he knew he'd never belong to Shlomo's group. But he was determined not to become a drone, condemned to heavy, dangerous work. He'd concentrate on the jobs that would keep him away from the Nazis and close to food.

Toivi shadowed a young, husky Jew, figuring that if the strong prisoner managed to stay healthy, he must be doing something right. Maybe it would rub off on him. So when Wagner called the husky lad, Toivi tagged along, as if they were a team. Wagner took them to a pile of pine branches near the main gate. Pointing to the bare spots in the thatched fence where the pine needles had dried and dropped over the winter, he ordered them to camouflage the fence to the left and right of the gate. Although the job was easy and unsupervised, it was highly conspicuous. If Wagner or any other Nazi thought he wasn't working hard enough or didn't like his weave, they could give him twenty-five lashes or send him down the tube to Camp III. Toivi started to look for another job.

One morning, instead of following the husky Jew, Toivi joined Selma and Chaim and the hundred other sorters. He found that sorting was safer than weaving branches, but it was not as close to food as he'd have liked, and it was too close to Franz Wolf and to Wagner, who slipped in and out of the barracks like a six-foot, four-inch shadow.

One corner of the sorting barracks was filled with suitcases carelessly piled into a cardboard and leather mountain. Only one Jew worked there to clean out the bags, scrape off stickers, cut identification tags, sort by size, and cull those that were broken, torn, or too old to be sold. It was more than one tired Jew could handle.

One morning, instead of going to the tables piled with Dutch clothes, Toivi began cleaning suitcases. The Jew in charge thought Wagner had sent him a helper; so did the Wolf brothers. Toivi had a new job. True, there was no food in the suitcases, but he was safe. Because he could hear anyone entering the barracks, he had enough time to look busy.

It didn't take Toivi long to cook up a scheme. As the suitcases were tossed helter-skelter, tunnels formed inside the pile, a labyrinth of leather. Toivi dug a little room underneath where he could rest or sleep. Soon he had a thriving business. Jews who had food, but no place to eat, would trade. If Toivi would share his safe house, they would share their food. Toivi joined the ranks of Sobibor smugglers.

Anyone caught smuggling food would be whipped or shot, depending on which Nazi did the catching and what mood he was in. But Toivi didn't care. For some strange reason that he couldn't understand, he loved the danger. And he knew exactly how dangerous smuggling could be, for one day he saw Wagner, who loved to pull random searches, stop a boy carrying a blanket filled with shoes. Wagner ordered the boy to spread the blanket on the ground. Pair by pair, the Nazi checked for food. He found a can of sardines in one shoe.

"Over here," Toivi heard Wagner tell the boy. "In."

The boy jumped into the ditch where Jews burned passports and papers, old clothes and broken toys. Wagner pulled out his pistol and shot the boy.

When the Dutch transports arrived every Friday night, Frenzel would barge into the barracks. "Up! Up!" he would shout, blowing his whistle like a traffic cop. "Let's go. Bahnhofkommando . . . Luggage carriers . . . Barbers . . . Up!"

With knots in their stomachs, the prisoners would dress quickly in silence, line up outside two by two to wait for their Kapos. The other prisoners would sleep until the five o'clock whistle.

One night, Frenzel drafted Toivi to work in the first of three sheds inside the tube to Camp III. "Stand here," Frenzel instructed him. "Tell them to leave their hand luggage."

The Dutch Jews had already left their large suitcases on the train or unloading platform, and had received claim checks from Abraham and his train brigade. But the Nazis encouraged them to take along their purses, valises, and shopping bags. "Handbags down," Toivi shouted as they filed through his shed, quiet and nervous. "Handbags down here."

Toivi was nervous, too. Frenzel had given him a dangerous job, the kind he had been trying to avoid. He stood less than a hundred yards from Camp III — the closest he had ever been — and the Nazis were edgy, as they always were until the new transport was under control. After the Dutch Jews passed through his shed, Toivi tossed their bags onto blankets, which other prisoners carried to the sorting sheds. He became a regular on the night brigade.

Sometimes Frenzel would pull him from the hand luggage job and send him to the last of the three sheds in the tube, less than thirty feet from the door to Camp III. It was a barnlike building with a door at each end and two rows of stools standing on the wooden floor. One of the Wolf brothers or Frenzel would be in charge.

Naked women and girls would come into the shed. Most did not have to be told to sit down. It took Toivi less than a minute to cut their pigtails or flowing locks with shears sharpened in Shlomo's shop before each new transport. The mounds of hair would later be bagged for Germany, where it would be threaded on bobbins and made into felt, or combed, cut, and woven into slipper linings for U-boat crews.

The Dutchwomen didn't resist, and in a way, it was merciful. They had been told that their hair would be cut to prevent lice from spreading. Some wept. Others, in the presence of men and boys, covered their breasts and squeezed their thighs together. They rarely talked, filing into the shed, their bare feet stepping over the piles of pigtails and black hair on the floor, sitting on the stools, hunched forward, eyes cast down in modesty. Then they filed out the other door.

Toivi had never seen a naked woman before, and like every fifteen-year-old, he wanted to. But as the women walked tentatively through the door, he cast his eyes down out of shame for them, for seeing them, for snipping their last shred of feminine dignity.

The Polish Jews were not fooled, and they tried to defend their nakedness with their tongues. They would curse the Nazis and shout at Toivi and the other barbers — mostly boys — "We're going to be murdered. Why don't you say something? Don't just stand there. Do something!"

Toivi would ignore their remarks, avoid their eyes filled with hatred and fear, and concentrate on clipping hair as fast as he could.

"Your time will come, too," they'd say, while Wolf or Frenzel shouted at them to shut up and keep moving.

"Cut," they would warn Toivi. "Cut."

Most of the time, Toivi could hear screams coming from the gas chamber, muffled but loud at first, then weak. Then silence. Or he would hear the plaintive wail of "Eli, Eli," the old song that expressed the Chosen People's relationship to their God.

"God, my God, why have You forsaken me," Toivi would hear them chant as they stood before the gas chambers.

Then, through the doubt and gentle reproach, he would hear them sing the affirmation of faith, as their forefathers had done for centuries: "Hear, O Israel, the Lord our God, the Lord is One."

It was a moan of pain by a people who had been beaten, robbed, and brutalized, torn from loved ones, shamed and rendered helpless by a false hope. Yet just when it seemed as if they might reject their God for delivering them into the hand of their enemies — into a world they did not understand or believe could ever exist — they would sing: "Hear, O Israel, the Lord our God, the Lord is One."

Toivi would endure it all for two hours, until Frenzel allowed him to go back to bed. At seven, he'd have to start sorting the loot taken the night before. Toivi could hear and see it all again as he tried to fall asleep: the screams, the silent tears on the cheeks of girls his age, the haunting cry of "Eli, Eli," which he had heard so often in the synagogue in Izbica. Nothing made any sense to him. Not the hope, the faith, the cruelty, nor God and the Nazis. Only life mattered. That's all there was. A thread.

*

One rainy spring night, it finally happened. Two Jews — a mason and a doomed carpenter with a broken arm — dug under the south fence behind the carpenter shop. Wagner was on vacation, leaving Frenzel in charge of the prisoners. During roll call, Frenzel stood in the yard draped in his black cloak, waiting for the Kapos and brigade leaders to report.

"Two missing," Shlomo told Frenzel.

"Where are they?" Frenzel demanded.

"I don't know." Shlomo wasn't lying; he had no idea they had escaped.

Frenzel called Josel. "Are they sick?"

"No," the medic said. He didn't know about the escape either.

Frenzel stomped away like a spoiled child. When he returned from the main office, his thin smile was gone. The guards had apparently found the hole in the sandy soil.

Frenzel walked down the column, pulling out every tenth Jew. Selma dug her nails into her palms as Frenzel neared Chaim. The Nazi passed him by, taking the Jew in front of Josel, moving past Itzhak and Eda, Bajle and Shlomo, Esther and Hella, Toivi and Abraham. Twenty prisoners stood waiting for Frenzel's next command, and although they knew what it was going to be, they did not protest, plead, or cry.

As Frenzel began marching them off to Camp III, Johnny Niemann came into the yard, riding crop twitching in his hand behind his back, walking so slowly (as he always did) that it seemed as if he had had an accident in his pants. Niemann signaled Frenzel to stop. The two Germans held a conference. Then Niemann counted every other condemned Jew and sent him back to the roll call.

No one was sure why Niemann had granted a reprieve to ten Jews. They suspected that Frenzel had exceeded his authority in a fit of anger, and that Johnny had to teach him who was boss. A few minutes after Frenzel left with the hostages, the Jews heard ten shots from Camp III.

The Nazis decided to take no more chances after that escape. They put padlocks and chains on the barracks doors, locking the Jews in for the night. They drafted a crew to dig a wide, deep ditch between the two outer fences of Camp I. And they mined the fields around the whole camp, as much a precaution against partisans who were becoming active in the Parczew as against another escape attempt. Wagner ordered Mordechai and his crew to paint signs saying DANGER! MINES! in German, Polish, and Russian. And he ordered Shlomo and his crew to cut long tubes and to weld one end closed, the other partly closed. "Priority," Wagner had warned Shlomo. The Nazis filled the tubes with explosives and planted a detonator in each.

The land mines were crude, but only temporary. Soon a team of Wehrmacht specialists came to Sobibor with the real thing. Their mines worked; every now and then a rabbit, hopping from the pines to nibble the spring grass in the open fields around the camp, would wander across the belt and set one off.

Shlomo and the Jews in his shop, who had been planning an escape for the spring, were devastated. Not only couldn't they break out at night, as they had hoped, but they now had a moat and a fifteen-yard chain of land mines to cross. Furthermore, the Nazis had kept their promise. If anyone escaped, they had warned, the rest of the Jews would pay.

Maybe they should start thinking of a revolt, a break-out, something that would give each Jew who wanted to escape an equal chance.

Chapter 17

Spring 1943

WHILE THE NAZIS were mining the fields around Sobibor, the Jews in the Warsaw ghetto a hundred miles northwest were attacking the Wehrmacht. Of the half-million Jews who once had roamed the ghetto streets, only fifty-seven thousand were still alive in the spring of 1943. Among them was a fighting force of under a thousand young men and women. Under instructions from General Sikorski, the Home Army had reluctantly given them arms — pistols, rifles, and eleven pounds of dynamite. The Polish Communists gave them a few more pistols and some hand grenades, and the Socialists gave them two thousand liters of gasoline, a batch of potassium chlorate, and whatever else they needed to make explosives. The Warsaw ghetto fighters also were able to buy a few guns and grenades from German and Italian deserters who were gunrunning.

In all, fewer than two hundred armed Jews in April attacked General Juergen Stroop's two thousand inexperienced soldiers. The Jews held out for a month while Stroop leveled all the ghetto buildings with tanks, flooded the sewers, scoured bunkers and basements with flame throwers, sent dogs into holes, and dynamited whatever looked like a hiding place.

In May, Stroop reported to Himmler that of the fifty-seven thousand Jews in the ghetto at the beginning of April, seven thousand had been killed and most of the others sent to Treblinka. He told Himmler that the Jews had killed sixteen of his soldiers and wounded another ninety (probably an undercount to save face).

Of the Jewish fighting force, fewer than a hundred had escaped to the partisans, skipped to the Aryan side of Warsaw, or survived in the rubble until the Russians came. The rest died in battle or committed suicide rather than be captured. All during the uprising, the Polish Home Army cheered safely from the Aryan side.

While the Nazis were mining Sobibor and the Jews in Warsaw were fighting the Germans, Allied diplomats were meeting in Bermuda (they had already made up their minds to do nothing) to talk about Jewish refugees, and Jan Karski was telling Washington what he had seen in Poland.

Washington knew about the Warsaw uprising, of course, since the United Press in Sweden had published the last radio communiqué from the Jews in Warsaw before their radio went dead:

The last thirty-five thousand Jews in the Warsaw ghetto have been condemned to execution.
Warsaw is again echoing to musketry volleys.
The people are murdered.
Women and children defend themselves with their naked arms.
Save us . . .

Besides meeting with Jewish leaders (Rabbi Wise and Nahum Goldmann), Catholic leaders (Cardinals Spellman, Mooney, Stritch, and the apostolic delegate), political leaders (the secretary of war, secretary of state, attorney general), Karski talked to General William Donovan, Chief Justice Felix Frankfurter, and President Roosevelt.

"Be precise," the Polish ambassador to Washington told Karski before he reported to General "Wild Bill" Donovan, chief of the OSS. "He's well informed."

Indeed Donovan was. When Sobibor opened its gas chambers in the spring of 1942, OSS field reports were already talking about "systematic liquidation of the Jews." Furthermore, the OSS had a man in London — Arthur Goldberg, future United States ambassador to the United Nations. Goldberg was a close friend of Szmul Zygielbojm's, the Jewish member of the Polish National Council. Goldberg reported regularly to Donovan what he had learned from Zygielbojm.

Karski didn't have to be precise, for Wild Bill showed no interest in either Poland or the Jews. All he wanted to know was whether the OSS had treated the courier well in Spain after his harrowing trip west.

"Everything okay?" he asked. "Any slip-ups? Any criticism?"

"It went smoothly," Karski told him. "I was pleased."

Donovan slapped his knee in pleasure. "My boys!" he said proudly. "My boys!"

Small and erect, with piercing eyes, Supreme Court Justice Felix Frankfurter listened closely to Karski.

"Young man, do you know who I am?" he asked the courier.

"Yes, sir. Mr. Ambassador said you are very important."

"Do you know I am a Jew?"

"Yes, sir."

"Good. Now, young man, tell me what is happening to the Jews in your country. I have heard many stories. I want to know."

As Karski told his story, dispassionately, like a schoolboy reciting a grisly poem, Frankfurter paced the room without interrupting.

"Young man," he said when Karski had finished, "I was made to understand that you have walked in and out of hell and that you are going back again. That being so, a man like me, talking to a man like you, must be totally frank." He paused. "I cannot believe you."

Polish Ambassador Jan Ciechanowski, who sat in on the interview, was incensed. He told Frankfurter that Karski spoke with the authority of the Polish government and that he was telling the painful truth.

"I did not say this young man is lying," Frankfurter replied. "I said I cannot believe him. There is a difference . . ."

Karski began to explain, but the justice held up the palms of his hands to push back the avalanche of truth. "No, no, no," he cried in pain.

The interview was over.

"Be brief," Ambassador Ciechanowski warned Karski on the way to the White House. Like General Donovan, President Roosevelt was well informed about the Jews; he had already met a Jewish delegation (led by Rabbi Wise) that had briefed him on the murder of the Jews, country by country, and had presented to him a twenty-page report, *Blue Print for Extermination*. Roosevelt had told them that he was deeply shocked to hear that two million Jews had already been exterminated, and he assured Rabbi Wise that the United States would take every measure to stop the murders "and save those who may yet be saved."

Roosevelt asked Karski careful questions about everyday life in Poland, the Polish underground, the morale of the Poles and Germans, the ultimate goals of the Soviets. But he listened in silence as the courier told him about the Jews in Sobibor, Belzec, and Treblinka in eastern Poland and the Poles and Jews in Auschwitz in western Poland. "I am convinced that there is no exaggeration in the accounts of the plight of the Jews," Karski told Roosevelt. "Our underground authorities are absolutely sure that the

Germans are out to exterminate the entire Jewish population of Europe."

"Tell the Polish underground," Roosevelt said, "that their indomitable attitude has been duly appreciated. Tell them that they will never have cause to regret their brave decision to reject any collaboration with the enemy, and that Poland will live to reap the reward of her heroism and sacrifice."

Not only was there no message for the Jews, but Roosevelt had misled Rabbi Wise. The United States did not intend to do everything in its power to stop the murder of the Jews and to "save those who may yet be saved." When the British Foreign Office suggested the bilateral Bermuda Conference, the State Department balked. Like the Home Office, it had been refusing to accept more Jews, even though it still had almost half a million openings under its European quota. The reaction to the Swedish plan was typical of State's stall tactics.

Bursting with forty-two thousand Jewish refugees, including almost all of Denmark's Jews, tiny Sweden had proposed a creative plan to England and the United States. A neutral country with good relations with Germany, Sweden said it would ask Hitler for twenty thousand Jewish children, provided that England and the United States shared food and medical expenses and agreed to help resettle the children after the war.

The Foreign Office agreed immediately, but the State Department stalled for five months, then submitted an amendment: the Swedes should include in the twenty thousand some Norwegian, non-Jewish children. By the time the amended plan reached Sweden — eight months after it first had been proposed — Sweden's relationship with Germany had become very strained. It dropped the plan.

When the United States couldn't delay the Bermuda Conference any longer, it tried to take credit for the idea (angering the Foreign Office, which was in dire need of good press), and it gave its negotiators secret order *not* to:

- offer to accept any more Jews into the United States,
- pledge funds for rescue operations,
- offer naval escorts for ships carrying refugees,
- offer refugees space on empty U.S. ships.

When the secret conference was over, the United States and England issued a joint statement, saying that the delegates had passed a number of concrete recommendations to help refugees of *all* nationalities, but that the recommendations must remain secret because of the war. They were: to revive the totally ineffective Intergovernmental Committee on Refugees so that it could study the problem in depth, and to ship twenty-one thousand

Jews already safe in Spain to North Africa to make room for more refugees.

"The Bermuda Conference was wholly ineffective as I view it," diplomat Myron Taylor wrote Secretary of State Cordell Hull in a secret memo. "And we knew it would be."

Word of both the refusal of the Allies to help the Polish Jews fighting the Germans in Warsaw and the failure of the Bermuda Conference finally reached Szmul Zygielbojm in London. As Feiner and Berman had instructed, Karski had met with the Bundist leader near Piccadilly. Zygielbojm and Karski had one thing in common. Both had been caught and beaten by the Gestapo, Zygielbojm in 1940 when he fled Poland because, as the founder of the Underground Resistance Movement, he was on the top of the Nazis' Warsaw hit list.

Zygielbojm was almost irrational when he saw Karski. "Why did they send *you?*" he ranted. "Who are you? You're not a Jew!"

When Karski explained how he had become a courier for the Jews of Warsaw and what the conditions were like there, Zygielbojm calmed down. He sat in his chair, legs apart, hands on his knees, leaning forward as if he were afraid he'd miss a syllable. His dark eyes didn't blink. No muscle seemed to move.

"You're not telling me anything I don't already know," Zygielbojm interrupted. "I know more than you." Karski then started to tell the Bundist about the reaction of British leaders to Berman and Feiner's demands. Zygielbojm exploded: "Don't tell me what is said and done *here*. I know that myself. I came to hear about what is happening *there*. What they want *there*. What they say *there*."

"Very well, then," Karski said. "This is what they want from their leaders in the free countries of the world. This is what they told me to say: 'Let them go to all the important English and American offices and agencies. Tell them not to leave until they have obtained guarantees that a way has been decided on to save the Jews. Let them accept no food or drink. Let them die a slow death while the world looks on. Let them *die*. This may shake the conscience of the world.' "

Zygielbojm took Feiner and Berman's order seriously. On May 12, just as General Stroop killed the last Warsaw ghetto Jews, and the Bermuda Conference closed without a crumb of promise, Zygielbojm committed suicide. In farewell letters to his friends and the world, he wrote:

> I cannot be silent. I cannot live while the remnants of the Jewish population, of whom I am a representative, are perishing. My friends in the Warsaw ghetto died with weapons in their hands in the last heroic battle. It was not my

destiny to die together with them, but I belong to them and in their mass graves . . .

Perhaps my death will achieve what I was unable to achieve with my life, and concrete action will be taken to rescue at least a few hundred thousand who remain out of three and a half million.

No concrete action was taken, and if the Allies were shaken by Zygiel-bojm's death, they didn't show it.

Chapter 18

Summer 1943

F RENZEL CAUGHT Toivi sneaking from Camp II to Camp I with a
can of sardines in his pocket.

"Kleiner!" the Nazi shouted. He liked to call the boy "Shorty." "Where
are you going? Come here!"

Frenzel was in a good mood that day, and rather than shoot, whip, or
search the boy, he picked up a two-by-four and began to pound him. Toivi
wasn't sure how far the Nazi would go — beat him to death, break his
arm, crack his skull — so he darted into his barracks in Camp I. To run
from a Nazi was death, too, but Toivi saw no choice.

Josel was in the barracks. "Help me," Toivi pleaded as he crawled into
his bunk, tight up against the wall to make himself invisible.

Frenzel followed. "How do you feel?" he asked. There was concern in
his voice, as if he felt guilty for beating a boy with a board.

"I hurt," Toivi said.

"Rest here, Kleiner. Then get back to work."

That was the closest Toivi had come to death since Frenzel had selected
him as a Putzer. (He never did shine Frenzel's shoes.) Toivi began to think
seriously about escape. Like so many prisoners, he fantasized about it during
the day, dreamed about it at night, and talked constantly about it behind
the barracks with his two Dutch girl friends.

Toivi saw a crew of forty men marching into a heavily wooded corner
of the camp. (The prisoners called it the North Camp.) Once, it had been

132

part of the pine forest, but when the Nazis built Sobibor, they put a barbed-wire fence around it in case they later wanted to expand. The North Camp was neither heavily supervised nor patrolled by Ukrainians. If there were any place from which Toivi could escape during the day, the North Camp was it.

One summer morning, Toivi joined the brigade marching there. The Nazis had missed a beat, and Dutch transports had failed to arrive on Friday two weeks in a row. With the camp routine broken, no one in Camp II missed him.

Toivi had learned a new survival trick. The Nazis had a passion for neatness and order, he noted. They loved to call the prisoners "dirty Jews." Indeed, most of the Polish Jews arriving in cattle cars were dressed in rags and covered with lice, since it was impossible to keep clean in a stinking, crammed ghetto with no sanitation. To the Nazis, it seemed to Toivi, neatness was the measure of the man. Wouldn't they give him better treatment if he became as passionate about cleanliness as they?

Toivi began to take great pains to shine his boots, even grabbing a new pair when his old ones became too scuffed. He washed carefully, combed his hair. He paid Judah, the barber, food for regular trims. Like a boy dressing for his first date, he selected his pants and shirts with great care from the piles in the barracks, making sure they fitted well. He even pressed his pants at night under his mattress. And he learned to walk as tall as a small lad could, head high, back straight, with bounce.

The Nazis were developing the North Camp into a weapons factory. Their master plan called for underground bunkers in which to sort, repair, and store the rifles and artillery pieces captured from the Russians, and barracks to house the prisoners who would eventually work there. The bunkers were already completed, the barracks under construction.

The weapons idea so excited Himmler that he suggested to General Oswald Pohl, the SS director of the whole camp system, that Sobibor be converted from a death camp to a labor camp specializing in weapons repair. Pohl discussed Himmler's idea with General Globocnik, then reported to the SS chief: "Your aim to install in Sobibor a depot for arms taken from the enemy can be achieved without transformation. We prefer everything stay as before."

Himmler agreed, and summer work in the North Camp began to move with breakneck speed. When Toivi joined the brigade there, Jews were chopping down pines to make room for the barracks, sorting guns in the bunkers, and building a half-mile road from the main gate to the center of the North Camp.

Sergeant Gomerski was in charge of both the North Camp and the forest brigade, which cut trees in the woods outside Sobibor for the pyres in Camp III and the stoves in Camp II. The former boxer was second only to Wagner in cunning and brutality. He usually worked with the woodcutters outside the camp, and Toivi was careful to avoid him.

Sergeant Daxler was in charge of the road crew. He was an older man, close to fifty, with gray hair and a small beerbelly. Unlike Gomerski, he was firm but not cruel. That didn't mean, though, that he wouldn't give out twenty-five or send someone to Camp III if he had to.

Toivi joined Daxler's crew, determined to land a cushy job. If Daxler said "Run," he'd run; "Faster," he'd speed up. Toivi would chop saplings inside the North Camp, trim off the branches, cut the logs down to fifteen feet, and lay them side by side, making a log road for trucks and artillery. He caught Daxler's eye, as he had hoped he would, and the Nazi put him in charge of the brigade. The fifteen-year-old boy was now a supervisor, just a notch below a Kapo.

It was an easy job, and Toivi felt good. He'd line up his crew two by two and march them to the woods, calling out like a drill sergeant, "One, two, three, left . . . One, two, three, left." Daxler loved it. Inside the camp, Toivi would order his brigade to sing German marching songs. Outside, guarded by Ukrainians, he'd tell them to sing Ukrainian folk songs, some pornographic, to soften up the Blackies. Toivi would stand there in the woods and order his brigade, "Cut this . . . Cut that," like an old forester.

One day Toivi marched his brigade through the main gate toward the North Camp, chanting, as usual, "One, two, three, left." Frenzel appeared from nowhere.

"*Achtung!*" he shouted.

"Halt," Toivi commanded his brigade.

"Bend over," Frenzel ordered. Confused and frightened, the boy bent over. Frenzel lashed him once with his whip.

"Straighten up," Frenzel said. Toivi obeyed. "Now, why did I beat you, Kleiner?"

Toivi didn't know, so he just stood there, staring at the Nazi in panic.

"Bend over!" Frenzel beat him again. "Up! Now, why?"

Toivi was sure the beefy German would beat him to death on the spot if he couldn't come up with an answer. What was he doing wrong? His pants were pressed. He was clean. His brigade was working hard. In desperation, he turned to the Kapo standing nearby. "What?" he asked. To run to a Kapo for help under the circumstances was an insult to Frenzel, but it was a risk that Toivi had to take.

"You were out of step," the Kapo said sternly, as if to scold the boy.

Snapping to attention and counting, "One, two, three, left . . . One, two, three, left," Toivi moved his feet to the beat of the cadence. Frenzel smiled a little more than usual, tucked his whip into his belt, and walked to another part of the camp.

Work in the North Camp wasn't exactly what Toivi had thought it would be. Not only was escape suicide, but Wagner and Gomerski had created a Strafkommando (penal brigade) to speed up construction. They kept the brigade at an even twenty, assigning prisoners to it (mostly Dutch Jews, whom they loved to taunt) under the slightest pretext — being one second late for roll call, not responding fast enough to a Nazi order, falling asleep in the job. Wagner and Gomerski made the Jews in the penal brigade do everything at a run, from carrying logs to toting clothes, even eating. Jews were condemned to it for three days. Few lasted that long. Wagner or Gomerski killed them on the job — they were unskilled labor — or sent them to Camp III when they collapsed from fatigue. As soon as one bit the sand, Wagner and Gomerski would find another Dutch Jew to replace him. By the end of the summer, more than fifty had been murdered.

Toivi decided to get out of the North Camp, the hottest spot in Sobibor. So when the log road was finished, he slipped back into Camp II, looking for a job as far away from Germans as possible. Between the sorting sheds and the new log road ran the ditch where two Jews burned passports and papers — the trench in which Toivi had seen Wagner shoot the boy he had caught with sardines in shoes. Toivi joined them. It was a hot, sultry, summer day, and the papers and rags were beginning to pile high. The two Jews liked Toivi, for he had frequently smuggled tins of milk or sardines for them, which they would bury in the sand near the ditch until it was safe to eat them.

When the Germans saw a third person raking and burning at the ditch, they didn't object. After all, they liked to run a clean camp. Eventually, Wagner built a small incinerator between the North Camp and the Officers' Compound, close to the east fence and the railroad to Wlodawa. With the incinerator inside a shed, it would be easier to keep the yard clean and to burn junk in the winter. Wagner put Toivi in charge, dubbed him *Feuermann,* and gave him as an assistant Karl, a young Jew who was blind in one eye.

It was a safe niche. Toivi had his own shop, keys and all, and, like Shlomo, he was providing an essential service. The work was easy, his shed relatively isolated, and he could still get food from the sorting sheds where he picked up junk to be burned. And he had *books.*

Toivi loved to read. Back in Izbica, a book was the best gift anyone could give him. And his mother, a former schoolteacher, had encouraged him to read. As a sorter in Sobibor, he had managed to find a book now and then, and, at the risk of his life, would steal away to a warehouse corner or to an attic and read. Now, as the "Fireman," he had all the books he wanted, because it was his job to burn them.

Frequently, Toivi would read while Blind Karl, as everyone called him, would stoke the fire and keep his good eye open for Wagner, who liked to pop in unexpectedly. If Toivi chanced to find a sex book, he was as happy as a prospector with a nugget. He knew little about sex and was too bashful to ask. If there was any mystery he wanted to crack before he died, sex was it. He remembered what his friend Josef had told him about his train ride to Sobibor.

Josef and his girl friend had never made love. They had kissed and touched in the ghetto, but had never gone much farther. When they ended up in the same boxcar to Sobibor (they knew they were going to a death camp), they held each other, pressing their bodies together in the crammed car. Josef's girl friend wept silently.

"I want to make love before I die," she had told him. "I want to die a woman."

They made love standing in a corner, with old men dying, babies crying, the frightened praying "Hear, O Israel," and the angry cursing.

"She went to Camp III a woman," Josef had told Toivi. And Toivi wanted to die a man. If he couldn't have a woman, at least he could read about them.

One day he found a German encyclopedia and flipped to the chapter on virgins. His eyes were riveted to the page.

"Wagner is coming," Blind Karl whispered.

Toivi tossed the book into the fire and ran to open the shed door for the Nazi.

"Sleeping, Feuermann?" Wagner asked.

Toivi wasn't sure whether he had a guilty look on his face, or whether Wagner was testing him. To say "sleeping" was a death sentence; to say "reading" wasn't much better.

"No, Herr Oberscharführer," Toivi said timidly. "I was just — just resting a moment."

Wagner picked up the iron poker next to the incinerator and shoved Toivi out into the yard. The Nazi began to swing the poker wildly. The first blow landed on Toivi's wrist. Either get beaten to death, he thought, or run. Toivi took his chances and dashed behind the shed.

Just then, Sergeant Beckmann was walking toward his office in the Administration Building in the center of Camp II. He was a slim, good-looking man, and even more meticulously dressed than most of the Germans, and much brighter. But he was no sadist like Wagner. Though he whipped Jews when he had to, he did so without relish. And he did his job when the new transports rolled in, like a good SS man and Nazi.

Wagner called Beckmann and ordered Toivi to lean over a water barrel. "Count twenty-five," he said, as he uncoiled his whip. Wagner and Beckmann took turns. Toivi felt doubly lucky. He got off with only twenty-five, and Beckmann hit like an old woman.

Wagner next called out Blind Karl.

"Over the barrel," he said. But Karl was so frightened by the angry giant with the whip that he just stood there, mouth open. Wagner knocked him to the ground, shoved his face in the sand, and, with his boot on Blind Karl's head, beat the boy with a fury. He didn't even bother to count.

Anything can happen now, Toivi thought. When Wagner's angry, he's unpredictable. And once he gets a taste of blood —

Toivi bolted across the yard into the Camp II tailor shop, where Jews repaired the second-class clothes taken from the transports before they were shipped to Lublin. He crawled under a table stacked with clothes.

"Feuermann," Wagner called, when he tired of beating Blind Karl. "Feuermann."

Toivi cringed in the corner like a trapped mouse.

"Go," the head tailor pleaded. "You must or he'll kill *me*. Please . . . go."

Toivi crawled out from under the table, and when Wagner had his back to the shop, darted into the sunlight.

"Yes, Herr Oberscharführer?"

"Where did you run to, Feuermann?"

Toivi thought fast. "To the dispensary."

"The dispensary? Why?"

"To rub my ass with talcum powder." He rubbed his buttocks as if he were in pain. Beckmann laughed and Wagner smiled. They whipped him a few more times for good measure and let him go.

"Two more days to clean this." Wagner pointed to the mound of rags, paper, and broken suitcases. Then he walked away, his long arms dangling.

Toivi sat on the pile of junk. He was shaking. He had survived with thirty lashes and a sprained wrist where Wagner had bashed him with the poker. It was another close call, but Toivi knew that being "Fireman"

137

was the safest job he'd ever find, so he decided to stay put. As long as the transports kept coming, there would be paper and rags, books and old suitcases to burn. And if there were no transports? Probably the end, anyway.

There were other advantages to working in the incinerator. The Jews who sorted clothes frequently risked their lives by stashing paper money and gold in the junk they sent to Toivi. It was one more way to make sure the Nazis didn't get them.

Toivi burned most of the money, but put aside enough to do business with the Ukrainians. In exchange for the gold he buried in a prearranged spot along the fence, Toivi would get vodka and kielbasa. He didn't drink, and he didn't need the homemade sausage, which the Ukrainians bought from Polish farmers for a pittance. He could always steal food when the transports arrived from the Netherlands every Friday. In fact, there was no logical reason for the boy to take such risks, except that, surrounded by danger and flirting with even more, he felt that the risks kept him alert. They gave him a feeling that he, not the Nazis, controlled his life, a sense of power, of dignity, of being equal to the guards. Weren't they doing what he was doing, dealing? He with them, they with the farmers. Dealing was another reason to live, to hang on, to hope.

*

One summer afternoon a transport of living skeletons in striped uniforms pulled into Sobibor from Maidanek, a concentration camp on the edge of Lublin. No one knew why the Maidanek Jews had been sent to Sobibor when Maidanek had its own gas chambers for Jews who could no longer work, or why the Nazis kept them in the yard instead of ordering them immediately to Camp III, as they always did.

After work that day, Shlomo stood at the fence and watched. It was the saddest moment in his sixteen months at Sobibor, and if he had had any tears left, he would have cried. The Maidanek Jews lay in the yard and in the corridor between Camp I and the Officers' Compound like a human mattress. No one spoke; there were no prayers. All looked alike, those skeletons. A few lowed like calves, but no one moved. The Nazis hadn't even bothered to assign a guard to watch them.

"Shlomo!" whispered someone close to the fence.

The goldsmith looked around, trying to find the cadaver that called his name.

"Shlomo, don't you remember me?"

138

The goldsmith peered at the eyes staring from deep inside a skull, skin stretched taut over a face.

"It's Majer from Pulawy."

Shlomo's cousin Majer had once been a tall, strong man. Now he was shriveled, and his back seemed hunched. In the face of such utter misery, Shlomo began to panic. If it hadn't been his own family there in the sand, he would have pushed the scene away, buried it in his mind. Instead, he lied. "Don't worry, Majer," he said, like a tape recording. "You're going to get a bath, new clothes. You'll rest and eat. Then work."

Why tell Majer he would die the next day? Why say the Nazis had fooled him to the stinking, starving end? Why tell him he was just another animal now, with no privacy, no hope, no love? Why add one more indignity to his cousin's suffering — the truth?

"Wait," Shlomo told Majer. "I have something for you."

He went to his food cache for a loaf of dry bread. He tossed it over the fence as close to his cousin as possible, but Majer was so weak, he couldn't crawl to it. The Jews next to the food attacked it like a pack of rats, pushing, clawing, fighting as the bread crumbled in the sand.

"I'll get another loaf," Shlomo told Majer. The sight of Jews scratching in the dirt made him want to retch.

But it was no use. When Shlomo threw the second loaf, this time even closer to his cousin, Majer couldn't move. The others attacked the bread once again.

Then a Nazi and a Ukrainian came into the yard to have some fun. They walked between the prostrate bodies as if they were out on a Sunday stroll. They smiled and jeered and beat the helpless Maidanek Jews with rifle butts, whips, and clubs. No one had the energy to resist or even to cry out. At least a dozen were beaten to death. When the Nazi and Ukrainian finally got bored, they left the Jews alone. By daybreak, only one out of ten could walk to Camp III. A few tried to crawl on all fours like dogs, still hanging on to the bone of hope that if they could only obey the Nazis just one more time, they would be safe at last. The others were either dead or dying or too weak to crawl.

The Nazis called out Abraham and the train brigade to load the rest of the Maidanek Jews into the miners' train. When the yard was empty, the Nazis sprinkled chlorine over the sand. It looked as if a freak summer snow had dusted the yard.

The Maidanek Jews were a symbol of the Polish Jews in the summer of 1943. Once three million strong, they were now a few thousand. After four years of Nazi occupation and terror, those still alive were mere skeletons, no longer able to crawl for food, walk to death in dignity, or even hope.

Then, on Friday, July 23, the last Dutch transport, number nineteen, came to Sobibor. The Polish transports had long since ceased, with a few stragglers from the Wlodawa work camp and ghetto just five miles down the road. Was this, then, the end? With no one else to kill, would the Nazis now send the Sobibor Jews to Camp III? To the gas chambers? To be shot? And if so, who would bury them?

The Escape

Chapter 19

September 1943

AS FAR AS Leon Feldhendler was concerned, the end had come as he had known it would, as he had sensed it would for weeks. If he and the other Sobibor Jews didn't break out soon, very soon, it would be too late. The transports had stopped. Himmler had kept his promise to Hitler to make Poland Judenrein, free of all Jews. Why did the Germans still need Sobibor? And the Russians were coming. Sooner or later, they would cross the Bug River. Would the Germans be so stupid as to leave the gas chambers and six hundred eyewitnesses?

The end was in the air, borne to Sobibor on the wings of whispers and rumors. The Jews in Warsaw, Feldhendler heard, had fought the Germans to the very end. There was no more ghetto there; just rubble. The last Jews in Bialystok also had attacked the Germans rather than be dragged off to Treblinka, he'd been told. There was no more ghetto there, either; just rubble. Feldhendler knew that Warsaw and Bialystok were the last large ghettos in eastern Poland where the Nazis kept a labor force. Apparently, they no longer needed the labor.

The end was in the air at the other two death camps as well. The Jews in Treblinka had revolted, according to his Ukrainian informant. They burned down half the camp, killed a couple of Nazis, but only a handful had escaped. The Germans had closed Treblinka permanently.

The last of the Belzec Jews were dead, too — the five hundred the Nazis had kept there since December to dig up six hundred thousand corpses and burn them. When Sergeant Paul Groth had brought the gravediggers to Sobibor by train, Kommandant Reichleitner was so afraid they would rebel that he locked up all the Sobibor prisoners and opened the boxcars one at a time. The SS and Ukrainians shot the Belzec Jews on the spot. After one carload had been murdered, the Nazis called out the train brigade to toss the bodies into the miners' wagons. Then, after locking up the train brigade again, the Nazis murdered another carload. Many of the last Belzec Jews had left notes in their pockets on scraps of paper: "If they kill us, avenge us."

Feldhendler wished he could. It was clear now that of the three death camps, Sobibor was the only one still open. But for how long? His Ukrainian contact had said there was a rumor among the staff that Sobibor would be closed by the end of October. In the light of what he already knew, that made sense to Feldhendler. The Jews had to escape by November in any case; the early winter snows would make a break nearly impossible after that. But when? And how?

Feldhendler, Esther's cousin, was a tall, handsome man in his mid-thirties, the son of a rabbi, who walked and spoke with a quiet air of authority. He had been in Sobibor for nine months and had made it his business to know everything — each move the Nazis made, the chain of command, where the land mines were buried, which Blackies could be trusted in a pinch, every escape idea, each shift in mood and morale. He sifted, analyzed, and schemed.

Young Jews like Esther, Toivi, and Shlomo looked up to him as to a surrogate father and moral leader. He led prayers on holy days and encouraged everyone. "Don't give up," he used to say. "Don't let them get to you. Resist. Fight back. Hold on." They listened carefully, for he was educated and well-bred, a man who thought about things and seemed never to act rashly. They felt a certain unselfishness in him, almost as if he had taken on his broad shoulders the responsibility for every Jew in Sobibor. And he had.

Ever since January, Feldhendler had been building a team — the Organization — to plan a break-out. A trusted group of leaders, all shop chiefs — Shlomo, Szol the shoemaker, and Mundek the tailor. But when the mason and carpenter had dug under the fence in the spring, and the Nazis had retaliated by killing ten Jews, locking the barracks at night, and mining the fields, Feldhendler knew the Jews' only hope was a mass escape. He and the Organization had talked seriously about several plans.

The first centered on Drescher, an eleven-year-old *Putzer*. He was the youngest boy in the camp, a shrimp, bright, gutsy, camp-wise. The Nazis treated him as the Sobibor mascot, their frisky, little Jewish terrier. Drescher and the other Putzers, who rushed to the Officers' Compound at five in the morning to shine boots, were to kill the Nazis in their beds, steal all the guns they could find, and smuggle them back to the Organization. Feldhendler would distribute the guns, and the Jews would make a break while the Ukrainians and Germans still alive were wiping the sleep from their eyes.

The second plan centered on Esther's friend Zelda, who worked in the North Camp, sorting and cleaning captured Russian guns. She and several other women who worked there would smuggle grenades under their dresses into Camp I. Key men in the Organization would blow up the canteen (while the Nazis and Ukrainians were eating), the Administration Building, and the officers' barracks, depending on how many grenades Zelda and her girls could smuggle. The Jews would then make the break.

The third plan centered on Feldhendler himself, who was the only member of the Organization to work in Camp II, sorting clothes. He and a few men he could trust would set several of the barracks on fire to create a diversion. While the Nazis and Ukrainians ran to put out the fire, the Jews would make a break.

The plans were risky, almost suicidal, but Feldhendler would pick one anyway, unless the Organization could come up with something better soon. That was unlikely. Furthermore, it was hopeless to expect the partisans in the Parczew Forest to spring them. A Jewish partisan group called Chil, under the command of Yechiel Greenshpan, crept to within a mile of Sobibor one night, carrying a forty-pound mine. They buried it under the railroad ties. When the tracks blew, the Nazis woke up all the Jews and herded them with machine guns into one corner of the yard. They stood there for hours while the Germans waited and watched. Long after the woods had stilled, Frenzel ordered the prisoners back to bed. "Partisans," he told them, as if to grind their last hope into the sand. "We drove them off."

If Jewish partisans couldn't free them, the Polish partisans — who, for the most part, hated them — certainly wouldn't, Feldhendler reasoned. The Sobibor Jews were on their own, as he had known for months that they would be.

The three escape attempts that summer didn't help his plans one bit. If anything, they had made the Germans and Ukrainians more wary. The Waldkommando, or forest brigade, was the first to make a run for it. Two Waldkommando Jews, Podchlebnik and Kopf, knew they couldn't last long under Gomerski, even with the extra food they got from their friends who worked in Camp II. Either Gomerski would kill them in one of his games —

145

he liked to make a Jew climb to the top of a tree, then order the others to cut it down — or they would just wear out and be sent to Camp III. They knew they had to act while they still had the energy to plan and run.

The Waldkommando followed a routine each day at lunch time. The Jews would sit on the ground to eat their bread, usually in two groups — the Polish Jews in one and the Dutch Jews in the other — while the Nazis and Ukrainians, forty feet away, ate cheese and kielbasa and drank vodka. It was at lunch time that the guards were the most relaxed, their machine guns and rifles leaning against nearby trees. One of the Ukrainians would randomly select two Jews to fetch water with him from a well in a neighboring village.

One day, Podchlebnik asked the guard who led the water detail whether he wanted to deal. Gold and jewels, the Jew told him. The Ukrainian's greed clouded his judgment, and he said yes.

"Pick Kopf and me to carry the water," Podchlebnik told him. "We'll bring the money. Tomorrow."

Kopf and Podchlebnik didn't tell their friends about the plan lest the Nazis smell something in the air. The plan could work only if they caught everyone by surprise — including their friends. The fewer who knew, the better. Besides, it would be every man for himself in the end, whether they knew about the plan or not.

At lunch time the next day, the Ukrainian walked over to the Jews. "You and you," he said to Podchlebnik and Kopf. They picked up their pails and headed into the woods, with the Ukrainian walking behind them, his Mauser pointed at their backs. Before they reached the village, the Ukrainian asked, "What do you have?"

"A gold watch," Podchlebnik said. "Take a look." He held out his left hand, his fingers partly closed.

The Blackie walked over and leaned forward to look at the watch. With his right hand, Podchlebnik slipped a knife from his boot and shoved it into the guard's stomach. Almost simultaneously, Kopf grabbed him from behind and slit his throat. The Ukrainian didn't cry out. They took his rifle and pistol, picked his pockets clean, and ran into the woods, looking for partisans. They felt their chances were good. They had money. They were Polish and knew the terrain. And they had guns.

When the Ukrainian didn't return, the Nazis got nervous. So they sent a second guard to see what was holding up the detail. The other Polish Jews also noticed that their water was long overdue. They watched the Nazis dispatch the guard. Knowing Podchlebnik and Kopf — both had been Jewish fighters before the Nazis had caught them — they were certain something was about to happen. They tensed like rabbits, waiting for the right moment to spring.

Within minutes, they heard the second Ukrainian snapping branches in the woods. They watched him hurry over to the Nazis. They couldn't hear what he was saying, but they could tell he was excited. They saw the Nazis, almost as if on cue, reach for their guns. One of the Polish Jews shouted, "Hurrah!" To a man, the Polish Jews split, and to a man, the Dutch Jews stayed put, hands on their heads. The Germans and Ukrainians sprayed the woods with gunfire, and while several guards corraled the Dutch Jews, the others ran after the Polish Jews. Three got away, two were killed, and thirteen were caught.

While the Polish Jews in the Waldkommando were making their break, Esther was cleaning the rust off bullets in the armory and stuffing them into ammunition belts. The armory was a small concrete building along the east fence, close to the main gate. The Germans stored their rifles, pistols, and machine guns there, logging each piece in and out. As usual, Wolodia, her Ukrainian guard, was there, cleaning guns. Wolodia hated the Germans, and he liked to talk war politics with Esther, who usually just nodded and kept scraping rust, afraid to agree or disagree with him. He was basically a good man — sometimes he even brought her bread and salami — but she was cautious. Who knew what he might say about her in the canteen when he was drunk?

Wolodia heard some shouts outside and looked through the barred window facing the main gate. "Wait till you see what's going to happen now," he told Esther.

"What?"

"Take a look."

The Jews from the Waldkommando were crawling on all fours through the camp gate, like dogs.

"It's going to be bad," Wolodia said. The Nazis began to blow their whistles for a midday assembly.

Feldhendler left the sorting sheds for the assembly. He was scared. Was this going to be it, he wondered. Is this the end? He was ready to give a signal to attack the Nazis and grab their guns. The other Jews also sensed that the end was near. Feldhendler could feel it.

Frenzel ordered the prisoners to form a semicircle. "Sit," he told the thirteen Polish Jews from the forest brigade. They plopped down in the sandy soil. "Hands on your heads."

Frenzel looked at the Dutch Jews from the Waldkommando. "Over

147

there," he ordered, nodding toward the others sitting in the semicircle.

Frenzel faced the semicircle, his back to the thirteen. "These men will be shot. They tried to escape," he said slowly in precise German. "Let that be an example."

He stepped aside. Three Ukrainians took positions ten yards from the thirteen Polish Jews. Selma squeezed Chaim's hand and closed her eyes, as he told her to. Toivi watched in shock and fascination; Shlomo boiled with anger. It was a scene none of them would ever forget. They had seen death in Sobibor every day. They had heard shots coming from Camp III. They had smelled smoke and seen fires in the night sky. But this was different. It was cold-blooded murder, right before their eyes. These were their friends.

The young Poles sat there, almost defiant. They did not plead for life or whimper. The only sounds were Frenzel calling, "Fire . . . Fire . . . Fire," and the voice of one Jew, fist in the air, crying, "Avenge us! Avenge us!" One by one, they jerked back as if hit by an invisible sledgehammer, and crumpled in the sand. When it was over, Frenzel drew his pistol and gave each the coup de grâce, as if he were paying tribute to men who had died like soldiers.

Once the shock of the assassinations wore off, the Sobibor Jews were angry rather than frightened — most at the Nazis, but some at Podchlebnik and Kopf. They had escaped at the risk of everyone else's life, even though they knew the Nazis would take it out on those left behind. Every one of them could have been killed — two freedoms bought with the deaths of hundreds. It had been that close.

The next day, the Germans found one of the Waldkommando Jews who had escaped wandering in the woods, disoriented and half-dead from running in circles. When two Ukrainians brought him back to the camp, Frenzel called "Radio," a Jewish supervisor in the sorting sheds.

"Whip him to death," Frenzel ordered, pushing the captured Jew to his knees.

Radio could have refused. But if he had, he would have been beaten to death himself, shot on the spot, or taken to Camp III, and the Waldkommando Jew would have been executed anyway. Frenzel called Toivi and a dozen other Jews to watch.

Radio took his whip from his belt, stood back ten feet, and began lashing. Frenzel didn't even order the condemned man to count. The whip whistled, then cracked like a .38 caliber pistol. By twenty-five lashes, the man's clothes were starting to shred. By fifty, he was raw and red. By one hundred, he was slumped over in the sand, motionless. Toivi didn't know whether he was dead or had just passed out.

"Enough," Frenzel ordered after he rolled the Polish Jew over with his boot. Two guards dragged the man away.

Frenzel had made no speech, nor had he gathered the whole camp into a semicircle to watch. He didn't have to. By lockup, every Jew in Sobibor knew that another Waldkommando Jew was dead, how he had died, and why.

Toivi had known the dead man from Izbica, and a great sense of pity ran through him. To be so close to freedom! To die so terribly and so alone! But the boy felt no anger toward Radio. Toivi knew that if Frenzel had ordered him to whip the man to death, he might have done it, too. For imprisonment at Sobibor was no longer life. And Toivi was no longer a person.

The Dutch Jews were the next ones to hatch an escape plan. Feldhendler never did learn precisely what their plan was. All he knew was that one day Wagner and Frenzel marched all the Dutchmen — with the exception of Van Dam, the artist — to Camp III and shot them, seventy-two in all. The Dutch and Polish Jews weren't close, so all Feldhendler had to go on was rumor, and rumor said that Jozeph Jacobs, a former officer in the Dutch Royal Navy, had bribed a guard to lead him and the other Dutch Jews out of the camp to Ukrainian partisans. Who betrayed Jacobs wasn't clear. The Ukrainian? Some German Jew? Perhaps a Polish Jew worried that everyone would be killed if the Dutch tried to break out?

The Kapos were the third group to get caught. One Sunday night, they began cutting the bars on a window in the barracks where Toivi and Josel slept. When the noise woke some of the other Jews, the Kapos called off the break. Monday morning, Josel saw a short German Jew in his fifties walk into the Administration Building, a two-story house the Nazis had dismantled in a ghetto, brought to Sobibor, and put back together again. A few minutes after the German Jew left, Wagner stormed into Shlomo's shop and dragged out a blacksmith. Then he rounded up the chief Kapo, Moishe, whom the prisoners called "the Governor," and another Polish Kapo. Wagner marched them to Camp III.

During the roll call that night, Wagner gave the little German Jew a whip, making him the new Oberkapo, and appointed a second German Jew to replace the other Kapo shot that morning. The Jews called their new chief "Berliner," because he spoke flawless German with a Berlin accent.

Berliner was a terror. He believed that Hitler was a national hero and blamed the Führer's anti-Semitism on the henchmen who surrounded him. He treated the Polish Jews with utter contempt, a master lording it over the slaves. One day at roll call, he had said, "I will lead you all into Camp III. *Alone,* I will see Berlin." The Sobibor Jews hated and feared Berliner.

Feldhendler was convinced that Berliner had snitched on the Kapos, maybe even on Jacobs, the Dutch Jew. That's all the Organization needed, he thought. Besides the locks at night, the fences, the moat, land mines, watchtowers, and machine guns — a stoolie. If only he had someone in the Organization with military experience. Someone used to commanding men in combat, who knew guns and how to use them. If he had such a man, then maybe . . .

Chapter 20

September 23, 1943

THE TRAIN FROM MINSK puffed into Sobibor on September 23 at nine in the morning. The locomotive slowly backed the cars with 1750 Jews into the camp. It was the first transport in weeks. Eleven Nazis stepped out of the Kommandant's white cottage next to the gate. Hubert Gomerski was in charge that morning. This was the first train from White Russia to cross the Bug into Sobibor. Would there be more as the SS liquidated the ghettos of Minsk, Vilna, and Riga before the Red Army could liberate them?

Gomerski planted himself like a boxer in front of the Jews, who had traveled the four hundred miles from Minsk in four days and nights without food or water. The German was under pressure to finish the barracks in the North Camp so that more captured Russian guns could be repaired faster. He needed a large group of strong men, for no one seemed to last there very long.

"Carpenters and cabinetmakers without families," he bellowed over the nervous din. "Step forward."

Lieutenant Alexander Pechersky confidently stepped from the pack. He was a big-boned man with a thin mouth, full but slightly sallow cheeks, and short-cropped black hair under his pointed Russian army cap. He stood tall and straight as he waited in his dirty green officer's uniform for Gomerski to inspect him as if he were a plough horse.

To Pechersky, it was all very familiar — the haughty, bored Nazis, the

151

guards filled with hatred, the barbed wire and dogs, hard work, little food, cruel games. The thirty-four-year-old Jewish officer had been in and out of German POW, work, and concentration camps for two years. To him, Sobibor was just another camp.

Gomerski looked at Pechersky with utter disgust. The Russian smelled of sweat, urine, and death. If there was anything Gomerski hated, it was a dirty uniform. But he wasn't surprised. After all, the Russian officer was a Jew, a strong and healthy one at that. As a Red soldier, the big Jew might be useful in cleaning and repairing Russian guns. So might the other POWs.

"Line up," Gomerski ordered the eighty men he selected. "March."

The German led them through the gate to Camp I and into a half-empty barracks.

"Pick a place," he ordered.

Most of the new men in the barracks were so tired from standing for ninety-six hours in the cattle cars that they stretched out on the bare wood bunks. But Sasha, as everyone called Alexander Pechersky, stepped out into the yard with his friend, Solomon Leitman. It was a warm, sunny fall day, and the fresh air smelled good. The pine trees beyond the fences had a soothing effect on the two Jews. They sat on stumps and talked about home and wives and children.

Sasha had a wife and daughter in Rostov-on-the-Don, but he didn't really worry about them. His wife was a Cossack, and their daughter, Elashenka, was safely tucked away with her grandparents in a Cossack village far from the German army and Himmler's Einsatzgruppen. Sasha missed Ela more than he could say. She had kept him alive. She had given him hope. She was his reason for wanting to live another day, kill more Germans, free Mother Russia. He reached into his cavalry boot and pulled out her picture. It was two years old now, smudged from sweat and dirt, and tattered from his pulling it every day from his pocket or cap or boot.

A bookkeeper before the war, and an amateur songwriter and composer, Sasha had been called up when the Germans invaded Russia. Two years ago, almost to the day, the Germans captured him at the battle of Smolensk. From then on, his life had been a miracle, almost as if Ela's small hand were protecting him.

In the first POW camp, Sasha caught typhus. He should have been shot, since the Germans routinely executed any prisoner with the fever. From somewhere he summoned the strength to stand at roll calls and fool the Nazis until he recovered.

Then he and four other POWs bolted from the line while marching to work outside the camp. The Germans caught him in the woods, but instead of shooting him on the spot — they usually taught other POWs a lesson by shooting anyone who tried to escape — they sent him to a penal camp. There, when he was stripped to the skin, the Germans saw that he was circumcised. They sent him to a labor camp in Minsk in White Russia.

The Minsk ghetto was the center of Jewish resistance in western Russia. The Jews who worked outside the ghetto in the ammunition factories or the gun repair shops smuggled weapons, piece by piece, back into the ghetto each night. Underground artists forged papers, and the underground radio in the ghetto kept in daily contact with the White Russian partisans in the woods around Minsk. More than ten thousand armed Jews were spirited out of the ghetto to join them or to form partisan units of their own. The wounded, Jews and White Russians alike, were smuggled back into the ghetto so that doctors at the Jewish hospital could heal them and send them out again to kill more Germans.

Sasha was assigned to a Minsk work camp on Seroka Street, which was separated from the main ghetto. He pulled an easy job as a maintenance man in the German-run hospital for German soldiers. There, he managed to steal extra food and regain his strength.

Somehow he survived the German games. When the bread rations were distributed, one of the Germans would order the prisoners to line up, one behind the other, nose to neck. Then he would rest his elbow on the shoulder of the man heading the line and shoot down the length of the column. Anyone who was slow to line up or who did not stand as straight as a sapling would be shot. Or sometimes at night, when the prisoners were asleep, the camp Kommandant would barge into the barracks with two German shepherds and set them loose. They'd tear into the blankets. Any prisoner who moved would be shot. Or sometimes the Nazis would nab a prisoner whom they suspected of stealing bread, and tie him to a barrel. Twenty guards would beat the soles of his feet with an ax handle for exactly one minute, each vying to see how many blows he could get in sixty seconds. The Kommandant would time each guard with his watch with true German precision. If the prisoner passed out, the Germans would revive him with ice water.

There were about five hundred skilled workers in the Minsk camp on Seroka Street — a hundred Jews from the ghetto, a hundred Jewish POWs, and three hundred non-Jews arrested for petty crimes. One of the skilled workers was Solomon Leitman, a Jewish Communist from Warsaw and a cabinetmaker. When the Germans blitzed into Poland, he fled east with his wife and daughter, who were killed in the Minsk ghetto.

153

It was hard for Sasha not to like the skinny little Jew with deep-set eyes. Intelligent and warm, he radiated trust and confidence. Pechersky, although a Russian, was not a member of the Communist Party, but he and Solomon had other things in common. They were both Jews who had seen their brothers and sisters brutally murdered by Germans in the ghettos and by the Einsatzgruppen. They both wanted a country where Jews could live in peace with their neighbors, without fear of pogroms. They both hated Germans. And neither had lost hope.

At night, they planned an escape from the work camp with other Russian POWs who considered Sasha their leader. But isolated from the ghetto underground by barbed wire, they had to plan a way out on their own. They knew that once they reached the forests, White Russian farmers who did not hate Jews would lead them to the partisans. Then they hoped to make their way back to the Red Army. But the Germans had other plans.

At four o'clock one September morning, while the cool fall air hung over Minsk, the Germans ordered the Jews from the Seroka Street camp, as well as another thousand from the ghetto, to line up in the yard. At first it was still, almost as if the Jews sensed something important was about to happen. Even the Nazis seemed civilized. No Jews were whipped or torn apart by dogs or scalded with boiling water for fun.

"You're going to the train station," the Kommandant said, twirling his whip in his hand. "You are going to Germany to work. Hitler will spare those Jews who work hard for Germany. You may take your families and your valuables."

The yard exploded with questions and shouts, good-bys and tears. The men marched to the station; women and children rode in lorries. The Germans seemed so decent that day. Was it possible that they would really spare the Jews?

*

While Pechersky and Leitman sat in the yard at Sobibor, chatting about better days, Jews began streaming out of the Camp I workshops for lunch, joined by the Camp II Jews who marched through the gate into the yard singing German songs.

"*Shalom,*" Pechersky called to those who passed by. No one answered. The other Russians came from the barracks and joined Sasha. For some reason, the Sobibor Jews seemed to be avoiding them, Sasha realized. That was odd, because in all the other camps there had been a sad camaraderie born of shared suffering and fear.

Leon Feldhendler leaned against one of the barracks, eyeing the Russians. He was excited by the POWs — soldiers, not just cooks and tailors and sons of rabbis. They were used to fighting and killing. They understood military discipline and the military mind. But could he trust them? Should he invite them into the Organization? Did they have a leader?

There wasn't much time to find out. It was the end of September, and the Polish winter would soon blanket the pine forests with snow. The Jews could be tracked, if they didn't freeze to death first. Food would be scarce.

As Feldhendler watched the Russians, one seemed to stand out. He was dressed in an officer's uniform, and the other POWs seemed to gather around him. Feldhendler leisurely walked over to Pechersky and stooped in the sand.

"Where are you from?" he asked in Yiddish.

"Minsk," Leitman said. "He doesn't speak Yiddish. Just Russian."

"Ask him why they won't talk to me," Pechersky told Leitman.

Leitman translated.

"We can't. Orders. Not until your comrades are taken care of."

Feldhendler decided there was no time to let the Russian gradually learn the truth, as other newcomers did. He'd give it to him straight, no frills, and hope that the awful truth wouldn't break the Russian. Feldhendler had seen it happen before, hundreds of times. The shock, the depression, the despair, and then the slipping of the will to fight the despair, to survive, if only for one more day.

Lieutenant Pechersky made it easy. "What's burning over there?" The Russian pointed to the northeast corner of the camp, where columns of gray-black smoke rose from the fences, drifting over the treetops into the cloudless fall sky. The air was still, and the smoke hung on the horizon as if an invisible hand kept pushing it down. To Pechersky, it seemed as if part of the camp was on fire.

"Don't look that way," Feldhendler snapped.

Pechersky glanced around the yard, then up at the towers. No one seemed to pay the least bit of attention to the smoke, almost as if it were part of Sobibor.

"Those are the bodies of your comrades burning," Feldhendler said. "From the train."

Pechersky almost fainted from the shock. He couldn't believe the handsome Jew with a brown mustache who spoke so matter-of-factly. His eyes uncontrollably scanned the smoky horizon. It was not possible. Was this some cruel joke?

"You're not the first and not the last," Feldhendler said. "The trains have been coming here for over a year and a half." He paused to let the shock settle in, watching the Russian closely.

"How . . ." Pechersky began.

"Gas."

Feldhendler explained in detail how the system worked. "No one in the camp has ever seen the gas chambers," he continued. "We know from notes written by those who worked there."

He went on to tell Pechersky what he had pieced together from notes and rumors. Not all of it was accurate:

"From what we can tell, everything looks like a bath, with faucets for hot and cold water, basins to wash in. As soon as they enter, the doors are sealed. A thick dark substance falls from the vents in the ceiling. There are horrible shrieks, which don't last long. Soon there are just gasps and convulsions. Mothers cover their little ones with their bodies. The Nazis observe everything through a small window in the ceiling. In fifteen minutes, it's all over. The floors open up and the bodies tumble into wagons below. The Germans have everything organized. The bodies are laid out in perfect order. They are sprinkled with gasoline and set on fire . . . We will also burn. If not tomorrow, then in a week or a month . . ."

Leon Feldhendler touched the Russian's arm gently, then left him to his own thoughts. It would take a few days before the Russian would bounce back — if he did. There was nothing to do but wait, be patient, and hope.

Although Sasha and Solomon were exhausted from the sleepless trip to Sobibor and the shock of the truth — beyond anything they could have dreamed — they couldn't sleep. They lay in their bunks, side by side, each wrapped in his thoughts.

"Sasha, what's going to happen to us?" Solomon whispered at last.

Pechersky did not answer. He was too sad to talk to his friend, to offer any words of comfort or hope. So he pretended to be asleep.

"Sasha? Sasha?" Solomon whispered.

Soon the barracks was quiet, but for the sounds of sleep. Sasha's eyes were open, and he stared at the rafters of his new home. He could not help thinking of Nellie, the two-year-old girl with curly locks who had been in his cattle car from Minsk. In his mind, he saw her enter the "shower," innocent and pure. He began to suffocate with her, sweating and gasping for air.

He drifted into a restless sleep and dreamed of Nellie, of flames like red hands, caressing her, holding her. Suddenly, the flames grew into horses, galloping and charging as if in a race. Out of the backs of the horses grew red Germans, who began to shout and chase after Nellie. Her face changed into the face of Elashenka. The Germans began to gain on her, those red horses and Germans of flame. There was nothing Sasha could do but watch. His Elashenka, his daughter, his hope, his life. He screamed, hoping to frighten the Germans away, the flames away, to make the Germans of fire stop.

"Sasha, Sasha, what's the matter? Wake up." He heard Solomon whispering. "Wake up."

Lieutenant Alexander Pechersky sat on his bunk and wept.

Chapter 21

September 24–26, 1943

AFTER SERGEANT FRENZEL counted noses at five-thirty the next morning, he assigned Sasha Pechersky and thirty-nine other POWs to the North Camp under Hubert Gomerski. Sasha was nearly exhausted. The long trip from Minsk, the sleepless night, the shock, and the uncertainty of his first day in Sobibor had gotten to him. At least he would be working with the other Russians and his two close friends, Solomon and Boris.

Frenzel ordered the Russians to line up four abreast at the head of the work column. "Sing," he commanded them. "In Russian."

The POWs waited for a signal from Lieutenant Pechersky.

"We're not sure what we're allowed to sing here," Pechersky told Kapo Porzyczki. Sasha could understand and speak some German — he had studied it in high school fifteen years ago — but he was far from fluent. Porzyczki, who spoke Yiddish, Polish, and German, and who understood Russian as well, translated.

"Sing whatever you know," Frenzel said.

Boris Tsibulski, who stood next to Sasha, was nervous. He was an excitable man, husky and powerful; before the war he'd been a miner in the Donets Coal Basin. During the war, when he was a scout in the Red Army, he had been captured near Kiev. He and Sasha had been close ever since their imprisonment in a cellar at the penal camp. Sasha liked Boris' open face and absolute loyalty. The other POWs considered the scout Sasha's first lieutenant and bodyguard.

"Which song?" Boris asked.

" 'If War Comes Tomorrow,' " Sasha ordered. It was a resistance song.

"Are you crazy, Sasha?" Boris was frightened. "They'll shoot us."

Pechersky didn't care. He wasn't going to begin his first day at Sobibor by backing down. He'd fight the Germans every way he could, not tomorrow or next week, but today. The first day. If he didn't, and if he didn't show leadership, set the tone from the start, he might lose the almost magic hold he had on his men. And if he was going to die at Sobibor, as the Polish Jew had warned yesterday, then at least he'd spit into the barrel of the gun that shot him. If the Germans wanted music, the Russians would give it to them.

"Start singing," he ordered.

Boris began timidly, watching Frenzel with one eye. Soon the other forty Russians chimed in. With each phrase, their voices grew more confident. And as their voices rose, their bodies straightened in pride.

> *If war comes tomorrow*
> *Tomorrow we march.*

Their pride grew to defiance. The song cheered them like good news from home, like a promise, a hope.

> *If evil forces strike,*
> *United as one,*
> *All the Russian people*
> *For their free native land will arise . . .*

The Ukrainians, who understood Russian, came running out of the canteen and barracks when the North Camp brigade marched through Camp II. It sounded as if some Russian company had invaded the heart of Sobibor. They marched in unison now, like soldiers, their heels digging into the sand, and their song rang out in the crisp fall morning as dawn spread white-gray fingers over the pine forest.

Leon Feldhendler suppressed the smile that began to curl under his brown mustache. The Russian was fighting back, he thought. The soldier had spunk; perhaps too much. He might have courage, but he was foolish. Did he have a death wish, too?

Feldhendler could almost feel the shock, the tension, the unspoken sense of triumph among the workers sorting in Camp II. No one looked up, but they stole furtive glances at each other. He could sense a skepticism under their pride. "Sure, the Russians got away with it this time. But will they last the day? Would the Germans break them at the woodpile? Would they try to push Gomerski as they had pushed Frenzel?"

Feldhendler went back to sorting clothes. For today, at least, his heart was lighter than it had been since he entered Sobibor nine months ago. Up to today, he had been a terribly lonely man, a leader trying to give hope and strength to everyone else. Now, there was someone in Sobibor who gave *him* hope, and he felt as if a great burden had been lifted from his shoulders. He would wait. There was nothing else to do.

Gomerski split the Russians into two groups. Half, including Sasha, were lucky. They worked inside the nine barracks still under construction. The others dug stumps to push back the woods inside the North Camp. Fifteen of them got twenty-five lashes because Gomerski thought they weren't working fast enough. When the Nazi didn't feel like whipping, Kapo Porzyczki took over, and he didn't spare the leather, either.

Sasha survived the first day. The beatings came as no surprise. Every camp he had been in was the same — leather whips, twenty-five lashes, count them yourself, miss a count and the German starts over — almost as if the Nazis were following some training manual chapter called "Whipping."

That night, Pechersky began a diary, coding his handwriting so that if the Germans found it, they would have no idea what it was. If he ever got out of Sobibor — and soon he would try — he wanted to make sure the world would know the truth. Little did he realize that the world already knew.

Leon Feldhendler sat in the women's barracks, chatting with the Organization and waiting for Drescher, the little Putzer who moved freely about the camp with the eyes and ears of a deer.

"He's making notes," Drescher told Feldhendler.

Feldhendler broke into a big smile. The Russian had survived the first day and was still fighting. But he would not be able to take the North Camp long, Feldhendler thought. No one ever does. The Organization will have to move quickly to help him, but not just yet.

The next morning, Frenzel pulled Pechersky and the Russians off the North Camp brigade and ordered them to cart coal from the tracks to the German and Ukrainian barracks and to the canteen. It was a good sign. It meant the Germans expected someone to be at Sobibor for the winter.

Frenzel became irritable during the lunch break. He wanted the coal moved quickly so that he could get the Russians back to the North Camp.

He had allotted the cook, Hershel Zukerman, only twenty minutes to dish "soup" for six hundred people.

Frenzel stood next to Zukerman, shouting at him. "Hurry it up! Come on! Keep it moving!"

From time to time, the German would poke Zukerman in the ribs with the handle of his whip. The cook dipped as fast as he could, spilling and slopping soup all over. Frenzel didn't care. It was almost a game now.

After fifteen minutes, only half the prisoners had been served, and the line waiting for lunch was a nervous snake. Would they all get punished because Zukerman was slow today?

Finally, Frenzel lost his patience, as everyone, including Zukerman, knew he would. "Outside," he ordered the cook.

He pointed to a spot in the yard. "Sit . . . Straight."

Zukerman sat, hands straight down and tight at his sides, feet tucked under him, like a child waiting to be punished by his teacher. Frenzel began to whistle a German marching song as he uncoiled his leather whip. Then, in time to the tune, he lashed the cook around the head and shoulders, not bothering to order Zukerman to count to twenty-five. It was a bad sign.

Zukerman quivered like a bowstring with each blow and moaned softly while the whole yard of prisoners watched, not daring to scream lest he be shot on the spot or beaten to death. The cook's face was covered with mean welts and the blood dripped into his eyes and from his chin into his lap. Then, without a word, Frenzel stopped. Zukerman struggled to his feet.

Sasha watched in silence like the others. He felt Zukerman's humiliation in the pit of his empty stomach, and he was alive enough to feel anger rather than defeat. He looked at his soup. It seemed to have turned to blood. With contempt and disgust, he poured it into the sandy soil. He was hungry, and without food — even watery soup — he knew he would never last. But he couldn't force himself to drink it. He wouldn't give Frenzel that satisfaction. He owed it to himself. When the other Russians saw their leader dump his soup, many quietly did the same.

Leon Feldhendler watched the beating as if it happened every day. Zukerman was lucky, he thought. He would recover. Josel would get some oil or salve for his wounds, and before long the cook would be busy preparing the evening meal, grateful to be alive for one more day. But what about the Russian? If Frenzel had seen Pechersky pour out his soup, he would have taken it as an act of defiance. It would have driven the

161

pampered Nazi mad, and there was no telling what he would have done.

The Russian had done a foolish thing, Feldhendler thought. Just like a novice prisoner, almost bordering on childish. Maybe the lieutenant was too reckless to be entrusted with the lives of them all. Feldhendler nursed his doubts quietly that night. He would not share them with anyone in the Organization — not yet, anyway. He would wait at least one more day before he'd make a move — if he decided to make one.

The next morning — the Russians' third day in Sobibor — Pechersky was assigned to dig stumps in the North Camp. Frenzel was in charge because Gomerski was out of the camp, and he was in a foul mood. He hovered over the forty wielding shovels and axes, just waiting for an excuse to pick on someone. Unlike many of the other Nazis and Ukrainians, Frenzel didn't play games to relieve his boredom unless there was a reason to punish someone. After all, he was an officer and gentleman. The non-Russians, who had been on the North Camp detail for more than a week, were emaciated and exhausted. Raising their axes with great effort, they simply dropped them on the stumps while Frenzel barked, *"Schnell! Macht schnell!"*

Work had hardly begun that morning when Frenzel, hands gloved like a butler and eyes as cold as his Walther pistol, quietly walked up behind the weakest man in the crew, a tall, skinny Dutchman who was so tired that he could hardly lift his ax. When he let it fall, it frequently missed the stump.

Frenzel gave him a taste of the whip. The Dutchman moaned, but didn't dare stop chopping. Frenzel seemed to enjoy the game, and each time the Dutchman's ax fell to a *"Schnell,"* he lashed the Jew across the head and shoulders. The Dutchman's cap fell to the ground, but he kept raising his ax and letting it fall.

Pechersky stopped working and watched. He knew Frenzel might beat him, too, but he couldn't control his anger, nor could he ignore the punishment. That was obviously what Frenzel wanted them all to do. Just accept the brutality.

Frenzel saw Pechersky resting on his ax. With a look of triumph, he booted the Dutchman to the dirt. *"Komm,"* he ordered Pechersky.

Knowing full well he was in trouble, Sasha decided that the best way to deal with this proud Nazi was with pride. He would not bow, quiver, or cower. He walked over to Frenzel and met the German's stare.

"Ja, Herr Oberscharführer?"

"You don't like the way I was punishing this idiot?" Frenzel asked. Kapo Porzyczki translated. "Well, then, you have exactly five minutes to split this stump. If you do it, you get a pack of cigarettes. If you miss by as much as a second, you get twenty-five."

Frenzel stepped back, crooked his arm, and studied the watch on the gold bracelet Shlomo had made for him.

"Begin!" he ordered.

Suppressing an urge to grab the Nazi by the throat and to squeeze the smile away, Pechersky imagined the stump was Frenzel's face. He sliced and pounded and beat. Everything was in a haze as he lost all sense of time and place, driven by the power of hatred, pride, and defiance. His back and hands began to ache, and the sweat streamed down his face into his eyes, burning and blurring. But the ax kept slicing the Nazi with a mad rhythm. Finally, Sasha stood up.

"Four and a half minutes," Frenzel said. He held out a pack of cigarettes. "I promised."

Pechersky knew he should take the smokes, but the thought of taking a reward from the Nazi, like a puppy who has just learned a new trick, made his stomach churn.

"Thanks," Pechersky said, "but I don't smoke."

He picked up his ax, wiped the sweat off his face with the sleeve of his Russian uniform, and, turning his back on the German, walked to his place in the chopping line. He waited for the blows, the whistle of the whip. There was only the sound of falling axes and the sawing and pounding from the barracks nearby.

Frenzel spun around and walked off, leaving Kapo Porzyczki in charge. He came back twenty minutes later with half of a fresh-baked roll and a slice of butter. He was still smiling. "Here, Russian. Take it."

Pechersky could see the envy on the faces of the Jews who had been in Sobibor longer than he, and he could smell the fresh bread. He knew he should take it. It would give him strength to live longer. He had earned it, hadn't he? The other Jews would not consider it a sign of weakness, for he had won; he had humiliated Frenzel in front of the Jews the Nazi despised. Would it be wise to add an insult to that victory? But a feeling of pride stronger than logic tugged at him.

"No, thanks," Pechersky said, not bothering to stop swinging his ax. "The rations here are more than adequate."

Frenzel lost his smile and his face flushed in anger. "You don't want it?"

"I'm just not hungry," Pechersky said.

Frenzel clenched his whip as if he were struggling to hold himself back. Once again, he turned abruptly and left the yard.

Some of the workers threw their axes down and surrounded the Russian. "Why didn't you take it?" they asked. "He could have shot you on the spot . . . He could have beaten you to death . . . You could have gotten all of us into trouble."

Boris and Solomon put their arms around Sasha and slapped him on the back. "Thank you, Sasha," Solomon said. "We're proud of you." They laughed and hugged him.

Kapo Porzyczki uncoiled his whip and started to walk toward the small group. Mean, and unafraid to use his whip, he didn't seem to tire as quickly as Frenzel did. So they all went back to work.

Word spread quickly throughout the barracks that night about the Russian officer's standing up to Frenzel. Each time the story was told, the Russian became bigger and tougher, and Frenzel smaller and weaker. Leon Feldhendler concluded that the Russian was no fool, that there was something special about him, that he must be able to sense how far to push the Nazis. Maybe he understood the German mind better than the rest of the prisoners. Whatever it was, it was working; the Russian had lasted three full days in Sobibor. He seemed to be settling in. Tomorrow, Feldhendler would make a move, cautiously, but still a move. There wasn't much time.

Chapter 22

September 27, 1943

PECHERSKY worked inside the barracks at the North Camp the next day. It was a break. Another day digging and splitting stumps would have exhausted him. The morning was unusually still. Both Pechersky and Kalimali sensed something was wrong.

"I'll meet you in the latrine," Kalimali whispered. "Make some excuse."

His real name was Shubayev, but everyone called him Kalimali. He was a charming Caucasian, tall and slim, with dark eyes and hair like a Gypsy's. Polish Jews like Toivi liked him, because hardly had he found a bunk in the barracks when he pulled out his mandolin and began to sing army songs like "Tachanka" or melancholy folk songs like "Chastuski."

"Did you notice all the Germans disappeared?" Kalimali asked in the latrine. "There's just the Polish Kapo there. What do you think it means?"

"I'm not sure," Pechersky said. "Let's look around. Watch the guards in the towers. Carefully, now! See if you can see who's stationed where. And when they change."

Kalimali left first; Sasha followed a few minutes later. There were still no Germans in sight. From time to time, Pechersky and Kalimali would stop sawing and pounding to look around. There wasn't much to see; the North Camp, surrounded by pine trees, was isolated.

Kapo Porzyczki surprised Sasha. "It's nothing special, Pechersky," the Kapo said. His lips were curled into a crooked smile as if he were pleased he had caught the Russian breaking the rules. Deliberately, Porzyczki made no move for his whip. *He* was boss now, and there were no Germans around to catch him being soft on Jews. Besides, he respected this Russian POW, and he had not given up hope of escaping from Sobibor, even though he had come a hair from death when Berliner had snitched on the Kapos. He was sure the Russian would eventually try something. He'd have to do what he could to protect the soldier, who just might be his own ticket out of Sobibor.

"Just another transport, Pechersky," the Kapo said. It was the first to arrive since the Russian transport four days ago. "All the Germans have to be there to take care of them."

"Where is it?" Pechersky asked. He sensed that the Kapo, like everyone else, was more relaxed without the Germans around.

"The gas chambers are over there, behind the barracks." Porzyczki pointed almost due west. "About a hundred yards or so. See that high fence camouflaged with branches near the guard tower at the corner?"

The guard tower was clearly visible through the trees, and once you knew a fence was there, you could make it out. Pechersky nodded.

"That's it. Camp III. The gas chambers aren't far from that corner."

Pechersky and his three close friends — Solomon, Boris, and Kalimali — stood gaping westward, straining to see between the pines. Porzyczki did not order them back to work. They didn't know what they expected to see; everything was as still as a forest pond.

Then it started. A woman's shriek like a sustained soprano note floated through the morning air. The scream seemed to echo for miles through the forest of the owls, bouncing from tree to tree, with nowhere to go. It hung there, so it seemed to Pechersky, for minutes, and then was drowned out by a sudden wailing of women and children. As soon as one cry died, another took its place. Then two and three more, until there was a symphony of screams and cries. Even the geese in Camp II began to honk, as if running from an imaginary fox in the yard.

Pechersky wanted to crash through the trees, beat down the barbed-wire fences, and smash every German and Ukrainian skull he could find. Anything to stop the wailing and the death. But he just stood there, trapped in a nightmare, listening, and straining to see some movement.

There was a lull, as if a Nazi had momentarily lifted the needle from a phonograph record. Then one pure sound floated toward heaven. It was a cry of absolute terror, frightening in its utter simplicity and emotion.

"Mama . . . Ma——" It ended in the middle of the word.

Pechersky's heart stopped. The tears began to roll down his cheeks. In his mind, he saw the child in panic, terrified among all those naked strangers and those black boots, looking for the one who had always protected her. He saw her being stampeded into a room and the door sealed in her face.

Then he thought of Elashenka. His dear, sweet Ela. The cry tore at his heart. His fingers squeezed the hammer until they hurt. He froze, paralyzed with fear — not afraid of his own death, but afraid that the cries of "Mama" would go on and on, that one of them might be Ela's, and that he, Alexander Pechersky, a soldier, a father, a strong man, would be unable to do anything. Just stand like a robot run by German orders, listening helplessly to the terrifying sounds of death. He hated and feared his own helplessness more than anything he had feared in his life.

He had already decided to escape. Now, he recognized that escape was not enough. He had to kill the Nazis and destroy their camp — for the girl who called "Mama," for Ela, for all of them. Above all, for himself, with whom he would have to live for the next hour or the next day or the next week — the rest of his life. He would not spend another minute paralyzed by such helplessness. He would *not* be helpless, and if he had to, he'd die proving it.

When Boris, Solomon, and Kalimali came over to him, Sasha was shaking. "Sasha, we have to get out of here," Boris said. "It's just over two hundred yards to the woods."

Between them and freedom stood one barbed-wire fence and a roving Ukrainian patrol. It looked dangerous but easy — they didn't know the fields were mined.

"The Germans are all busy," Boris continued. "We can cut through the fence with the axes. Hack any guards that get in our way."

Pechersky believed the chances of escape were fair, and if it had been yesterday, he might have agreed to try it. But not today, not after what he had just heard. He couldn't run out on the others, leave the Germans just sitting in the canteen, sipping vodka and waiting for the next transport, and the next.

"We might be able to make it." Sasha put his arm around Boris' shoulder. "But what about the others? You know the Germans will kill them all, don't you, Boris? No, my friend, when we go, we'll all go together. The whole camp. Some will die. But those who make it will get even for them."

Boris felt calmer, as he always did in the face of Sasha's logic. In his mind, he knew that Sasha was right, but his heart told him to run. "We can't wait too long, Sasha. Winter is coming, and there will be tracks in the snow, and . . ."

"Patience," Pechersky said. It was a standard joke between the two. Boris was a bull who always wanted to move immediately. The planning could come later. Pechersky thought things out. If there wasn't time, he'd rely on his instincts. So far, Sasha had always been right; he was still alive after two years of Nazi camps. Although Boris was loyal, he lacked judgment. Sasha had to tell him exactly what to do. And when he did, Sasha could count on Boris to follow those instructions to the letter.

"Don't breathe a word, any of you," Pechersky cautioned. "We're new here. We don't know whom we can trust. When the time comes, I'll tell you what to do. When and where."

Boris, Solomon, and Kalimali felt relieved. They trusted Sasha, his integrity and his judgment. They'd wait. And they knew it would not be long.

That night in the barracks before lockup, Solomon and Sasha talked, alone at their bunks, sometimes in whispers, analyzing what they already knew about Sobibor after four days — the fences, the Kapos, the routine, the barracks, the guards. It wasn't much, but they would observe and look for an older prisoner they could trust. Then they'd pump him discreetly.

*

September 28, 1943

Just before the final whistle for work the next morning, Leon Feldhendler joined Solomon Leitman in the yard.

"*Shalom aleichem.* How's the work going?" Feldhendler asked.

"Like a clock. You wind it, it runs."

The work whistle blew.

"Time to get ready," Leitman said.

"Wait a minute. I must talk with your friend."

"Which one?" Leitman asked. He knew the Jew with the brown mustache meant Pechersky.

"The one who doesn't understand Yiddish. Bring him to the women's barracks this evening."

"Why there?"

"He's handsome." Feldhendler winked. "Why shouldn't he spend a little time with our women?"

The final whistle blew, and the two Polish Jews took their places in the work line for Camp II and the North Camp.

Feldhendler had decided to give the Russian more exposure, to watch him react with the non-Russian Jews, to evaluate how they responded to him. It would be the last test. If the Russian handled himself well, he'd ask him to join the Organization. There'd be no beating around the bush anymore, just a straight "Do you want to join us?"

Feldhendler was certain Pechersky would come, if only out of curiosity. He had purposely veiled the invitation with innuendo. The suspicious skinny Jew from Warsaw wouldn't miss it. Feldhendler came closer to believing there would be an escape than he ever had before.

Later that morning, Solomon whispered to Sasha, "Ask for permission to go to the latrine right after me."

Pechersky knew that Leitman must have something important to say or he wouldn't have taken the risk.

"I talked with the Jew we met on the first day," Leitman said in the latrine, telling Sasha about the invitation. "The girls are eager to meet you." He laughed while they pissed.

"Let them go to the devil," Sasha said. He was irritated. The message could have waited until lunch break. There were only so many times you could use the latrine trick without making the Germans suspicious.

"I think it's important," Leitman said. "Otherwise I wouldn't be here. It wasn't just idle talk. The Polish Jew has something in mind. I'm sure of it. It was the way he spoke, almost in a whisper."

"Who is he?"

"He sorts clothes in Camp II. His name is Leon Feldhendler. He's the son of a rabbi. Everyone seems to know him."

"Okay," Pechersky said. "We'll go together. You'll interpret for me."

The women were waiting for Pechersky that evening. They were curious about him. Some had seen him around, especially those who had marched from Camp I to Camp II with him. Others had just heard about him, and what they knew was skimpy — a Russian, a soldier, handsome and tall, who had stood up to Frenzel. There was a sprinkling of men in the barracks as well, relaxing with their girl friends or flirting.

As soon as Pechersky and Leitman walked through the door, the women began to pepper them with questions.

"Who are you?"

"Where are you from?"

"Who's winning the war?"

"When will it end?"

They were hungry for news, these isolated women, most of whom had lived in ghettos or labor camps before coming to Sobibor, where rumor was the only source of news.

Pechersky looked around. The women's barracks was built exactly like the men's, but it was quite different. The women had dressed up for the occasion. He could smell perfume. Leaning against a wall stood Kapo Porzyczki, talking to a young woman, his cap cocked over his eye, the one

169

that always seemed to be half-closed. Feldhendler sat on a bunk in the corner with another man. They were watching him. One young girl, slight, with short-cropped chestnut hair, stood out. She seemed confident, almost defiant.

Pechersky knew what the women wanted to hear; it was what he wanted to hear, too. That the Germans were losing the war, that the Russians were driving them toward the Bug and would be there soon, that the war would be over before the year was out, that they would be rescued and would live happily ever after. They wanted that hope, that silver fantasy, to hold on to. They needed it. Others can give them that, Pechersky thought. From me, they get the harsh truth.

Solomon translated into Yiddish, and some of the women translated the Yiddish into German or Dutch for those who didn't know Russian or Yiddish. The women seemed to hang on to his words.

Between June and September 1941, Pechersky told them, the Germans had crossed the Bug and fanned out into the Soviet states, capturing city after city, army after army — Riga and Novgorod in the north, Lvov, Kiev, Minsk, and Smolensk (where he was captured) in the center, Odessa in the south. The Germans drove east without mercy, and it seemed their supplies would never run out. He told them about the German and Ukrainian killing squads — the Einsatzgruppen — how they rounded up the Jews and shot them in ditches.

The battered Russian army and air force caught their breath, he told them, and regrouped. The guerrillas behind the wide Russian-German front line began to pick away. Gradually, the Russian army began to slow the Germans. It recaptured Rostov, his home town, resisted at Sebastopol, and dug in at Moscow. German tanks got within twenty miles of Moscow before they were mired in the autumn mud. Like Napoleon's army, the Wehrmacht got caught in the clutches of the Russian winter, without enough food or clothes. Their guns froze. Russian guerrillas harassed them at night. Slowly, the Red Army drove the Germans back.

Near Finland, in the north, Leningrad was still holding out after two years of German siege. People were dying of hunger and typhus, but the rest fought side by side with the Red Army. They would not surrender.

And there is Stalingrad, he told them. The Germans besieged the city on the Volga for five months. Then the Red Army surrounded the German Sixth Army and captured over a hundred thousand starved, frozen, abandoned, and beaten Germans. Another seventy thousand were killed in battle or froze and starved to death or committed suicide.

Earlier this year, Pechersky told the women, the Red Army held firm in Kursk, fought the Germans in the biggest tank battle of the war, and won. At least a half-million Germans died in the battle of Kursk.

"We are still pushing the Germans home," Pechersky said.

He could see the women were delighted every time he told them how the Germans were defeated, how they starved or committed suicide. The huge numbers impressed them. He purposely dwelled on the siege of Leningrad, emphasizing how the civilians refused to give up, how they fought back side by side with the army. But he did not want to give the women false hope. At the rate the Red Army was moving west, he told them, it would be a year before it reached Sobibor.

"The Germans have their backs to the Dnieper River now," he said. "That's more than six hundred miles from here."

It was like pissing on a fire. Enthusiasm and hope fizzled and smoked.

"They say there are partisans in Russia. They're fighting the Germans all the time," someone said timidly. "Why don't they attack and free us?"

Pechersky told them about the White Russian and Jewish partisans around Minsk. "The Germans are afraid to leave Minsk without an armed convoy," he said. "Every night the partisans blow up bridges and trains and ammunition dumps."

The question was important, and Pechersky did not want to dismiss it lightly. He knew that the White Russian partisans would not risk their lives and ammunition to free six hundred Jews. Frankly, there were more important military targets — bridges, troop trains, supply depots. If he were commander of a partisan unit, he wasn't sure whether he'd risk attacking Sobibor. Perhaps some Jewish partisan group might. He wasn't sure about that, either. Furthermore, he suspected that the Germans would liquidate the camp if they felt it was a partisan target. And as for the Ukrainian partisans across the Bug, it was hard to say whom they hated more, Germans or Jews. No, partisans offered no hope, and the sooner the women — and Feldhendler in the corner — understood that, the better.

"The partisans have their own tasks," Sasha said carefully. "No one can do our work for us."

All during the evening, Kapo Porzyczki stood by the wall, watching and listening. He had sized up the Russian correctly. Sasha did have something in mind. His little speech was a clear signal. The only questions were: Where, when, and how could he, Porzyczki, become part of it?

Leon Feldhendler was impressed, too. Beneath the bragging, the pride in Russia, the subtle Communist propaganda, was a message: resist, fight back, don't give up, and don't wait for help from the outside. The Russian sounded confident and smart. He was the Organization's man. No doubt.

Pechersky waited for Feldhendler to approach him, but the son of the rabbi didn't. Just before lockup, Pechersky and Leitman left for their own barracks. Sasha knew Solomon had been right. He had been tested. Well, if Feldhendler had listened, he couldn't have missed the message.

When Shlomo came into the barracks wearing his silk shirt, polished black boots, and a satisfied look on his face, as if he were returning from a night out on the town, Feldhendler told him about the meeting in the women's barracks and what the Russian had said. Feldhendler was excited and worried.

"The Germans are sure to wipe out the camp," he said. "They'd never let the Russians find it. We'll all be killed. As in Minsk."

Feldhendler had heard a rumor that the camp would be liquidated on October 15, just three weeks away. He wasn't sure whether there was any truth to it; it could be a trick to incite a riot so that the Nazis and the Ukrainians could have a little fun. Besides, the rumor wasn't logical. Why the hurry to build the North Camp, why all the new bricks, if the Germans were going to blow up Sobibor? Yet the Organization could not discount the rumor completely.

Feldhendler continued, "We can't just keep talking. The Russian is our man. I want to ask him to join us. To plan the escape. To lead it."

"I'll ask the others," Shlomo said.

The goldsmith knew they would agree, and he went to sleep smiling. It was finally going to happen. He could feel it; he knew it. They didn't have a choice. Live for a few more weeks or months, then be killed. Try to escape now, and take the chance of surviving. Hope was fast running out. A thousand thoughts of revenge and freedom filled his mind. His mother and father, the Jews of Maidanek, the corpses, the children, the beatings, Gomerski, Frenzel, Bauer, the games. He saw himself killing Germans with his bare hands, with knives, with axes, with grenades and pistols and rifles, cutting fences, running across fields, blowing up bridges, getting shot defending Nojeth, Moses, and Jankus, being pinned to the barbed-wire fence, shouting "Fuck you" as he died, sleeping with a woman in a soft bed under an eiderdown quilt, a free man and woman. He smiled, and as he smiled, the fear and hope fought each other. He was sixteen, strong and smart. He had survived the ghetto, the selection, almost two years in Sobibor, Wagner and Gomerski, Klat, Niemann, the Red Dumpling, and Groth. He would survive again and again. He was sixteen, and he felt immortal.

Chapter 23

September 29, 1943

AT SIX THE NEXT MORNING, Frenzel ordered all the Jews into one long column, three abreast, and marched them to the railway platform to unload bricks. The Germans were in a hurry that day because a new transport was waiting on the side track outside the gate. There were moans from the train, and hands stretched out, seeking water and bread. Pechersky felt like strangling the first Nazi he could reach; he still wasn't used to the horrors of Sobibor. All he could think of was the children. He didn't have to imagine anything. He had been on such a train just five days ago — and it had seemed like a lifetime. Most of the older prisoners barely glanced at the train. Their emotions had already been numbed, and they had enough energy left only to make it through the next ordeal.

The Germans ordered seventy to seventy-five men onto the platform to toss bricks to the Jews below. Each worker — man and woman — had to hold six to eight bricks, run two hundred yards, stack them where ordered, then run back for another load. There was pushing and swearing and crowding. The Nazis and Ukrainians whipped the prisoners for each mistake. Anyone who dropped even one brick got twenty-five lashes. For the next fifty minutes, whips cracked in the early morning air. Soaked with sweat, prisoners gasped for breath as they ran, trying not to trip on the Jew in front of them, worrying about stumbling, concentrating on the two hundred yards ahead of them, breathing much easier as they returned to the platform with empty hands, hoping against hope that they wouldn't drop a brick,

173

that the Jew who tossed the bricks from the platform had a good eye, that some German would be looking at someone else, eyeing the platform on each return to see how many bricks were left.

After the bricks had been unloaded, Frenzel once again assigned Pechersky, Solomon, Kalimali, and Boris to the North Camp. Shortly after work began there, one of the Russians who was chopping stumps outside sneaked into a new barracks where Sasha was working.

"We're escaping," he said. "Right now."

"How?" Pechersky tried to stall the Russian. "Who said so?"

"We just talked it over." He nodded to a group of Russians digging and chopping side by side. There were no Germans around; they were all processing the new transport. Kapo Porzyczki was in charge, and, as on the previous day, he seemed relaxed without Gomerski or Frenzel present.

"There are only five guards now," the Russian continued. "We'll get them with our axes and head for the woods."

"It sounds easy enough," Pechersky said. It was obvious that the Russian was counting on him to go along. "But the guards are spread all over the place. You kill one, the others will open fire. If you make it, how will you cut through the fences? What if the field is mined? They'll get you one way or another. Then they'll kill the rest of us. If we really think it through, if we take our time — we can come up with a better plan."

Pechersky let his warning and offer sink in. "You can do whatever you want," Pechersky said. "I won't try to stop you . . . But I won't join you either. When I go, I want to make sure I have a good chance of making it."

The Russian returned to his group, and Pechersky watched as they talked among themselves, gesturing and pointing. Porzyczki stood, hat cocked over his bad eye, and watched. Sasha was counting on two things: that the Russians didn't have a leader, and that they still respected him. He hadn't lied. They would never make it. They would endanger the lives of the rest of the North Camp brigade, and kill any chance for a well-planned break-out.

After a minute or two, the Russians went back to work quietly. The escape was off, but Pechersky wasn't happy. He didn't know how long he could hold his men in check. They had all been in camps before, and they knew that once lethargy creeps in, you lose hope, and once you lose hope, you no longer even think about escaping. Just surviving. And that was nothing but slow death.

That night, Pechersky and Leitman were not surprised when Feldhendler sat on the bunk next to them. They were expecting him.

"You made a deep impression on the women," Feldhendler told the Politruk, as the Polish Jews now called Sasha. Although he was no Communist, he had sounded like a Communist commissar to them. They meant the nickname as a compliment. "They understood what you meant by 'No one can do our work for us.' It was not a very wise thing to say. Kapo Porzyczki was there, too. Be careful with him."

"Why?" Pechersky played his hand coolly. "I only do what I'm told around here."

"I understand what you're trying to say," Feldhendler said. "So let's be frank. I've been watching you. Not long ago, Frenzel dropped a hint that Hitler had issued a decree to spare some Jews. We're part of those to be spared, Frenzel told us. None of us really believes that." He watched the Politruk's face for some kind of reaction, but the Russian looked uninterested. "I sense you're up to something. You'd better think it over. What do you think will happen to the rest of us if you escape? The Germans can't risk letting the world know what goes on here. They'll kill us all at once. That's clear."

"How long have you been here?" Pechersky asked.

"Close to a year," Feldhendler said. It was the first question of importance that the Politruk had asked, a signal that he was fishing in the right pond. Feldhendler didn't blame the Russian Jew for being cautious. He trusted the Politruk, but the Russian had no reason to trust him.

"What makes you think I'm planning some kind of escape?" Pechersky asked. He got up as if the conversation were over. The next move was up to Feldhendler.

"Wait a minute," Feldhendler said. "Don't run off. You wonder why *we* haven't escaped? I'll tell you. We've thought about it more than once. Even developed some plans. But we didn't know how. You're a soldier. Take over. Tell us what to do, and we'll do it. I make the offer in the name of a resistance group. We trust you. Think it over."

"Thanks for the warning about Porzyczki," Pechersky said. "I'll think it over. I'll give you my answer tomorrow night."

Pechersky didn't have to think it over; he had already made up his mind. He liked the rabbi's son with the open and honest face. Feldhendler had taken a great risk in approaching him, and he seemed as concerned about the fate of the rest of the Jews as he did about his own. But Sasha wanted one last chance to talk over the offer with Solomon, who'd heard Feldhendler in Yiddish, not just in translation. Maybe Leitman had picked up a nuance he'd missed, some small inconsistency, some reason not to trust the Polish Jew.

September 30, 1943

They met the next night in the carpenter shop. Present were Feldhendler, Shlomo, Szol, chief of the shoemakers, Mundek, chief of the tailors, the chief of the carpenters, Sasha, Solomon, and Kalimali.

"Why me?" Pechersky asked, after Feldhendler had introduced everyone to him.

Feldhendler was prepared for the question. "We need someone whose spirit hasn't been broken yet by the Nazis. Someone who doesn't consider himself a slave," he said. "Most of us believe it's more important to live one more day than to fight for a future. We know you won't sit back and take it. Do nothing. Besides, you're a soldier, an officer. You're used to leading, fighting, killing."

"I am honored," Pechersky said. "I accept."

Feldhendler told the Politruk about the uprising in Treblinka. He didn't have many details, except that the prisoners had revolted and burned some of the camp. The news had been a boost. The Organization knew now that something could be done, that the Germans were not invincible. They *could* be killed with sticks and stones. Some Jews *could* get away. If it had happened at Treblinka with Stangl as Kommandant, why couldn't it happen at Sobibor?

They all agreed that whatever plan they adopted would have to include all the prisoners. The Organization would not try to escape as a group, leaving the rest to be killed. If the others did not want to run when the time came, that was their choice. They also agreed that no plan could help the Jews in Camp III. Any attempt to break into that isolated bastion would risk the whole operation and condemn everyone to almost certain death. Finally, they agreed that Pechersky should draw up a plan and present it to the Organization for approval. They would give him all the help he needed to create the master plan, because they knew the camp and he did not. Once the plan was accepted, they would follow the Politruk's orders like soldiers.

Pechersky asked Feldhendler whether the Organization had any escape ideas of its own. The Polish Jew told him about the *Putzer* plan, the attack on the canteen, and the diversion plan. They had misgivings about each one, he said.

Pechersky told them that their instincts were right. It would be too risky to entrust the success of a plan and the lives of everyone to Putzers, mere children. To kill face to face is not easy for men, and there is no way to

176

foretell how children — even those hardened in Sobibor — would react. The likelihood that they would panic was great.

Blowing up the canteen, Pechersky said, would kill some Germans and Ukrainians, but it would offer practically no chance of escape. The other Nazis and Blackies would seal off all corridors, then probably kill everyone.

A fire might destroy half the camp, but the camp could be rebuilt, Pechersky said. The Germans knew that. Besides, that's what the prisoners tried in Treblinka, so the Germans would be wary. It would be hard to fool them.

Pechersky told them he had some escape ideas of his own, but that it was too premature to discuss them; he needed more details about the camp.

"Are the fields mined?" he asked.

"Yes," Feldhendler said.

Pechersky had thought they were. As soon as he had seen the ditch around Camp I, he knew it was an antitank trench. The Germans would not try to protect themselves against tanks without mining the fields.

"Where are they? How many?"

"I know the men who dug the holes," Feldhendler said. "I'll get a map."

"I'll need to know everything," Pechersky said. "The guards — how many, how they are changed, what kind of ammunition they carry, where they store their ammunition when they're off duty. Who the leaders are — German and Ukrainian. Routines. Any kind of routine."

Feldhendler agreed to get him the information later. They wanted to keep the meeting as short as possible.

"Feed it to Solomon," Pechersky said. "Casually. He'll be my liaison. Talk to him in the bread line. Before roll call. In the yard. In the women's barracks. Any way you can. Make it short. He'll get it to me."

Feldhendler liked the idea of dealing with Leitman. The little Jew from Warsaw was gregarious. He liked to talk, meet new people. He spoke Polish and Yiddish and Russian. He was likable, the kind of person you trusted easily. Besides, it made the Politruk even more unobtrusive. It was a nice touch.

They agreed that secrecy was vital to the success of any plan. The fewer who knew that something was up, the better the chances were that no one would let something slip when a Nazi, Ukrainian, or Jewish snitch could overhear. Their group meetings would be few and very short, with lookouts posted. And for the time being, no one outside the Organization would be told anything. When the time came, others would be told what to do and when.

They agreed.

"I'll need a cover," Pechersky said. He knew that if the Germans suspected an escape, they would watch him for the same reasons that the Organization had selected him to be their leader. He was a soldier. He commanded respect. And he had already stood up to the Germans. "A woman who doesn't understand Polish or Russian. That way, I have an excuse to be around the women's barracks, and I won't stand out in the crowd."

"I'll find you someone," Feldhendler said. He was growing more and more confident in his choice of the Politruk. The Russian was clever and precise.

Feldhendler brought up the Kapos. Whom could they trust? Whom should they be wary of?

They all agreed that Bunio, in charge of the Bahnhofkommando, could be trusted if they needed him. Porzyczki was touch and go. He had tried to escape, so he had guts. But he beat the Jews with too much enthusiasm, and he wouldn't hesitate to send someone to Camp III if he had to. On the other hand, he had never squealed on anyone, as Berliner did. No one knew Kapo Spitz very well, but he was a German Jew, and therefore not to be trusted. Berliner, on the other hand, was a real threat. Everyone agreed on that. He was not only a stoolie; he was suspicious and smart, like Gomerski and Wagner.

"We have to take care of him," Feldhendler said. He looked at the Politruk. "We'll do it."

Chapter 24

October 1–3, 1943

T OIVI WAS ASLEEP in his bunk after the evening roll call. His friend, Fishel Bialowitz, shook him awake. "Keep your eyes open," he said. "They're coming to take care of Berliner."

Toivi sat on the edge of his bunk. A few minutes later, Kapos Bunio and Porzyczki walked in. They chatted with some of the prisoners who were sitting around resting. Then Porzyczki beckoned Drescher over with his finger.

"Go to the women's barracks and get Berliner," he ordered the Putzer. "Tell him I sent you. Say there's someone here who needs twenty-five . . . Fast."

Drescher trotted out.

Porzyczki hated Berliner more than anyone in Sobibor, for Porzyczki had been part of the Kapo escape plan that summer. To him, it was a miracle that Wagner hadn't dragged him off to Camp III with his friend, Oberkapo Moishe. Why he was spared, he didn't know. But he did know that he could have been murdered and that Berliner had been the stoolie.

Drescher trotted back into the tense barracks.

"He won't come," the boy told Porzyczki. "He said he was busy."

"Go back. Tell him I said he'd better come. It's urgent."

Berliner sauntered in, walking as tall as a five-foot, four-inch man could, his face stern and puffed with authority.

"All right," he threatened, whip in hand. "Who's lying down here?"

179

Mundek and Shlomo came into the barracks; two other Organization members kept guard outside. Porzyczki grabbed Berliner around the neck from behind.

"*You're* lying down," he said, forcing the German Jew onto one of the barracks benches made in the carpenter shop. Porzyczki was a husky man. Lifting Berliner was for him like tossing a bale of straw.

"You're joking," Berliner gasped. "You're joking."

Porzyczki pinned his arms and shoulders to the bench. Mundek the tailor grabbed his feet. He lay stretched out on his back as if he were in a strait-jacket. Kapo Bunio began to beat him on the stomach, careful not to make any marks on his body. Between muffled groans, Berliner cried, "Pity! Please! Pity! Pity!"

There were about twenty prisoners in the barracks. They went berserk. Some stayed in their bunks, lest they get caught if a German walked in. A dozen others joined Shlomo and Bunio at the bench. They fought to get their punches in. Their hatred for Berliner, the Nazis, the Ukrainians, Sobibor itself, poured into their fists.

"Did *you* have pity on us?" they chanted. "Did you?"

"Are you tired, Berliner?" they taunted, imitating his sneering Kapo voice. "Do you want to rest?"

"Twenty-five, Berliner," they called. "Count."

They beat Berliner with the crazy fury of their pent-up emotions. When the German Jew quit resisting and his body lay limp, Porzyczki and Mundek let him go. Everyone stood silent, stunned by what they had just done. They thought Berliner was dead from the beating. Then, slowly, he began to stir. His eyes opened, dazed, confused. He struggled to his feet and staggered to his cubicle near the barracks door.

Porzyczki, Bunio, Mundek, and Shlomo followed him, carrying the light pine bench. Berliner was lying on his bed, in pain, still dazed, almost as if he had lost consciousness. But his eyes were open, and he moved. They couldn't leave him like that, in case he regained his senses and turned them in.

They could easily smother him; he was too weak to resist. But the plan had been to rupture his spleen, liver, and kidneys so that he'd bleed to death internally. Then there would be no marks on his body. No one thought of changing the plan, so Shlomo put a blanket over his head to stifle any groans or screams. Porzyczki grabbed the bench and began to pound Berliner on the stomach. When the Kapo finished, Berliner was still breathing, but was so battered that he'd never be able to walk. It was just a matter of time. By morning, he would be dead, and Porzyczki would report him missing at roll call. Shlomo neatly covered Berliner with a blanket, as if he were sleeping. Then they left as if nothing had happened.

The next morning, Berliner was still breathing. Porzyczki reported his roll call tally to Frenzel as usual. "The Oberkapo is sick, Herr Oberscharführer. He's in bed."

Frenzel wasn't suspicious. It was business as usual. Those who worked in Camp I went to their shops; those for Camp II, the North Camp, and the Waldkommando lined up to be led through the gate and across the Officers' Compound. They marched through the gate to the beat of the marching song:

> *Es war ein Edelweiss,*
> *Ein kleines Edelweiss.*
> It was an Edelweiss,
> A little Edelweiss.
> *Hol-la-hi-di, Hu-la-la,*
> *Hol-la-hi-di-ho.*

Porzyczki reported to Frenzel once again, after the midday roll call. "The Oberkapo is still sick in bed. Everyone else accounted for."

Frenzel still didn't seem suspicious. Neither did the other German Kapo, Spitz. After all, Berliner was not a young man, and even Kapos could get sick. That afternoon, Frenzel went to the tailor shop at the request of Mundek to try on a new uniform. Mundek set the hook.

"I hear that poor Oberkapo is sick," the chief tailor said. "Too bad. He's been telling everyone how important he is. He's been saying how much he respects Herr Oberscharführer Wagner, but that he doesn't think much of the rest of the SS."

Frenzel was vain, and there was a power struggle between him and Wagner. His muscles tightened at the gossip.

"Check with the Spengler," Mundek suggested. "He heard the Oberkapo boasting, too."

"Get him," Frenzel ordered without moving a muscle inside his new uniform.

"Yes, Herr Oberscharführer?" Shlomo asked. "You wanted me?"

Mundek broke in before Frenzel could open his mouth. "Isn't it true that the Oberkapo has been saying he only respects the orders of Herr Oberscharführer Wagner and — "

"Yes, it's true," Shlomo cut in. To set the hook even deeper, he added,

"The Oberkapo is proud of being a German Jew. He believes he's better than the rest of us because he's German. He considers himself on the same level as an SS Scharführer."

Shlomo could see that he had gotten to Frenzel. No Jew could ever equal *any* German, especially not a sergeant in the elite SS. Shlomo decided to go for broke. "The Oberkapo's also been bragging that *he's* really the boss in Camp I," the goldsmith said. "He's been saying he's more of a boss than Frenzel, and that Frenzel is an idiot."

Frenzel couldn't hold back his anger any longer. "Is that so? Is that so? Well, you're going to see the end to that kind of shit!"

He stamped out of the tailor shop. Shlomo and Mundek smiled in relief. They knew Frenzel was too vain and angry to smell a setup. Besides, the Nazi wasn't very bright, not like Wagner, who, thank Lady Luck, was on leave. They doubted whether Frenzel would become suspicious of anything now — or even care if he learned that the Jews had murdered Berliner.

"Check out Berliner," Shlomo told Josel that night. He was ready to ask the medic to poison Berliner if the Oberkapo wasn't dead.

"He's still alive," Josel said. "He can move. But it's a matter of hours now. He pissed blood."

Berliner was dead by the morning roll call when Porzyczki reported to Frenzel. "Herr Oberscharführer," he lied, his face serious and concerned, "the Oberkapo is still sick in bed. He barely moves."

"Is that so?" Frenzel said. "Is that so? Then take that piece of shit to Camp III."

Mundek and Kapo Bunio followed Porzyczki to the barracks. They wrapped Berliner in his own blanket and carried him to the miners' train.

"Sobibor. High wall plaited with branches covers the gas chambers. The railway leads behind the wall. Only half a train can enter there; the transport must be separated into two parts. Time for discharging, 20 minutes."

Eighteen pencil drawings about Sobibor, sketched by an artist named Joseph Richter, were found in Chelm after the war. The sketches were done in 1942 and 1943 on scraps of old Polish newspapers and Nazi posters. They were dated and signed, and the captions on the back were written by the artist, about whom nothing more is known. The originals are in the vault of the museum of the Ghetto Fighters' kibbutz. Some of them are reproduced here by permission.

Unless otherwise credited, all photos are by the author.

"Lubin. Here Jews were transferred from lorries to cattle trains . . ."

Facing page, top: "At the station in Uhrusk an old Jewish woman ran away. She had her right arm broken. The [Austrians] did not want to dispatch her. It was done by the Ukrainian police. One is digging a grave near the railway. Another waits to shoot her. She begs, 'Only a little vodka.' "

Facing page, bottom: "The train goes to Sobibor. We stand near the railway in railway employee uniforms; we hold hacks and other tools. We stay without movement and in a visible place so as not to be taken for Jews escaping from the train. Far away there is the smoke of burning bodies. This is the forest behind Stulno."

"A little window of a wagon. They ask for water. Guards watch them. We sit in a train on a parallel railway. I am drawing slowly on newspaper."

"Train from Holland. They don't know anything. Pullman cars, comfort, in an hour they will die."

Gustav Wagner (Courtesy of Thomas Blatt)

SS Sergeant Karl Frenzel (Courtesy of
Thomas Blatt)

Shlomo as a partisan (Courtesy of Stanislaw Sjmajzner)

Sasha Pechersky in Red Square, 1981

Mordechai Goldfarb holding the portrait he painted of his brother, who died at Sobibor

Selma, Chaim, and Emilchen Engel, 1945

Selma and Chaim, 1981

Eda and Itzhak Lichtman in front of their home in Holon, Israel

The spur inside Sobibor where Jews were unloaded from the boxcars

The Sobibor train station

The forester's tower

Thomas Blatt (Toivi) standing on the Road to Heaven, explaining Sobibor to a group of children

The memorial statue of a woman and child in Sobibor

Chapter 25

October 3–7, 1943

HER NAME was Luka. She was a German Jew, but most of the prisoners thought she was Dutch because she had come on a Dutch transport. She was eighteen, with short chestnut hair, poised and perky. Pechersky remembered her from the first night in the women's barracks. She stood out not only because she was beautiful, but because she had seemed defiant and confident. She was a perfect cover. Everyone would envy Pechersky, for Luka had no lover, even though many of the men wanted her and tried to get her.

At first, Solomon translated for Pechersky and Luka, to get them acquainted. Since everyone who knew the Politruk knew he couldn't speak or understand Yiddish, Solomon would not be conspicuous if he was seen with the two of them, chatting in the evening in the barracks or outside in the yard. Gradually, Luka and Sasha learned to communicate in simple German, flavored with gestures and signs.

Sasha and Luka met every evening in the women's barracks or outside on the benches. Solomon would mix with the other Jews, and members of the Organization would casually seek him out to pass on details about the camp. Sasha would evaluate the information and then send Leitman back for more. Luka never caught on. It seemed only natural to her that Sasha would have a close friend like Solomon who talked to him often, and besides, she liked the skinny Jew from Warsaw with the kind, understanding voice.

Pechersky learned where the mines were buried, and from their description concluded that his guess had been right: they were antitank mines, which blew upward rather than outward. That was an advantage; if someone stepped on one, the explosion would not necessarily kill everyone within a hundred feet. The antitank mines were so sensitive they could be exploded with stones. Besides, some were always duds. The mines were a big problem, Sasha realized, but not an insurmountable one. And there was one chink in the armor. The Germans would never mine the field right behind their barracks. If Russian tanks or partisans or escaping Jews set off the mines, ᵗhe shrapnel could rip through the windows or pine walls and kill the officers inside. What the Germans had planted behind their barracks were probably signal flares.

"Find out what the Jews do in the shoemaker barracks and in the tailor shop," he told Leitman one night. "Who supervises the workers. Whether the Nazis visit the shops on a regular basis."

Solomon came back half an hour later. "The shops are supervised by members of the Organization," he said. "The Germans and Ukrainians ask for boots, uniforms, shoes for their wives. They come in for measurements and fittings. No one checks the shops regularly. Sometimes Wagner or Frenzel pops in."

Solomon went on to explain that in Camp II, the Germans and Ukrainians visited the warehouses, especially after a new transport, to look for clothes or souvenirs or things to sell. He told Sasha how the valuables were collected and stored in the Administration Building.

"The Germans are greedy," Solomon said. "They can be tempted."

Pechersky savored the information. It opened up all kinds of new possibilities. Ideas bumped against each other in his mind. "Find out how the furlough system works," Pechersky said. "See if there's some pattern. Get everything you can."

Besides surprise, routine and pattern were vital to any escape, Pechersky knew. If he could find a moment when the Germans would be less watchful, when he could predict their actions and reactions, then the Jews might have a chance.

Sasha looked around the yard. So far, everything was moving like a clock — as smooth as the Nazi machine itself. He watched Solomon mix with the others, chatting here and there. He smiled at Luka sitting next to him. The intrigue and planning were the only things that had kept him alive for the past two weeks. They gave him hope. They helped him survive the long days of uncertainty and fear and grueling work. And then there was Luka, graceful and beautiful, almost innocent, in the corrupt, cruel world of Sobibor. He was growing fond of her, and he hated the lying and deception of their relationship. But he could not tell her the truth or get emotionally involved with her. They could not become lovers, no matter how much he wanted her. It had been so long since he had had a woman. But he needed all his energy for the escape. Nothing could get in the way of that: the lives of six hundred men and women depended on him. He needed to be free to concentrate on the job — mentally, physically, emotionally.

"How old are you, Luka?" Sasha asked one evening. They were sitting outside the women's barracks on a stack of pine boards. She was smoking the cigarette she had gotten from one of the Dutchwomen who sorted in Camp II. Luka worked in Camp II, feeding lettuce to a hundred Angora rabbits and cleaning their pens. They were Frenzel's pets, and he was as solicitous of them as a sable rancher.

"Eighteen," she said.

"And I'm thirty-four," Sasha said. "Almost old enough to be your father. You must obey me like a father." His feelings toward her were mixed. He wanted her, yet he felt as if she were his own daughter. He wanted to protect her. He was planning an escape not only for Solomon or Boris, Kalimali or Feldhendler, or the little goldsmith. It was for Luka, too.

"Good," she said, with a perky nod of her head. She was growing to like this gentle but firm Russian. "I shall obey you."

"Then stop smoking." The contradiction of Sasha's demand never dawned on him. Here he was in a yard surrounded by barbed wire, guard towers, machine guns and whips, the smell of death, and he was worried about her health.

"I can't," she said. "Nerves."

"Nerves, nothing. It's just a bad habit."

"Please, Sasha. Don't say that. You know where I work? With the rabbits. Through the cracks in the fence, I can see the naked men and women — even the children — march to Camp III. I watch them and begin to shake as if I had typhus. But I can't turn my face away. I can't close my eyes. Sasha, sometimes they call out, 'Where are they taking us?' as if they sensed I was there listening. I tremble when they call out to me. But I just peer at them through the crack. Should I cry out, Sasha? Tell them they are going to their death? Would it help them, Sasha?"

It was not a question, but a cry of pain. The strength of her emotion made him want to fold her in his arms and tell her not to worry, he would take care of her. He would get her out of this hell. He would put an end to the Nazis, to the gas chambers. But he just sat there and listened. His soft eyes told her what he was thinking.

"No, Sasha," she continued. "At least they die without crying, without screaming. Without humiliating themselves before their murderers. But it is so horrible. So terrible, Sasha."

That evening, Luka told Sasha she was not a Dutch Jew but a German Jew from Hamburg. Her father had been an anti-Nazi, and when Hitler came to power, the Gestapo ordered his arrest. He went into hiding.

"They beat and tortured Mother," she said matter-of-factly. "Me, too, but we would not tell them where Father was. Later, we escaped to Holland."

When the Nazis took Holland, Luka explained, her father managed to escape again, but the rest of the family was caught and sent to Sobibor. "Both of my brothers went to Camp III," she said. "My mother and I were selected . . . Tell me, Sasha, where will it all end?"

He wanted to tell her about the escape; ask her not to give up hope, to believe. But he had been sworn to secrecy, and he let her question dangle.

For the next several days, Pechersky sorted out the information he had gotten from Feldhendler, and he and Leitman whispered late into the night, analyzing what they already knew.

The Organization controlled all the shops in Camp I and held the leadership in Camp II. This would be the strongest factor in any escape plan, and Pechersky would somehow have to build on and around it. The problem was that no one in the Organization except him and Kalimali was used to killing. If the plan called for cold-blooded assassination, he wasn't sure that the Organization could be counted on.

The loyalty of the Kapos as a group still had to be tested. Berliner was out of the way, and Porzyczki had helped kill him. That gave the Organization something to hold over his head if they needed him or if he became a problem. Kapo loyalty would have to be solved at some point, because it would be difficult to plan and execute an escape without the help of some Kapos.

How the rest of the Jews would react to a break-out was unknown. There were informers; there always were. No one knew precisely who they were. Some of the prisoners were too weak to try to escape — or at least that's what they'd probably tell themselves. Perhaps the German or Dutch Jews, who didn't speak Polish, would balk at leaving the camp, reasoning that the risk of capture and death outside the camp in the woods was greater than the risk of death inside. Perhaps some German Jews would rather stay than flee, convinced they were special and that the Germans would treat them as such. The reaction problem was insoluble. Any successful plan could not be built on the assumption that all or even most of the Jews would run. Secrecy was the key. Would the Organization have the discipline to keep the plan quiet? Could they control their nerves and act casual for days on end? Would they talk in their sleep? Whatever the case, Pechersky and Leitman concluded, the Organization must not learn of the details, the date, and the time until the very last minute.

Because the Germans got so much leave, there would never be more than fifteen to twenty in the camp at any given time. Thus, if every German were armed with a machine gun — and that was unlikely — there would be no more than fifteen to twenty to worry about. Since no one knew the leave schedule, there was no way to plan an escape around who was gone and who was still in the camp. At any rate, the three Nazis to fear the most were Reichleitner, the Kommandant, whom the Germans and Ukrainians respected and feared, and Wagner and Gomerski, who were smart, suspicious, and totally unpredictable.

The two hundred Ukrainians, all heavy drinkers, were docile, leaderless, indifferent. The Jews could count on a certain number of them being drunk. They were also dependent on both rigid routine and orders from the Germans. Two things were certain: they would not act independently, and they would not offer the Jews any help. Although they hated the Germans, most of the Blackies hated the Jews at least as much. Those who didn't, wouldn't lift a finger to help if it involved any risk. In fact, it would be in their interests not to help the Jews, for if some escaped — even a few — the Nazis would take it out on the guards. They were Blackies because they were willing to sell their loyalty to the strongest side. They would defect to the partisans or the Russians if it was expedient. But with the front still six hundred miles away, it wasn't expedient.

The Ukrainians on duty did not carry machine guns, since the Germans didn't trust them. But no one knew how many rounds the guards carried for their semiautomatic Mausers. Thus, it was difficult to say how many Jews might be killed if the Ukrainians in the towers were good shots. Pechersky didn't worry much about the rifles anyway; it was the machine guns that bothered him.

The weakest point in camp security was the main gate. There was only one fence, no ditch, and no mines. It gave the Jews the chance to run across the tracks, behind the Sobibor station, and into the woods. Or down the tracks beyond the mines and then across the fields into the woods. The front gate was also the biggest risk. It was guarded day and night by a German with a machine gun.

187

There were only two practical times to escape — at night or just before dusk. That would give those who got out the chance to get as far from the camp as possible before daylight.

The concrete armory, which stood close to the east fence in the Officers' Compound, was not impregnable. Inside were machine guns, grenades, rifles, pistols. But anyone who tried to break into it would be completely exposed. Any guard from the tower would shoot immediately, without doubt. Furthermore, the lock could not be picked in advance because no Jew ever had an excuse to approach it. The lock would have to be shot or blown off if they wanted to get the guns and ammunition. If they did capture the armory, though, they would be better armed than the Nazis and Ukrainians.

Even though the prisoners at Treblinka had revolted, the Germans at Sobibor seemed smug. They did not increase security after the Treblinka episode. They didn't seem to fear having POWs around; it was almost as if they were saying, "We dare you." And they didn't seem to be concerned that to run an efficient camp, they had created a pool of smart, emotionally and physically strong, lucky Jews who hated them more than they themselves hated the Jews. These were survivors, who were willing to take risks, Jews who knew the camp better than the Germans did, for with few exceptions, they had been there longer.

The escape strategy had to have a clear focus — revenge, freedom, or both. Did the prisoners want to kill as many Germans and destroy as much of the camp as possible, assuming that they would never get out anyway? Should they opt for freedom, and not run the risk of killing any more Germans than they had to? Or should they try to kill and destroy, hoping that some Jews would escape? Pechersky was torn between escape and revenge, so he and Leitman decided to work on two plans. Then they would select the more feasible one.

*

Pechersky brought Boris in on the first plan, as much as he feared doing so. He needed Boris' mining skills, but he also knew the big, lovable bear was hotheaded and had a loose mouth, especially after he'd had vodka. Sasha took the chance, and when Plan One was ready, he told Leitman to arrange a meeting with Feldhendler — no one else.

They met over chess after work on October 7. Leitman sat next to them, translating and glancing around the yard.

"Can we trust the workers in the shops — tailor, mechanic, shoe, carpenter?" Pechersky asked.

"Yes, in the tailor shop, shoe shop, and carpenter shop," Feldhendler said. "The chiefs trust the Polish Jews under them there. But I'm not sure about the mechanic shop. There are a lot of foreign Jews working there. Shlomo doesn't trust them. He's certain someone once squealed on him to Berliner. But he doesn't know who."

"Forget the mechanic shop," Pechersky said. "Concentrate on the others. Here's what I want you to do. Tomorrow morning, ask two Germans to come to the shoe shop and tailor shop for measurements or fittings. Make the appointments for four and four-thirty. Call in whoever has work being done there. Or whoever's next on the list for a new suit or pair of shoes. Do everything just as you usually do. Nothing out of the ordinary. Don't make the Germans suspicious. Then ask Frenzel to come to the cabinetmaker shop to inspect something at four-thirty. It has to be a good excuse. Take no chances with Frenzel."

Feldhendler nodded and moved a chessman. He knew better than to ask why, and he was excited that something was happening. It was clear to him that the Politruk had something definite in mind.

"Check the time when they come," Pechersky said. "I want the exact time, down to the minute. Don't keep them there longer than ten minutes each. Tell the chiefs not to tell anyone in the shops what we're doing. Report back to Leitman."

Feldhendler tried to concentrate on the chess game, but his mind was asking a hundred questions. Then, as if to satisfy the Polish Jew's curiosity, Pechersky said, "I'm working on a plan, but it's not ready yet. We'll discuss it soon. Until then, I've an alternate plan."

Pechersky explained that the mechanic shop was only fifteen feet from the first fence. There were twelve feet between fence one and fence three. From the third fence to the end of the minefield was another forty-five feet. "Figure twenty feet from the shop wall to the stove and add twelve feet just to be safe. That comes to just over a hundred feet from the stove to freedom." Pechersky paused. He spoke in a low, calm voice as he studied the chessboard and made his moves. He didn't look up.

"We dig a tunnel," he said. "The stove will cover the entrance, and the noise in the shop will drown out any noise we might make digging. The tunnel has to be exactly thirty-one inches deep. Any deeper, we hit water. One of my men is a miner. He figured it out. Shallower — we hit the mines. We need to hide nineteen cubic yards of dirt. We'll begin to store it under the floor. Later, we'll find other places. The miner will supervise the digging so that the tunnel is absolutely perfect. We can finish in twelve to fifteen days."

Feldhendler was clearly disappointed. The Organization had thought of a tunnel, too, but rejected the idea. The ground was too sandy, and they didn't think they could keep the tunnel a secret for so long. But with a miner supervising, it might just work. The mechanic shop, however, was the worst place to dig, given Shlomo's suspicions about an informer.

Pechersky noticed the disappointment in Feldhendler's face. To show that he, too, understood the risk, he said he realized that six hundred people would have to crawl through the tunnel, thirty-five yards apart, between eleven at night and dawn. Then they would have to sneak to the woods three hundred yards away. "Some of the prisoners may panic," Pechersky added. "There might be fights over who goes first. Some may refuse to escape. There's no telling what they may do. Anyone could betray us at any time, and we'd be sitting ducks."

Sasha could see that Feldhendler was relieved that he understood all the risks. Besides all that, they'd have to find a way of breaking out of the locked barracks in the middle of the night.

"We'll need about seventy knives and some sharp axes in case the plan fails and we have to fight," Pechersky said. "Get Shlomo to start working on them. A few a day. We have time. We'll pass them out just before we break."

The more Pechersky talked, the better the alternate plan sounded. The worst thing that could happen was that someone would turn them in before the tunnel was finished. If so, it was doubtful whether the Germans would kill all the prisoners. Life would go on almost as usual until another escape attempt. If they got caught trying to get through the tunnel, there was a good chance some would make it. Some Germans would die trying to stop the rest. What more could they ask for? It was better than waiting for death.

"There's another thing," Pechersky said. "Solomon and I need to be assigned to the carpenter shop as soon as possible. There are a few things I need to check out for myself, and I have to be close to the digging. I have to make decisions immediately."

"It will be arranged," Feldhendler said. "But there may be a little problem. Kapo Bunio knows something is up. He asked one of our men in the Bahnhof-kommando if he could escape with us. Our man said he didn't know anything about an escape. Our man says he thinks it's a good idea to include Bunio. He can be trusted. He's a good man."

"What did *you* say?"

"I told him no decision without checking with you first. 'The Politruk is in charge,' I said."

Pechersky was pleased. "I've given the Kapos a lot of thought. It would be good to include them. They can move around more freely than the rest of us, and the Germans trust them more. But we'd be taking a terrible risk . . ."

Solomon was getting nervous. "Leave the Kapos for another time," he cut in. "We'd better move. We've been sitting here too long."

Feldhendler and Pechersky pushed a few more chessmen.

"Checkmate," Feldhendler said.

Chapter 26

October 9, 1943

It was Yom Kippur. All day long the Orthodox Jews in the sorting sheds in Camp II prayed and fasted. That night, before sundown, Feldhendler led them in some of the traditional holy day prayers. There was no rabbi in Sobibor, and Feldhendler knew the service by heart.

The Orthodox Jews were a minority, certainly fewer than a hundred. After their prayers, as they gathered to break their fast and celebrate with the food they had squirreled away, they took quite a ribbing from the agnostics like Shlomo.

"Better pray to the Politruk," the nonreligious Jews joked. "Only he can help you now."

"We're praying to God to help the Politruk," the Orthodox Jews answered.

For the Politruk, it had been a good day. Shlomo had sharpened the knives Feldhendler had gotten him from the Camp II storage rooms. There were hundreds of them there, from pocket knives to Dutch switchblades to Jewish ceremonial knives. Shlomo had also sharpened and stashed away a dozen axes. Every evening, the forest brigade left one set of axes to be honed. In the morning, they picked up the other set. There were always extras around. And then, all the Nazis — including Frenzel — who had been invited to the shops to try on boots or to be measured for a uniform or to inspect furniture in the carpenter shop had appeared on time for their appointments. The Politruk now knew his second plan had an excellent chance of succeeding, at least partially.

192

It had also been a bad day. Thirty Jews working in the North Camp had each gotten twenty-five. Among them was Grisha, a hotheaded young Russian Jewish POW who was caught chopping while sitting down. Pechersky was worried about Grisha because he didn't think he could keep the reins on the young Russian too much longer.

While Pechersky was sitting on his bunk, thinking about his plan and worrying about his men, Kalimali burst into the barracks. He was nervous and scared.

"Eight men are getting ready to make a break," he told Pechersky. "They asked me to come along. You'd better do something. And quick."

"Who's behind it?"

"Grisha. He's in the women's barracks right now."

Pechersky strode into the barracks calmly, as he usually did. The room was crowded; a lot of men were visiting. He spotted Luka chatting with several of the Dutchwomen. "Let's sit outside for a while," he told her. They had a hard time getting to the door. "What's new?" the women asked. "What's going on?" They sensed that something would happen soon.

Pechersky shrugged. "You know as much as I do," he said. As he passed Grisha, he whispered, "Luka wants to see you."

No sooner had Luka and Sasha settled on a pile of boards in the yard than Grisha followed. "What do you want," he asked Luka in Russian. She didn't know what he was saying.

"Not her," Pechersky cut in. "Me." He grabbed Grisha by the arm and led him a few feet away from Luka. "Kalimali says you're going to make a break tonight."

"Join us," Grisha invited.

"What's the plan?"

"Simple. The area near the latrine has no lights. We'll cut through the fence behind it. Crawl over to the guards. Kill them and run."

"It *is* simple. But you forgot one thing — the fields behind the shops are mined. Antitank mines. And suppose you do make it, what about the rest of us? The Germans will kill everyone."

"Who's to blame for that?" Grisha asked. He was bitter. "Why are they sitting around? They had their chance — months and months ago."

"Did you offer them a plan?"

"I haven't been here that long," Grisha said. "Why haven't they tried to get out before?"

"Listen to me, Grisha." Pechersky's voice was threatening. He knew the brash Russian was the kind of man who would respond to strong leadership. Doing nothing, waiting, made him restless. "Forget your plan. People are already working on a better one. Don't interfere."

"Who? Who's working on it?" There was a smirk on the young man's face. "You, maybe?"

"Maybe."

"Where? Over there on the boards with her?"

Pechersky let the insult pass. "Knock it off. I want you on my team. I need you, Grisha. You're strong. I trust you. You'll be one of my leaders. I'll give you an assignment when the time comes. An important one. That's all I can say now."

"Well, we're not waiting. We're getting out tonight."

"All right," Pechersky said, without a trace of anger. "Since your mind is made up, fine. I'll level with you. Our preparations are almost finished. It's only a matter of days. The plan is to take out the Germans. Do you want to kill that plan? Spit on the rest of us because you and your friends think you can cut through the fence, kill a couple of guards, and cross the minefield without help? Do you know where the mines are? I do, and I'm warning you, Grisha. I'll put lookouts all over. If I have to, I'll — "

"Kill me, Sasha?"

"Yes."

"Then I have nothing more to say."

Grisha turned and walked back into the women's barracks. Sasha called Kalimali and Solomon over to him. "Put some lookouts near the latrine. Set someone on Grisha. Watch his every move. Don't let him out of your sight. If he tries to make a break, kill him. Don't hesitate for a minute. Just him. The others won't try anything if he's dead."

Pechersky sat next to Luka on the pile of boards.

"Sasha, what were you and he talking about?" she asked.

"Nothing much."

"You're lying. You were arguing. I saw you. I can see in your eyes that you're lying. And what about all those other conversations while you're sitting out here in the yard or in the barracks with me? You think I don't understand? You're using me, aren't you, Sasha?"

"Let's say you're right." He could not look at her face. He wanted to tell her about the escape. He wanted to warn her to get ready, to be hopeful. But he had been sworn to secrecy. Besides, the more she knew, the more difficult it would be for her to look and act natural when he was around, as if she were unaware of what was going on, the planning, the scheming right under her nose. He needed her innocence. It was all part of the cover, and that made him feel even worse. "Didn't you tell me that you wanted to see the Nazis torn into tiny pieces?" he asked.

"I did, Sasha. But I'm afraid. What if you fail? What if they drive us all to Camp III? I wish we could escape. But that's impossible. Impossible, Sasha."

She began to tremble. He could feel her through his jacket. He wanted to fold her in his arms as he would Ela, as he would a lover, kiss her on the head, and say, "Hush, now. It will be all right. We can do it. We *will* do it. I'm the leader. You trust me, don't you?" But he just sat there stiffly.

"Why us?" she said, over and over. "Why don't they let us live? Why?"

He could not answer.

"You don't trust me," she said. "Do you? When I was a child — I was just eight years old then — the Gestapo tortured me to tell them where my father was hiding. They did unspeakable things to me. I wouldn't tell them. And now . . . You, Sasha — "

With tears in her eyes, she fled back into the barracks. Sasha went to his bunk to wait for news about Grisha and to think about the thin, defiant girl. Just before lockup, Solomon sat down beside him.

"Everything is okay," he said. "Grisha backed down. No trouble."

October 10, 1943

It was Sunday, a day of rest for the Nazis and the Jews. Sasha and Solomon sat around in the barracks or in the yard, refining their final plan. Sasha would present it to the full Organization the next night. He wanted to be sure of each detail.

As part of the overall plan, they talked about sneaking someone into the Nazis' garage to wreck the jeeps and trucks — cut some wires or take out the distributors — so that the Nazis wouldn't be able to chase them once they got out. But they discarded the idea. It was too risky. What if they got caught in the garage? It was an unpredictable place, and Jews weren't allowed there. Even if they could get in and out without being seen, Erich Bauer, the camp driver, could always walk in for a jeep. If he couldn't start it and figured out what had happened, he would alert the others. The escape would be over in a matter of minutes.

They talked about two POW marksmen killing two Ukrainians just before the changing of the guard and putting on their uniforms. The POWs would climb the towers, kill the Ukrainians there, and take their rifles. If the plan worked, the Jews would command at least two towers and could shoot at the Germans and Blackies below. But Sasha and Solomon dismissed that idea as also being too risky. Not only might they find it difficult to isolate the two Ukrainians to be killed, but someone could detect the Jews in the Blackie uniforms before they climbed the towers. Besides, someone might get suspicious if the guards who finished duty did not come down. The idea was just too complicated.

They thought of dressing a couple of POWs in SS uniforms. (The tailors could always put together two uniforms in a pinch.) The POWs in SS uniforms could lead a work brigade right up to the main gate, kill the guard there, and hold the gate open for the rest to run through. But Sasha and Solomon dismissed that as well. Again, too risky. If the POWs were detected, the rest of the Jews would be sealed in Camp I and Camp II. It would be the end.

The more complex the plan, Sasha and Solomon concluded, the less chance it had of succeeding. The final plan had to be simple.

That night, Kapo Porzyczki invited the Politruk to come to the blacksmith's shop for Russian music and food. The blacksmith had stolen a phonograph from a Camp II barracks filled with goods for Lublin, and Porzyczki had filched some Russian records, flour, and sugar. Pechersky sensed the Kapo wanted to talk.

Sasha, Solomon, Porzyczki, and the blacksmith sat around the table in the shop, ate pancakes sprinkled with sugar, drank vodka, and listened to the music playing softly in the background. The conversation was stiff and awkward. After a few embarrassing lulls, Porzyczki nodded to the blacksmith to leave, and Pechersky waved Solomon outside.

"I want to talk to you," Porzyczki said when the other two men had gone. "You probably know about what."

Pechersky sensed the Polish Jew was running scared. "What makes you think so?" he asked.

"And why are you so afraid that I might guess?"

"Unfortunately," Pechersky said, "I find it difficult to talk to you. I don't understand Polish, German, or Yiddish."

"Hardly an excuse," Porzyczki said. "You don't seem to have a problem talking to Luka. And I understand Russian. I speak it poorly. But you can understand me, soldier. If you want to."

"Why should I want to, Kapo?"

"Quit playing games and listen. I want a straight answer. Something's stirring. I feel it. The workers are restless."

"They have good reason," Sasha said.

"Yes, they do. But before you came, it was not so noticeable. It's clear you're planning something. An escape, to put it bluntly."

"You're guessing, Porzyczki. Just guessing."

"You are doing it carefully, Russian. You avoid gatherings. You don't hold long discussions with anyone, except maybe over chess. You spend the evening with little Luka. She's a good cover for you." Porzyczki paused. "I heard your remark last week: 'No one will do our work for us.' "

Pechersky knew the Kapo had heard those words, for Feldhendler had warned him to be careful of the Polish Jew. No one was really certain where his loyalties were, except that he would do whatever was best for Porzyczki.

"I could have killed you for those few words alone," the Kapo said. "But I didn't. I didn't do that, did I, Russian? I know you don't think much of me, so I won't try to defend myself. But I know what you're up to. You talk only to the little Warsaw Jew, Leitman. He's your mouthpiece. No one suspects him. You sleep next to him. You discuss your plan at night. I know that. But I'm not going to turn you in, Russian."

Porzyczki waited for Pechersky to speak. He knew his logic was making perfect sense.

"Keep talking," Pechersky said. "I'm still listening."

"Sasha, take me along. With me, you can pull it off easier. We Kapos move all over Camp I and II. We can talk to anyone. The Germans trust us. They don't even watch us."

Pechersky didn't answer.

"Why not?" the Kapo pleaded. "I don't believe the Germans. Frenzel makes all kinds of promises to us Kapos. He gives us privileges. But when the time comes, we'll be right next to you in the line to the showers."

"I'm glad you understand that," Pechersky said. "But why come to me with your problem?"

"You're the leader, soldier. Let's not waste time on useless talk. We want to help. We want to go along."

" 'We?' " Pechersky asked. "Who's the 'we'?"

"Me and Kapo Bunio."

"And Kapo Spitz, the German Jew?"

"He can't be trusted."

Ever since Feldhendler had told him to watch out for Porzyczki, Sasha had eyed him closely. Jacket wide open, cap at a jaunty angle, the Kapo strutted about the camp as if he were an SS officer. His whip was always in his hand, and he didn't hesitate to use it. He had a yen for one of the women, and had pestered her until she gave in. Maybe he had even threatened to send her to Camp III if she didn't go to bed with him. Pechersky wouldn't put it past the cunning Polish Jew. But still, as Feldhendler had pointed out, Porzyczki had never informed on anyone.

"Tell me," Pechersky asked unexpectedly. "Could you kill a German?"

The Kapo thought for a moment. "If it were vital to the plan — if I had to — yes."

"And if it weren't?"

"Hard to say. I never gave it any thought before."

"Well, it's time to go to bed." Pechersky wouldn't give the Polish Jew a yes or a no until he talked first to Solomon, then to Feldhendler. "Good night."

Sasha and Solomon discussed the Kapos in the barracks that night. They knew that they would have to make a decision one way or the other tomorrow night during the Organization meeting. They agreed that the Kapos would be very useful, maybe even crucial to the plan. But could they be trusted?

Pechersky leaned toward bringing Porzyczki in, because the Kapo had said that he wasn't sure whether he could kill a German. If the Kapo were a traitor, he would have said, "Of course. Anything you ask." It was a thin reason for so important a decision, but Sasha had only his instincts to rely on. He considered himself an excellent judge of character. The Polish Kapo wanted to get out of Sobibor as badly as he did, maybe even more. Porzyczki would be more dangerous if he weren't part of the plan.

In the end, Sasha and Solomon agreed that they didn't dare take him in, didn't dare not to, and didn't dare kill him.

Chapter 27

October 11, 1943, Morning

SELMA WAS SICK with typhus, and Chaim was worried. At first, he and Ulla were able to help her to the latrine, keep her temperature down with cold compresses, and make sure the red rash over all of her body, except her face, the palms of her hands, and the soles of her feet, would not break open and become infected. If it did, she could get gangrene. Day after day, Chaim propped her up during roll call and let her rest in the sorting sheds until he saw a Nazi coming.

But over the weekend, her fever had peaked at 104° F., and she was so delirious that she hardly knew she was in Sobibor. Josel had taken her temperature and written a sick card for her. If she didn't recover in three days, he'd tear it up and write another one. By Monday morning the fever had broken, leaving her weak and still a little delirious.

For some reason — maybe because Wagner was still away on leave, and he didn't want the Jews to think he was soft — Frenzel was suspicious when the Kapos reported during the Monday morning roll call that fourteen Jews were sick. Whip in hand, he charged into the barracks, shouting, "Up! Up! Up!"

Chaim stood by helplessly as Frenzel tramped from the men's to the women's barracks. He wished he could attack the Nazi, tear the whip from his hand, and beat him away from Selma, because he knew this was the end. The sick men were standing in a haphazard line in the yard. That meant only one thing — Camp III.

Selma was the only sick woman in the barracks. Frenzel smiled at her as he always did and said, "Go to work. You'll be all right." She was too sick to be frightened or relieved. She knew only in a vague sort of way that Frenzel had been nice to her, saved her again. She managed to get up and weave out the door. When she recognized Chaim, she grinned at him in her tomboy way and joined him in the line. He squeezed her hand.

Like a doctor with too many patients, Frenzel peered at the faces of the sick standing in the yard. Indeed, they all looked weak — some had red spots — but he had seen several of the same men sick a week ago. When it dawned on him that Josel had been tricking him with his sick cards since spring, Frenzel began searching the roll call line-up for the medic. Josel tried to look as insignificant as the grains of sand on which he stood.

"Your turn is next," Frenzel shouted, riveting his eyes on Josel. The Nazi had no time to fool around with the medic today. "There's no place for you to hide. I'll get you."

Josel knew Frenzel meant it. He would try to avoid the Nazi, but he was certain his days were numbered unless Frenzel went on leave. The German might be slow to act, Josel thought, but he didn't forget easily. And if there was anything that angered him, it was someone who made him look foolish. Josel knew about the escape plan. If only the Politruk and Feldhendler would hurry, he thought. They might be his only hope.

As Frenzel began marching the sick — if one could call it marching; they had a hard time standing, much less walking in military formation — the wife of one of the sick Dutch Jews broke from the roll call line. "Murderer! Murderer!" she screamed at Frenzel. "Take me with him! I will not live without him! Murderer! Scum!"

She caught up with her husband, gently put her arm around his shoulder, and walked off with him toward Camp III. She held her head high, proud, defiant. Frenzel did not try to stop her, nor did he wipe away his little smile.

After Frenzel returned without the Jews, the North Camp brigade, including Boris and Sasha, lined up for work. Standing next to the gate with a bandaged right hand was SS Sergeant Greischutz, the new commander of the Ukrainian guards. He had been wounded by a Russian airplane while returning to Sobibor from leave. While he was gone, SS Sergeant Goetzinger, the old commander, had been assassinated by the Ukrainians, and the Nazis never caught on. Esther knew about the murder from Wolodia, the Ukrainian in charge of the armory.

One day she had been cleaning bullets there when Wolodia came in for guns for the weekly military maneuvers held outside the camp. He had winked at her as he dragged out one of the large machine guns, the kind mounted on a jeep or a caisson. "Wait till you see what's going to happen now," he had told her. Esther was too scared to ask what.

The next day, after the news spread through the camp that an explosion had killed Goetzinger, Wolodia said to her, "You see. I told you something was going to happen."

Pechersky considered the death of Goetzinger a small victory for the Organization. With a new commander, the Ukrainians would be even more confused in an emergency. Furthermore, he had learned from Feldhendler that both Kommandant Reichleitner and Sergeant Gomerski had gone on leave, and that Wagner had not yet returned. That meant that Johnny Niemann was in charge of the camp, that Frenzel was still in charge of all the Jews, and that life in the North Camp, without Gomerski, would be easier.

Unwittingly, and in a drastic way, the Nazis had solved another of the Organization's problems — what to do about the Jews in Camp III. The Organization didn't want to leave them there after an escape, but it couldn't take them along. Now, there was no way to free them, for Frenzel had announced at roll call that all the Jews in Camp III had been killed for trying to escape. Pechersky and Feldhendler believed that the Jews were dead, but not because they had tried to break out. Once the transports had stopped, the Jews weren't needed any longer, so the Nazis had got rid of them. Then they cooked up the escape story to scare the Camp I Jews. Well, at least the prisoners in Camp III would not be murdered because of Pechersky and Feldhendler. And that was a very small consolation.

More than even Pechersky himself, Boris seemed to have enjoyed the irony of Greischutz's being wounded by a Soviet plane. So when Frenzel ordered the Russians to sing, Boris whispered to Sasha, "Let's sing the 'March of the Fliers.' "

"You start it," Pechersky said. "Tell all the others to join in."

Boris winked at Sasha. " 'We were born to make a fairy tale come true,' " he intoned, like a cantor in a synagogue. Then, just as they passed Greischutz, the others chimed in, " 'Always higher, and higher, and higher. We strive to match the flight of our birds.' "

Greischutz, who understood Ukrainian and knew the song well, began to seethe. Mouth twisted in hatred and whip dangling at his side, he ran up to the column. But his injured right hand made it difficult for him to swing the leather, and his blows were weak. That made him even angrier.

Frenzel thought it was a good joke. He put his arm around the Nazi's shoulder and smiled at him the way he smiled at Selma.

Evening

That night, the Organization met in the carpenter shop, with lookouts in the yard. Pechersky was ready to unveil his plan, and the room was tense and excited. The Kapos were the first order of business.

The Politruk told the Organization about his chat with Porzyczki and polled each member for his opinion. The consensus was to invite the two Polish Kapos — Bunio and Porzyczki — to join the escape, but not the German.

"Get Porzyczki," Sasha ordered one of the Polish Jews. Porzyczki was more important than Bunio, who could not move around Camp II as freely. "He has to hear this. We'll need him."

As soon as the Kapo sat down, the Politruk said: "We've decided to count you in, Porzyczki, even though we're not sure of you. I think you understand the spot you're in . . . If we fail, you'll be the first to be killed. Either by the Germans or by us."

"I know," Porzyczki said. "Don't worry."

"Good. We understand each other."

Pechersky turned to the whole group. "Here's the plan, comrades. In the first part, we kill off the German leaders. One by one. Without the slightest sound. One moment of wavering, and we're finished. It has to be done in one hour. Any longer, some German might notice another is missing and sound the alarm. My Russian soldiers will get them with axes. They're used to killing.

"In the second part of the plan, we make the break. We'll have a few pistols by then. Any questions so far?"

No one spoke, pleased that it was finally happening — what they had dreamed and whispered about for months. It was too late to turn back; the momentum would carry them forward.

Pechersky knew it would. He had counted on it; it was important that they believe the plan could and would work. He didn't. He knew they'd kill a few Germans, but they'd never make it to roll call. So many things could go wrong, that surely one would. If the Organization was lucky — really lucky — a handful might just make it to the woods.

"Now the details," he continued. "At three-twenty, Porzyczki will find an excuse to take two Russians from here — the carpenter shop — to Camp II. I'll pick the men at the last minute. They'll kill as many Germans as possible by the time they hear the first signal for roll call."

Pechersky had learned from Feldhendler that there was no predictable routine in Camp II to build around. The assassination plan there would have to be loose and flexible. That was the weakest link in the chain — and the strongest. Unpredictability could either help or destroy them.

"Feldhendler will be responsible for getting the Germans into the warehouses on some pretext," Pechersky explained. "The executions must be finished in one hour unless I order otherwise. Feldhendler is in charge of who gets killed where and when. The Russians do the job. All major problems are brought to me unless there's no time. I'll be in the carpenter shop all day. Clear?

"If any Jew in Camp II looks like trouble, silence him. Do what you have to. Kill him, if necessary. I don't want anyone passing from Camp II to Camp I after three-thirty unless Feldhendler or I send him."

Pechersky paused to read their faces. He had seen many soldiers before an important mission, and these were the faces of soldiers. Tense, excited, frightened, almost awed by the task that lay ahead of them. Did they realize they were going to die, he wondered.

"Little Drescher will be the liaison between me and Feldhendler," Pechersky continued. "He will report to me by four o'clock. Who is dead, how many, any problems. Then, just before four, the telephone wires connecting Camp II with the Officers' Compound will be cut. At both ends. That will delay repairs. The phone lines to the outside will be cut at the same time. That means once we get out, the Germans won't be able to call Lublin or Wlodawa for help.

"The electricity will be cut just before the first roll call signal. We'll have a better chance in the woods if the Germans can't see what the hell they're doing. Feldhendler will pick the men to cut the phones and the generator. Pick the usual men so everything'll look natural."

No one objected.

"At precisely four, we begin killing Germans here in Camp I. Invite them into the workshops one by one . . . by appointment . . . but only those who have a *reason* to come. No one should be suspicious. Don't invite anyone to Shlomo's shop; we've got a leak there.

"Two Russians will hide in each shop. They'll do the killing. By four-thirty, it must all be over here, too."

Their excitement was high now. Pechersky could sense it. He continued to give orders as if he knew exactly what he was doing. They must trust him.

"Tell those in your shop who must know," he said. "It would be risky if they were taken by surprise. If any Jew tries to run, goes crazy, stop him. Silence him — yes, even kill him. You have no choice.

"At five o'clock, the second part of our plan begins. The workers in Camp II will march back for roll call as usual. No matter who leads them — Bunio, Porzyczki, or Spitz — everything must be as usual. March, sing, look tired. Anything but nervous. No slip-ups. Don't hesitate to use your whip, Porzyczki."

The Kapo smiled at the dig.

"Just before five-thirty Porzyczki will blow the whistle for the roll call. That's the escape signal. We will line up as usual. Frenzel will be dead, so Porzyczki will take over. Then, we'll do one of two things. Surprise will be our best weapon.

"We'll line up four abreast. A team of Russians will head the column. They'll have the pistols we take from the Nazis. Porzyczki will march us right to the main gate, as if he were leading us out to the woods. Just like the Waldkommando. The Germans and Ukrainians should be so confused without their leaders, they won't try to stop us. If we're lucky, we'll walk right out of Sobibor. The road is not mined. While we march out, the Russians will attack the armory and shoot off the locks. If we can get inside, we'll be better armed than the Nazis. We'll blow up the whole camp.

"If something goes wrong before we get through the gate, we scatter. Every man for himself. Feldhendler will see to it that a few men have wirecutters for the fences. Encourage those who are running to throw stones at the mines. The best place to cut through the fence is behind the officers' barracks. I'm sure there are only signal flares buried out there. Also along the main gate, right or left. There are no mines there, either."

No one asked Pechersky the obvious questions. What happens if the Nazis discover the executions before roll call? What if Porzyczki can't get all the Jews to line up and march for the main gate? What would they do if they reached the woods without guns or maps?

"Solomon and I have thought it through," Pechersky said. "It is the best plan. We have no other choices. No one has objected. So it is agreed, then. We'll meet here tomorrow night for a final briefing. I'll set the date then. And remember. Not a word to anyone. Wife, lover, brother, or friend."

There was no further discussion, and they left the meeting one at a time. Pechersky knew their heads must be filled with doubts, for only one thing was certain — they would kill some Nazis. How many, before they got caught, he couldn't say. Who, he didn't know.

Another thing was almost certain — they would never make it to the roll call. Something would go wrong. Some Nazi was bound to be missed.

Some Jew would panic and give the whole thing away. Maybe the cut phone wires would be discovered. Maybe some Nazi would die screaming his head off, or run out of the shoe shop or tailor shop, head bashed but still alive. Or maybe a Nazi would see an ax hidden under someone's jacket. No, Pechersky thought, they'd never make it to roll call. But at least they'd take some Nazis with them when they died. At least they would die fighting like the Jews in Warsaw, Treblinka, Bialystok. And if the Nazis did discover the plan, some Jews still might cut through the fences and make a dash for the woods. Pechersky doubted that any would make it. But it was worth the risk.

Once in the yard, Pechersky called Kapo Porzyczki aside. The Politruk had noticed that in the last several days the Ukrainians on duty were handing over their bullets — it seemed like five rounds — to their replacements during the changing of the guard. That could mean several things. The Nazis didn't trust the Blackies; they weren't expecting a revolt; and the Ukrainians off duty would have to chase the Jews with unloaded rifles.

"Get me assigned to do some repairs in the Ukrainian barracks tomorrow," the Politruk told Porzyczki. "I want to check something out."

Chapter 28

October 12, 1943

PECHERSKY picked his way through the Blackies' barracks on the pretext of testing the doors for warp. Each barracks had two rooms. In the larger, the rank and file slept on bunk beds, warmed by two wood stoves with round plates that could be removed to heat water. Along the walls were gun racks partly filled with Mausers, each holding five or six rounds. In the smaller room, the Ukrainian officers slept in single beds. There was one wood stove there, and the guns were stored in a closet.

No one was inside the officers' quarters. So Pechersky quickly closed the door behind him and took a rifle from the closet rack. As quietly as he could, he slipped back the bolt. The chamber was empty. He searched the closet for bullets, but found none. So he assumed that if the officers' guns were not loaded, the rifles of the rank and file wouldn't be, either.

Pechersky was pleased. He doubted that the empty guns would be a big advantage for the prisoners, but the news would encourage the Organization. Just one more small sign that luck was on their side.

They met briefly that night. Pechersky rehearsed the basics of the plan:

Kill all the Germans you can in Camp II between three-thirty and four-thirty. Feldhendler is in charge. Cut all the phone wires in two places just before four, and the electricity just before roll call. Kill the Germans in the Camp I shops between four and four-thirty. If we get caught before the roll call whistle, it's every man for himself. Line up four abreast, Russians up front. Follow Porzyczki to the main gate. Walk right out of the camp.

If we get caught, break for the fences. The Russians will take the arsenal.

Pechersky then added a few new details: Porzyczki will assign the Russians to work in the new barracks in Camp I. The carpenters will hide planks and a ladder in the weeds behind their shop in case the prisoners can't get out of Camp I. The first ones over the fence will lay the planks over the ditch. Off-duty Ukrainians don't have ammunition in their rifles. Don't hesitate to knife them if they get in the way.

Pechersky paused, waiting for questions. "We break tomorrow," he said at last. The room was as tense as a hair trigger. "Wear extra clothes. It will be cold in the forest. See Feldhendler. He'll get whatever you need."

Shlomo was swept up in the excitement of the plan. "I can steal some rifles," he said. The words slipped out like a piece of butter. He hadn't planned to say them; in fact, he hadn't even thought about smuggling guns. His boldness made him shiver. He had no idea how he could get them.

"Have some Russians meet me in the kitchen just before roll call," he told the Politruk. "I'll have the guns then."

Pechersky didn't want to tell the boy that if he wasn't dead by roll call, he'd be fighting for his life in some corner of the camp. Nor did he want to say that even if he managed to smuggle the rifles, he'd never find ammunition. But anything that would raise the morale of the Organization at this point, Pechersky thought, was worth the risk.

"Good luck," he told the boy. He'd send a couple of his men to the kitchen just in case the goldsmith did smuggle the guns and did find some bullets — if there was anyone to send by five o'clock.

The meeting was over. They shook hands, wishing each other good luck, each hoping that he'd kill a Nazi tomorrow, hoping that he'd make it through the fences, across the minefield to the forest of the owls, hoping he'd be the first to tell the world about Sobibor.

Although each member of the Organization had been sworn to secrecy, the Politruk was the only one to keep the vow. Not only hadn't he told Luka; he hadn't even briefed the men he had picked to kill the Nazis. The other members of the Organization leaked the plan, but not necessarily the details, to friends.

*

Feldhendler told his cousin, Esther, so that she would be sure to wear extra clothes and a good pair of boots. Esther told her friends, Eda, Hella, and Zelda, and a few other women she trusted.

Drescher told some of his young friends so that they, too, could get ready. One of Chaim's Polish friends told him, but he decided to wait until the morning to tell Selma. She was much better now; even able to work. Her fever was gone and the spots were disappearing. Every hour she was gaining more strength and spunk. He wanted to make sure she got a good night's sleep.

Shlomo had told Nojeth about the plan as soon as he had first heard of it. "Get four sacks of gold and money ready," he had told his cousin. If the four of them — Shlomo, Nojeth, Moses, and Jankus — were going to survive in the forest, they'd need money to buy food from the Poles. "Bury them close by."

To Shlomo's surprise, Nojeth was delighted with the plan to kill Germans. He'd been hiding a knife in case he'd have the chance to stick a Nazi before he escaped. He still believed in God and prayed each day, Nojeth told Shlomo. But didn't Samson kill the Philistines with the jawbone of an ass? Well, the Dutch switchblade was his jawbone, Nojeth said.

Shlomo had also told his younger brother, Moses. The boy had grown taller and stronger than Shlomo, and just as hard. The suffering in Sobibor had filled him with hatred for the Nazis, and he would bite his way out of the camp if he had to. Moses took the news like a professional assassin.

Finally, Shlomo told two Jews in his shop whom he trusted absolutely. "Keep your ears open," he had said. "If you hear any whispering about the plan among the others, let me know. We have to be prepared to kill them if necessary. Keep a knife on you at all times."

That night, after the final meeting, Shlomo hid the axes and knives where the Politruk had told him to. The Russians would pick them up in the morning, after Sasha had given everyone his assignment. Then he told Jankus about the escape (he had kept it from his nephew because he wasn't sure how the lad would handle the news). Jankus shivered like a wet puppy.

It was hard for the Jews who knew about the plan to sleep that night. Their feelings were mixed. Most weren't completely convinced that they would survive, even though they didn't share their doubts with the others. But they were happy in a frightened way. They would avenge their mothers and fathers, wives and children, brothers and sisters. They would teach the Nazis a lesson. They were men, not shells of men who had once been human. They would fight for their dignity and die with pride. With Nazi blood on their hands. If there was a God, He'd forgive them.

October 13

Dawn broke sunny and clear, and the fifty Jews who now knew about the escape tried to act as if October 13 were just another Wednesday.

They watched Frenzel at roll call to see whether he seemed suspicious or nervous. He didn't.

The brigades marched through the gate for the North Camp and Camp II as usual. Porzyczki assigned Solomon and nineteen other Russians to the unfinished barracks in Camp I, and Pechersky to the carpenter shop. From there, the Politruk could get a clear view of the yard and could see anyone approaching the shop. He had desperately wanted to kill Frenzel himself, but Feldhendler had vetoed the idea. The Politruk had to be free to handle problems, Feldhendler had argued. He should not have to worry about a tough and dangerous assignment. Furthermore, if the Politruk did kill Frenzel, what assurance could he give that his head and heart would be clear enough to lead the rest of the revolt?

Feldhendler was right. Once a soldier is in the heat of battle, it is almost impossible to keep his mind on the war. That's the job of the generals behind the lines. Besides, Pechersky knew that he hated Frenzel so much that he would be consumed with the thought of killing him, and that once he axed the Nazi, he might not be mentally and emotionally free to make all final decisions.

The first problem of the day arrived at nine o'clock that morning. A train filled with SS officers pulled onto the spur outside the camp. They all headed for the canteen. They had come from the Osow work camp, eight miles away. None of the Jews could figure out why they were in Sobibor or how long they would stay. When they hadn't left by noon, Pechersky called off the escape, even though the likelihood of the plan leaking in the next twenty-four hours was high. It was suicidal to try to escape with all those SS there. Besides, he doubted that the Nazis would keep their appointments at the shops now that their daily routine had been broken. So, like a clock shattered by a bullet, the escape plan stopped.

The Organization met briefly that night, after the SS guests had left. They discussed what the visit had meant. Some thought the SS just had a day off and took their leave at the death camp, where the food was good and where there was always plenty of wine and vodka and a few Russian girls. Others argued that they had come to plan the liquidation of Sobibor.

Pechersky saw that the Organization was discouraged, almost depressed from disappointment and emotional strain. "No matter what, it happens tomorrow," he said. "We break. Same plan. No changes."

Feldhendler objected. "But tomorrow is the first day of Succos," he said. "The Orthodox Jews will object to breaking out on the holy day."

Succos follows on the heels of Yom Kippur, the Day of Atonement.

The holy days commemorate God's protection of the Jews who had escaped from Egypt and wandered in the desert for forty years before they found the Holy Land.

Pechersky didn't know whether Feldhendler, the son of the rabbi, was speaking for himself or for other Orthodox Jews, but he didn't miss the irony of escaping on Succos. For some lucky Sobibor Jews, it would be a day to celebrate a new leaf, to thank God for His protection as they searched for the Promised Land of freedom won for them by the Red Army.

"The Nazis kill Jews on holy days, don't they?" Pechersky asked Feldhendler. "Well, we can kill Nazis on them, too."

It was settled. October 14 would be the day, no matter what. No matter whether Wagner came back or not. No matter whether it rained or not. No matter who might be sick. No matter whether Himmler himself visited Sobibor.

The barracks hummed with whispers late into the night. The sense of excitement and fear and hope was the highest it had ever been in Sobibor. There would be no turning back. Their fate was in the hand of God — and of the Politruk.

Chapter 29

October 14, 1943, Morning

ONCE AGAIN, day broke bright and clear. Frenzel never noticed that some of the Jews were wearing good boots and winter clothes. Josel tried to avoid the Nazi's eye; Frenzel had reminded him only yesterday that his turn was coming. "You can't hide from me," the Nazi had said. "Don't try." If Josel could make it until five o'clock without Frenzel spotting him, he'd have a chance.

Shlomo told Nojeth, Moses, and Jankus to meet him in the kitchen after work, before roll call. Then he called Nojeth aside. He reminded his cousin to bring the four bags of gold and told him about his promise to smuggle rifles. "If I don't make it to the kitchen," he said, "take care of Moses and Jankus. You're older. Stay with them."

Nojeth promised. He thought the whole plan was crazy and that none of them would ever leave Sobibor alive, but he knew that staying in the camp would surely mean death.

Chaim told Selma. "Wear extra clothes and get a good pair of boots," he warned.

Chaim wasn't surprised when a friend had told him they were going to make the break; he had known for over a month that the Organization was planning something. He even knew about the Putzer plan, the fire diversion plan, and the plan to bomb the canteen and officers' quarters. Once the Russians came, however, he noticed how Feldhendler and Shlomo, Szol and Mundek, walked around more confidently. Chaim didn't know

211

the details of the escape yet, but he'd find out. His and Selma's lives would depend on it.

Chaim was prepared for the escape, too. In bandages wrapped around his legs, he had wads of paper money and gold coins, and in his eyeglass case, some diamonds. During the eleven months he had been in Sobibor, he had never given up the hope of breaking out some day. How, he had never been sure. He wasn't a leader, he knew that; but he was a good soldier, a good follower. There was a twinge of disappointment that he had not been included in the planning of the escape and in the Organization, and that he had not been given an assignment, as others apparently had. But Selma was worth it. He made up his mind that if he was called on to do anything, no matter what, he would. And he would break out with Selma, holding her hand. He'd drag her through the gate or fence if he had to. He loved her, and he would either escape with her or die with her in the yard or on the fences or in the fields.

"Meet me next to the medicine shed," he whispered. "Be there at four o'clock sharp. On time. I'll tell you what I know then."

Selma was frightened. It was more than just the thought of dying. It was that she didn't know anything — how, when, where, who — and the uncertainty gnawed at her. Besides, she wasn't completely well yet. Would she hold Chaim back? Would he die because of her? And if they made it to the woods, how would they live? She was a city girl from Holland, had never really been in a forest before. Although the thought frightened her, she had Chaim to protect her. She would do exactly what he told her. He had taken care of her so far, and he'd take care of her again. She squeezed Chaim's hand — "bride and groom," Frenzel still called them — and they marched off to Camp II, singing:

Es war ein Edelweiss,
Ein kleines Edelweiss.
Ho-la-hi-di, Hu-la-la,
Ho-la-hi-di-ho.

One by one, Pechersky called his soldiers into the carpenter shop to give them their assignments. Boris was the first.

"I know you better than anyone else," Pechersky said. "I don't have to waste words. You go to the shoe shop. Take your hatchet. Remember, do it without a sound. And don't forget to take their pistols."

Pechersky gave Boris a Russian hug. He had no worries about the big, simple miner. Let the Germans beware.

Kalimali was next, and Pechersky was counting on his cool head and

212

brains. The Caucasian had graduated from the University of Rostov as a transportation engineer, and his education was an asset.

The least certain part of the escape plan was the executions in Camp II, which were open-ended. Besides, Camp II was close to the Officers' Compound; in the center of it stood the Germans' Administration Building. And more than two hundred Jews worked in Camp II. Once a Nazi was killed, it would be difficult to keep it a secret. Anything could happen at any time, and Pechersky would not be there.

"I'm going to give you the toughest job," he told Kalimali. "Porzyczki will come to the barracks and get you around three-twenty. You'll be assigned to work alongside Feldhendler. He'll line up the Germans you have to kill. I'm sending another Russian with you. Take your hatchets. Remember, you'll be killing the first Nazis. It should give courage to the others. If anyone over there gets scared, replace him. No one should be forced to kill."

They shook hands silently.

Pechersky saved Frenzel for Solomon's crew in the barracks under construction. He called in the skinny Warsaw Jew, even though he was not a POW. He trusted Solomon's judgment, and he wanted to make sure they'd get Frenzel quietly and at the last minute. If anyone would be missed at Sobibor, with Wagner still on leave, it would be the smiling butcher.

"Invite him inside to look at your work," Pechersky told Leitman. "Find some good excuse. You don't have to kill him yourself. Assign one of the Russians there, if you want. I leave that up to you. Just get him."

"I understand," Leitman said. "It's done."

Early Afternoon

At one o'clock, before the plan was set in motion, Frenzel walked into the carpenter shop to check the work. He saw the shop chief dressed in a new suit. Pechersky hadn't noticed that. The chief figured that since he wouldn't be able to take much along when he escaped, he might as well wear his best.

"Is there going to be a wedding here?" Frenzel asked. "Why are you all dressed up?"

Pechersky kept working as the chief carpenter tried to make a joke of his new clothes. If they had to kill the Nazi now, they would. Frenzel had laughed, but Pechersky wasn't so sure that the Nazi didn't suspect something. Wagner would have, he thought. And Gomerski. But, then, Frenzel was not very bright.

Frenzel inspected the furniture the carpenters were making and left without a word. Pechersky waited for a whistle or a gunshot or a group of Ukrainians to come marching through the gate, but the camp routine did not change. They had survived the first crisis. What would be next?

At two o'clock, a Nazi with a machine gun came into Camp I and led away Kapo Porzyczki and three prisoners. No Nazi used a machine gun to guard the Jews; it was too dangerous. A smart prisoner could grab it and open fire. Before he could be stopped, he might kill a half-dozen guards and Germans. What was going on? Did the Nazi sense something? Would he bring Porzyczki back? Sasha needed him by three-twenty if the plan was to move on schedule.

For a tense hour, Pechersky waited in the carpenter shop, peering through windows and doors into the yard. He listened for shots, watched for smoke, for anything unusual. He kept an eye on the watchtowers, because he knew that the Ukrainians up there would be the first to signal if something was wrong. But everything seemed normal.

At three o'clock, Kapo Bunio walked through the gate and headed for the carpenter shop. This is it, Pechersky thought. It must be bad news. Bunio is walking too fast. He should be more casual.

"Everything's okay," Bunio told the Politruk. "They took Porzyczki to the North Camp to supervise. The prisoners are piling wood over there."

"Why the machine gun?" Pechersky said. "Do they suspect?"

"There're no Ukrainians in the North Camp today. The German wanted to be sure, so he took the gun."

Pechersky relaxed. "Do you realize that Porzyczki was supposed to take Kalimali to Camp II at three-twenty?"

"Yes."

"Well, you'll have to take him."

"Impossible," Bunio said. "I have no right to go there. That's off limits for me."

"You have to," the Politruk ordered. "If anyone asks, say that Porzyczki's in the North Camp and there's something that has to be done in Camp II. Make up some good excuse."

Bunio started to go to pieces. "Why not postpone the escape until tomorrow? Porzyczki will be back then. He — "

"No, today. Not tomorrow. That may be too late," Pechersky said. He recalled the rumor that Sobibor would be liquidated on the 15th. He didn't necessarily believe it, but he wasn't about to take a chance. Besides, he doubted that the secret, if one could call it that, could be kept for another twenty-four hours. "There's no backing out. You'll do as I order."

Pechersky was ready to kill Bunio if he either disobeyed or threatened to give the plan away.

"All right," Bunio said. "I'll do it."

At twenty past three, Pechersky watched Bunio lead Kalimali and another Russian through the gate. Everything still seemed normal. The guards in the towers looked as bored as usual. In ten minutes, it would begin.

3:30

Toivi was in the incinerator shed.

"They're coming," Wycen whispered to him, even though there was no one else inside to hear them. Feldhendler had told Toivi to cover the windows with rubbish just in case the Organization decided to kill a Nazi there. Blind Karl had been assigned to work elsewhere, and Wycen was Toivi's new assistant.

Toivi peeked through the cracks between the boxes covering the window. He saw Kalimali, Bunio, and another Russian walking toward the clothes storeroom. Then he watched Sender, one of the Jews from the sorting barracks, walk toward his shop. Toivi opened the door.

"Go to the gate," Sender ordered the boy. "Stay close to the Dutchman guarding it. Try to keep him there. Try to keep anyone from entering or leaving. If he gives you trouble, call me. I'll be nearby, watching."

Toivi had a knife in his boot, but he wasn't sure he could use it on a Nazi, much less on a Jew. He liked the Dutch Jew. He joined him at the gate, as Sender had ordered him to.

Toivi made sure he was facing both the clothes storeroom and Sender, and he tried to keep the Dutch Jew's back to the barracks. He didn't think the Dutchman would necessarily blow the whistle on the escape, but he might notice some commotion and then do something to draw the attention of the guards. He might even panic, because his wife was also in Sobibor.

"Maybe there'll be a new transport tomorrow," Toivi said. It was the safest topic of conversation, and they chatted about why the transports had stopped.

Joseph Wolf, the dumbest German and the easiest to fool, was the first Nazi the Putzer invited into the storeroom to try on a new leather coat. The German didn't suspect a thing. When he walked into the warehouse, everything looked normal. There were six Jews there, piling clothes in bins. One of them approached him with the coat, another stood behind him to help him into it. Then Kalimali and the other Russian, axes raised, crept out from the bin where they were hiding. Wolf fell without a sound.

Two Jews then dragged Wolf's body into a bin and covered it with clothes. Two others covered the blood with sand, and Kalimali and the other Russian rushed back into their hiding place.

Next, the Putzer called Sergeant Beckmann, who was crossing the yard, to see whether he wanted a new leather jacket that seemed to be made just for him. Toivi watched Beckmann head for the storeroom, then hesitate. The Nazi turned around as if he sensed something was wrong or had just remembered he had something more important to do than to try on clothes. He walked to his office in the Administration Building, just a hundred feet away.

The Dutchman started to get suspicious. As much as Toivi had tried to keep his back to the storeroom, the Dutch Jew had seen Wolf enter. "I wonder why he didn't come out?" the Dutchman said to Toivi. "I'd better check."

There was no time for Toivi to call Sender. He had to move quickly. "It's a revolt," the boy blurted. "Wolf's dead."

The Dutch Jew didn't try to cry out or bolt. If he did, Toivi would have to kill him, and he wasn't sure he could.

"I want to warn a friend of mine," the Dutchman said. As the man made a move to leave the gate, Toivi motioned to Sender. The boy wasn't sure whether the Dutchman wanted to warn a friend or the Germans. Sender rushed over. "Come with me," he warned, sticking a knife in the Dutchman's ribs. "Be quiet or I'll kill you." He led the Dutchman into the luggage barracks, where Toivi had once worked.

After Wolf had been killed, Drescher sauntered through the gate, down the corridor, into the yard of Camp I, and toward the carpenter shop. Pechersky watched him through the window. It seemed as if the boy were walking in slow motion. The Russian tried to read his face. Was there a problem? Had it begun? But the boy didn't look excited. He didn't seem frightened. In fact, he looked frighteningly cool for an eleven-year-old lad.

"Got one," the Putzer told the Politruk. The boy smiled from ear to ear. "We may have a problem. Beckmann seemed suspicious." When the Putzer realized that Pechersky probably didn't even know who Beckmann was, he added, "He works in the Administration Building. He wouldn't go inside the storeroom."

Drescher waited for instructions. If they had a problem with the Nazi, Pechersky thought, they would have to take care of it from Camp II. He was too far away to tell them what to do.

"Tell Feldhendler to handle it as he sees fit," the Politruk said. "Tell

216

him we're ready to begin here. Tell him 'Happy hunting.' And send me Luka."

No sooner had Drescher left than Leon Friedman walked through the gate with climbing cleats on his shoes and a safety belt around his waist. He entered the infirmary, where Josel was waiting.

All morning Josel had baby-sat the German Kapo. Feldhendler had told him to keep Spitz busy and to report back if he sensed that the German Jew suspected anything. Josel liked Spitz and thought he would be the last person in Sobibor to turn them in, but he obeyed. Spitz suspected nothing.

Josel had once saved Friedman's life. Like many shoemakers, who did most of their work in the wintertime, Friedman had doubled as an electrician before he came to Sobibor. There, he took care of the telephones and sorted shoes in Camp II. One day, Friedman had come to Josel with a boil on his groin that was so painful he could hardly walk. Fortunately, Josel had some contraband anesthetic. After spraying the boil, Josel lanced, cleaned, and bandaged it. The wound had healed, and Friedman never forgot.

As he sorted shoes, he checked under the heels of each for gold and diamonds. Every week, he'd bring the loot to Josel, who would bury it in the yard close to the infirmary. On the evening of October 12, the day before the escape was supposed to take place, Josel dug up the jar and hid it in the Dutch tile oven in his infirmary. Now, when Friedman entered just before four o'clock, Josel divided the money and jewels equally. Friedman was trembling with excitement and fear.

"Calm down," Josel told him. "You can do it. Everything will be all right."

The shoemaker gave Josel a hug and a kiss on both cheeks, then walked across the yard to the only telephone pole. He swung his safety strap around the pine pole, snapped it onto his belt, dug his spikes into the wood, and climbed to the top. Among other things, he cut all the phone wires. To the guards in the towers below him, nothing seemed unusual.

While Friedman was climbing the pole, Chaim strolled over to the medicine storeroom in Camp II, where Selma was waiting nervously. She was so happy to see him that she didn't seem curious about what was going on. While puttering around in the utensil barracks, he had overheard members of the Organization talking. He knew they were worried about Beckmann.

"Two Germans are dead already," he told Selma. "There's no turning back now. Wait here for me until roll call. Don't move. I have to be able to find you."

Chaim went back to the barracks. Kapo Porzyczki's younger brother and another Polish Jew were there, edgy and excited. They seemed to be waiting for someone. Chaim picked up pieces of their conversation: "Beckmann . . . Should we wait . . . Where is he . . . Did he chicken out . . . Need a third person . . . Can't do it with just two."

Chaim volunteered. He was not a killer, but there was no turning back, as he had just told Selma. If Beckmann caught them or was too suspicious, he'd raise the alarm. They'd all get killed.

"Got a knife?" the younger Porzyczki asked.

Chaim nodded.

"Come on, then. Let's get it over with."

Chapter 30

4:00

AT PRECISELY FOUR O'CLOCK, Johnny Niemann rode into Camp I on Cilly, the chestnut mare. He reined up in front of the bakery next to the tailor shop and eased himself to the ground.

"Hold the horse," he told Israel, the baker, who had been expecting him. "I won't be long."

Then, with his riding crop behind his back, Niemann slowly walked into the tailor shop. As soon as he disappeared through the door, Israel gave Cilly a slap on the rear. The mare bolted through the gate for the stables.

Pechersky watched from the carpenter shop. He felt relieved that something was finally under his control, something he could watch and see. With Reichleitner still on leave, Niemann was in charge of the whole camp. If they could kill him, there might be a few minutes of confusion when they broke. And a few minutes could mean life or death.

Mundek brought Niemann his new uniform as soon as he entered. The head tailor held the jacket while Niemann slipped into it. He turned the Nazi around so that his back would be to the mirror. Niemann allowed himself to be pushed and turned and patted like a bride being fitted for her wedding dress.

Pechersky had assigned Yehuda Lerner to kill the assistant Kommandant. Like Leitman, Lerner was a Polish Jew from Warsaw, not a Russian POW. And like Solomon, Yehuda had met Pechersky in the Minsk camp. He

219

had been part of Sasha's escape team there as well. The Politruk trusted him.

While Mundek was fitting Niemann, asking him to hold perfectly still for a moment, Lerner tiptoed out of the back room, where the tailors slept, and split Niemann's head with one slice of the ax. Then he gave the Nazi one more blow for good measure. As he and the other Russian dragged Niemann's body into the back room and stuffed it under a bunk, Mundek and the other tailors mopped up the blood with pieces of cloth.

Hardly had Niemann entered the tailor shop than Fallaster walked into the shoe shop next door. Szol and Itzhak were pleased that the Politruk had given them the hard-of-hearing Nazi who ran the miners' train and who worked mainly in Camp III. Fallaster was in a good mood.

"Beautiful day outside," he told Szol. "It's warm. The sun is shining. My boots, are they ready?"

"Yes, please. Sit down," Szol said into his ear. "Try them on. I hope they're a perfect fit."

Fallaster took the boots. "Well, *Schuhmacher,* I'll be going home in five days. You must make a pair of slippers for my *Frau.* Remember that."

"Of course," Szol said. "I hope Frau Fallaster will be pleased with my work."

Boris was working at a shoe bench; Grisha was standing near the door. As Fallaster grunted and tugged at his new boots, Boris hit him with the flat side of his ax. The Nazi wasn't dead and tried to scream. But only a long moan came from his throat. Szol pounced on him, covering his mouth. Boris and Grisha finished him off and dragged him into the back room. There was no time to wipe up the blood, so Itzhak and Szol covered the floor with old pieces of leather.

Boris took Fallaster's pistol and walked nonchalantly to the carpenter shop, as if he were returning from the latrine.

"Here, take this." He handed Pechersky the pistol. "It will come in handy."

The two Russians hugged and kissed.

"How did Szol do?" Pechersky asked.

"Like a professional."

"Then hurry back in case someone else comes in."

Luka passed Boris in the yard. She was out of breath. "You wanted me?" she asked Sasha.

"We're breaking in less than an hour," he told her, trying to hide his emotion. "Change into men's clothes. You'll be cold in a dress."

"Who's escaping? What are you talking about, Sasha?" She was shocked.

220

The news and excitement hadn't reached the rabbit pens where she was working that day.

"Don't waste my time with questions, Luka. The whole camp. All of us. We've already killed half a dozen Germans. This is no time to have doubts."

"I know, Sasha. But I'm afraid. All I've known is death. Don't listen to me. Just do what you have to."

"We've just begun to pay them back, Luka. Wait until we get out of here. We'll get them. Be strong. Please . . . for me."

"I'm afraid, Sasha." The girl was trembling. The sky was clouding over, and it was starting to get colder. "Don't look at me like that, Sasha. Not for myself. For you. I'm afraid for you. I don't care what happens to me anymore." She threw her arms around him, pressed her face against his chest, and broke into tears.

Pechersky grew stern. He didn't have time for Luka. They were in the middle of an uprising, and his men needed him. "Pull yourself together," he ordered her, as if she were a naughty child. "Aren't you ashamed? Go change! When you hear the signal, you'll come out and you'll take your place by my side. Understand?"

"Yes, Sasha."

"You must live, little Luka. This is the only way. *We* must live. Take our revenge. Run, now, quickly."

Luka returned a few minutes later with a broom. "I took this along in case anyone asked me why I was coming here," she explained. Then she pulled a man's shirt from under her blouse and handed it to him.

"What's that?"

"Put it on," she begged.

"Why?"

"Sasha, p–l–e–a–s–e! Put it on. It will bring you luck."

"I don't believe in good luck charms, Luka. And I don't have time. I — "

"No!" she snapped defiantly. "You will put it on." She began to unbutton his jacket. "If you won't do it for me, do it for your daughter. You once told me she is dearer to you than anything in the world. This shirt will protect you. And if you're safe, we'll be safe."

Pechersky slipped into the shirt, then put his officer's jacket over it while he watched out the window. A smile lit up Luka's thin face. She kissed Sasha on the lips and ran off to the women's barracks to wait for the roll call whistle.

One of Shlomo's assignments was to check the tailor shop to see whether everything was all right. If not, he was to report to Sasha. No one knew how Mundek and the other two tailors would cope with the assassination and with a Nazi under their beds.

The tailors were fine, but the hat-maker, who also worked in the shop, had begun to hallucinate. He had taken a large pair of scissors and had dashed into the back room. The little Jew became covered with blood as he attacked Johnny Niemann's body with the shears. With each stab, he shouted the names of his wife and children who had been killed at Sobibor.

Shlomo and the tailors pinned the hat-maker's arms to his side and took away his scissors. Then they tied and gagged him. The problem was solved. Shlomo felt no need to bother the Politruk. If the hat-maker was still a threat at roll call time, they'd have to leave him tied, hoping the Nazis would have pity on him when they found him next to Niemann.

Shlomo walked back to his shop to get the stovepipe he had carefully selected. It was time to steal guns. With the large pipe over his shoulder like a cannon barrel, he walked out of Camp I to the Officers' Compound. No one stopped him, since one of his jobs was to repair the wood stoves in the barracks there, and that included cleaning and replacing the stove-pipes.

4:15

Hand still bandaged, Sergeant Greischutz walked through the gate toward the shoe shop for the Ukrainian guards. As chief of the guards, he got better service there than he did in the SS shoe shop nearby, where he had to wait his turn. In the Ukrainian shop, Greischutz was number one.

As soon as Greischutz sat down to try on his new boots, Semyon Rozenfeld and Arkady Vaispapir slipped out of the back room and split his skull. They dragged him away and, with the back room door cracked, waited to see whether anyone else dropped by. They didn't have long to wait.

Klat, the young Ukrainian whom Shlomo had paid to carry messages to and from Camp III, was looking for his boss, Sergeant Greischutz. One of the other Blackies in the canteen had told him that Greischutz had gone to the shoe shop. Klat barged in unexpectedly. Since the shoemakers didn't have a pair of boots for him to try on, they explained that Herr Oberscharführer Greischutz had left minutes ago and was probably in another shop. They maneuvered Klat so that his back was to the door. Rozenfeld and Vaispapir rushed him. Klat did not cry out. They dragged him into the back room to join his boss.

For Pechersky, who was watching who went into the shops and didn't come out, things were moving smoothly. With Niemann dead, the Germans were leaderless. With Greischutz dead, the Ukrainians were leaderless. That left Frenzel. Once they killed him, there would be no Nazi in the yard for roll call, and no one to stop them from marching right up to the main gate. But so far, Frenzel had not returned to inspect the work in the new barracks, as Drescher had asked him to.

Sasha was becoming somewhat concerned. Why didn't the Nazi show up? Was he suspicious? With Wagner gone, was he just too busy? Was he looking for Niemann? Had he found out the phones weren't working? There was still time — it wasn't even four-thirty — but if they failed to get Frenzel, there could be one big problem in the end.

While the Russians were killing Klat, Shlomo was entering the Ukrainian barracks next to the armory and parallel to the railway station. Over his shoulder was the stovepipe. Inside, he was laughing, for at least five Nazis were dead — he didn't know exactly who and how many. If he had to die today, at least he'd have the last laugh. But he was also scared. If he got caught, it would probably mean an escape before five o'clock. The Politruk would have no choice but to tell the others to run for the fences. Maybe gun smuggling wasn't such a hot idea. Maybe he should just go back to his shop empty-handed.

The larger room, with bunk beds, was empty. The rifles stood in the racks like toy soldiers waiting for a bugle call. The Ukrainians were on duty, drinking themselves under the canteen tables, or humping the prostitutes they kept in the houses across the tracks. The officers' bedroom was also empty.

Shlomo set the stovepipe on the lower berth of one of the bunk beds and pulled a half-dozen rifles from the rack. He could fit only two guns into the stovepipe, because the bolts were open, and he wasn't sure how to close them. So he wrapped the stovepipe and three rifles in a blanket and began to search for bullets. When he couldn't find any in the larger room, he ran into the small room. Time was running out. In approximately half an hour, the bugle would call the Camp II workers to line up for the march back to Camp I.

After rummaging everywhere for ammunition, he finally found bullets buried in the closet. The officers must have been squirreling them away like hickory nuts, just in case they needed them. He stuffed as many as he could into his pockets. What should he do now? he asked himself. If he tried to cross the yards, he'd stand out like a rabbit on the minefield. If he stayed, what would he do if a Ukrainian or Nazi walked in?

Shlomo decided to wait until the bugle call. That way, if he got caught, the Germans would think he was acting alone. Or would they? He pushed the blanket under a bed and got busy checking out the wood stove like a good little tinsmith.

4:45

Kapo Porzyczki returned from the North Camp with the prisoners who had been chopping wood there. Hot on his heels was SS Sergeant Friedrich Gaulstich. Solomon, who was still waiting for Frenzel, saw the Nazi. Since he had no idea why the German came into the yard — he usually worked in the office, and the Jews hardly ever saw him — he called to him from the doorway. "Herr Oberscharführer, I'm not sure about the rest of these cabinets," he said. "I need your advice. The lazy Jews are standing around doing nothing. Can you come in for a minute?"

Gaulstich hurried toward the barracks. Kapo Spitz tagged along. If the Jews weren't working, a Kapo might be needed to whip them into shape. Pechersky dashed out of the carpenter shop. Spitz was a threat. They were less than an hour away from the escape. They couldn't take a chance.

"Get Spitz out of here," Pechersky ordered Porzyczki. "Fast! Don't let him go into the barracks."

"Hey, Spitz," Porzyczki called. The German Jew turned around. Porzyczki grabbed him by the elbow. "Don't go in there," he whispered.

"Why? What's going on?" Spitz tried to pull away.

"If you want to live," the Pole warned, "don't stick your nose into this. Most of the Germans have been killed. We're watching your every move from every barrack. I'll slit your throat." Porzyczki jabbed a knife into Spitz's ribs, just far enough so that the Kapo could feel the point.

Spitz quivered but obeyed. A Russian joined the two Kapos in case they had to take care of Spitz right out in the yard.

When Gaulstich stepped into the barracks, Solomon moved quickly from behind the door and sliced him with the ax. The Russians dragged the Nazi into a corner and waited for Frenzel. Drescher had gone to the German a second time to remind him he was needed in Camp I, but Frenzel hadn't made a move to follow the Putzer.

Meanwhile, Beckmann was still in his office in the Administration Building. He had gone in at three-thirty, after he had refused to look at the leather coat, and had not come out again. Feldhendler had decided it would be best to kill him even though there were Nazi bedrooms in the Administration Building. It was close to roll call time, and Feldhendler didn't want to risk the SS man getting suspicious now, when they were almost ready to launch the escape.

Kapo Porzyczki's younger brother rapped on Beckmann's door; Chaim and another Jew stood to the side.

"Yes?" Beckmann shouted.

"This is Porzyczki. We have a problem in the warehouse. Can I come in?"

"Yes, yes, come in." Beckmann sounded impatient.

The three Jews entered the office and closed the door behind them. Beckmann was standing in front of his desk. He seemed surprised that three men came in, but he was not alarmed. His whip and pistol hung at his side. Porzyczki was well known in Camp II because of his brother.

"What is it?" Beckmann said. "What — "

Porzyczki grabbed the Nazi's right arm, hammer-locked it behind his back, yanked his pistol, and spun him around to face Chaim and the other Jew.

Chaim began to stab Beckmann as he struggled in Porzyczki's grip. Beckmann's eyes widened in disbelief. As the dagger began to plunge, he screamed and squealed.

"For my father!" Chaim shouted as he slashed. "For my brother! For all the Jews!"

Blood spurted over Chaim's face and jacket. Twice, he hit bone. The knife bounced back, cutting his own hand and wrist. Soon it was quiet. The three Jews dragged Beckmann's body behind the desk. There was no time to hide it or wipe up the blood.

Selma stood in front of the medicine shed. Between worrying about Chaim and being frightened of dying, she thought about her cousin Minnie. Selma had stopped in the laundry to see her earlier in the day. "I have some nice fresh mushrooms," her cousin had said. "I'll fix them tonight. Come over and have some, and bring Chaim." Selma had wanted to tell her about the escape, warn her to wear warm clothes, to bring food or money. But Chaim had told her to keep the escape a secret. Grateful that at least she and Chaim knew, Selma felt guilty about not telling Minnie.

Selma had watched Chaim, Porzyczki, and the other Jew walk over to the Administration Building, and she had sensed that something important was going to happen. Then she heard screams from inside, piercing, squealing almost like a pig in a slaughterhouse. She fought for breath. "Oh, my God! My God!" she kept saying. "Chaim! Chaim!

While Beckmann was screaming, a truck turned the corner and headed toward the Administration Building. Erich Bauer was behind the wheel. Selma held her breath, as if her breathing would spook Bauer. He's bound to hear, she thought. "Oh, my God! My God! Chaim! Chaim!"

5:00

Kalimali and Kapo Bunio returned from Camp II. The young Russian went right over to the carpenter shop to report to Pechersky. "We finished off four," he said. "The telephone wires are cut. The electricity is off permanently."

"Where are the pistols?" Pechersky asked.

"I have one. The other three are still in Camp II. Feldhendler is waiting for the bugle call."

"Send Solomon out," Pechersky ordered. "You stay inside."

Pechersky stood at the crossroads alone. What should he do about Frenzel? Wait for him? Send him another message? Sound the bugle and play the rest by ear? If Frenzel came into the yard for the roll call, they could finish him then. Pechersky leaned toward waiting a little longer. Solomon disagreed.

"The devil take him," Leitman argued. "Sooner or later, he'll get what he deserves. It's time. Every second is precious now."

Pechersky stopped and listened for a minute. The guards in the towers didn't seem to think anything was amiss. There were no Nazis in sight. The sky was getting cloudier, as if it were about to rain. Pechersky took a deep breath and nodded to Porzyczki. This was it.

"Now!" Porzyczki called to Judah, the barber. He climbed the foresters' tower, fondled his bugle, then blew it for the last time.

The Jews in Camp II poured out of the barracks and warehouses and began to line up haphazardly. And just as Bauer passed Beckmann's office in the truck, Chaim came out and joined Selma. Bauer didn't see him.

Chaim was covered with blood, and shaken. "Beckmann," he said as Selma desperately tried to wipe the blood from his face, hand, and jacket. Then she tore a handkerchief and tied the cuts on his left hand and wrist.

There were no Germans or Ukrainians around in Camp II; Porzyczki and Bunio were already in Camp I. Feldhendler was worried that it might look strange to the Ukrainians in the towers if no one led the Jews to Camp I. Everything had to appear normal, the Politruk had warned him.

"Line up," Feldhendler shouted. "Line up." He waited. "March," he shouted. Then he began to sing:

Es war ein Edelweiss,
Ein kleines Edelweiss.
Hol-la-hi-di, Hu-la-la.

Four by four, they headed for Camp I. The formation was ragged. There was tension in the column, but nothing appeared out of the ordinary to the guards in the towers.

Just before the bugle sounded, Shlomo cornered two Putzers who were cleaning the Ukrainians' barracks. When they saw him come out of the officers' quarters, they became frightened.

"I'm going outside, and I'll stand under the window," Shlomo told the boys. "When I say so, hand me my blanket."

They knew what was wrapped inside. If the Nazis caught the Spengler smuggling guns, they would kill them, too. So they refused.

"You'd better!" Shlomo flashed his knife. "Or I'll kill you both."

When Judah sounded the bugle like an archangel, Shlomo walked out of the barracks and stood under the window. "Now," he said. The Putzers handed him the pipe and rifles in the blanket, and he slung them over his shoulder, just as he had done when he had left Camp I. As he walked briskly to catch up with the column marching back, he didn't see a German or a Ukrainian. But his pulse still raced. If he could just make it through the first gate. If he could just make it down the corridor. If he could just make it through the gate into Camp I. Then he'd be safe.

Chapter 31

5:05

SHLOMO was too excited to feel lucky when he finally reached the kitchen, where Jankus, Moses, Nojeth, and a half-dozen Russian POWs were waiting. He unwrapped the guns and emptied the bullets from his pockets.

He was so excited and pleased with himself for stealing the guns that he decided to keep a rifle for himself.

"I got them," Shlomo told the Russians. "I want one." He held the Mauser tightly.

"You don't even know how to shoot the damn thing," one of the Russians said.

"I don't care. Show me how."

"We'll make better use of it."

"I don't care. Show me how to shoot the damn thing."

They did. And before they left to join the other Russians, Shlomo loaded the rifle and filled his pockets again with ammunition. Then he turned to his family. "We'll all stick together." He had a gun now, and he would protect them. They waited in the kitchen for the roll call whistle, which would signal the march to the main gate or, if the Politruk decided, a break for the fences.

Esther, Bajle, Eda, Hella, Zelda, and half a dozen other women waited in the laundry. Esther had been working in the garden that day, but she left early — just in time to see Niemann enter the tailor shop — to make sure she wouldn't be left out when the action started. She didn't think her chances of survival were good, but she had had a strange dream the night before. And the dream had given her hope.

Her mother had walked into the barracks, in her dream, and stood next to Esther's bunk. "Mama, you know we're going to escape tomorrow," Esther had said. "I don't know if I'll make it."

"Follow me," her mother had said. She led Esther through the main gate to a barn on a farm that Esther recognized. "Stay here," her mother had said. "Here, you'll survive."

As Esther waited behind closed doors for the signal, she made up her mind that if she ever got to the woods, she'd head for that barn.

Toivi stayed in the yard, drinking in the excitement and watching the Politruk. The yard buzzed. Some of the Jews were already lining up for roll call. Those who knew about the escape were telling others. Some ran inside the barracks to hide. The yard was a bowstring waiting for the archer.

5:10

There were still five minutes to go. The plan was to blow the whistle fifteen minutes before roll call. Kapo Porzyczki would then lead the Jews toward the main gate. Frenzel was still nowhere to be seen. Nothing unusual seemed to be happening in the towers or anywhere else, as far as Pechersky could tell. He couldn't believe his luck; he never had thought he'd see five o'clock without the Nazis opening fire. But the yard was ready to explode. He couldn't risk waiting any longer. "This is it," he told Porzyczki. "Now."

When the Kapo blew the whistle, Kapo Spitz went to pieces. "It's not time for roll call," he began to shout at Porzyczki, as if he were angry that the Polish Kapo had exceeded his authority. "It's not time yet!" Porzyczki slipped a knife into his stomach to shut him up.

Sasha recognized there could not now be an orderly march to the main gate. It was time to surprise the Nazis and Blackies by stampeding the fences. He jumped up on a table and shouted. "Our day has come. Most of the Germans are dead. Let's die with honor. Remember, if anyone survives, he must tell the world what has happened here . . ."

Just as Sasha was finishing his little speech, a Ukrainian in Camp II ran up to Erich Bauer, who was standing on the back of his truck supervising Jacob and David, two young boys he had commandeered after the bugle call to unload cases of vodka.

"*Ein Deutsch kaput!*" the Ukrainian screamed. "*Ein Deutsch kaput!*"

Jacob and David bolted like deer. Bauer opened fire. He got David, but missed Jacob.

Almost at the same time as Bauer fired, a Jew shouted, "Hurrah! Hurrah!" and a tornado hit the yard. Jews ran in all directions. One group, including Esther, Mordechai, Hella, Zelda, Eda, and Abraham, headed for the fence behind the carpenter shop. Like Crusaders attacking a castle wall, they threw up the ladder the carpenters had left in the weeds, and began to stream over the fence.

Several hundred others surged for the main gate, yelling, screaming, shooting into the air, clubs raised. They ran straight into Albert Kaiser, a Ukrainian guard on a bicycle who was pedaling toward the Camp I gate and shouting something that sounded like "Hey, you sons of bitches. Didn't you hear the whistle?"

The first Jews to meet Kaiser knocked him off his bike and slashed him with knives. One of the Jews close to Toivi cut off the guard's belt and took his pistol.

By the time the mob reached the Officers' Compound, the mines began to explode in the south field behind the carpenter shop. Then the Ukrainians opened fire. One of them shot Esther, who had already crossed the minefield and was fighting, half out of breath, to run a few hundred feet more to the forest of the owls.

Russians armed with pistols and two rifles assaulted the armory, but Frenzel, who was hiding behind a barracks, opened fire on them with a machine gun. The Russians retreated and tried a second time, but Frenzel held them off. They headed for the fence.

The rest of the Jews, a crazed mass by this time, a body without a mind, rushed the main gate. A German with a machine gun opened fire on them, too. Those up front wanted to turn back. Those in the rear kept pressing forward, afraid they would get shot in the back. The fences began to fall under the weight of the Jews, who could almost taste freedom. Toivi was in the crowd, close to the front. As the Jews behind him pushed, he fell, pinned to the barbed wire.

Sasha looked for Luka, but the mob had swallowed her. Shlomo lost Jankus, Moses, and Nojeth. Eda and Itzhak were separated. But Chaim was still holding tightly to Selma's hand.

As the mines in the field to the right of the main gate began to explode, a small group of Jews with wirecutters snipped the barbed wire behind the Merry Flea and the Swallow's Nest, crawled through the fence, and fled across the field. As Sasha had predicted, there were no mines there.

Soon it was quiet, except for the shouts of the Nazis and Ukrainians and the groans of the wounded. One hundred and fifty-nine Jews were still inside Camp I, trapped there by fear or by a decision to stay behind where it might be safer. Dead bodies were stretched on the barbed wire like scarecrows. The yard in the Officers' Compound was strewn with at least a hundred dead and dying Jews. The fields were dotted with bodies and pieces of bodies.

But in the woods, panting, too frightened to feel happy, were three hundred Jews. All alive and free.

The Forest

Chapter 32

Sasha

S ASHA led the attack on the arsenal. SS Corporal Karl Werner Dubois, recently transferred to Sobibor from Belzec, tried to stop the Russians single-handed. A Russian clubbed him, nearly knocking out one of his eyes. He fell and played dead. Then Frenzel opened fire with a machine gun. Sasha and his men scattered for cover behind the garage and the Ukrainian barracks. He fired at Frenzel with Fallaster's pistol, but missed.

Sasha saw the fence to the right of the main gate collapse like cardboard under the sheer weight of more than two hundred men and women. He saw three or four Jews cutting through the fence to the left of the main gate, where there were no mines.

Some of the Jews, including his own men, were caught in the yard of the Officers' Compound, afraid to run out or back to Camp I, trapped by their own indecision. "Run!" Sasha shouted from behind the garage. "Run! Don't just stand there!" He watched them scatter.

Sasha took one more shot at Frenzel, but missed again. Then he darted across the Officers' Compound to the Swallow's Nest. Before he crawled through the hole in the fences that some of his men had already cut, he took one last look at Sobibor. Crouched in the sand on one knee and aiming a rifle at a watchtower was Shlomo, the little goldsmith. Sasha heard him fire and saw a Ukrainian go down. He wasn't sure whether the guard had been killed or wounded, or whether he had just ducked as the bullet whizzed by. There was no time to find out. He crawled through the fences and ran across the field without mines.

When Sasha reached the woods, he stopped to catch his breath and to look back. Men and women were still racing across the three hundred yards of open field, most trying to run in a crouch. Bullets kicked up the dirt around them. Some fell.

Sasha began looking for Luka. He hadn't seen her since the mob swallowed her. Had she made it? Was she still in the woods? He waited for a few moments to see whether he could spot her crossing the field. Then, as he searched the edge of the woods, hoping to find her sitting by a tree, panting for air, he stumbled on Boris and Arkady Vaispapir.

"Where's Luka?" he asked. "Did you see her?"

"No," they told him.

"And Solomon?"

"Him neither."

When the last shadows in the field reached the woods and Luka wasn't among them, Sasha, Boris, and Arkady began running again, deeper into the forest. It was raining lightly now. The dogs would never be able to sniff them out. Behind him, Sasha could still hear shots. The Germans are probably killing the wounded and anyone else they can find, he thought. Trying to keep the sounds to his back, he kept running. Soon the gunshots became weaker and weaker, then stopped. The forest of the owls was silent, except for the sound of other Jews crashing through the trees all around him. Sasha could hear them stumble, curse, cry out.

When the shooting began again, Sasha knew that the Germans were sweeping the forest for lost Jews. The hunt was on. Darkness and a good head start were on his side.

Around seven o'clock, seventy-odd Jews had gathered in a clearing. Sasha took stock as he rested. Besides himself, there were two other Russians in the group. Among them, they had five pistols and two rifles. Sasha wasn't sure he could control such a large group of undisciplined Jews, but he would try, even though it would be dangerous. He owed them that much.

It was time to move on. Where to, Sasha wasn't sure. He had no idea where he was. It had stopped raining, but the sky was cloudy, and there were no stars to guide him. Whatever he did, he thought, he'd have to inspire the others or they would panic.

"We'll walk all night," he announced. "Single file. No talking, no smoking, no lagging behind. We're not stopping for anyone. No running ahead. I'll lead. Boris and Arkady will follow me. If the man in front of you hits the dirt, hit the dirt. If the Germans shoot flares over us, hit the dirt immediately. No one must panic. We'll protect each other. *No panic,* no matter what."

With Sasha in the lead, the long line began to pick its way between the trees. By now, the sky had cleared. A harvest moon, like a bright kerosene lamp, cast dull yellow patches on the forest floor. Around midnight, Sasha heard airplanes overhead. Using the North Star as a compass, he steered south.

It wasn't working, as Sasha had known it wouldn't. The Jews behind him were whispering from fear. Every once in a while, someone who had strayed from the line or had fallen behind would shout, "Moshe, where are you? Josef, where are you?"

They would have to break into smaller groups or no one would survive, Sasha thought. As it was now, they were like geese in a barnyard. Sasha would wait at least until he knew where he was and until he had taken them farther from Sobibor so that they would have a chance against the Germans. He was a soldier, not a nursemaid. He had gotten them out of Sobibor, but he would not spend the rest of the war leading them around the forest. He would cross the Bug, find the Red Army, and kill more Germans.

From time to time, another Jew would find Sasha and the others. "Did you see Luka?" he'd ask. "Did you see Solomon?"

"No," each would say before staggering into the line.

Suddenly, they were out of the woods and in an open field that stretched for two miles in front of them. Still in single file and with the moon as their flashlight, they began to cross the field. Halfway through, they bumped into a canal, five or six yards wide. Sasha fell to the ground, and those behind followed like dominoes. "Check it out," he ordered Boris.

"It's too deep to wade across," the scout said when he returned. "I saw some men about fifty yards to the right."

"Have a look," Sasha ordered Arkady.

The Russian slithered away on his belly. The other Russians waited, pistols drawn.

"Sasha, Sasha, they're ours!" Arkady was excited. "Kalimali is there. They're floating across on stumps."

Sasha managed to bob his whole group to the other side. He was relieved that they had found the stumps, even though the ditch was only fifteen to twenty feet wide, because he couldn't swim and he didn't want his men to know that. It was his job to worry about them, not theirs to worry about him.

"Did you see Luka?" Sasha asked Kalimali after he had crossed. "Solomon?"

"I didn't see Luka," the Russian said. "But I found Solomon. He was shot trying to cross the field. He got about a mile into the forest, but had to give up. Just couldn't run any farther. He begged Feldhendler to shoot him. He wouldn't. Feldhendler took him along."

The news tore into Sasha like shrapnel. To break out of that hell, to skirt the mines, to cross the field, to smell the pines, and then to be too helpless to run the rest of the way to freedom. As a soldier, Sasha knew Solomon would never make it. He'd either slow the others so they'd all get caught, or he'd bleed to death or catch pneumonia or turn gangrenous.

They were like brothers, he and Solomon. Together they had created the whole escape plan, piece by careful piece pasted together out of whispers in the night as they lay side by side in the crowded barracks. Solomon's clear mind, his courage and serenity, his loyalty, had buoyed Sasha. With Solomon, he had shared the fear, the loneliness, the responsibility. Solomon had given him strength and hope. Now he, Sasha, was free, and the skinny Warsaw Jew was near death. It wasn't fair. It wasn't fair. But how like Solomon to ask to be shot rather than risk the lives of the others or falling into the hands of the Nazis again. He had always wanted to die on his terms, not theirs. And he would. At least Solomon had been granted his death wish.

And Luka? Had she been shot, too, wounded in the field like one of the rabbits she tended? Sasha touched the shirt she had given him. She had trusted him so much, his defiant little Luka with the chestnut hair. Was she dead, too? Now he was glad that he wore her gift next to his heart.

There was no time to think of her or Solomon. There was nothing he could do for them, but he could still help the others. He gave the signal to move on, and they trudged another three miles before they heard the rumble of a train. They were standing in a treeless field dotted with leafy shrubs. It began to drizzle again, and daylight was trying to break through the crust of the horizon. Sasha hit the ground. It was October 15.

Boris, Arkady, and Kalimali slithered over to him. "They'll be after us as soon as it's light," Sasha whispered. "What do you think we should do?"

It was an easy decision. The woods around the field were a thin line of birches and scraggy pines. The Nazis would have no trouble quickly combing them clean. An open field next to the railroad would be the last place the Nazis would look for runaway Jews. The best thing they could do would be to lie motionless under the bushes, camouflaged by the branches, resting, sleeping, waiting. But first, they would scout the fields and tracks.

Sasha and Kalimali broke to the west, Boris and Arkady to the east. Sasha and Kalimali covered about five hundred yards before they hit a farmer's field. Beyond it, the woods were thick again. They crept back.

Half an hour later, Boris and Arkady returned. "The tracks are a hundred yards away," Boris reported. "To the right is the station, about half a mile down the tracks. Between where we were and the station are some Poles. They're working on the tracks. We didn't see any Germans or Ukrainians guarding them."

Sasha spread the word to the others to take cover. Then he sent two scouts to creep close to the station and to report back immediately if anything suspicious was happening. He changed the guards every three hours.

As he rested under a bush, Sasha could hear the Poles pounding on the tracks. Every now and then their voices floated across the field, low and muffled. Airplanes buzzed overhead all day, but no Nazis came close to the field. No one but the scouts moved until dark.

At nightfall, when all was still, the Jews crawled out and stretched. They were rested, but wet and hungry. Boris was running a fever. Just as they were ready to move out single file — Sasha and Boris up front, Kalimali and Arkady in the rear — two men came weaving across the field toward them. Two crouched shadows in the moonlight. From the way they approached, Sasha could tell that they were not Germans, but men on the run. As the other Jews hid, Sasha and the Russians waited to pounce on them.

They were two more Russians from Sobibor. "We reached the Bug," they told the Politruk.

"Why didn't you cross?" Sasha asked.

"Some farmers told us the Germans were crawling all over the place. They fanned out late last night. All the bridges are heavily guarded."

"Did you see Luka?" he asked. By this time, the question was automatic.

"Yes," one of the Russians said. "In the woods with some Polish Jews. They said they were going to try to make it to Chelm."

Sasha's heart leaped against Luka's shirt. He felt younger and lighter and happier. She was alive. Breathing free air again, like him. Where was she now, he wondered. Who was leading her to Chelm? Did he know the way? Would she make it?

He could go home now, across the Bug, back to the Red Army, to fight for Russia, for Luka, for all the Jews.

After walking most of the night, they stopped at the edge of the forest, opening onto another meadow. Long before daybreak, Sasha gathered the Jews around him. "We'll break into small groups," he told them, "then scatter in different directions. It will be our only chance. That way we'll draw less attention. Some of us will make it."

He could see they were frightened. He, his soldiers, and their guns had given them a false sense of security.

"I'll take a group to reconnoiter," he said. "I'll find out where we are and buy some food. I'll need some money."

He passed his pointed Russian army cap, and the Jews tossed in gold, rubles, zlotys. Then he chose nine men to take along — all of the Russians and all of the guns but one. He'd be back soon, he said.

But he wouldn't. As a Russian just a few miles from his homeland and as a soldier a few hundred miles from the Red Army, he felt he had no choice. Besides, what more could he do for them? He had gotten them out of Sobibor. He had led them away from the Germans. They were free and as safe as he could make them. They had survived before he met them. Now, they'd have to survive after he left them.

Again using the North Star as a guide, Sasha led his men east, toward the Bug. Once he found the river, he'd wait for the best time and place to cross into the Ukraine.

Before long, he spotted a village. At daybreak, when the cottage lamps began to flicker in the windows and the dogs to greet the morning, he and another Russian knocked on a door for food and directions.

"Be careful," the farmer said. He quickly closed the door behind them. "There was an escape at Sobibor, where the Germans burn Jews. The Germans are searching everywhere."

Sasha didn't tell the farmer he was a Jew and that he had a nodding acquaintance with the camp. If the farmer thought he was a Russian partisan, so much the better. There would be no telling what the man might do if he suspected the officer was a Jew.

The farmer told them where to go, how to get to the Bug, and which villages to avoid. "Go to Stawki," he told them. "It's next to the river, and the farmers there will help. They hate the Germans."

Sasha paid the farmer for the food and led his men back into the woods to wait for night. It was October 16.

On the evening of October 19, they reached Stawki, a hamlet less than a mile from the river bank. Sasha and two of his men approached a one-room cottage. The others waited nearby, ready to fire one shot if there was trouble.

The room was flooded with warm lamplight. A young man about twenty, with long, light hair tumbling over his forehead, stood behind a table cutting tobacco, his shirt unbuttoned. In one corner, a crib hung from the ceiling with a string stretching to the floor. A young woman was rocking it gently, her foot tugging the string as her hands plied the spinning wheel. By the stove in another corner sat an old man.

"Good evening," Sasha said. "May we come in?"

"Come in," the woman said in perfect Russian.

"It might be good if you covered the window," Boris suggested.

"It could be done," the woman said.

The old man spoke up. "Take a seat."

The woman, her husband, and her father-in-law waited for Sasha and Boris to explain why they had come. "Perhaps you can tell us where we can cross the Bug?" Boris asked.

"I don't know," the husband said.

Sasha turned to the old man. "You, Pop. You've been around so long, you must know. They say that near Stawki there's a shallow spot."

"Well, if that's what they say, then why don't you go there?" the old man said. "We don't go to the river much. They won't let us. Rest a while. We're not rushing you. But we don't know a thing."

They talked for an hour. Sasha told them that he and Boris had escaped from a camp, and they wanted to go home now. They had no reason to fear, he said.

"My son had escaped from a POW camp, too," the old man said.

"Listen to me, Pop," Sasha said. "If your son escaped, it was because someone helped him. Why not help us?"

The old man gave in. "All right, we'll show you," he said finally. "But if you're caught, you never met us."

"Agreed," Sasha said.

The young man took over. "I won't lead you all the way to the river, but I'll point the way there. You won't have any trouble finding the spot. But I warn you, the shore is patrolled. There was an escape from a camp not far from here where people are turned into soap. The Germans are searching under every rock.

"If you make it, you'll be lucky. I hope you do, from the bottom of my heart. But if you don't, please don't get us all killed. That's all I ask."

"My friend, and you, Pop," Sasha said, "how can I find the words to thank you? I can never express what I feel." He paused. "Let's get going before the moon rises."

"Wait," the young woman said. "I want to give you some bread to take along."

241

Sasha took the bread and thanked the woman, and the old man made the sign of the cross over them like a priest.

The young man led them east toward the river for about fifteen minutes. Then, after giving them specific directions, he left. They found the river within five minutes. The bottom was muddy, and when they tried to walk, air bubbles fought to the surface, creating a sound like a plunger in a clogged sink. They moved to another spot.

Sasha waded to the middle of the river. The bottom was stony, the water waist-deep, and the current swift, flowing north, a black tugging streak. Sasha paused and listened for voices or footsteps. He was more frightened than when he had shot at Frenzel and crawled through the fence behind the Swallow's Nest. If he told his men he couldn't swim, they would insist on carrying him across. That would make them even more conspicuous. He'd take his chances with the current. As he stood in the middle of the river, thirty yards from either shore, he motioned his men to follow.

When they reached Russia, Boris was in bad shape, shivering with high fever. Sasha knew his friend was too sick to go on. He probably has pneumonia already, Sasha thought. If he started to cough, he could give them away. If he didn't, he would probably die in the cold.

Sasha left Boris with a friendly farmer. Boris was in Russia now. He was safe, even though he was behind the German lines. The Ukrainian farmers would nurse him until he was strong enough to find his way to the Red Army or the Russian guerrillas fighting behind the German lines.

Within a week, Sasha and his men found the partisans. Their leader searched and interrogated Sasha for hours, then for days. The leader couldn't take a chance. He had to satisfy himself that Sasha was not a deserter and that he could be trusted, for the lives of his men and their guerrilla operations depended on it. In the end, the leader welcomed Sasha and his men into the group. There were over a thousand guerrillas in the unit, and the leader assigned Sasha to a group of four hundred. The other Russians he kept with the main group.

Sasha became part of a demolition team that dynamited German troop trains. When the Red Army came closer, he fought the Germans from behind while the Red Army attacked from the front. Then, under orders from headquarters, his unit broke through the lines and joined the Red Army.

Four months later, Sasha stepped on a mine, almost blowing off his right leg. In a hospital far behind the lines, it was touch and go. But the surgeons saved his leg, and when it had healed, they sent him home to Rostov and to Ela. He still wore Luka's shirt.

Chapter 33

Toivi

SOMEHOW Toivi found himself between the two fences to the right of the main gate. He didn't know how he got there and didn't care. All he knew was that he had only one more fence to get through, and he'd be out of Sobibor. Nearby stood Shlomo, rifle tight against his right shoulder, coolly trying to pick off a Ukrainian from a watchtower, like a farmer shooting a pigeon off his roof.

Someone just in front of Toivi beat a hole in the barbed-wire fence with a shovel. Toivi's head and shoulders were through the opening when the Jews behind him rushed the fence. Some tried to climb over it; others washed against it like a tidal wave. The fence collapsed, leaving Toivi with his face in the sand and his leather coat, which he had selected with care for the escape, snagged by a hundred barbs. Feet raced over his arms and back. Moments later, mines began to explode in front of him.

While stragglers jumped the barbed wires around him, Toivi slipped out of his coat. It hung on the fence as if someone had just tossed it there to dry. Toivi ran straight for the woods, crossed the mine belt covered with little craters and dead Jews, past the signs saying DANGER — MINES. He fell once, twice. Each time, he thought he had been hit. When he finally reached the forest, he looked back at Sobibor. The field was empty now. He had been one of the last Jews to cross.

Toivi found Sasha and followed him through the forest, to the railway tracks, and across the canal. Like the other Jews, he was frightened when

Sasha left to buy food and get directions. He waited in the woods until dawn. It was obvious that the Politruk was not going to return and that the rest of them would have to split into small groups, too.

As young as he was, Toivi understood one thing clearly — his escape from Sobibor had just begun. Most Poles would turn him in without a scruple. And most partisans would kill him rather than let him forage in their turf or take him in.

The Jews argued. The older and weaker ones wanted to team with the younger, more resourceful ones. And the younger Jews didn't want to be slowed down by older men who wouldn't take chances, who would try to boss them around, and who would spend most of the time complaining. Toivi decided to team with little Drescher, Wycen, the seventeen-year-old lad with whom he had worked in the incinerator, and Kostman, who was twenty-one.

After tramping through the woods for a short while, Toivi and his three friends saw smoke rising from a clump of cottages. The boys began to argue. They were lost and hungry, but should they risk knocking at a door? Would the Poles turn them in after taking their money? How would they defend themselves, without a gun? All they had were knives.

Little Drescher was in no mood to quibble. He left the others and knocked on the first door he came to. Toivi watched from the woods. When Drescher came out of the house, instead of returning to the others, he kept right on going. In a way, Toivi was relieved that Drescher had deserted them; the boy was so young and so small, he would have become a problem sooner or later.

After trudging for another hour in the early morning light, Toivi found a lonely cabin and a barn at the edge of a field. The three boys were no longer as frightened as they had been. For several hours now they had been on their own, no Sasha to protect them. They had survived, and they grew more confident with each hour. Besides, they desperately needed to know where they were.

They knocked. When no one answered, they walked in. There was just one room with a table, two chairs, and a bed. On the down quilt stretched a tomcat; under the quilt a boy lay sleeping. After all those months at Sobibor, the cabin looked like a palace to Toivi. He wanted to crawl under the quilt and sleep until the war was over. He even envied the cat.

A young woman came in and, without seeing them behind the door, walked over to the bed to awaken the boy.

"Good morning," Toivi said. Startled, she turned to face him.

"Good day, gentlemen," she said in formal Polish.

"We would like to buy some food."

"As you see, I am poor," the woman said. "I live alone on this farm without a husband. But I'll give you what I can."

She brought bread and milk. When they drained their tin cups, they asked for more. Saving just enough for herself and her son, she filled the cups again. Kostman offered her a gold ring to pay for their breakfast.

"What for?" she asked. "For the food? Nonsense. You were hungry. I fed you what I could."

They pressed her to take the money. After all, she was poor, they said. She had a son to support. A war was on.

The mother seemed insulted. "Jesus said, 'Give food to the hungry, water to the thirsty.'" She waved away the ring.

As they got up from the table, the woman said, "I suppose you boys are from Sobibor, where they burn people. They searched the next village yesterday. You'd better get away from here."

"How far are we from the camp?" Toivi asked.

She knitted her brow and stared at a spot on the wall as if she were trying to add up the miles. "Sobibor . . . Sobibor . . . Must be about two miles. On a clear day you can see the foresters' tower there if you stand behind the barn."

Toivi felt weak. He had run and crawled and stumbled through the forest for four full nights — almost eighty hours — only to find that he could see Sobibor from where he stood if the sky was clear. He felt like crying, like screaming. They'd never make it now. Never! But he was not about to give up.

"How do I get to Lublin from here?" he finally asked the woman.

The three boys hid in the woods until dark. Toivi took charge. This was his part of Poland. He knew the towns and cities; he knew the roads. He decided to head for home, for Izbica, as if something invisible were drawing him there. At least he knew people in Izbica, and he was more certain he could find someone to hide him there than in a strange village.

They hit the highways. It was fast, though risky. Yet certainly not more risky than running in circles in the forest where he didn't know a soul. On the blacktop, Toivi knew exactly where he was and where he was going. The two boys followed him.

By midnight, they found a road sign: IZBICA, 12 KILOMETERS. Only seven and a half miles, and Toivi would be home again. Not that he had a home to go to anymore, with his mother, father, and brother all dead.

But just the thought of being surrounded by the familiar was comfort to the boy. From here on, Toivi knew the road the way he knew the streets in the shtetl.

They burrowed into a haystack to sleep the rest of the night away and to stay dry, for a steady fall drizzle had begun to chill them, and Toivi did not have a coat. The next morning, they slipped back into the woods until they reached the outskirts of Izbica. Toivi suggested that he visit an old family friend in the Christian part of town and offer her a large sum of money if she'd hide them. She had known and respected his father, Toivi explained. She was a good and honest woman. Kostman and Wycen agreed, but first they stripped Toivi of all his gold, money, and jewels, lest he be tempted to desert them as Drescher had done. Wearing Kostman's coat, collar turned up to hide his face, Toivi walked into Izbica.

The boy hardly recognized the shtetl. The Christians had dug up the yards and torn up the homes, looking for hidden treasure. They had stolen the furniture and dishes, the doors and the window glass.

"Who's there?" the family friend asked when Toivi knocked.

"My God!" she said when he told her. "Go away. I'm afraid."

"Please . . . Open the door."

The bolt slid back and the door opened a crack. "What do you want?" she asked.

Toivi told her he'd pay her a great deal of money if she'd hide him. She said she would never take money from him, but neither would she hide him because she was afraid of the Germans. They would kill her if they caught her. A neighbor could turn her in.

Toivi asked her for food. She brought him a crust of buttered bread. When he tried to put it in his pocket so that he could divide it later into three equal parts, she objected.

"Eat it now," she said. "Right here. Or give it back."

She was afraid that someone would catch him, she explained, and that he would say where he had gotten the bread. Then they would drag her off and shoot her. Toivi ate the bread, thanked her, and threaded his way back to his friends.

Early that night, the three boys broke out of the woods less than a mile behind Izbica, crossed a wagon-rutted dirt road, and crawled to the lip of a hill. About three hundred yards away stretched an orchard, a cottage, and several small barns. As they approached the farm, a dog began to bark. The cottage was empty, lamp-lit, and a bowl of soup was on the table. The boys looked into the barns and stables, stood in the yard, and called, "Anyone home? Anyone here?"

When no one answered, they went back into the house and, standing, ate the soup. "Let's go," Kostman said, worried that they might get caught. The dog was still barking outside. The feeling was eerie. As they left the cottage, Toivi spotted a flashlight beaming in the bushes.

"Farmer!" he called. "Farmer!"

A tall, broad-shouldered man stepped out. His name was Bojarski. When he saw that they were only boys and probably Jews, he called to his wife and daughter. The girl recognized Toivi, with whom she had gone to the public school.

Bojarski invited the boys inside for supper. Toivi asked him to hide them. They'd pay, he said.

Bojarski hesitated. They should go back to the forest, he said finally. He'd consider the deal and give them an answer in the morning.

Just after dawn, they crept back to the farm. Bojarski gave them breakfast, hid them in a pile of straw, and brought them lunch. That night, after a bath and supper, Toivi spread part of their loot on Bojarski's table — diamonds, gold, platinum jewelry. German and American paper money, rubles, francs, guilders. That, added to what Toivi didn't show the farmer, amounted to several hundred thousand dollars. Bojarski's eyes grew bright with greed.

The girl tried on several rings; the woman, diamond earrings. But Bojarski still couldn't make up his mind. The risk was great, and there was no telling how long he'd have to hide the boys before the Russians came, he said. He needed one more day. They could sleep in the straw pile.

At midnight, Bojarski woke them. "All right," he said. "The Russians will be here soon."

After they gave him about one quarter of their money, Bojarski led them to an outside corner of his barn, yanked a plank from the wall, and told them to crawl inside. He had made a den for them. The roof was a tabletop covered with straw; the back and two sides were a thick pile of straw; the front wall, the side of the barn. The floor was covered with leaves.

Things went smoothly for three weeks in the den, where they lay or crouched. Bojarski fed them regularly; at night, he let them out into the yard to exercise. They paid him to buy them a down quilt, a kerosene lamp, and cigarettes. But when they asked him to lead them to the partisans so that they could fight the Germans, Bojarski stalled. He didn't know anyone he could trust, he said. It would be very dangerous to try. He had his wife and daughter to think about.

The boys became suspicious and concluded that he didn't want them to leave their nest until he had bled all their money from them. Before long, Bojarski was asking whether he could "borrow" a pair of boots, a jacket, a shirt. He never returned them, and soon all they had between them was underwear, trousers, and one sweater.

One night, they heard the dog bark louder and longer than usual. Voices filtered through the barn wall from Bojarski's house. Then, several people entered the barn and began poking the straw with a stick and tossing things around.

"Any strangers here?" a voice asked Bojarski.

"No," the farmer said. "No one."

"Then why do you seem so rich lately?" the voice asked, "and so well dressed? Everyone can see it. They want their share. Come on, give us the Jew. We'll finish him off."

Bojarski began to cry, and between his sobs he kept swearing that he wasn't hiding Jews.

Toivi knew that if the men in the barn found them, they'd kill them all, including Bojarski, for their money. The men continued to probe their nest, and every now and then the stick would break through the straw into their room and wiggle in front of their noses as they lay pressed against the barn wall. Had they come so far, survived so long, only to be shot by greedy, Jew-hating Polish Christians? They didn't pray. They didn't dare move. They breathed as quietly as they could and waited. When the dog stopped barking, they knew the men had gone.

Bojarski returned. "You see now?" he complained. "A bit longer and all of us would have been killed. What do we do now?"

Toivi told him that the men were clearly convinced that he wasn't hiding anyone, and that they would never return. When Toivi offered him more gold and promised to give him the title to his house in Izbica after liberation, the farmer quieted.

Then one day Bojarski crouched next to the hideout and whispered that the Russian front was approaching and the Volksdeutsche were fleeing Izbica. The Russians will be here soon, he said.

As the days crawled by, Toivi could hear guns in the distance, then a silence broken only by the occasional barking of Bojarski's dog. It was just Russian partisans, the farmer explained later. He was so upset and angry that he no longer allowed the boys out at night, and he began to feed them only once a day. The boys kept track of time by placing straws in a jar.

Christmas came and went. When the boys ran out of kerosene and cigarettes, Bojarski refused to buy more for them. They begged him to lead them to the partisans or to someone who would, but Bojarski refused. What could they do? They had no clothes. It was winter. They'd freeze. The farmer could track them in the snow if they ran. Besides, where would they go? No matter how bad Bojarski became, he was still all they had.

Bojarski became more and more unpredictable. One day he would bubble with enthusiasm. "Boys, I'm with you all the way," he'd say. "I'll keep you until the Russians get here. They've started their offensive. If everything goes well, they'll be here in two weeks."

Another time he'd be low. "If I'd known this would last so long," he'd complain, "I'd never have taken you in . . . What a shame and a disgrace it would be for my family if people knew I was sheltering Jews."

The boys knew it was a game, a sick trick to squeeze more gold out of them. They paid, and paid gladly all winter, for they preferred to dribble him the money than to have him rob and kill them, as most other Poles would have done. They felt lucky. They had a den. They were strong. They'd outlast the farmer. And besides, their supply of gold and diamonds and guilders would stretch longer than the war.

It was five months since they had stood up straight, walked in the yard, smelled fresh air, bathed, or even seen the sun. None of them had gotten sick. They continued to ask Bojarski to return their clothes, to let them into his house where they could wash and shave, to give them a gun and let them go. One day he'd promise them everything but the gun; the next, he'd say no. They sensed that he was reaching a decision; that his greed and fear were gnawing away at his patience. But they had no choice. Money was their only protection. It was also their worst enemy.

It was April 23, 1944. They had lived in the den for five and a half months. The Russians hadn't yet crossed the Bug River. That night they were unusually hungry, for Bojarski hadn't fed them for several days, and he had pounded nails into the boards, sealing them inside their pen. They were now in a prison, and Bojarski was their jailer. It was late, but Toivi couldn't sleep as he lay next to the outside wall, dreaming of hot bread and listening to the wind whistle through the cracks. Without a shirt to wear, he was getting cold, so he tried to snuggle between Kostman and Wycen, as he used to do in the dead of winter. But Kostman wanted more room. They exchanged places. Before the boys could drift back into sleep, they heard footsteps in the yard. Probably Bojarski, they thought. He must be bringing some food. Maybe he wasn't such a bad fellow after all.

The footsteps stopped at the outside entrance. Kostman, next to the wall, stretched on his stomach to peek through the peephole they had dug in the straw. Someone began to rip off the boards. Then there was absolute silence, as if Bojarski were listening for the sound of their breathing. They waited for the farmer to whisper.

A gun exploded, and Kostman screamed, "Goddamn!" He lay on the floor, gurgling as if he were drowning, and, thrashing in the grip of a convulsion, sprayed blood all over Toivi and Wycen. They pressed into a corner. Kostman became silent, and in a moment of total shock and terror, they realized he was dead. Would they be next? Maybe whoever shot Kostman didn't know there were three of them. Maybe he would leave. Just go away.

They heard the footsteps again, then voices. Someone began to strip away the straw around them. Like two mice, they burrowed deeper and waited.

"They aren't here," a voice said.

Toivi could feel the straw being pulled from around him.

"I got one," someone said, flashing a light in Toivi's face and thrusting a pistol against his head.

"No, please," Toivi pleaded. "Please! Let me live!"

The young man with the gun looked him straight in the eyes. "Where's the first one?" he asked.

"Dead."

"And the other one?"

"Next to me."

Toivi heard the gun explode. His ears went deaf, and he felt a hot poker of pain under his jaw. Without a moment's thought, almost as if he had been doing it all his life, he closed his eyes and let his body go limp. Seconds ticked by. He felt no pain, not even panic. He wasn't sure whether he was dead or alive. His uncle had once told him that for three days after you die, you can still hear and feel. Was he dead, then?

Toivi opened one eye a slit, just enough to see the man who had shot him talking with another man. Should he ask the man to finish him off? It would be better than dying slowly or being buried alive. He continued to play possum.

Someone slipped a noose around his feet and dragged him through the hole in the barn wall. He was blocking their way to Wycen. Lying on his back in the mud, a cold rain washing his chest and stomach, he watched the silhouettes digging into the den. He sat up until he heard footsteps, then dropped back into the mud.

"Might be better to give him another bullet," Bojarski said.

Toivi recognized the farmer's voice and tried to stiffen his body like a corpse. Would he ever be able to control his trembling? They'd feel him. They'd know he was still alive.

The man who had shot him bent down to put his hand over Toivi's mouth. Through the slits in his eyelids, the boy saw the hand coming and held his breath until he thought his chest would split. The man released his hand and checked Toivi's fingers for rings.

"Let's not waste a bullet," the man told Bojarski. "This one's stiff already." He walked back to the hole in the barn wall.

Toivi began to shake uncontrollably in the mud, from relief, from fear, from cold. He saw others in the yard, including the plump shadow of Mrs. Bojarski. There could be no escaping now. He'd have to lie there and wait. Maybe they'd just leave him in the mud and rain until daylight.

"Don't shoot!" he heard Wycen cry. "Don't — "

Three loud shots, a scream, then a muffled shot and silence. The men dragged Toivi into the barn and rolled him face down on the floor. The blood from the wound in his jaw began to flow freely. He heard the men overturn the tabletop (their roof) as they rummaged through the straw like children on an Easter egg hunt.

"We'll go through the Jew rags tomorrow when there's light," someone said. "They won't rot. We'll search the straw then."

Before they left, they pulled off Toivi's pants.

"Kostman? Kostman? Are you still alive?" Toivi whispered in the straw. He found the body, and touched it. His friend was still. He pulled the bloody overalls off Kostman's body and wriggled into them. Then he dug into the straw for Wycen, who had kept most of their money and valuables in a leather purse. After four shots, Toivi thought, Wycen was surely dead.

Toivi found Wycen face up. As he leaned over the body to roll it so that he could get into Wycen's pockets, Toivi thought he felt some breath.

"Shmuel, are you still alive?"

Wycen's eyes popped open. "Oh, it's you," he almost shouted. "I thought it was them."

"You okay?" Toivi asked.

"Yes," he said. "Only one bullet hit me."

"You got the money?"

"I buried it in the straw."

They dug for the purse and, when they found it, crawled out into the rainy night and ran to an abandoned brick factory in Izbica, where Toivi used to play as a boy. It seemed so long ago. Only when they reached the factory did they sit down to rest. Toivi felt his jaw. The bleeding had stopped, and there was only a small hole. He figured that the bullet had ricocheted from his jawbone back into the straw.

Toivi looked at Wycen's wound. The first three shots had missed the boy, but he had screamed anyway to make it sound as if he had been hit. The fourth shot had burrowed into the knuckle of his index finger as he had covered his face with both hands. An eighth of an inch of the bullet stuck out of the bone.

The boys knew they were lucky. They knew that if they could avoid infection, they would live. They also knew that Bojarski would be combing the town and the forests for them. They were witnesses to a murder, and they still had money.

Toivi and Wycen decided to split. That way, if one got caught, at least the other could still get away. Wycen headed back into the woods. (Toivi would never see him again.) Toivi knocked on the door of Roman, a Catholic schoolmate with whom he used to play. Roman talked his father into hiding Toivi in the barn. They brought him food, iodine, and bandages.

Three months later, in July 1944, the Russians came. Soldiers in green, walking, riding bikes, in jeeps, on tanks with lids thrown back. The Germans had fled west to the next town, to other fields. It was over. Toivi was free. He had survived, as he had always felt he would.

But for what? For him, there was no more Izbica. His mother and father were dead. His brother, whom he had loved so dearly, was gone, a handful of ashes in Sobibor. He had no relatives. He was one of the last Jews of Izbica.

Toivi had dreamed so long of this day, hoping to see the green uniforms, to watch the Germans run, to hear the tanks and the airplanes overhead, to smell the victory. He should have been dizzy with joy. But all he felt was a profound sadness.

He was empty and alone.

Chapter 34

Esther

When the Jew cried "Hurrah! Hurrah!" and Camp I exploded, Esther had to make a quick decision. Should she follow the mob toward the main gate or head for the south fence behind the carpenter shop?

She chose the carpenter shop. Someone — Esther wasn't sure who — flung the ladder against the fence. She scampered up like a squirrel and jumped. Her close friend Samuel followed. She crossed the ditch on a plank and squeezed through the second fence. Samuel followed. The mines in front of her began to explode, and she prayed that God would help her step in the right spot.

The Ukrainians opened fire on the crouched figures in the field. Most of the Jews did not zigzag like soldiers. They headed for the woods like arrows. Esther felt pain sear through her hair just above her right ear. Blood began to trickle down her neck. She didn't know how badly she'd been hit, only that the pain disappeared quickly and that the warm sticky blood kept flowing.

Esther began to feel sick and weak. She reached to hold on to the girl running next to her. "Leave me alone!" the girl screamed as she pushed Esther away. Esther stumbled forward. "Leave me — " As bullets tore into her, the girl fell on the field.

Esther kept running until she broke into the woods. Samuel looked at her wound. The bullet had just grazed her, leaving a little ridge above her ear like a furrow in a newly ploughed field.

Nine other Jews, all trying to decide what to do, where to go, how to foil the Nazi chase, joined Esther and Samuel. The others who had made it over the fence behind the carpenter shop had scattered. Esther told them she didn't care what *they* were going to do, but she intended to go to Janow, where a friend owned a large farm. That's what her mother had told her to do in a dream, she said. That's where her mother had promised she'd be safe.

It was irrational to stake her life on a dream, Esther knew. But this was no time for logic. She had followed her instincts ever since the Germans invaded Poland four years ago, and she was still alive. She would follow her instincts now.

The other ten Jews — all men, including Samuel — couldn't come up with a better plan, so they tagged along. Esther had told them that if they made it to Janow, which was close to the Staw work camp, the farmer would hide them. At least they had a definite place to go and the name of a farmer who would not betray them to the Germans. What more could they ask?

They began running, walking, resting. When they felt lost or discouraged, the men would complain. "You're going to get us all killed, looking for that farmer," they'd say. But they followed her anyway. Once they met what appeared to be friendly partisans. Some of the men wanted to join them, but Esther refused. Her mother had told her to go to the farm, she said, and to the farm she would go. They tagged along.

After three nights of wandering and two days of sleeping, they found an isolated farm at the edge of Novosiolki. It was Sunday morning, October 17. The eleven Jews caucused in the forest. Should they ask for food? Should they ask the farmer to hide them? They decided that only three should approach the house. If the farmer saw eleven, he surely would send them away. And if he betrayed or killed the three, the other eight would be free.

Esther, Samuel, and Avram knocked on the door. The farmer made the sign of the cross and invited them inside — quickly, so that no one would see them. He knew about the escape from Sobibor, he said. He was just on his way to Sunday Mass. Would Esther like hot water to wash her bullet wound? He'd be back soon.

Esther cleaned the scab matted with hair. Samuel cut her pigtails and clipped the hair around her ear. Then they waited. Was the farmer looking for the Germans or the Polish Blue Police? Was he selling them for a kilo of sugar? Or would he really help them? They waited.

When the farmer returned, he dabbed Esther's wound with salve and invited the Jews to join his family for a huge Sunday morning breakfast.

"Will you hide us?" Esther asked after they had eaten. "We have money."

"Yes." The man did not hesitate. It was as if he had expected the question.

"First," Esther said, stubbornly, "I have to go to Janow to a farmer. He's a friend. Can you show us the way?"

"My son will take you to the main road," the farmer said. "If that farmer doesn't want you, you come back here. I'll hide you."

Esther offered him money, but he shook his head. He made the sign of the cross over them again before they left so that God's power would protect them against the Germans they both hated. On the way to the main road, they stopped in the woods to pick up the other eight men, but they were gone. Esther figured that they had thought that she, Samuel, and Avram were dead or had deserted them, and that they had struck out on their own. She hoped they'd find friendly partisans. As for her, it was Janow. Esther thanked the farmer's son, and the three Jews waited in the woods for nightfall.

It took them eleven nights to walk to the farm owned by Stefan Marcyniuk. After World War I, he had escaped from a Communist prison and, almost penniless, had lived in the attic above the flour mill owned by Esther's father.

"How are you going to make it?" Esther's father had asked him one day. "You live in an attic. You don't have a job. Your wife is expecting a child."

"I don't know," Marcyniuk had said. "I'm a baker by trade. If only I had half a sack of flour, I could bake bread and sell it."

"I'll give it to you. Pay me back when you can," her father had offered.

In a few years Stefan Marcyniuk had become one of the richest men in Chelm. The farm in Janow was one of his investments. He and Esther's father had become as close as brothers. To the two religious men, it made no difference that one was a Jew and the other a Christian. They respected each other's religious beliefs, their children played together, and their families celebrated religious and secular holidays together. Esther knew Marcyniuk would welcome her as if she were a lost daughter.

When Esther found that no one was home at the Marcyniuk farmhouse, she knocked on the caretaker's door. The man thought they were partisans. "Take anything you want," he told them. "Just don't shoot me."

Esther caught on quickly. It was better that he believe they were partisans than Jews. "I'm not looking for you," she said. "I'm looking for the owner. I'm going to kill him."

"Why? What did he do?"

"None of your business. Where is he?" Esther demanded. "We have something to settle."

"He doesn't live here. He just comes once or twice a week."

"All right, then give us some bread and we'll be off."

It was a beautiful farm, huge by Polish standards. A wooden fence enclosed the farm itself, which opened onto a tree-lined dirt road. The farmhouse had two stories, with a single dormer poking out the roof. Surrounding the house were a large barn filled with straw, a cattle barn, and two chicken coops. In the square that made up the barnyard sat two haystacks. And beyond the barns and yard were the well and two ponds and a string of other buildings.

Esther suggested that they hide in the large straw barn. From there, they could see the yard, house, gate, and road. "We'll wait for him," she said.

For three days and nights, they watched and waited. They saw partisans creep into the yard to steal chickens and eggs. Samuel was getting edgy. "Let's go with them," he suggested. "At least we'll have a chance to make it."

"Go if you want," Esther said. "I'm waiting here." Samuel stayed, for Esther was his rabbit's foot. In Sobibor, she had saved his life twice in one day.

*

Samuel was working in the stable, feeding and grooming Cilly, the mare, and Emil, the gray gelding. Wagner found some of the gold Samuel had stashed in the hay. Wagner also suspected that two cooks were planning an escape, so he concluded that all three were plotting together.

Wagner strode into the barracks where Esther was working. "I just killed two from the kitchen," he told her. His boots were flecked with blood. "Next — Solomon."

Solomon was Wagner's nickname for Samuel.

"If you kill someone, I'm sure you're right," Esther said to calm him. For some strange reason, she could talk to the unpredictable Nazi and he listened. "But why Solomon?"

"Money in the hay," he said. "An escape."

"Why would Solomon want to escape? He has it so good here. Food and nice clothes. What would he eat if he escaped? What would he do? He can't even read."

"So smart," Wagner said. "You're trying to confuse me."

"No, I'm not."

"Why the money?"

"Solomon never had money before," Esther said. "Maybe he just wanted to hold some real money in his hand. Besides, you don't even know for sure that he's the one who took it."

Wagner's anger drained in the presence of Esther's logic. He ordered Samuel to load all the hay back into the barn by himself before nightfall. It was an impossible job.

Esther cornered Wagner later in the day. "The horses have to go into the barn to eat and sleep," she reasoned. "They're hungry. Samuel can't get the stable ready for them."

"So?"

"Nothing. It's just that the horses are standing out in the cold. Look at them! Maybe someone should help Samuel so the horses don't get sick."

"Get help, smarty," he said. "Trying to confuse me again?"

*

Samuel had never lost his faith in Esther's uncanny knack for saying the right thing at the right time. He wasn't about to leave her now.

On the third evening, Samuel went to a neighboring hamlet to buy milk, bread, and vegetables. It was dark as a well when they ate, sitting on top of the straw piled twenty-five to thirty feet high, almost to the peaked roof of the barn. Samuel reached for the second bottle of milk. When he couldn't find it in the dark, he and Avram slid down the pile to hunt for it in the straw or on the floor.

"I found it," Samuel called up to Esther in Yiddish.

Just then, someone reached out from the straw like an octopus and grabbed Esther. "Who is it? Who is it?" she cried. She was frightened out of her wits.

"Never mind who," a voice answered in Yiddish. "Just sit still and be quiet."

"Idel?" she asked. "Idel!" She was shocked. It was her brother's voice. She was certain of it. For almost a year now she had thought he was dead, caught by the Nazis after he had escaped from the Staw work camp. "It's me, Esther."

Twisting her arm behind her back, the man held a knife to her throat. "You're going to sit right here until daybreak. If your friends try anything — "

Esther waited and prayed. When light seeped through the barn cracks, dusty and dull as fog, the man studied her features. "Esther," he said, over and over. "Esther." He hugged her. He ran his hand over her cheeks

257

and her cropped hair. They held each other like lovers and cried.

Esther told Idel about her dream. He told her how he had escaped and walked to the farm as she had, and how Marcyniuk, who had feared he was dead, had received him as if he were his son.

He told her that, like a beaver in a pond, he had built a house under the straw. He lifted a wad of straw from the top of the pile like a cork from a bottle. Inside, he had dug five tunnels. Three went to the barn walls so that the fresh air could come in and he could see out. A fourth ran to the front of the pile, which faced the barn door and the floor below. The fifth was a shaft plunging straight down the center of the pile to the floor, where he had dug a room four feet into the earth. In that room, lined with feed and flour sacks, he slept.

"When Marcyniuk comes," Idel explained, "I'll tell him you're here with a boy friend. I won't say there's another man. We'll share the food he gives us."

Esther slept on a cloud of love that night. She had Idel back. She was warm and safe and had food. Her mother had been right. In the barn, she would survive.

The next day, Stefan Marcyniuk whistled outside the barn. It was his signal that he was back and the coast was clear. Idel told him about Esther and Samuel. He knew that his friend loved Esther, but would he accept Samuel? Would he take a risk on a complete stranger?

Marcyniuk folded Esther to his chest. Yes, he had heard about the escape from Sobibor. Who hadn't? But he had long given her up for dead. Of course she could stay. And her friend, too. "If God has put us all together," he said, "I won't divide us."

The winter and spring passed peacefully. There was just enough space in the room under the straw for the four of them to sleep side by side. Marcyniuk or his son brought them food and news about the war. The front was moving closer to the Bug. The Russians would be in Janow soon.

One day, late in June, when the wheat was already high, the nervous Germans bivouacked in Marcyniuk's barnyard. Esther and Idel, Samuel and Avram took turns watching their every move. The situation was dangerous. Even if the Germans didn't discover them, they knew the Wehrmacht was following a scorched earth policy wherever it could. They feared that the soldiers would burn the wheat and the beautiful farm rather than leave them for the Red Army. And a haystack afire would be worse than a bullet in the back.

"The first chance we have, we'll run," Idel ordered. He had become their leader now. In their basement room, they kept a three-day supply of food, in case they might have to flee their nest. But before they could bolt, a gun went off. Two German soldiers had been sitting in the yard cleaning their rifles. One of the guns fired, and a soldier bit the dust. From where he was watching, Idel couldn't tell whether it was an accident or murder. Neither could the other Germans, who set up a military commission to investigate the shooting — right in the center of the barn. All day long, German officers called in eyewitnesses to the shooting, one by one. Then, late in the afternoon, one of the officers thought he heard a noise in the straw. He ordered some noncoms to start ripping apart the pile. The Jews drew their knives. At least they would take a couple of Germans with them. They had surprise on their side. But when the Germans didn't find anything suspicious, and when they saw that the straw was packed as tightly as silage, they gave up.

That night, as the Germans continued their interviews, Idel motioned to the others to slither quietly into the basement bedroom. There was nothing they could do but sleep. If the Germans were going to burn down the barn, their underground den would be as safe as any place in the straw. Besides, if they lasted the night, they'd be rested and fresh in the morning to run — if they had the chance.

Idel was the first to wake up. The barn was as still as a meadow. He motioned to the others that he was going to crawl up to see whether the Germans had gone. Esther shook her head, afraid the Germans would hear the straw rustling. A minute later, Idel noisily slid back into the cellar grinning.

"They're gone. Let's go, too."

Carrying their emergency rations, they jumped to the barn floor, where they found three rifles, three loaves of bread, and three tins of onions. Scooping up the extra food and the guns, they ran into the wheatfield behind the barn.

"Let's stay here and get some sun," Esther suggested. Their faces and arms were as white as a bride's veil, and she was afraid that if they had to melt into the countryside, they wouldn't blend. Like seals warming themselves on a rock, they sunned themselves pink.

Suddenly, gunfire shattered the hot July day. Machine guns pounded around them. Grenades exploded to the front and the rear. Artillery whistled overhead. The Germans and Russians were having it out again, and they were trapped in the middle.

Idel and Esther, Samuel and Avram were so used to crises by this time that they didn't bother to panic. If they were going to be killed, what

259

better way than by a bullet shot from an unknown gun, sudden and easy. They lay in the wheat, waiting, listening, trying to figure out who was winning.

Just before nightfall, they heard dogs barking and Germans shouting. "Run . . . Quickly . . . Move it . . . Get going . . ." Then, the only sound was wheat whispering in the wind.

At dark, they crept back to the barn, where Marcyniuk was poking in the straw and calling "Idel? Esther?"

"I thought they'd got you," he said when he saw them. His face broke into a smile of relief. "Better get back inside for the night. You'll be safe until morning."

The next day, just after dawn, he returned. "I've dug a bunker for you in the woods," he said. "The Germans are burning everything in sight."

They lived underground in the woods until the Russians and Germans decided to fight somewhere else; then they returned to their straw nest. Hardly had they settled into their old routine when a company of Germans, driving five hundred Ukrainian slaves whom they had snatched from their farms to dig trenches, bivouacked in the barnyard. The fence around the farm made a neat little prison, and the Germans couldn't pass it by.

The Ukrainians were so exhausted that most of them just plopped down in the yard. A few came into the barn to pull straw for beds. The Jews waited in their bedroom. They were certain that this time the Germans would burn down the farm. After a few minutes, the German in charge called the Ukrainians to attention. The men in the barn filed out.

"This is it," Idel whispered. "Let's get out of here. Let's run out the back for the field."

He pushed out the straw plug.

"Are you hiding from the Germans?" a tired Ukrainian asked.

Idel almost dropped his knife, he was so startled. "We have knives," he warned the man. "If you try anything, we'll kill you."

"Oh, don't worry," the Ukrainian said. "I hate them more than you do."

Idel relaxed. "Can we give you anything? Some food?"

"Bread," the Ukrainian said. "Go back inside. I'll keep a lookout for you. Don't worry."

Soon the other Ukrainians returned to the barn and continued tearing at the straw for bedding. One of the tunnels collapsed, but only the Ukrainian who had talked to Idel noticed.

"Hey, you want some bread?" he called to the others.

They almost attacked him. "Where did you get it?"

260

"I found it sitting here," the man said. "The owner must have slept here last night."

"Let's pull out the rest of the straw. Maybe he hid more inside," they said.

"Forget it," the man said. "I looked carefully. This is it."

The Ukrainians shared the bread and rested in the barn for three more hours. Then, late in the afternoon, the German officer called them to attention once again.

"Listen, we're leaving," the man told the straw. "I'll stay here until the last minute. Don't worry! And good luck."

"Would you like some money or some more bread?" Idel asked him.

"I can't take it. It would make them suspicious."

Idel peered through the cracks in the barn wall. The Ukrainians were lining up. Someone called to the man in the barn.

"Just a minute," he shouted back. "I have to fix my shoe. My feet are swollen."

When all the others had lined up in formation, the man walked out of the barn, then turned as if he were looking for something. He nodded so slightly that if he hadn't been looking for it, Idel would never have seen it.

The next day, Marcyniuk shouted to them. It was over. The Russian front had moved past them during the night. They were free.

Chapter 35

Shlomo

SHLOMO fired four shots, but didn't wait to see whether he had hit the Ukrainian in the tower. He hugged his Mauser, crawled through the hole in the fence behind Sasha, and ran to the woods as fast as he could. After he caught his breath, he looked around for Moses, whom he had seen dart safely across the field. He had also seen Nojeth, Jankus, and Bajle go down. He assumed they were dead.

When he couldn't find Moses, Shlomo ran after Sasha. There was no time to feel angry or lonely. He hoped that Moses would make it somehow. The Politruk was his hope now, and he followed the Russian deeper into the woods.

When Sasha went off on the pretext of searching for food and directions, a Russian demanded Shlomo's rifle. The goldsmith refused. He had earned it, he told the Russian. He, not the Russian, had smuggled it out. He had fought his way out of Sobibor with it and had carried it through the forest. It made him feel important and safe.

"But you don't know how to use it," the Russian objected.

"You're going to have to fight for it," Shlomo warned. He pressed the gun tighter to his chest.

"Then come with us," the Russian invited. He could see that the boy was serious. The Russians could use all the guns they could get. Maybe the boy would give it up if he were separated from the Polish Jews.

But the Polish Jews protested. "Let him stay," Leon the blacksmith said. "We need at least one gun. What if someone attacks us?"

The Russian agreed.

Until the Politruk returned with food, Shlomo would be the new leader. It was ridiculous, Shlomo thought. One gun to protect sixty people. Well, it would be only for a few hours. Then the Politruk would take command again.

Before dawn, while the forest was still black, Shlomo heard gunfire about two miles away, coming from the direction in which the Politruk had gone. Shlomo waited and the Jews argued. Some said the Russians had been killed. Hadn't they heard gunfire? Others were convinced that the Politruk had deserted them. What should they do?

Shlomo suggested that they break into smaller groups, as the Politruk had suggested before he had left. But there was great confusion and a hail of protest. Everyone wanted to cling to Shlomo, since he had the only gun and more than twenty rounds of ammunition. "Forget about the Politruk," Shlomo told them. "Forget about crossing the Bug. We're Poles, not Russians. If we stay together, we'll draw too much attention. We'll get caught and killed. Then there'll be no one to tell the world about Sobibor. Besides, as a group we'd never be able to agree about where to go next. Smaller groups can make that decision easier."

The Jews agreed with Shlomo in principle, but began to argue about who would go with whom. Eventually, Shlomo ended up with seventeen men (the largest group), including two blacksmiths and two tailors. The other forty-two Jews broke into smaller groups and struck out on their own.

Since he had no plan, Shlomo wandered through the woods by night and slept by day, until he heard diesel motors. He told the others to lie low while he crept to the road. He saw trucks and soldiers. The Germans began shouting orders and shooting into the trees. Shlomo hurried back to the other Jews, and they buried themselves as deeply as they could under branches and leaves.

The Germans swept the forest, crashing quickly for two or three hundred yards right past Shlomo and his men, then slowing down and firing ahead of them as they walked in a straight line. Shlomo listened for cries of pain from the wounded. But since there were no noises other than Germans walking, shouting, and shooting, Shlomo concluded that the soldiers were blindly searching for Jews, hoping the gunshots would frighten some into running.

The Germans passed Shlomo a second time as they returned to the road. They were walking quickly now, talking among themselves and not paying attention to where they were stepping. Shlomo could hear them pile back into their trucks and move off to another part of the forest. He lay still until nightfall, when the forest was quiet. He knew that if he had not been so close to the road — the least likely spot for a runaway Jew to hide — the Germans surely would have caught him.

Late that night, Shlomo found an isolated house at the edge of the forest. Determined not to be caught by surprise, he circled the house several times, rifle ready, flashlight shining in his hand. The two other Jews with him had their knives drawn. When the coast looked clear, Shlomo broke into the house and searched it room by room. The only person he found was a frightened old man. "Don't shoot," he cried when he saw the gun. "Don't kill me."

"We're partisans," Shlomo said. "All we want is food. We won't hurt you."

The old man quieted and gave Shlomo the stale bread he had begged that day. Shlomo and the others pounced on it. Other than leaves, it was the first food they had eaten in four days. Shlomo gave the old man a gold coin and left.

Later that night, the eighteen Jews bumped into a swamp so large they couldn't find their way around it. It was drizzling, and there was no moon to silhouette the reeds and trees. All night they waded through mud and high grass, lost, thirsty, and almost crazed with hunger. By daybreak, they found a high, dry spot in the swamp, from which they could see a hill and trees straight ahead. They knew they'd be out of the mud the next night, so they made beds of grass and slept peacefully. No one would ever think of looking for them on an island in a swamp.

The next night they trudged once again through the mud, stumbling on mounds and into sinkholes. Leon the blacksmith had an old bullet wound, and his leg was throbbing so badly that he could barely walk; Shlomo's new boots had shrunk so much that he got blisters. He took them off and walked barefoot.

Before morning they broke out of the swamp, climbed the hill, and walked through a woods carpeted with pine needles and birch leaves. The more they walked, the thinner the woods became, until they could see light ahead of them through the birch branches. Shlomo crawled on his stomach and parted the leaves.

His heart sank. About three hundred yards in front of him stood the foresters' tower, the main gate, and the south fence. He was back at Sobibor.

Five nights of running, of fear and fatigue, of pain and hunger, and he was back, standing barefoot, at the edge of hell. Now what would he do?

Shlomo crept deeper into the woods; he couldn't bear to face Sobibor. Just being close to the camp made his skin crawl in fear. But after his emotions settled enough to free his mind, he began to think through his latest problem. Maybe it was fortunate that he had run in a giant five-day circle. Where would the Nazis be least likely to look for him? Right across from the main gate, of course.

Shlomo and the other Jews rested all that day, and at night headed south, trying to keep the railway tracks to their left. Soon they found another isolated house at the edge of the forest. It was night, and Shlomo knocked.

"Who is it?" There was a noise as if people were scrambling to hide.

"Partisans," Shlomo said.

The door opened a lamp-lit slit. "Come in," a voice said. "What do you want?"

"We need food," Shlomo said. "And directions. Where are we?"

"Near Sobibor."

"I heard there is a camp there," Shlomo said innocently.

"Yes. I don't know much about it," a Pole explained. "A lot of trucks and trains go there. At night the sky is bright all around. I hear it's a work camp."

"What's going on there with the fires?" Shlomo asked.

"I don't know exactly. But it's strange. The Germans just ordered sixteen coffins for the place a few days ago."

Shlomo wanted to smile and slap his knee, but he controlled himself like a wise old partisan. One thing was certain — the coffins weren't for the Jews.

"You won't have any trouble hiding in the forest," the Pole said. "There are a lot of partisans around. You'll be able to find a larger group."

Shlomo and the others ate some of the food and kept the rest as reserves. They knew it would take them days to get to Lublin, where they had decided to go for want of a better plan, and the fewer doors they had to knock on, the safer they'd be. They would avoid all towns and villages if they could. If they had to buy food, they would approach only isolated homes at night. That way, they'd run less risk of being betrayed; and if they were, they'd have a head start on the Germans and the Polish Blue Police.

Before dawn, they camped near a lake, and when it was light, they saw a lone Pole approaching. "Can you help us?" Shlomo asked. "We're partisans and we want to join up with a larger unit."

"I'm a partisan, too," the Pole said. He had a pistol tucked in his belt. "I'll tell my group about you. I'll come back tomorrow and let you know if they'll accept you. Wait here. Rest."

"Can I buy your pistol?" Leon asked, offering the Pole a fistful of gold, ten times more than the gun was worth. The Pole agreed.

Shlomo was peeved. "Now he knows we have a lot of money," he chided Leon after the Pole disappeared into the forest. "He'll probably come back to rob and kill us. I don't think we should wait around. I don't want to be a dictator, but I just don't trust the man. I'm leaving. If the rest of you want to stay, then stay."

All but Leon agreed to leave the lake. "I want to join the partisans as soon as I can," he said. "This is the best offer we've had. Besides, all the Poles have been good to us so far. I'll take my chances with this one."

"Don't decide so quickly," Shlomo told him. He had admired and trusted Leon from the first day they met in the mechanic shop. It was Leon who kept urging Shlomo to escape. Shlomo didn't want to lose him now. "Just think it over while we rest."

"There's nothing to think over," Leon said. "I've made up my mind."

Shlomo and the sixteen other Jews left Leon by the lake and continued walking toward Lublin, crossing roads and railway tracks, always tramping in the forest at night. At Izdebno, not far from Izbica, Shlomo decided to approach another isolated house to buy food, because their supplies were low. He picked Mayer and Jankiel to go along.

After he had purchased the food and just before he reached the others, waiting in the woods, Shlomo heard loud voices. He knew it couldn't be the other Jews; they had agreed to talk only when necessary and then in whispers.

Shlomo slid on his belly toward the voices until he could make out forms in the moonlight. Twenty men in uniforms and with drawn guns had surrounded his friends. Their leader was speaking Polish. Shlomo hoped they were not Polish Nationals or Home Army partisans; if they were, his friends were dead.

What should he do? Hide until they were gone? Sneak away while they were still talking to the others? Could he desert them, his friends, after all they had been through together? Didn't they depend on him and his gun?

"We're also partisans," he heard the carpenter from Sobibor say. He didn't sound very convincing. "Our leader has a gun."

That was it! Shlomo didn't have a choice now. If the partisans hated Jews, they'd hunt him down for his gun and money. He slipped the rifle

266

in the bushes and walked into the circle with Mayer and Jankiel at his side.

"Put up your hands," the Polish leader ordered the Jews. He motioned his men to search them.

"You," he said to Shlomo after his men had taken the gold from their pockets. "Where's the gun?"

"Over there in the bushes."

"Get it."

It was hopeless to try to run. The Poles had him covered. And if he escaped, they would certainly kill his friends. He obeyed.

The Polish chief caressed the gun and fired a few shots into the air. Shlomo knew the Poles were going to kill him. They had his gold and his gun. Why would they spare him and the others? Shlomo tensed. He wasn't frightened now. All his senses were alert, ready for the worst, to run or to fight or to hit the dirt.

"Fire!" the Polish leader commanded.

Before the first shot could ricochet off the trees, Shlomo dove to the ground. Someone fell on top of him. He heard moans, death rattles.

"Let's go," the Polish leader said.

Shlomo heard the men snapping branches and crunching leaves as they moved deeper into the woods. He waited for what seemed like half an hour, until everything was perfectly still. None of his friends was moaning now, or twitching on the ground. He lifted his head slowly. Everything seemed safe. Then he stood. Mayer and Jankiel popped up, too. Like Shlomo, they had played dead. The other fourteen Jews were already cold.

Shlomo didn't bother to plan his next move. He, Mayer, and Jankiel just ran and ran as far from the Polish partisans as they could. Only when they were out of breath and their sides hurt did they stop and ask: What now?

Without a gun, it would be risky to ask Poles for food. They could be lucky and find a good one, but most probably they'd find Jew-haters. Defenseless and almost penniless, they'd be unable to appeal to the Poles' greed or fear. They'd have to live on the cabbage leaves and beets the rabbits and the farmers had missed.

Shlomo was deeply hurt. His gun had been the only true friend he had, part of his new life, the symbol of all he believed in now — hate and revenge. It had been his security, his hope, the source of his pride, his manhood. Everything had been against him but his gun — the cold, the mud, the uncertainty, the Germans, the Poles. If he had eaten, it was because of his gun. If he had gotten directions, it was because of his gun. And if the

Poles had not betrayed him, it was because they respected his gun. Wasn't there one Pole in Poland who'd help a Jew without a gun?

There was one, Jankiel said. An old Polish farmer who used to order clothes from Jankiel and his brothers. He was a good man, experienced and well traveled. He had even lived in America for a while, but had missed his farm so badly that he had returned to Poland. He would help. In fact, Jankiel and his brothers had made a pact that if they ever escaped from the camps, they'd meet at the farmer's house.

"I think I can find it," the tailor said. "Let's go there."

Jankiel rapped lightly on Josef Albiniak's window. When the old man recognized the tailor, he hugged him. "Come in, come inside," he invited the three Jews. After introducing them to his wife, children, and aged mother-in-law, and feeding them, Josef led them to his farm nearby, where he had built an underground bunker covered with hay for emergencies.

"How can we contact the partisans?" Shlomo asked Josef. The boy was determined to fight the Germans.

"It's difficult and you must be very cautious," Josef warned. "There are some Jewish partisans, but not around here. The others don't like Jews. They would probably kill you."

None of that surprised Shlomo.

"Your best bet is to join the Russian partisans behind the German lines," Josef continued. "They take Jews without a question. But it won't be easy to get to them. You rest first. I'll try to help you find them — if I can."

Shlomo, Mayer, and Jankiel slept all the following day. The next night, Josef brought them back to his home, where his wife had a banquet waiting.

"My sons," Josef said after dinner — his voice was serious and fatherly — "I'll hide you until the war is over, even if it lasts longer than I do. I want you to know that. When it *is* over, I'll travel the world with you. I'll tell everyone I hid three Jews, survivors of Sobibor. I would be proud to do that."

Shlomo was touched by the old man's kindness and courage. But he had made up his mind while still in Sobibor that if he escaped, he'd hunt and kill Germans. Although he appreciated the risk Josef was taking by keeping him, he was determined not to wait out the war hiding under ground or in a haystack, but to find a partisan group who'd give him a rifle or a stick of dynamite and show him where the Germans were. Since he and Jankiel still had some gold — the Poles in the forest had made a superficial search — Shlomo made a deal with Josef's sons-in-law — two gold pieces for a pistol. If he had a gun, Shlomo thought, the Nazis would never take him alive; he would not give them the final satisfaction of taking his life. He'd die on his own terms.

Shlomo asked Josef to buy him a pair of boots and some cloth, and Josef's wife to make clothes for him, Mayer, and Jankiel. With new boots and clothes, a pistol, and a well-rested body, he'd find the partisans even if he had to crawl to the Bug on his stomach.

One day soon after the three Jews had arrived at the farm, Josef told Shlomo that he wanted to build a room under his kitchen floor. The three Jews designed it — a four-foot-high cell with a small stove and ventilation pipe, a table, a lamp, and some chairs. The dirt would be buried under the compost heap in the yard.

When they moved into their new home, they stayed in the cell all day; at night, they joined Josef and his family, who were warm and friendly. They even seemed proud to hide three Jews. Sometimes Josef's two sons-in-law would come into the cell to talk about war, politics, and the future.

Whether at the dinner table or before the fire or in the hide-out, the conversation always returned to the partisans. Even Josef's sons-in-law tried to discourage Shlomo from leaving the farm. They were both members of the Home Army, they said. Their groups hated Jews. They'd kill Shlomo or turn him in if they ever found him.

But Shlomo wouldn't give up. "You're able to walk around freely," he said. "You can go from village to village and from city to city. Do you ever see any Jews?"

"No," they said, as if they had rehearsed their answer.

"Where are the millions of Jews?" Shlomo was shocked. He knew Jews were being killed at the other camps, but he had no idea of the extent of the slaughter.

"Most have been killed," one of the sons-in-law said. "Some are still in work camps. A few are partisans. A very few, like yourselves, are hidden."

The news hit the three Jews like a mudslide. They were discouraged, angry, sad. They argued and debated, and with each argument they became more determined to fight back.

Mayer was growing impatient. The long hours underground in a new prison were making him irrational. He told Shlomo and Jankiel that he knew a farmer not far away who he thought would hide him. He had made a pact with his brother, he said. If they escaped, they would meet there. Maybe his brother was free, too. Maybe he'd find him at the other farm. Then they could join the partisans together, side by side.

Shlomo and Jankiel tried to dissuade him. You'll never find a better

269

place than this farm, they said. You'll never find a kinder and more courageous man than Josef. Some Pole may catch you and kill you or hand
you over to the Nazis before you find your farm. If you do make it, the
farmer may betray you or turn you away. Stay with Josef. Here you're
perfectly safe.

Mayer wouldn't listen. So one night he thanked the farmer, said good-
by to Shlomo and Jankiel, and left. Shlomo would never hear from him
again.

Before long, the desire to kill Nazis and the feeling of confinement got
to Shlomo, too. He began talking about searching for partisans on his own;
it was clear now that Josef and his sons-in-law would not help him find a
group. He had a pistol, a little gold, good clothes, and perfect health. Besides,
he was beginning to distrust one of Josef's sons-in-law. It was just a feeling,
an intuition. He sensed that the man hated Jews as much as the other
members of the Home Army, but wouldn't betray him out of respect for
Josef. If the man could find a way to kill him without hurting Josef, Shlomo
was sure he would.

Jankiel argued with Shlomo, using the same points Shlomo had used
with Mayer. But in the end, they both agreed to leave. They felt like prisoners
again, and they knew that the Nazis could trap them any time. Was this
what they had escaped from Sobibor for? To hide in a new prison? To
wait for the Nazis to catch them? To depend on luck and the good will
of a family whose own lives hung in the balance? At least in the woods,
they'd be on their own, with fresh air and the sky above them. There,
they could fight back or run.

Shlomo went in one direction and Jankiel in another. (Shlomo would
never hear from or about him again.) The goldsmith felt confident, free,
and safe. He had a friend — his gun. And as his hatred drove him night
after night, he thought of only one thing — revenge. He'd find the Russian
partisans and he'd kill every German he saw. He'd drive them across the
Bug, across the tabletop flat plains of Poland, right to Berlin. Then he'd
piss on Himmler's desk.

Chapter 36

The Partisans

 IN OCTOBER 1943, there were two Jewish partisan groups with bases in the Parczew Forest, to which more than four thousand Jews had fled. One was led by Samuel Gruber (Mietek), the other by Yechiel Greenshpan (Chil). Besides being Jewish, Gruber and Greenshpan had one important thing in common: both had been corporals in the Polish army and had received military training.

Gruber was drafted in 1936. He loved the army so much that he wanted to make soldiering his career, but because he was a Jew his chances for acceptance into the officers' training program were slim. Instead, he joined a *hakhshara,* a farm that trained Jews for kibbutz life in Palestine.

When the Germans invaded Poland in 1939, Gruber was called up, wounded on the Slovak-Polish border, captured, and sent to Stalag 13A, outside Nuremberg. When the Germans told all Jewish POWs to step forward, Gruber tried to pass as an Aryan, but his fellow Poles turned him in. The Nazis sent Gruber to the Lublin ghetto, where the Judenrat assigned him to help the Germans build the concentration camp at Maidanek.

With escape in mind, Gruber managed to get himself reassigned to work in a hospital for wounded Germans. There, he began to steal the pistols of the soldiers who were on the critical list. Then, realizing that he and his friends could never escape from Lublin without the help of the Polish underground (he didn't know the forests), he asked the Poles to sell him guns, ammunition, and guides. The Polish underground agreed, promising to prepare a bunker in the Janow forest (close to where Esther would later hide).

Not trusting the Polish underground, Gruber sent an advance party of forty armed men to inspect the bunker and to buy the rifles. But when Gruber's scouts crawled into the dugout, the Poles tossed in grenades, opened fire, and robbed them of their pistols and money. Two of Gruber's men escaped back to Lublin.

With no other resources, all Gruber could do was try to work with the Polish underground once more. He and twenty-two men planned another escape attempt at the end of October 1942, about the time that Jan Karski was visiting Belzec, disguised as an Estonian guard. But Gruber still needed rifles, so he asked the underground to sell them. The Poles agreed, telling Gruber to send one Jew to a certain spot at a certain time. When the Jew appeared, the Poles robbed him and sent him back empty-handed.

Gruber still wouldn't give up. "I don't know about you," he told his men. "But I know about me. I'm leaving. I have a pistol and a couple of rounds of ammunition."

He filled a sack with bread and carrots, and hired two Poles as guides, figuring that they wouldn't try anything funny with twenty-three Jews (some with pistols) watching their every move. The Poles led the Jews to a forest just north of Lublin. There, the Jews adopted Christian names (Gruber took Mietek or Michael) and discussed their strategy. But before long, the two Polish guides began to needle the Jews. "Listen," they'd say. "You can't be partisans without even one rifle. Unless you can find a way of getting us some fast, we're leaving." So Mietek gave them the last of his band's cash, watches, and valuables to buy guns in Lublin. He never heard from them again.

As winter approached, Mietek forgot about fighting Germans and concentrated on surviving. Posing as Polish partisans, he and his men made contact with the farmers and villagers around the forest, developing a food and clothing supply line. And they accepted into their band a Jewish lad who had escaped from Maidanek inside a dung wagon.

When the Polish villagers found out he was a Jew, Mietek moved his men to a thicker forest east of Lublin, where it was safer for Jews. Hardly had they settled in it when they heard voices.

"Amcha?" Mietek called.

"Amcha!" someone answered.

Amcha ("Your people") was the password that the Maccabees had used when they fought the Syrians in the second century B.C. Persecuted Jews have often used it since then.

Mietek broke into a clearing in the forest, where he found a camp of a hundred Jewish men, women, and children who had escaped from the town of Markoszow near Lublin. Led by two Russian POWs, the Jews had rifles, pistols, and a machine gun. The younger Jews foraged for food; the others lived in forest bunkers.

Mietek was now ready to start fighting Germans. He understood full well the obstacles that Jewish partisans faced, the most serious of which was the Polish Home Army (Armia Krajowa) — an underground network of 270,000. Although the AK did not have partisan units in the fall of 1942 — its strategy was to arm and wait until the German occupation began to crumble and then to pour out of woodwork and haystacks — it had members in almost every village. One third of the AK had once belonged to the National Armed Forces, which were bitterly anti-Communist and anti-Semitic. Forced to choose between killing a Jew, a Communist, or a German, the Polish Nationals would pick the Jew almost every time. The rest of the AK were a mixed lot. Some hated Jews; others tolerated them; some welcomed them as freedom fighters against the Germans.

With few options open to him, Mietek made contact with Genek Kaminsky, leader of the Polish Communist underground, which welcomed Jews. Kaminsky told Mietek that the Poles around Lublin had pirated hundreds, if not thousands, of rifles when the Polish army surrendered to the Germans in the fall of 1939. Why not get guns from them and form his own all-Jewish partisan unit?

By threatening, begging, and beating, Mietek squeezed ten rifles out of the farmers. Then he sent his most Aryan-looking Jew back to the Lublin hospital to smuggle out more pistols. The Jew returned a few days later in an army truck driven by a German held at gunpoint. In the back of the truck were eighteen more Jews and a load of guns, blankets, and German uniforms. With a rifle and uniform apiece, Mietek and his band of forty were no longer Jews on the run, but partisans ready to fight.

Mietek faced a problem during that winter of 1942–43, when the snows were deep and footprints difficult to hide. The Polish villagers and farmers, who knew by this time that Mietek was a Jew, began to collaborate with the Germans against him. They set dogs on his men, organized defense teams to kill them, and rang church bells to alert the Germans or the police. Almost every day, Mietek would lose one or two partisans.

One night, a group of Poles attacked a party of Mietek's men who were foraging for food. All but two escaped. The Poles stood the two captured Jews against the wall and executed them. For Mietek, it was — finally — the last straw. He was armed and ready to fight the Germans who occupied

Poland and who were killing innocent Jews and Poles alike, but he couldn't, because he had to spend all his energy fighting Poles. It was time to take a stand, to teach the Poles a lesson.

Mietek and twenty armed men surrounded the village where the two Jews had been murdered, and ordered all the villagers into the square. Mietek made a speech. The Poles ought to be ashamed of themselves, he said. Instead of killing Germans who are raping their country, they are killing Jews, their own countrymen. The Jewish partisans are forced to make an example of the village. Everyone must leave.

Mietek and his men let all the livestock go free, burned the village to the ground, and spread handwritten leaflets over the countryside, explaining why they had burned the village and warning the other Poles to expect the same or worse.

Even though Mietek had guns and men eager to kill Germans, he did not have a real partisan unit; most of the Jews in his group and in the forest refugee camp were untrained, undisciplined, disobedient, and careless with their weapons. If he was going to fight, not just survive until the war was over, Mietek would have to whip his men into a tough, disciplined unit. He had heard that the partisans in the Parczew Forest just east of him were good guerrilla fighters and were well armed with guns and explosives. Maybe it would be good to join them. They could help arm and train his men. So late in December 1942, Mietek took a team of thirteen volunteers, crossed the Wieprz River, and rested in a barn at the edge of the Parczew.

Mietek was the first to wake the next morning, only to learn that his sentry had fallen asleep and that the farmer had betrayed him. Germans and Polish Blue Police had surrounded the barn. Mietek quietly woke his men and gave the order to attack. They broke out of the barn firing. Before he zigzagged into the woods, jumping snowdrifts like a moose, Mietek saw one German go down. He saw the boy from Maidanek fall, wounded or dead, then two more of his men. Henry, the Jew running beside him, got hit in the palm; Mietek was knicked in the finger, then shot in the calf. Henry and Mietek skipped through the snow.

When Mietek broke through the trees onto a road, he found two more of his men, one wounded. The four Jews hitched a ride from a rich farmer who happened to be passing, and the man dropped them off at his manager's house to get their wounds cleaned and dressed. The farmer told Mietek he'd return for them in the morning.

He did — with the Germans. Mietek and two of his men escaped through a tunnel and over a wall. One was killed. When Mietek reached the Wieprz

River, he found seven of his men waiting. While searching for their three wounded comrades, they had come across a forest ranger's house, filled with a dozen half-drunk Germans, and had tossed a grenade inside. Even though Mietek had lost four men, there was one consolation: they had fought their first battle with the Germans and had lost their virginity, only two months after escaping Lublin. *Now* they were real partisans.

Mietek had no choice but to recross the Wieprz, report back to the refugee community in the forest, and hole up with "Drop," the Polish farmer who had always welcomed him. While his wounds were healing, Mietek had long conversations with Drop's aged father, who had lived in eastern Poland under the Russian czars. The old man tried to explain to Mietek why the Poles in the area hated Jews so much. The Russian Orthodox priests, the old man said, had taught the farmers that Jews were both Christ-killers and dangerous revolutionaries. The Poles and Ukrainians in the area believed their priests. The Germans were merely exploiting those old fears and hatreds.

While Mietek and his men were recuperating with Drop, some Poles led the Germans to the Jewish refugee camp in the forest. The Germans killed everyone except fourteen men who were out on patrol at the time.

When Mietek healed, he set up camp in the forest and took into his unit a band of young Jews who had escaped from the town of Kalmionka. He now had forty to fifty men.

Mietek developed a set of clear strategies. He wouldn't try to maintain another refugee camp for women and children, the sick and aged. That was too dangerous and tied him down too much. He would place them with those farmers whom he had learned to trust. Next, he would find and kill the Poles who collaborated with the Nazis against the Jews. There would be no mercy, even if the traitors were women or youngsters. Finally, he would begin picking off German patrols and stealing their weapons.

In the spring of 1943, Mietek began to suffer losses he couldn't understand. His men would go out on patrol in twos and threes and never return. Through his intelligence network, Mietek learned that the AK was beginning to recruit partisan units in anticipation of the Red Army's crossing the Bug to liberate Poland. Mietek knew it was time to head for the Parczew once again. Kaminsky, the leader of the Communist underground, had advised him to join Yechiel Greenshpan, who commanded a tough, all-Jewish partisan unit there. Mietek had agreed.

But first, there was one more important job to do. Mietek had heard that the Germans were drafting for forced labor all the young Polish men they could identify from records. Using the explosives he had found (parachuted by the Russians or the Polish army in exile), Mietek and his men blew up town halls in Garbow, Kalmionka, and Markoszow. Then, after sabotaging a German armament train and killing all the German prisoners he took, Mietek led his men across the Wieprz once again, looking for Greenshpan.

*

In one way, Yechiel Greenshpan was luckier than Mietek. Born in the Parczew and a member of a Jewish family that traded horses with the villagers and farmers, Greenshpan knew every swamp and wagon rut in the forest, and, more important, which farmers could be trusted and which could not.

In another way, Greenshpan was worse off. The first partisans in the Parczew had been Russians who escaped from the more than a hundred POW camps in eastern Poland. The Ukrainian minority who lived at the edge of the forest welcomed the Russian POWs, who, at least until late 1942, hunted, raped, and killed the Jews for guns, food, and money.

Furthermore, in the middle of 1942 (just as Sobibor was opening), the Germans began to sweep the Parczew for partisans and for Jews who had escaped from the ghettos. That angered the Russian POWs even more, for they knew that what drew the Germans to the forest, endangering them, was Jews, not Russians.

Greenshpan and his unit of fifty well-armed men decided that their first goal was to protect the sick and old Jewish refugees and the women and children from the Russian POWs and the Germans. In a camp deep in the forest, they collected almost a thousand Jews. Greenshpan assigned several men to guard and feed them.

Life in the forest camp, called Tabor, was not easy. Food and medicine were scarce. Most of the time, Greenshpan and his men were fighting Germans far away from Tabor, and the handful of partisans guarding it were no match for the Germans and the Polish Blue Police. On one raid alone, the Germans killed several hundred sick and aged Tabor Jews who could not flee fast enough.

In mid-1943, Greenshpan joined forces with the Polish Communist partisans as a separate, all-Jewish unit — People's Guard Unit Chil. Greenshpan's decision to coordinate his fighting with the Polish Communist underground was logical: he received better weapons, including explosives, and more important assignments, including sabotage. And he got protection against Home Army anti-Semites, because the AK had issued an order to kill the Jewish partisans, whom it considered no more than "well-armed gangs."

In the fall of 1943, while Chil's group was blowing up factories, trains, and bridges, the Sobibor survivors began to dribble into his camp in twos and threes — more than a dozen in all — sick, half-starved, frozen.

*

On October 14, Abraham from the train brigade was kneeling at the fence to the right of Sobibor's main gate with a pair of shears he had taken from Shlomo's shop. "Cut the wires!" he heard the Jews around him shouting. "Cut the wires!" But before he could, the fence caved in under the weight of bodies pressing against it.

When he crossed the minefield, Abraham found a large group of Jews at the edge of the forest. Among them were Yehuda Lerner, who had just killed Johnny Niemann; Hella, who worked in the laundry; Aizik, an eighteen-year-old construction worker from Wlodawa, five miles north; and a Russian Jew with a pistol. They decided to walk to Wlodawa, cross the Bug — the town sits on the west bank of the river — and join the Russian partisans.

They trekked through the woods, wandered in circles, and ran. At dawn, they found themselves back at Sobibor. As they lay in the underbrush, they heard Sergeant Frenzel talking to a peasant. "We'll get them all," the Nazi was saying. "There's a reward of four hundred zlotys per head." Although the peasant knew the Jews were hiding nearby, he didn't turn them in.

After arguing about what to do and where to go, they broke into smaller groups. Lerner, the Russian with the pistol (they both had been in Minsk with Sasha), and two others went one way to look for partisans; Hella, Abraham, Aizik, and three others went in another direction.

Lerner's group wandered in circles for weeks, until they stumbled on Mordechai (the painter), four other Sobibor Jews, and four Russian POWs. They banded together to look for partisans — Jewish, Russian, Polish Communist. It made no difference, as long as they weren't Home Army or National Armed Forces. All they wanted to do was to fight the Germans.

Soon they met a group of Poles who said that they were partisans and that their larger group would welcome the Jews. But that night, while Mordechai, Lerner, the Russian Jew, and one of the Russian POWs were hunting for food, the Poles attacked, killed, and robbed everyone else, including one woman. A few days later, a friendly farmer directed Lerner, Mordechai, and the two Russians to Chil.

Meanwhile, Hella, Abraham, Aizik, and the other three Jews wandered from farm to farm, hunting for food, directions, and a place to sleep. Eventually, the Polish underground found them and killed three — two men and a woman. Abraham, Hella, and Aizik survived and found a Polish farmer who offered to take Hella (with blond hair and brown eyes, she passed easily for a Pole), but refused to hide Abraham and Aizik. They agreed to part.

Abraham and Aizik eventually wandered into Chil's group, but Aizik had a detour. He and a Jew he found wandering in the forest were betrayed by a Pole to a civilian German farmer, who chained them in his barn, forcing them to act like dogs or be handed over to the SS. They had to crawl on all fours, even bark. The farmer fed them as if they were dogs — little bones in a dish, some mush, old potatoes. Aizik and his friend found a piece of a knife and worked on the chain until they cut it through. Then they waited until a Saturday night (the SS slept late on Sunday), when they broke out. With chains still around their necks, they found Chil.

The last three survivors to reach Chil were almost dead from cold, hunger, and exhaustion — Eda, Ulla (Selma's friend), and Katty, a Dutchwoman from Sobibor. They had been wandering around the forest for over a month. Eda, who was a good nurse, sold her services to farmers and villagers for food. Everywhere they went, they asked for directions to the partisans, but no one wanted to help them. Then one day, when the snow had already blanketed the forest, a Pole finally led them to Chil.

The partisan leader sent the three women to Tabor. Eda, in particular, was in bad shape. But a surprise awaited her at the camp. Itzhak, the shoemaker she loved, had also found Chil, and was now a fighting partisan.

Not long after the last Sobibor survivors trickled into Tabor, Mietek joined Chil. By this time, both Jewish units were tough, experienced, and disciplined. They had earned a reputation with the Polish Communist underground and the Soviet partisans across the Bug as brave and reliable fighters. The youngest in the Mietek-Chil forces was just twelve; and among the 150 people in the combined unit were twenty armed women, who fought alongside the men. Ulla and Katty were fighters. Eda was still too weak to fight.

The Mietek and Chil units became two companies in the Holod Battalion of the People's Guard, making up one third of the battalion's strength. Chil's and Mietek's partisans, including the Sobibor survivors, fought side by side. They cut telephone poles and lines between Lublin and Wlodawa; they attacked police headquarters and government posts in Kaplonosy and the town of Parczew; they blew up at least four army troop trains; and they hijacked German supply trucks on the highway, driving the vehicles into the forest, where they transferred the matériel into horse-drawn wagons and killed the German prisoners.

When the Holod Battalion fled from the Parczew to avoid being caught between the retreating Germans and the Red Army, Chil and Mietek were ordered to follow. They refused. Chil would not abandon his refugee community in the forest. Mietek was not about to cross the Wieprz River to be betrayed by the Polish anti-Semites who infested the farms and villages he had fled.

By the end of July 1944, Chil's and Mietek's were the only partisan units still left in the Parczew Forest. Behind them to the west were the German reserves; in front of them to the east was the German front line. Before long, they were completely surrounded by Germans.

On the night of July 22, the Jewish partisans and the refugees they guarded camped in a wheatfield, hoping that the Germans would be too afraid to leave the cover of the forest. The next morning, the Jews were free. The Red Eighth Army had passed them during the night, and they were now behind the front line in liberated Poland.

The 150 Jewish fighters joined the Russian and Communist partisans in a grand parade in Lublin, to the cheers of the Jewish refugees they had protected. They were the remnant, and among them was Leon Feldhendler, who, together with his men, had joined the Polish Communist partisans in Krasnik.

Of the four thousand Jews who had fled to the Parczew between 1940 and 1944, only two hundred were still alive. The Sobibor survivors who had fought with Chil and Mietek had a near-perfect record. Of the dozen or so who had found Tabor, only Katty Gokkes had been killed.

A Chil partisan described how the Poles in Lublin received the Jewish fighters after liberation. "When we reached the first streets, we were welcomed with flowers," he said. "But on the next street, we were shot at by members of the Polish National Armed Forces."

279

Chapter 37

Selma and Chaim

SELMA AND CHAIM stumbled through the forest. They had no idea where they were or where they were going. There was no time to think; they could only run. Selma was dripping with sweat. She peeled off her second sweater. Then she stopped to take off her second pair of woolen pants and throw them to the ground.

They heard screams and shots behind them, and no matter where they ran, they couldn't seem to shake them. Finally, they heard voices and chatter and whispers. They stopped and strained to hear. The whispers were in Yiddish.

Selma and Chaim broke into a small clearing where eight or ten Sobibor Jews stood, arguing. One had a gun.

"You're not coming with us!" warned the Polish Jew with the gun. He eyed Selma suspiciously. "We don't want her."

He pointed the gun at Chaim. It was clear that he didn't trust her. She could give the others away because she didn't act, speak, or look Polish, and after all, they were in Poland.

But before the Jew with the gun could shoot, Selma stepped in front of Chaim. She sensed that they wouldn't kill her before Chaim's eyes, for there was no telling what he'd do. They'd kill him first, then either abandon or shoot her, too.

The Jew with the gun was taken aback, and before he could recover,

Chaim grabbed Selma's hand. "You go on by yourselves," he told the man with the gun. "We don't want to tag along."

Tugging at Selma, Chaim turned his back on the gun and ran through the trees. He waited for a shot, but all he heard was chatter.

Chaim decided to look for the Ukrainian farmer for whom he had worked in 1940 and 1941, after the Germans conquered Poland. The Ukrainian and his wife, who knew he was a Jew, had treated him fairly. He was counting on the fact that their kindness had been sincere. Besides, where else could he go?

Chaim found the North Star and headed south, away from Sobibor. He and Selma walked in the woods by night and slept by day for ten days. At first, they heard shots behind them, then only the sounds of night — an occasional dog barking on a nearby farm along the edge of the forest, an owl hooting at the harvest moon, a doe snapping branches as she picked her way through the forest to her favorite watering hole.

Selma was frightened half to death. A city girl from the crowded Netherlands, she had never been in a forest before. She had visions of wild animals attacking them, of Germans trapping them, of partisans shooting them for their money, and in the shadows she kept seeing the face of Karl Frenzel.

When the nights grew colder, Selma cursed herself for throwing away her extra clothes. Why hadn't she listened to Chaim? He was always right. She was wet and chilled to the bone. The insides of her fine leather boots were wet, and her feet swelled so badly that she couldn't slide them back inside the boots. That slowed them both up.

Like the other Jews, Selma and Chaim had money but no food. So every morning before they bedded down, they would ask a farmer to sell them bread and a place to sleep. One farmer let them stay in his barn all day, on their word that they would go on their way at nightfall. He had small children, he explained. He couldn't take the risk of getting caught by the Germans or of being betrayed by a neighbor.

Another time, they spotted a haystack in a field away from a farmhouse. Chaim studied the farm from the woods; it seemed serene and quiet. They crept to the haystack and crawled inside, exhausted and wet. Suddenly, they woke. They held each other tightly and listened. Someone was poking in the stack. Then they heard the laughter and squeals of children. Chaim grabbed Selma's hand, and they fled back into the woods.

Another time, two farmers in a wagon came rumbling along the road at the edge of the forest. Chaim flagged them down and paid for a ride. No sooner had he and Selma jumped on the wagon than the farmers took off like pioneers for a land claim. Chaim crept to the front of the wagon and listened to the two Poles arguing. He heard enough to realize that they were debating how best to kill them and take their money. When the wagon slowed to negotiate a turn in the road, Chaim and Selma jumped and rolled into the woods.

On the morning of October 24 — ten days after the escape — they approached one more farmer, discouraged, half-starved, covered with lice, and frightened.

"Can you hide us?" Chaim asked. "We'll pay."

"No," the farmer said. He looked them over carefully. There was no greed or hatred or even suspicion in his eyes. "I'm too close to the road. The Germans pass by almost every day. But I have a brother farther back. He has a barn. Maybe he'll hide you. I'll take you there tomorrow."

Chaim and Selma had no choice but to believe him and to hope for the best. He gave them something to eat and led them to his barn. The next morning, with Selma, dressed in a black coat and a babushka, sitting beside him on the wagon, and Chaim in the rear, covered with branches, the farmer drove them to his brother, Adam.

Adam and his wife, Stefka, agreed to hide Selma and Chaim until the Russians came. It was clear to Chaim that Selma had caught Adam's eye. Perhaps he felt sorry for her and didn't have the heart to condemn her to almost certain death. Whatever the reason, it was one of the greatest ironies Chaim had seen so far. His fellow Jews had nearly killed him because they thought Selma would cause their death; now he was alive because a Polish farmer had taken a liking to her.

Adam and Stefka gave them food and a bucket of water so that they could bathe. Then Stefka led them to the hayloft above the cows, gave them a blanket, and took their clothes to delouse and wash them. The rules were simple. Selma and Chaim were to whisper only, never come down from the loft unless Adam or Stefka invited them to, and move around as little as possible during daylight. They would be fed once a day, and they'd have a bucket for a toilet. Chaim gave Adam and Stefka most of his gold.

Although the barn was cold, the smell of manure nauseating, and the rats huge, they had a roof, a little food, some straw, and each other. Unless Adam and Stefka decided to turn them in, they'd be safe.

As far as Selma was concerned, Chaim was her husband. He was a good man; he had cared for her at Sobibor, nursed her through her typhus, took her with him at the risk of his own life. They had talked about Holland and her family hotel in Zwolle, the ocean breeze, the flowers, the laughter and freedom. They had planned to go there someday to live and raise a family.

They had never talked of marriage; marriage was only a rule, a society regulation. But there were no rules in the war against the Jews, and there was no longer a society for them; for each, there was just the other. And though they had never slept together, in all the important ways their lives had been interwoven like hair in a braid. "Bride and groom," Frenzel had called them, and they were.

Selma gave herself to Chaim in the straw. The loft was the only privacy they had ever had in the seven months they had known and loved each other. There was no big decision, no long discussion, no passionate moment. Just two people who loved each other, needed each other, because that's all they had; two people who took care of each other, suffered together, escaped together, hid together, and lay together under the straw, holding on to each other, taking comfort in each other, and waiting for tomorrow, for another day, for the Russians.

Selma began a diary there in the loft, writing with a pencil in small neat letters in a two-by-four-inch notebook that Chaim, the practical one, had taken from the sorting warehouse. "My darling husband," she began to call him in her journal.

To while the time away, Selma and Chaim would write love letters to each other. He studied German, writing down next to her diary entries the words she taught him. He continued to teach her Yiddish, and she kept working on his Dutch. Stefka gave her a ball of yarn and needles, and she began to knit a pair of socks and a sweater.

They stayed in the loft for nine months, and though it was relatively peaceful for the first six months, it was hard. They had barely enough food to keep them alive, and on the days Adam or Stefka gave them more bread than usual, they couldn't save any; the rats ate it faster than they. It was freezing in the barn, even under the hay, and because they couldn't bathe, there was no way to control the lice. They both developed severe cases of scabies from the insect bites, and the itching drove them crazy. Even though they kept paying Stefka to buy ointment in Chelm, she never seemed to get enough.

Then one day Stefka demanded the rest of Chaim's money. When Chaim told her he had no more, she and Adam brought Selma and Chaim down from the loft and forced them to spend two days with the pigs while they searched the hay for gold. Then, satisfied there was no more, they let Selma and Chaim go back to the hay.

A stork used to perch on the barn roof, motionless for hours, like a sentinel guarding the farm or watching for Germans. It was an interesting bird, black and white with an orange bill and one leg tucked under its wing. To relieve the boredom, Selma used to peek at it through a knothole in the wall. One day she made too much noise and the stork flew away.

The next day Adam stormed into the barn. "You have to leave," he said.

"Leave?" Chaim asked. His stomach tightened. "Why?"

"The stork is gone. That's a bad sign. Something terrible is going to happen. He used to sit on this roof. It must be you."

Chaim was relieved. "We scared him away," he told Adam. "We were watching him through the hole."

"All right," Adam said. "We'll wait. If he comes back, you can stay. If not, out."

The stork returned with a sad surprise.

"I think I'm pregnant," Selma wrote in her diary on April 14, 1944. "My breasts are getting bigger. It will cost us our lives. These people will never keep us here. We cannot have a child here. I've been lying here and crying for three days now. There's nothing to do but wait and see what will happen. We can't walk on the street. They'll shoot on sight. We can't go to a doctor. No doctor would dare help a Jew.

"We've known each other for only a short time and would like so much to live together like human beings. We have no family; everything is gone. God, help us out of this misery. We have seen thousands go to their deaths, and we are bringing a new person into the world. Now we will join the dead. Why didn't I die a year ago in Sobibor? I wouldn't have had all this misery. But I still have my husband, my darling husband."

Although Selma tried to hide her pregnancy from Stefka, she couldn't fool the farmer's wife. Stefka had been half-expecting it. After all, what are a naked man and woman, huddled together under straw day and night for the whole winter, going to do? Stefka noticed Selma's face filling out and getting a little puffy. She knew it wasn't from eating too much.

"You're pregnant," she told Selma one day. It was a threat. "You'll have to go. With a baby up here, it's too dangerous."

"No, it's not true," Selma said, pleading. "I'm not pregnant."

There was no arguing with the practical Stefka, so Selma began to work on Adam. For the past three weeks they had heard guns in the east, and the sounds seemed to be getting closer each day. She begged the farmer to let them stay. "I'm only three months pregnant," she said. "The Russians will be here before long. We'll be free then. Safe from the Germans. We won't have to hide anymore."

Adam was a reasonable man and he liked Selma. He said he would see whether he could convince Stefka to wait. "But the child cannot be born here," he warned. Chaim and Selma knew he meant it.

Then, on Selma's birthday, Adam came to the loft with some homemade potato vodka. "My brother was here," he said. He was already slightly tipsy. "The Russians have crossed the Bug. Everything along the river is on fire. The Russians are in Poland."

Selma and Chaim were so happy that, even though they didn't usually drink, they felt like celebrating. Selma was only four months pregnant, and the Russians were just miles away. They and their baby would live. Undernourished as they were, they got so drunk that they almost rolled out of the hayloft into the cow manure below.

Then, on the night of July 23, 1944, while they batted away the flies with a handkerchief and lay awake because of the oppressive heat, they heard the front moving toward the farm, yard by yard. They could almost see it and feel it. The barn shivered. There was constant artillery fire, machine-gun chatter, and grenade explosions. There were Russian airplanes overhead. The war surrounded them. Trucks and jeeps roared down the road in the distance.

At daybreak, they peered through the crack in the east wall and saw Germans running across the fields. Then they waited and waited for what seemed like a year. A lone Russian captain stepped cautiously out of the woods. He waved, and soldiers poured into the field. Chaim and Selma dressed quickly. They had been saving their clothes for nine months for this day. Selma's stomach was so big she couldn't button her trousers. They scampered down the ladder into the arms of the first Russian soldier they saw. Overhead, a Russian plane was dog-fighting a Messerschmitt.

"We're free!" Chaim hugged Selma.

Indeed they were. Penniless and pregnant, but free.

Chaim and Selma stayed with Adam and Stefka for two more weeks, until the front had moved well beyond the little farm at the edge of the forest. Chaim worked in the field; Selma did what she could around the house and yard. But one day Adam told Chaim that he had heard some villagers say over vodka that they were going to kill any Jews they could find, including him and Selma. Though Chaim wasn't sure whether Adam was telling the truth or just trying to scare them away, he couldn't take a chance.

First, they fled to the old Jewish ghetto in Chelm, where they met Josel and a few other Sobibor Jews. Then Chaim was drafted into the Russian army, and Selma was devastated. She was pregnant, had no money, couldn't speak Polish, and was convinced that both she and the baby would die if Chaim went to fight the Germans on the western front. To avoid conscription, Chaim worked in an army hospital as a nurse's aide, but the blood and the screaming made him sick.

He grew a mustache, bought false papers, and they hid in the town of Parczew, in the middle of the Parczew Forest. Ulla came to visit them. Selma and Chaim were married there, and their son was born there. It was a difficult delivery. Chaim was away hustling food and money, buying small items like shoelaces, soap, shoe polish, even guns, and selling them to the Russians — anything to scrape up enough money for food and a few clothes.

Selma walked five miles to a Red Cross center in a village school when she thought her time had come. She couldn't speak Polish, and the doctors and nurses didn't speak Yiddish or German or Dutch. She got her labor instructions in sign language as she lay on a cot for five days and nights. When she screamed in pain, the Red Cross told her in signs to shut up or they'd throw her out. Then, when the baby's head had already lowered, they walked her down the hall to the delivery room.

They called him Emilchen — Little Emil — and Selma was depressed. Winter had descended on her with a fury. There was no glass in the window of the one room on the second floor where they lived, and only sawdust for the stove. The two pots she had leaked. With Chaim gone for as long as five weeks at a time, she was lonely. She cried away most of the winter.

When Chaim heard that the Polish Nationals still in the Parczew Forest were rounding up and killing Jews in the neighborhood, they packed up Emilchen and fled to Lublin, to the home of Podchlebnik, who welcomed them with open arms. Ever since he had escaped from the Waldkommando, he had been building up a trading business by buying wagons of sugar and potatoes and vodka, and selling them to the highest bidder, frequently door to door. His apartment was a refuge for penniless Jews from Sobibor. Even Leon Feldhendler lived nearby.

One night the Polish Nationals raided the Lublin ghetto. The Jews in Podchlebnik's house, warned in advance, had just enough time to snap off the lights and hide their money under Emilchen's mattress.

"Podchlebnik? Podchlebnik?" the Poles called as they rapped at the door. No one inside moved. Selma was afraid that Emilchen would start to cry. They waited in dreadful silence. It was just like old times, hiding in attics and cellars waiting for the Nazis to pass. When no one answered the door, the Jew-hunters went to other rooms, other doors, other houses. The next day, Selma and Chaim learned that several Jews had been robbed and killed, among them Leon Feldhendler.

Soon after the raid, Chaim told Selma that he had managed to get them passage on a refugee train to Odessa. From Odessa, he said, they would board a Dutch ship for Holland. Selma began to cry. Home at last. It would soon be over. Three years of jails, prisons, camps, hiding, fearing, and hating. She had lost a mother and two brothers — maybe three. She had found a husband and a child. She had nightmares and memories. But at last she could start over again. Pick up her life back in Zwolle, with her husband and child.

It took from January to May 1945 to travel to Odessa through Rumania. The train was jammed with refugees; food was scarce. To wash diapers, Selma warmed water in the locomotive, next to the firebox. Once, when the train had stopped and Chaim was in a town hunting for fresh milk for Emilchen and she was washing dishes, the train started up without warning. Emilchen was on it. Selma and Chaim ran alongside the tracks to catch up.

Then Selma caught diphtheria and gave it to the baby. When the train reached Chernovtsy in northern Rumania, its first major stop, all the passengers were sent to a transit camp. Selma and Emilchen went to the hospital. But before they were completely rested and nourished, the train left for Odessa, and Chaim had to sign them out in a hurry.

Odessa, the resort city on the Black Sea, was a joy. It was neat and clean, beautiful after Sobibor, the forest, the hayloft, the house in Parczew, the stinking, crowded refugee train. The British Red Cross nursed Selma and Emilchen back to perfect health. For the first time since she had left Holland, Selma felt healthy, free, happy, and glad to be alive.

There was still one small problem. Chaim was Polish. If the refugee authorities found out, they would turn Chaim back, and she would be forced to choose between him and Holland. The decision would be easy. She'd never leave him, not her Chaim, even if it meant spending the rest of her life in the Poland she hated and under a red flag.

The Dutch captain of the ship offered to help. "Don't worry," he told them. "Just don't say a word to anyone. When we board, I'll go with you. I'll get you back home."

Departure day came, and Selma was almost as nervous as she had been in Sobibor on October 14. Poland was a prison for her — another Sobibor, a kind of slow death. She didn't know how she could live there any longer, with all her memories of death and hatred. "My God," she whispered, "help us."

Amidst the noise and confusion, the tears and happiness in the harbor, she carried Emilchen and held on to Chaim's hand. With the captain at her side, she walked up the gangplank to freedom. No one stopped her.

Selma and Chaim celebrated that night and sang Dutch songs and cried. Selma even managed to find some fresh milk for Emilchen. The ordeal was over. They were going home to a free Holland, to the hotel in Zwolle. The ship passed Istanbul, through the Sea of Marmora into the isle-studded Aegean, with the sun shining on the hot white shores and houses, and fishing boats crawling between the islands, as they had done for centuries. It was like a fairy tale come true.

Then Emilchen began to vomit. At first, Selma thought he was seasick, because she herself was beginning to get dizzy. But Emilchen grew worse. Within twenty-four hours, he was dead. The fresh milk had been contaminated.

The Dutch captain wrapped him in white cloth like a tiny mummy, gathered the refugees and the crew around, and read the ceremony from his ship's manual. It was a beautiful day — the sun bright, the water a strange blue, almost shining. Then he slipped Emilchen into the water off the Isle of Naxos, a jewel in the sun.

Chaim and Selma could barely control their grief. Their one beautiful thing after all those months of hell had been taken from them: Emilchen — their child.

The
Remnant:
A Personal
Epilogue

Chapter 38

Toivi

How many of the fewer than fifty men and women who had escaped from Sobibor and had survived the war were still alive? Where were they? Would they be willing to relive Sobibor for me? Where should I begin?

I decided to contact Thomas Blatt (Toivi) first. I had found an article in *Listener* magazine about Gustav Wagner. The author, Tom Bower, a BBC correspondent who had taped a television special on the Nazi, named in the article three Sobibor survivors living in the United States. According to Bower, Thomas Blatt had been collecting memorabilia about Sobibor for years and wasn't camera-shy. If Blatt had talked to Bower, wouldn't he talk to me? And if he was still trying to keep alive the memory of Sobibor, wouldn't he know who the other survivors were and where they lived?

Mr. Blatt's wife answered the phone. "Tom has left for work," she said. "Who is this?"

I gave her my name. "I'm writing a book about Sobibor, and I'd like to interview your husband."

She paused, as if I had taken her breath away. "Why?" she asked finally. "Why a book on Sobibor? Do you have a publisher?"

I tried to explain, but she was guarded. "I'll tell him you called," she said. "Try tomorrow morning around eight-thirty."

When I called at precisely eight-thirty the next morning, Mr. Blatt had already gone to work. Why had he left early if he knew I would be calling?

With some reluctance, Mrs. Blatt gave me her husband's number at work.

Although Mr. Blatt heard me out with no enthusiasm, I sensed an ambivalence, a certain weakening, as if he wanted to say, "No, I don't want to be interviewed," but couldn't.

This phone call, I knew, might very well set the whole course of my book. "I need your help," I said. "If I come to Santa Barbara, will you talk to me?"

He wavered. "Okay, I'll help. When will you come?"

I was so relieved — and frightened, in a way — that I couldn't work the rest of the day. I knew that Sobibor was going to be painful for me, too. I knew that my emotions would be bent and twisted before I finished the book, that my mind would be stretched in ways it did not want to go, that I would have to confront the painful issues of indifference, hatred, brutality, and genocide. I would hear stories of almost unbelievable suffering. Somehow, I'd have to remain objective, detached, a skeptical interviewer trying to dig deeper into people's personal nightmares. Would they trust me with their pain?

Two days after Christmas, I walked into Blatt's auto stereo shop on a busy corner of the Santa Barbara business strip. It was the most hectic time of the year for him, with customers dashing in and out to get their new stereos installed or to shop for after-Christmas bargains. The phones rang constantly.

Toivi was standing behind the counter. At fifty-three, he was a strong-looking man with powerful arms and hands nicked from pliers, wires, and stubborn screws. His face had a healthy, ruddy color, and he had a full head of brown hair combed into a big wave reminiscent of the 1950s.

Tom was a very successful businessman who had earned his money the hard way. After the Red Army liberated Poland in 1944, he became a Polish officer and chased and arrested Nazis. After the war, he changed his name to hide his Jewish heritage, and worked in the Polish government office of cultural affairs. But he felt guilty trying to pass as a Christian, even though he knew that if he didn't, he would always be an outsider in Poland, as he had been before the war.

When the Communist government eased its restrictions on Jewish emigration to Israel, Tom left Poland, without a penny in his pocket. A friend in Israel took him in and helped him find a job. On a kibbutz, he met Dena, an American Jew who spoke Yiddish and wanted to learn Hebrew. They married in Israel but decided to live in the United States.

It was difficult for Tom in Los Angeles. He couldn't speak English; he had no trade; he and Dena had little money. Sometimes, they both took two jobs, and they began to save for a house. Tom worked as a janitor and in a factory, his immense curiosity stifled, his mind wasted; he was bored to the point of suicide. He and Dena eventually bought a house, and Tom worked for one of the pioneers in the auto stereo business. Eventually, he opened two stereo stores of his own.

Tom still had all the characteristics of Toivi. He was friendly and had an inquisitive mind that sought adventure. We sat in easy chairs next to the shop door and talked. We'd hardly get deep into conversation when he had to jump up to help customers while his two assistants installed radios and tape decks at the rear of the shop.

When I told Tom I wasn't Jewish, he seemed amazed. But he recovered quickly.

"That's good," he said. "It will make your book more credible. The best book I've ever read on the Holocaust was written by a non-Jew — Gitta Sereny. Did you read her book?"

I had read and admired *Into That Darkness: From Mercy Killing to Mass Murder.* It had some valuable new information about the Sobibor Kommandant Franz Stangl, who had been convicted of war crimes and sentenced to life in prison. Sereny had interviewed him just days before he died of a heart attack.

Between customers, Tom quizzed me about my book. How would I approach it? Was I writing fiction? What would I try to say; my message? Why was I writing it? I could tell I was being tested and judged.

I knew I had passed when Tom shifted from being friendly but guarded to being friendly and totally open. The more I listened to him talk about Sobibor, the more apparent it became that Tom wanted to trust me, almost needed to. There was a compulsion to talk about Sobibor. I sensed he had to tell his story, their story — the story of his mother, father, brother, and the other Jews of Izbica. The world had to know. Not that six million Jews died in the Holocaust, but that two hundred and fifty thousand had died in Sobibor on the Bug River, and that his entire family was among them.

We were interrupted so often at the shop that a serious interview was out of the question. Tom was offended that I hadn't given him my flight number so that he could have met me at the airport, and that I had spent the night in a motel. He insisted that I be his guest.

"My wife will pick you up for dinner," he said. "Have your bags packed."

Dena dropped by around six, and we drove along the beautiful Santa Barbara beach. She pulled into a park so that we could face the sea and watch the sun sink, large and rosy. I was on trial again.

Dena was an honest, blunt woman with a round face, dark eyes, and black hair streaked with gray. She told me she didn't think a non-Jew could write a sensitive book on Sobibor. "You'd never understand," she said, as the sun painted the smooth sea a golden orange. "I don't know how you would interpret the information."

She told me that the Sobibor story could be twisted and used against the Jews.

"Do you blame me for being skeptical?" she asked. "I don't know anything about you."

"No," I said. "I guess you'll just have to trust me."

"But how can I trust you? I don't know you."

She was right. I was asking a lot of her and Tom. People have been writing against the Jews ever since Gutenberg. Intellectuals have twisted history, journalists have written half-truths, and scholars have denied there was a Holocaust. Why should she trust me with her husband's private pain?

I listened to Dena carefully, trying to understand her point of view, hoping I would find the right words to bridge that gulf between a Christian with a pen and the Jew who had learned to distrust in order to survive.

Dena began to lecture me about the Holocaust, the anti-Semitism of the Poles, about the inaction of London, Washington, and the Vatican in 1942 when they knew that Jews were being gassed like lice. When she realized that I was well informed, she began to trust me — a little. She told me about her childhood in Montreal, the prejudice, the hatred. How she couldn't get a room in student homes because she was a Jew. How one landlady told her she could live in her rooming house if she wouldn't talk to any of the other women, stay to herself, and use the maids' entrance, lest someone find out she was a Jew. The experience was still painful for her to talk about.

"I haven't told many people about that," she said. "I'm telling you because it's important for you to know about anti-Semitism. What it is. What it does to a person."

I sensed there was more to Dena's doubt than my being a Gentile, and it didn't take me long to find out what it was. That evening after dinner, I plugged in my tape recorder and began to interview Tom seriously. My plan was to go over a translation of the published version of Sasha Pechersky's short diary, line by line, checking it for accuracy and fleshing it out. Then, to get at the structure and physical details of the camp — the buildings, the jobs, the routine, the Nazis, the Ukrainian guards. Next, when Tom understood my thoroughness and competence, to talk about his personal experiences at the camp. I knew it would take days.

Hardly had I tossed out my first questions when Dena warned Tom not to give me too much information because it would ruin *his* book.

It was out in the open now. Tom had written a diary in Polish, I learned, and Dena wanted him to publish it. He had already published two short articles based on his diary and had finished a third one, still unpublished but copyrighted. Although most of his diary dealt with his life before and after Sobibor, Dena saw my book as a threat.

I sensed that I was caught in the middle of something larger than an unpublished diary. Tom had begun it in the late 1940s, yet he had never shown it to an American publisher. It sat in his study or in a desk drawer somewhere. Every time Dena urged him to be cautious, not to tell me all, he'd say, "It's my story. I can do whatever I want with it. Leave us be." I knew I had to dig under the diary to find the sore spot.

"Why not finish it?" I asked Tom. "Publish it."

I had grown to appreciate Tom. He was smart; his memory was excellent. He was concerned that the truth about Sobibor be known. Exaggerations or technical errors in a book like mine, he told me, would destroy its credibility. I found him to be balanced, critical, and enormously curious. In a word, he was an ideal person to interview, and I had come to trust his judgment and the account of his own experiences.

When Tom talked about Sobibor, his voice would change, and he'd become Toivi. One moment he would speak with passion; his eyes would blaze with an anger that did not show in the rest of his face. The next moment, his voice would almost whine, or become flat and colorless. When I asked a painful question that he preferred not to answer, his voice would become strained, almost a whisper, and his answers clipped and to the point.

I asked about the autobiographical account. Tom became evasive and contradictory. The question was important to me: I didn't want to live with the idea of his not publishing his life story because I was writing my own book.

He would finish it, he said. But he was too busy now. Besides, it would only have a small section on Sobibor. He *wouldn't* finish it, he said, because it was always growing, changing, as he grew and changed.

"I can't," he said finally. "I'm not sure why. It's psychological."

I dropped the topic. I knew by now that I'd have to get Tom away from home if I was to understand him and his experiences in Sobibor. In four days, I had superficially covered only a third of the topics I wanted to.

"Who else should I talk to?" I asked him.

Without a moment's hesitation, Tom said Sasha, Shlomo, Eda, and Josel.

Sasha lived in Rostov-on-the-Don, Shlomo in the middle of Brazil, Eda in Israel, and Josel in the United States. I didn't speak Russian, Portuguese, Yiddish, Hebrew, or Polish.

I had read Shlomo's book, *Hell in Sobibor,* which he'd published in Portuguese in 1968. An interview with Shlomo, I knew, was essential for my book, for the only two key members of the Organization at Sobibor still alive were Shlomo and Sasha. I asked Tom whether he'd go to Brazil with me. He agreed. Would he call Josel for me to break the ice? He agreed.

I was ready to leave. The trip had been a partial success. I was beginning to understand Tom-Toivi.

"Do you have an alarm clock?" I asked Tom the night before I left. I had to be up at five to catch my flight.

"I'll wake you," Tom said. "I don't need an alarm. I just tell myself what time to wake up and I do."

"I prefer an alarm," I said.

"Okay." He laughed. "I'll see you at five."

He did. It seemed almost as if he slept with his eyes open, afraid Wagner or Frenzel would catch him napping. I was not far from the truth.

"I think of Sobibor often," Tom told me on the way to the airport. "When I meet someone, I ask myself, 'What would he be like in Sobibor? What would he have done?' "

Tom turned his face toward me in the dark car. "You seem like a nice man, Richard. I wonder what you would have been like there?"

The question bothered me for days. I wanted to think that I never would have betrayed my fellow prisoners, never surrendered my soul to Wagner or Frenzel, inspired others like a Feldhendler, been a leader, maybe even a hero like Sasha.

But I had no answer. Sobibor, with its fear and degradation, its brutality and terror, was so far from the pale of my experience, I couldn't even imagine what I'd have been like or have done. Neither could I imagine what I'd be like if, like Toivi, I had survived. What would the experience have done to me? How would I see the world, other people, the future?

I knew who I was, but not what I could become if I were dragged from the realm of the familiar and thrown into, as Shlomo had put it, "hell in Sobibor."

*

Shortly after I returned home, Tom called to say that Josel had agreed to be interviewed. I was elated. He could tell me not only about his own escape, but also about the details of the Berliner killing, his role in the escape, all about the dispensary, the nursing. He had a dimension that few of the other survivors had.

Josel was cordial on the phone. "How much time do you need?" he asked when I called him at his office on a Friday afternoon.

"Six hours," I said. "I can do any follow-ups by phone or letter."

"All right," he agreed.

"How about Monday?" I asked. I wanted to get him before he could change his mind.

"Tuesday is better."

When I called him on Monday to give my arrival time, he was edgy and nervous. "I've been going through hell ever since you called," he said. "My stomach has been churning. I haven't been able to sleep, thinking about the interview. I'm sorry, but I can't go through with it."

"I understand," I said with disappointment. And I did understand.

I wrote Josel a week later, telling him again that I understood and respected his feelings. Couldn't we compromise? How about an interview only about the escape? I promised not to go beyond that, and told him we could do it by phone if he didn't want to meet me.

Josel called back. "I'll help you," he said. "But don't push me. I will write something for you or record something on tape. I promise. It may take some time."

I asked him a couple of lead questions, and Josel went on to talk about his escape from Sobibor for half an hour. I took notes furiously, cursing the fact that I didn't have my recorder attached to the phone.

"Do you know any other survivors in the United States?" I asked him before he hung up.

"Have you talked to Esther and Samuel?"

"No," I said.

"They are very sharp and reliable. But don't call them. It's too much of a shock. Write first."

He gave me addresses and phone numbers.

"Can I say you referred me to them?"

"Yes," Josel said.

Chapter 39

Shlomo

SHLOMO (STANISLAW) SZMAJZNER was grinning and waving through the glass in the Goiania terminal. He was almost bald, with a graying mustache and a tanned face. His shirt was unbuttoned down to his belt, and he was as trim as a man of twenty.

Shlomo bear-hugged Tom Blatt. "My brother," he said. *"Mein Bruder."*

Tom paced as he waited for his bag. "Slow down," Shlomo told him between puffs on the Parliament that hung on his lip as if glued there. "You're in Brazil now."

We drove to Shlomo's six-room apartment with a huge deck overlooking the young capital city of the State of Goias in Central Brazil. In 1947, Shlomo had planned to emigrate to Israel, as far away from Poland as he could get. First, he had visited relatives in Rio de Janeiro — and stayed in Brazil for thirty-four years.

Shlomo opened a jewelry store in Rio, and during the next ten years built it into a thriving business, married a Brazilian Jew, and began raising a family.

In 1958, with the advice and help of friends who were politicians in Goias, Shlomo bought a jungle island between two rivers near the Amazon Basin, which he developed into a ranch with eighteen hundred head of cattle. He was the first white man most of the Indians there had ever seen.

When the government fell in 1967, and again on the advice of his friends,

Shlomo sold the ranch, fearing that he might lose it. He moved to Goiania, where he became executive director of Induprel, a paper-recycling plant on the outskirts of town, owned by his political friends.

Shlomo had a cold supper waiting for us — local cheeses, fresh rolls, smoked cured ham, salami, fruit, and sparkling water and beer.

"You're in my home, now," Shlomo told us. "You're not to spend a penny while you're here."

We easily avoided Sobibor that first night, as if it were an ugly shadow Shlomo and Tom didn't want to look at or admit was there.

I went to bed early. I was tired after twenty-four hours of travel — an overnight flight from Washington, D.C., to Rio, and then a flight to Goiania with a change of planes in Brasília — and I knew Shlomo and Tom had a lot to talk about together. They did — until three in the morning. Shlomo got up at six and was off to work by the time I rose for breakfast.

Late that morning, Pedro Ludovico stopped by to visit. He was a law student in Brasília, about a hundred miles east, had studied briefly in the United States, and had spent several months in Tom's home in Santa Barbara. Shlomo joined us later in the morning.

We were a Babel of sounds. Tom and Shlomo spoke Yiddish. Tom and I, English. Shlomo and Pedro, Portuguese. Pedro and I, English. Shlomo and I, German. Again we avoided Sobibor while Shlomo tried to size me up and decide how far he could trust me. We discussed anti-Semitism, and like water around a rock, our chatter swirled by a deeper question that lay just under the surface. Could it happen again? Could there be another Sobibor?

Both Shlomo and Tom had definite opinions. Shlomo said he had never experienced prejudice in Brazil, and that the solution to anti-Semitism was assimilation. "Let those who want to be Orthodox Jews go to Israel," he said. "Let the others assimilate."

Tom disagreed. Anti-Semites will always find who the Jews are when they want to, he argued. History shows that. Jews will never be safe. Assimilation is a myth.

Shlomo conceded that anti-Semitism is learned and that he was worried that the Arabs, who were becoming very interested in Brazil, would teach the Brazilians to hate Jews.

Tom was even more pessimistic. He pointed out that German Jews before the war, like Brazilian Jews today, represented about 1 percent of the population, and that, like Brazilian Jews today, had been assimilated.

"Look what happened," Tom argued. "When someone like Hitler wants to find Jews, he will. There's no safety. No solution."

Pedro and I listened for the most part, as if we were on the edge of a question that didn't really pertain to us, somehow glad it was their problem, not ours, yet knowing deep down that it *was* our problem.

We broke to have a midday dinner with Pedro's family. Throughout the meal, I watched Shlomo carefully. Even here, in the genuine hospitality of a dinner with friends, Shlomo could not get away from the Jewish question. It crept into conversations; it was there by implication. I could feel Shlomo's self-consciousness, almost as if Sobibor had burned into his psyche with every lash of the whip: "You're a Jew. You're a Jew. Don't you forget it. Don't you forget it. We'll get you. We'll get you."

*

That night, we finally spoke of Sobibor.

"I would never talk to you if it weren't for Tom," Shlomo said. "I'm doing it as a favor to him."

"I know," I said. Shlomo seemed wary of something.

"Why do you want to write this book?" It was a question Dena, Tom, and Josel had asked. Wherever I went, Jews would ask it over and over, never completely satisfied with my answer. They would listen and nod, but there would always be a question staring at me from puzzled eyes.

It was clear to me by this time that Shlomo was proud of his own book, the only full-length story of Sobibor ever published. I sensed that he felt that if the English-speaking world wanted a good book on Sobibor, it should translate his. I was on trial again.

The story of the uprising and escape from Sobibor is unique; it has never been told fully in English, I explained. It is a story of resistance, hope against all odds, a scream for human dignity, and revenge. Those aspects attract me, I said. Furthermore, I am concerned about the rise of anti-Semitism around the world, and would like to write a true, accurate, honest, and frank book about what anti-Semitism leads to. I explained that I had read his book and found it excellent, but it was one man's story, told from one vantage point. I wanted, I said, at least seven stories, told from other vantage points. Then I would weave them together after I had sorted out discrepancies.

Shlomo cut my lecture short. He smiled. "I trust you, Hicard," he said. "Hicard" was his Portuguese equivalent of Richard. "Ask," Shlomo said. The ice was broken.

Shlomo laid a bar stool on its side and sat on it. It was hot and humid. Both Shlomo and Tom had taken off their shirts, and it was obvious that Shlomo was proud of his physique. He looked at me and waited. There was a sadness in his smoky brown eyes that would never completely disappear, even when he was angry or laughed his hollow laugh.

"Hicard," Shlomo said, "I am *in* Sobibor now."

Like Tom's, Shlomo's mind was sharp and precise. He clearly distinguished between facts, personal opinion, and hearsay. When he didn't know something, he said so. When I told him things others had written about Sobibor, he would listen intently. "That's true," he would say simply. Or, "Not true." His voice left no doubts — definitive, strong, and self-assured.

I asked long questions in English, translated by Tom into Yiddish. Short questions in faulty German. Shlomo would answer in Yiddish, and when he felt he needed to emphasize something, he'd point directly to me and speak in German, sometimes too fast for me to catch it all with precision.

I queried him about his book, asking for clarification, new information. I asked him specific questions about other things I had read, such as, "Did you put on German uniforms as part of the escape plan?"

"Not true!" he thundered. "Not true!"

There was both tension and excitement in Shlomo's den, surrounded by quadraphonic speakers, tuners, tape decks, and close to a thousand records and cassettes, neatly arranged in a case that covered one whole wall. Shlomo would jump up from his stool, pace the length of the room, always gesturing, usually angry, his voice at times rising to a shout, defiant, as if I were a Nazi — his enemy. Several times, he stormed out of the room still talking and smoking, even though he had had a serious heart attack some time ago. Words tumbled out in an endless stream, and he would not give Tom time to translate into my tape recorder.

It was a difficult experience for Tom, too. He and I both sensed Shlomo's agony. There were a few times when we thought Shlomo was going to walk out, he was so edgy and belligerent. Besides, Tom had to fight the urge to join the conversation, to question Shlomo himself, to contradict him, to clarify some points. Most of the time, Tom succeeded in biting his tongue. "I'll explain later," he'd tell me when he wanted to say something.

Whenever Shlomo would digress — he would do that a lot — Tom would sense my frustration. "Don't push," he'd say. "He needs to break the tension."

At a particularly angry point in the interview, about the role of the Poles in collaborating with the Nazis against the Jews (Shlomo considered them worse than the Germans), he stomped out of the room. I had covered less than 10 percent of the subject matter I wanted to probe, and I thought it was all over; that Shlomo couldn't take any more.

A few minutes later, he returned with a photo album and flipped the pages to a picture of himself in his Russian partisan uniform, holding a carbine tightly across his chest. The photo had been taken just months after his escape from Sobibor. I had forgotten what a sixteen-year-old soldier looks like.

He flipped to another picture of him and Yehuda Lerner in partisan uniforms. "He killed Niemann," Shlomo said with pride.

Shlomo wore a medal on his chest in the second picture.

"What's that for?" I asked.

"Bravery," he said.

"What did you do?" I asked.

He avoided the question, as he always did when there was something he did not want to talk about. Instead, he fished out a photocopy of his Russian papers, identifying him as a partisan.

We talked some more about Sobibor. Tom and I each had a Scotch; Shlomo, who rarely drinks now, had coffee. The conversation seemed more relaxed as Tom and Shlomo reminisced. There were no smiles or laughter, no tears, but an intensity as heavy as the humid summer night. At eleven, after two hours of interviews, Shlomo said abruptly, "We stop here. Mark your place. We'll begin again tomorrow."

We sat around the kitchen table. Shlomo brought cheese, fruit, and rolls. "Eat," he said to me with a quick nod, as if he were giving me an order. I drank a bottle of mineral water instead.

He dragged out a shoebox full of black and white snapshots of his jungle ranch, seven hundred miles north of Goiania. Most of the pictures were variations of the same theme — Shlomo with a rifle or a fish or a deer, in his jeep, next to his jeep, with his son Norberto, cattle, a few Indians. His rifle seemed to be everywhere. After showing the pictures, Shlomo put on a primitive headdress he had gotten from his Indian friends, explaining with pride that the Indians rarely gave those away.

I excused myself and went to bed. I needed to conserve my energy so that I would be fresh the next day. My feelings that night were mixed. I was pleased that the interview was getting somewhere, that I had Shlomo's cooperation, but I felt like an invader. I had dragged Shlomo back into his hell. I had him on the rack, stretching the old hatred and anger out of him. My only comfort was that he had agreed to talk and that he controlled the timing of the interviews. I was not forcing him to say anything. At the same time, I was afraid that the interview might turn out to be too much for him and that he'd clam up. Shlomo was capable of doing that. Just saying, "Enough," and walking out of the room.

He was up again at six. When he returned for lunch, I sensed depression in both him and Tom. Part of it was the lack of sleep; part was Sobibor. I could feel Shlomo getting very belligerent, even hostile, when we touched on topics other than Sobibor.

"What's next?" I asked Tom. "Will he talk some more?"

"I don't want to push," Tom said. "He's very edgy."

We taped for an hour and a half. I decided to drop the heavy stuff and move on to easier topics. The talk was light, breezy, and relaxed as Shlomo told me about the uprising and escape. There was pride in his voice and eyes. His hatred for the Nazis and the Poles seethed under the surface like a sulfur spring that, from time to time, erupted in an angry burst. The fires of revenge had not abated after thirty-seven years.

Later that night, after we had covered the escape and uprising, I began to explore more sensitive topics. The phone rang. It was Norberto in Rio. Shlomo was clearly pleased to get a reprieve from the relentless questions. Then the doorbell sounded. Shlomo came back to apologize. Two friends had stopped in. He grinned, as if to say "Too bad, Hicard."

I took the opportunity to interview Tom, who understood that I needed to know much more about his experiences than he had told me in Santa Barbara.

"I was a very young boy when I came to Sobibor," he said. "My conscience hadn't been formed yet. I had a strong will to live. I never doubted I would survive. I was so convinced I would that on the day of the uprising I went to the little train. The cars were loaded with canned goods. I filled my pockets."

Tom was in a reflective mood, so I picked up on it. "Do you think you left Sobibor a better or a worse person for the experience?" I asked.

"I don't know, Richard," he said. "Seeing dead people didn't matter to me anymore. Killing didn't matter. Sobibor changed my outlook. I used to believe in God. In my little town, when I would return home and it was dark, I was afraid of demons. I'd run down the street with a prayer on my lips, because according to Jewish tradition, if you have God on your lips, devils can't hurt you. I came from a religious home. This was my basic change. I no longer believe in God."

Tom was pensive and quieter than I had seen him before. There was no bitterness or anger in his voice. He spoke in matter-of-fact tones, with a barely detectable sorrow. I could feel his sense of loss, an emptiness like a hole that had never been filled. I tried to dig deeper, but Tom repeated his answer: "That's all."

"Did you need any special qualities to survive in Sobibor?" I asked. I would return later to how Sobibor had changed his life.

"Simple luck and maybe daring," he said. "Even at the camp, I took risks. I fed myself well. It was dangerous to steal food. I risked it. I smuggled food from Camp II to Camp I. I was always looking for an easier job. I tried to keep myself clean. The Germans liked that. I walked straight and fast. They liked that, too. Maybe that was my way of surviving."

I wasn't satisfied with his answer. It was clear to me that Tom had never really asked himself that question; if he had, his answer would have been more precise. I tried again. "Was there something special about you? Did you have some kind of special survival instinct?"

Tom thought for a long moment. He was sitting in the hot den with his shirt off and the air conditioner running. Tom hates heat, and the warm, humid air of Central Brazil was getting to him. He was already telling me how eager he was to get back home.

"I believe I did," he said at last. "But others with attitudes like mine went to their deaths — " He touched his jaw where the slug from the gun in Bojarski's barn was still lodged. He had found out after the war that the bullet hadn't ricocheted from his jawbone but had buried itself there. I felt the lump.

"Wasn't *this* luck?" he asked.

Tom returned to my earlier question without prodding. "Maybe if I had been older, things would have been different," he said. "I didn't know any other world. I grew up in a small town and didn't know anything about life. Then came the war and five years of hatred, beating, death. I accepted all that as normal."

Tom paused, pleased with his own insight and the impact that his observation had made on him. "I didn't know about courts until after the war. I actually thought that if someone does wrong, you just shoot him and that's the end of it."

Like Shlomo, Tom was still consumed by Sobibor. These days of talk had not been easy for him. Each night he went to bed with the terrors of Sobibor on his mind. The Holocaust — any aspect of it — touched a nerve. He had once told me that every time he read a new book on the Holocaust — and he always seemed to have one around — his family could sense it. He chuckled humorlessly. "My son used to say 'Keep away. Dad's been reading about the Holocaust again.' "

I thought the time was ripe to explore those feelings. "Is Sobibor still part of your life?" I asked. I wasn't sure where he'd take the broad question.

"I was only in Sobibor six months," he said. "But if you add to that all my dreams since then, it would be five times that amount."

"What do you dream about?"

"At least once a week," he said, almost relieved that someone was asking about his terror in the night. "The dream makes me feel as if I'm still in Sobibor. You see, Richard, I am still a prisoner. I feel I would betray my parents, my brother, my friends, if I pretended that Sobibor never happened, as some survivors have. I feel it would be some kind of an insult."

He paused, and then answered my question directly. "I have one basic dream with variations: I have a chance to escape from Sobibor. I am walking close to the fence. The Germans are all looking the other way. I could run away, but I don't.

"The general theme is — I don't take the risk. Then the Germans come to execute me, and I feel very sad. Not guilty or angry, but sad, because I lost a big opportunity.

"That's it. Lately, I've been having a variation of the dream. Wagner sends me out of the camp to get some photographic materials for him. It is the first time he's sent me out. I could go free, but I come back."

Tom paused. The silence was heavy; it was as if we had reached some important breakthrough, something deeply personal, covered with layers of feelings so complicated that they couldn't be separated. Tom began to analyze his own dream. "I think I understand where it's coming from," he said. "When they took me to Sobibor, while I was on the train, when I saw the fires, I asked myself, 'Why didn't you run away? Why didn't you sleep in some other town last night?' . . . That's the same feeling in my dream. That sadness."

"Will it ever go away — this dream and that feeling?" I asked.

"I think I could get rid of it maybe today or tomorrow. But I don't want to. Maybe I'm a masochist. I think I'll get rid of it when I finish my diary, which I began many years ago. I'm still working on it. When I finish, the dreams will stop."

We were back to his diary and to Tom's dilemma of whether to publish it or not. In Santa Barbara, he had told me that for some reason he couldn't really finish it. In Shlomo's den, quiet and pensive, he admitted that if he did, he was afraid there might be no reason to live anymore, that his body might quit, give up on him. He might just die.

I repeated an earlier question, sensing that Tom was ready to answer it now. "Did you come out of Sobibor a better or a worse person?"

"I became a pessimist," he said without hesitation. "Every nice feeling about people has disappeared. I'm worse. Being a pessimist isn't so bad. It's only an outlook. But — but killing someone is not a big deal anymore.

If I see someone suffering, I no longer can feel pity. I used to — before Sobibor . . . All feelings of pity are dead. When I was a child, I used to give . . . give . . ."

"Alms?" I suggested.

"Alms to beggars. Now I can pass them by without turning my head." There was a sadness in his voice, as if he could feel his own loss.

I changed the topic to the discussion Tom, Shlomo, Pedro, and I had had on the first day about the possibility of another Holocaust. I wanted Tom's views without Shlomo's angry interruptions.

"One of the smartest sayings is 'History repeats itself,' " Tom said. "From experience, I believe the Holocaust will happen again. Maybe not in our generation, but it will be worse. There is a history of killing from primitive times all the way to Sobibor. There will be one difference in the future — we will not go like sheep. We will fight, and this is the only thing that makes me feel better.

"I'm not a religious person. If I were, I would think God was using the Jews to bring out the good and evil in other people. The fact is that when Jews assimilate, they fade away. Maybe they need a jolt to pull them together. It's a miracle that they survived for so many generations as Jews."

I was struck by how Tom had suddenly switched to "they" when he came to the topic of Jews and religion, as though he had separated himself from his tradition and roots. I sensed a conflict. Tom saw himself as a Jew, wanted to feel as a Jew, was proud of being a Jew, and yet had cut himself off from the religious traditions of his family, his forebears, his whole race. There was a tug of war I didn't understand or perhaps couldn't understand. Or maybe it was an inner dynamic that even Tom didn't understand.

When Shlomo walked back into the room, for once I wasn't happy to see him. Tom and I had been exploring important areas I felt I might never have the opportunity to probe again.

"Ask him the questions you asked me," Tom said. "I want to hear what he has to say."

Shlomo was delighted with my questions about how Sobibor had affected him; it was as if he had been waiting for someone to ask them. His answers were organized and clear.

"There are four things needed for surviving," he began. "Luck, guts, brains, and a strong will to live . . . I hated the world after Sobibor. All humanity without exception. I was against all men." He was almost shouting at me from across the small room. His brown eyes were deeply angry. "I left Sobibor a worse man. I had little experience in life before I came.

306

While I was there, I saw only the worst of life. That filled me with hate. *Everything* died in Sobibor." Sadness forced the anger from his eyes. "Softness . . . tenderness . . . pity. Only hate. If I had been older? . . . It might have been different. But Sobibor was my school."

I asked Shlomo whether he had changed since the end of the war, more than thirty-five years ago. I knew the anger, the cynicism, the hatred, the thirst for revenge were still there. He didn't answer my question entirely or all at once.

"At first, I only wanted revenge," he said. "I was fortunate. I had a chance to release my anger."

Shlomo was referring to his year as a sixteen-year-old Russian partisan, a proud and satisfying year, when he tried to fight his way back to sanity. He didn't really want to talk to me about what he had done to "release his anger" except to say that he had killed Germans. All he would do was smile that sad smile and say, "That's another book, Hicard."

When Shlomo and Tom reminisced about Poland after the Russian liberation in 1944, I got an insight into what Shlomo may have been like just after Sobibor. The two had met in Lublin and decided to visit Bojarski. Tom thought that the farmer might not have spent all the gold and diamonds that he, Wycen, and Kostman had given Bojarski. Tom and Shlomo wanted to get what was left of the money and then execute the farmer.

Shlomo, two Russians, and Tom knocked on Bojarski's door. They were all dressed in Russian uniforms.

"Where's Mr. Bojarski?" Tom had asked.

"In town," his wife said. Her daughter stood next to her. They were frightened, because they recognized Toivi.

"We'll wait!"

Mrs. Bojarski nervously poured them vodka. Russians had a reputation for drinking every drop they could find, and if they couldn't find any, they'd drink perfume.

Shlomo got impatient and took over.

"Where'd your husband hide the money?" he demanded.

"I don't know," Mrs. Bojarski said.

"If you don't tell us, we'll kill her," Shlomo threatened, pointing to the daughter.

Tom became upset. He knew that Mrs. Bojarski had known and approved of Kostman's murder. She had accepted the money with as much greed as her husband. But Tom couldn't bring himself to shoot the girl. She was innocent.

Shlomo grabbed the girl. Mrs. Bojarski quickly told him where the money was buried. Shlomo and Tom dug it up. There were still thousands of dollars' worth of gold and diamonds. They split the money, as agreed. Then Shlomo ordered the girl to follow him behind the barn, close to the spot where Toivi had been shot in the jaw. Shlomo cocked his rifle. The girl's mother pleaded.

Tom could not go through with it. He begged Shlomo not to execute her, and, reluctantly, Shlomo lowered his gun.

"I would have done it," Shlomo told me. "Just like that."

Tom wasn't sure why he couldn't agree to killing the girl. Somehow, he said, he had felt she wasn't really guilty of anything except being in Poland. Besides, Tom had felt a little embarrassed and shy in her presence. "Her father," he admitted, "I would have shot without hesitating."

"Who is guilty and who is innocent?" he asked me rhetorically. "My mother? My father? What did they do? Who is guilty, Richard?"

"God, maybe?"

"Yes, He is the guiltiest of them all."

I wanted to get back to the question of whether Sobibor still dominated Shlomo's life, and if so, how. Because it was a painful question, I skirted it. "Are you glad you wrote a book about your experiences?" I asked.

"My book was the best thing I did in my life." Shlomo didn't even pause for breath. "The best therapy. I promised myself to tell the truth, even if it hurt someone. Because of the book, the pressure was released with much of the pain. I told Tom, 'Publish your diary. It will save your life.' "

There were contradictions in Shlomo's frank answer. He seemed to be saying that he had gotten rid of his pain and anger, yet I could see both in his eyes and hear them in his voice.

Shlomo noticed how he had been pacing, sitting, and jumping up. "You see how restless I am?" he said. "Tom is like that. We are all like that. Those of us still alive. If I'm going to live a few more years, I must forget about Sobibor. But I can't. I must talk about it."

Shlomo calmed down, sat, and puffed on his Parliament. The den was strangely quiet except for the hum of the air conditioner. I self-consciously scratched at my yellow legal pad, waiting for something to happen. Once again, I felt we had reached a crossroads. We were beyond Sobibor. We stood in the *new* Sobibor, the prison created by a prison, the new hell that in some ways was worse than the old, for there was no escape but death.

Shlomo suddenly jumped up, very excited, eyes burning like coals. In

German, he shouted at me, "Hicard, what would you do if someone killed your mother, your father, sister, and brother? What, Hicard?"

The words were almost a plea.

"I don't know," I answered in German, then switched to English. "I think I'd go crazy with hate. I'd want revenge."

"Thank you, Hicard! Thank you," he said, as though I had forgiven him.

Then Shlomo asked the question I had been expecting all day. "Do you think I'm normal?"

"What's normal?" I said. "I don't accept that word. You're special. You've suffered in a special way that the rest of us haven't. You have special feelings."

Shlomo nodded and smiled. He seemed pleased. I knew he wished he weren't so special. I also knew I was violating his inner sanctum; I had entered a very private place, where I had no right to be.

The contrast struck me with full force. We sat under a cloud of self-doubt and pain and loss, surrounded by the music Shlomo loved so much — Mantovani, "Russische Balalaika-Musik," Bernstein and the New York Philharmonic, "Chanson d'Amour," tangos, sambas, and boleros, the sound track of *Lawrence of Arabia*. I sensed that Shlomo felt he didn't have much to live for, that he was floating on the wave of life, carried forward, no longer fighting for control, retreating to the otherworldliness of love ballads and childhood memories, not certain when the wave would hit the shore or where, not caring what would happen when it did.

"Hicard, you have taken two years from my life," Shlomo said finally. "Tomorrow we finish. That's it!"

*

The next morning, I was in the den, poring over my notes, when Shlomo returned from the paper factory for lunch. It was eleven o'clock, and Shlomo was more tense than I had seen him.

"Where's Tom?" he asked.

"Still sleeping," I said.

"*Ach,*" he said in disgust. He had gotten up at six after less than two hours of sleep.

Poor Tom was exhausted. He was having trouble resting, and it wasn't just the heat, the humidity, the all-night traffic on the street below. "You only hear what we say," Tom had told me the night before. "I can see it and feel it. I can't turn it off. If I had known it was going to be like this,

I wouldn't have come. All I ask in return is that you give me credit for helping you."

I promised I would.

As we ate lunch, Shlomo suddenly relaxed, even though he was extremely tired. Maybe it was because we were going to the travel agent that afternoon to make reservations for Tom's and my return flights. It was the first sure sign that the interview would soon be over.

I told Tom I still had twenty questions to ask Shlomo.

"He still has fifteen questions," Tom told Shlomo.

"Okay," Shlomo said. "Let's work."

We went to the den. Shlomo took off his shirt and stretched out on the floor. He answered my questions directly, didn't digress, and didn't volunteer one extra detail. I felt rushed and under pressure to finish, to get my ticket, to get out of his house, out of Goiania, out of Brazil. Shlomo was like a horse, hired for an hour. He sensed he was on the way back to the stable.

"One last question," I said to Shlomo after I had picked over my list. "I know how you feel about Leon Feldhendler." Shlomo had told me that he considered Feldhendler his spiritual leader and held him in utmost respect. "But I don't know how you feel about Sasha."

"Will you accept a false answer?" Shlomo asked.

"No," I said. "I have to ask the question. But you don't have to answer it." I waited. "Did he desert you?"

Shlomo picked his words carefully, trying to be honest out of regard to me and trying to be diplomatic out of gratitude to Sasha.

"I respect him," Shlomo said. "Without him, we would not have survived. More than this, I will not say. I can't talk about someone who did, say, ten good things and maybe one bad thing. It wouldn't be fair. Tom and I can talk about it. But it's painful. It hurts me. It hurts Tom."

Once again, Shlomo had reminded me that I was an outsider, that there were things I could never understand, feelings I could never share, so intimate that I could only see their shadow, secrets I could not learn.

"The leaders are Feldhendler and Pechersky," Shlomo said with finality. "My role was small. I got the rifles."

*

It was hot and sticky. Tom was cranky because of the heat, the lack of sleep, the tension, and my obsession with questions and work. I felt relieved that I had finished with Shlomo, but I still had to talk to Tom.

We began that night after Shlomo went out to visit friends. Tom took off his shirt, lay under the air conditioner on the floor, held the mike in his hands, and answered my questions with absolute candor. He seemed relieved that at last the ordeal was coming to an end.

"I've had it today," he said after about an hour and a half. "We can finish tomorrow."

He turned on the color television to a soccer game. I had a Scotch, Tom a glass of Zubrowka, imported Polish vodka. Our minds were numb. All we wanted to do was unwind.

Shlomo came back around nine. He turned off the sound on the TV, and we began to chat. Within fifteen minutes, we were back to Sobibor. It was as if the talk over the past five days had stirred memories and emotions into a whirlpool, and the waters of pain were still swirling.

"After Sobibor, I've never laughed," Shlomo said out of the blue. He got up from the floor and walked over to me. I was sitting on the cabinet filled with drawers of cassettes. The wall above me was covered with records. He pointed to his bare, brown stomach. "I cannot laugh," he repeated. "I cannot love. I have slept with women, but there was no love. A woman is an object." He looked me straight in the eyes. "Is that normal? Is that normal?"

Shlomo didn't wait for an answer. "Sometimes I wonder why I didn't go crazy after Sobibor." He paused and said softly, "I am still in Sobibor."

Both Shlomo and Tom talked about the Poles, and they were very bitter. They didn't consider themselves Poles. They were Jews — different, separate, hated. They had both known some good, kind Poles, but not many.

"After the Russian liberation," Tom told me, "as the Jews came out of the woods or the barns or returned from Russia, the Poles used to ask, with contempt, 'There are still *more* of you?'"

He turned to Shlomo. "Do you remember that?"

"Yes," Shlomo said. "The best time of my life was as a Russian partisan. The best time of my whole life." He got up again, paced the room, clutching an imaginary carbine to his chest. "I was in control of my life. Not others . . . Me!"

Again Shlomo pulled out an observation buried deep in his memory. "I never saw anyone at Sobibor cry," he said. "Never. Seventeen months. Never."

"Neither did I," Tom said.

During a lull in the conversation, I asked Shlomo about the capture and trial of Gustav Wagner; both Wagner and Kommandant Franz Stangl had been high on the list of Simon Wiesenthal, the Nazi-hunter.

*

After the destruction of Sobibor in October 1943 put an end to Operation Reinhard, Stangl, Wagner, General Odilo Globocnik, Captain Franz Reichleitner, Captain Christian Wirth, Sergeant Hermann Michel, and 120 other death camp personnel were transferred to Trieste and assigned to the most dangerous job their superiors could find — antipartisan combat. As Stangl told Gitta Sereny in 1971, "We were an embarrassment to the brass. They wanted to find ways and means to 'incinerate' us."

Sobibor's other Kommandant, Franz (the Idiot) Reichleitner, and death camp inspector Christian (the Savage) Wirth were both killed by partisans. (Stangl believed that Wirth may have been murdered by his own men.) Stangl, Wagner, "the Preacher" Michel, and Globocnik survived Trieste.

Globocnik committed suicide when the Allies caught him; Michel fled to Egypt after the war and is presumably still there; Wagner found a construction job in Austria; Stangl was arrested as an SS officer and sent to an Austrian open prison. On May 30, 1948, he filled a knapsack with food, walked out of the prison, and picked up Wagner.

A good mountaineer, Stangl knew the Tyrolean Alps well from his youth. He and Wagner crossed into Italy and made their way to Rome, where they had heard that a German Catholic bishop, Aloïs Hudal, was helping Catholic SS officers to escape. Hudal was the rector of Santa Maria del Anima and the Vatican-appointed confessor to the German Catholic community. He was also a close personal friend of Pope Pius XII who had been apostolic delegate to Berlin and who spoke German fluently.

When Stangl and Wagner reached Rome, they had no idea about how to find Bishop Hudal. By pure chance, Stangl spotted in a crowd a former SS man who had also escaped from an Allied prison.

"Are you on the way to see Hudal?" Stangl's *Kammerad* asked. He told Stangl where to spend the night and where to find the bishop.

"You must be Franz Stangl," Bishop Hudal said as he walked into the room where Stangl was waiting. The bishop held out both hands. "I've been expecting you."

Bishop Hudal, who died in 1963, found living quarters for Stangl, gave him money and, within two weeks, a Red Cross passport, issued to stateless persons. Soon after, the bishop got Stangl a visa to Syria, a boat ticket, and a job in a textile mill in Damascus. (Before the war, and before becoming a policeman, Stangl had been a master weaver.) Stangl and his family lived in Syria for three years. They weren't lonely; also hiding there were many Germans who, like Stangl, had fled Europe. In 1951, Stangl emigrated to Brazil, where he worked first in a textile factory, then as a supervisor of preventive maintenance in a Volkswagen plant in São Paulo.

In 1967, Simon Wiesenthal paid a former Gestapo agent $7000 to tell him where Stangl was hiding. The simple fact was that the Nazi wasn't hiding. He had been living openly in Brazil under the name Stangl and was registered at the Austrian consulate in São Paulo under his name.

Wiesenthal told the press after Stangl's arrest, "If I have done nothing else in my life but get this evil man Stangl, then I would not have lived in vain."

Next, the Nazi-hunter turned his attention to Gustav Wagner, who, un-known to Wiesenthal, lived on a farm at Atibaia, just thirty miles from Stangl's house. Wiesenthal knew Wagner had been hiding in Brazil since 1950 because Stangl had so testified during his trial in Duesseldorf. Wiesen-thal asked the Brazilian police to find Wagner — he, too, was living under his own name — but the police said they couldn't. Suspecting that Wagner was being protected, Wiesenthal decided to play a waiting game. If Wagner felt no one was looking for him, maybe he would make a mistake. So over the next decade, the Nazi-hunter spoke constantly about Joseph Men-gele, the infamous Auschwitz doctor, but never about Wagner.

On April 26, 1978, someone complained to the police that "Communists" were holding a secret meeting at the Hotel Tyll in the mountains north of Rio de Janeiro. The police broke into the hotel and found sixteen German-speaking men — some had come from as far away as Britain — singing an old Nazi anthem, the "Horst Wessel Song." When the Germans explained that they were only celebrating Hitler's eighty-ninth birthday, the police released them.

Two Rio reporters covering the raid on the Hotel Tyll photographed each German and sent the pictures to Wiesenthal in Vienna. One of them was Gustav Franz Wagner. Wiesenthal decided to smoke Wagner out. He convinced the journalists that one of the Germans in the pictures — a dark man with big ears — was Wagner. (It wasn't.) The journalists ran the photo, identified the man as Wagner, and printed his Nazi ID number and a brief history of his Nazi activities.

The Germans in Brazil "eliminated" the dark man with the big ears. But Wagner, fearing that Israeli agents were after him, called the police and offered to surrender on a São Paulo street corner. Germany, Israel, and Poland had each requested Wagner's extradition.

Shlomo was watching the evening news when he saw Wagner's face on the screen. He nearly went crazy with anger, realizing that for almost thirty years he had been breathing the same air as Wagner. He jumped on the first plane for São Paulo, because if someone did not positively identify the Nazi as Sobibor's Gustav Wagner within a few days, the police would have to release him, and he could then run off to Paraguay or bury himself in some remote Brazilian village.

Shlomo found Wagner in the holding tank with several other prisoners. "Hello, Gustl," he said, using Wagner's more intimate name.

"Who's that? Who said that?" Wagner seemed confused.

"It's the little Jewish goldsmith from Sobibor."

"Yes, yes, I know you. I saved you," Wagner said. "You and your three little brothers."

The police held Wagner, and Shlomo eventually testified at the extradition trial, where Wagner admitted that he was a Nazi and had served in Sobibor. "I know what happened there," he told the court. "But I never went to see. I only obeyed orders."

The Brazilian Supreme Court ruled that neither Poland nor Israel had jurisdiction over Wagner, and that Germany's extradition documents were flawed. Wagner was a free man once again.

Then, in October 1980, Wagner's attorney announced that the Nazi had committed suicide on the farm in Atibaia where he worked as a farmhand. Shlomo hinted to me that Wagner's death was no accident. Did the Israelis get him? Did Brazil's *Kameradenwerk,* the Nazi underground, get him? Did the Jews get him? Shlomo declined to explain his cryptic remark.

Shlomo recalled how Tom had phoned him from California when he had learned that the Brazilian government would not extradite Wagner.

"Can I buy a gun in Brazil?" Tom had asked Shlomo.

"Don't worry," Shlomo had said. He didn't want Tom to do anything rash. "Wagner'll be taken care of."

Tom told me later that he had thought many times about hunting down and killing the Sobibor Nazis. He said he didn't know whether he would have actually done it, but he could have because to him it wouldn't have been murder. But if he'd been caught, he said, that might have affected his family, especially his children. "We all dreamed that if we survived," he once said, "we'd cut Wagner slowly to pieces and make him suffer a slow death. But if we did that today, we'd go down to his level."

The next day, my last in Goiania, I finished interviewing Tom. His voice was emotionless and flat; his eyes showed nothing. He was reluctant to expand his answers, and when I touched on something especially painful, his voice became very soft.

One such painful memory was the death of his parents. It was the last subject of our interview. "There's a mental block about them," he told me. "There has to be. I had never allowed myself to think in the ghetto what a terrible loss it would be if *one* of my parents died. I just couldn't imagine the pain. I couldn't even think about it. Then, in a matter of minutes, my mother, my father, my brother died. And I didn't even think *one second* about them. Nothing. It must be nature's way. If I started to think, maybe I couldn't begin to handle it."

"Do you feel guilty about not having felt deep sorrow over the loss of your family?" I asked.

"I feel very guilty that when I said good-by to my mother, the words I said were stupid." His voice was soft and pained. Tom had told me many painful things about Sobibor in the more than ten days I had been with him, both in Santa Barbara and Brazil — murder, humiliation, greed, degradation, beatings. But this was the closest I had seen him come to tears. I expected them to flow, but it was as if his sockets were dry, and the pain and memories, no matter how hard they pushed, could not produce a single tear. I remembered what Shlomo had said the previous night: "I never saw anyone at Sobibor cry."

"Other than that, no guilt," Tom continued. "Why? Should there be? I couldn't help anything."

"What were those last words?" I asked gently.

Tom paused for a long while, then said, "I hate to repeat them to you."

I didn't push anymore. I had found at least one of Tom's Sobibors, the one he would never escape from. A son's last words to his mother, the words she was to carry in her ears to the gas chambers, words that, once spoken, can never be recalled or changed, only replayed in one's mind. There was nothing I could say or do. I turned off the tape recorder and tried to look busy.

Shlomo came home, and after lunch I told him I'd like to hear some music. I had been surrounded by records and speakers for days, but had never given Shlomo the chance to show off his equipment. He was delighted. After all, this was Goiania, not New York or Paris or Tel Aviv, and here he had the best records in every language.

Shlomo played Brazilian sambas and danced around the room with an imaginary beauty. He cut off the sambas before even one side had been played and switched to Brazilian folk songs. He hummed along. "I love music," he said. Then he switched to a cassette of modern Hebrew music that his son had recorded in Israel. Shlomo seemed to lose himself in his music, leave Sobibor for a few brief hours, touch a different part of his soul, meet a part of himself he had never really known, the gentle side, the joyful, the playful.

Then Shlomo put on a cassette of Hebrew religious music. There was a mood in the den that I hadn't felt before. Shlomo closed his eyes and, as if he were standing before the Wailing Wall in the Holy City, rocked back and forth to the plaintive cry of a people questioning their God, asking the reason for all the suffering, not understanding, yet never losing faith in Him.

Then Shlomo sat on the arm of the couch. Tom was stretched out on the other end, his feet propped on a stool. I was lying on the floor on my back, a huge pillow under my head. Except for the music, the room was empty and sad. I had never seen either Tom or Shlomo so still for so long.

I felt the loneliness and sadness, too, and for a brief moment, I no longer felt like an outsider looking into a world I had not experienced and could not understand. I felt close to Shlomo and Tom. Three agnostics, we shared the same loss. Once, in the life of each of us there had been a religious warmth, a haunting beauty that had surrounded us in our youth. Once, there had been a closeness, a peace, a continuity, a rootedness, a sureness beneath the prayers and melodies and pleadings with God. They were gone now, no longer part of our lives. They had left a hole that could not be filled by our work or the comfort of our adult loves.

Tom couldn't take the sadness. He walked out to the balcony into the afternoon heat and humidity.

The cantor intoned, "Eli, Eli" in a rich tenor voice. Shlomo hummed along.

"My God, my God, why have You forsaken me?" the cantor sang. They were words of doubt and gentle reproach. Then he broke into the affirmation of faith, as his forefathers had done for centuries before him. "Hear, O Israel, the Lord our God, the Lord is One."

Tom returned to the room as if the "Eli, Eli" were a terrible magnet of memories and dreams, drawing him back to Sobibor.

"*They* sang that," Shlomo said softly.

He didn't have to tell me who "they" were. The long lines of women, children, and men had never really left us.

"Yes, I have heard it myself," Tom said. "Often."

Chapter 40

Esther

T HE FIRST TIME I met Esther Terner-Raab, she was crying. It was at the International Liberators' Conference, sponsored by the United States Holocaust Memorial Council and held at the State Department in October 1981. Esther was a member of a panel discussing uprisings. When she began to talk about Sobibor, her voice cracked and her emotions took over.

The conference was unusual for many reasons, among them the fact that Communist-bloc countries had sent to it military delegates who as soldiers had liberated the camps. Although the Russian and Czech speakers at the conference described the camps and the condition of the prisoners when they freed them, never once did I hear them say the word *Jew*. If I had not already known that six million Jews died in the Holocaust, I would have gotten the impression that the only prisoners in the camps were non-Jewish Russian, Polish, and Czech civilians. Since I did not attend all the workshops and plenary sessions, I checked my observation with Jan Karski, the Polish underground courier, who gave a talk at the conference. He also had thought it both strange and symptomatic of Communist-bloc attitudes that major participants at a conference on Hitler's Final Solution avoided saying *Jew,* almost as if they had been coached.

The second time I met Esther, I was angry. It was in her spacious Vineland, New Jersey, home. We were sitting in the kitchen, and my tape recorder was plugged in. Although she had readily agreed to the interview, she wasn't sure whether she would allow me to use her name.

317

"Why not?" I was surprised and disappointed because, like most writers, I don't like the idea of false names or anonymity. They tend to lessen the credibility of any story.

"I got a letter," she said. "Who needs that?"

The Vineland newspaper had printed a short article about Esther. One of the readers had written her an anti-Semitic diatribe. After the murder of her parents, the months of terror in Sobibor, the uncertainty in Stefan Marcyniuk's barn, the destruction of her Jewish community — after all that — she still felt that she had to hide, not in a straw pile in Poland, but in New Jersey, almost forty years later.

As we sat in her kitchen ("It's cozier in here," she said), Esther was nervous, and her face showed signs of strain. She was not looking forward to dredging up old memories. "Not for a million dollars would I go through this," she said.

But like Tom Blatt and other survivors I had talked to, Esther was anxious that the Sobibor story and her personal story be told with accuracy. Her older son was especially interested. "You ought to see his Holocaust library," she said. "He was one of four children of survivors interviewed on a television show in Chicago."

Esther told me about her three companions in the barn after the escape from Sobibor. Her brother Idel (Jerry Terner) is still alive, Samuel Lerer is a New York City cab driver, and Avram Kohn lives in Australia. She also told me that Wolodia, the Ukrainian guard who supervised her in the armory, fled Sobibor on the night of October 14 with one of the Russian women the Nazis had held as prostitutes (Esther met both of them after liberation in Chelm), and that her close friend Zelda Metz, who had lived near Vineland, died recently. After breaking out of Sobibor, Zelda had bought false identity papers proving she was an Aryan.

Esther missed Zelda. "We used to sleep in the same bunk in Sobibor," she recalled. "Zelda slept on one side of me, and Mrs. Shapiro [chaperone] on the other."

Esther doesn't laugh easily, but her face brightened a little as she recalled a story about her and Zelda. Once they were picking mushrooms in the woods outside the fence at Sobibor. When they had filled a few boxes, they brought them to the canteen. The Nazi in charge told them to wash the mushrooms and put them in the cellar that served as an icebox. When Esther and Zelda walked into the basement, they saw a large pot of soup cooling there. They were delighted.

"We spit in it and washed our hands in it," Esther said. "Don't ask me what else we did to that soup . . . And they *ate* it."

Two of the Jews who had escaped from the forest brigade after the Ukrainian guard was killed — Podchlebnik and a man named Hoenigman — also used to live near Esther. The Nazis had killed all the Polish Jews in the Waldkommando in retaliation.

"Zelda held a grudge against Podchlebnik and Hoenigman until her last breath," Esther told me. "She felt it was too high a price to pay for two lives."

Podchlebnik was dead. Hoenigman, who was very sick, moved to Florida a few years ago. Esther had lost track of him. Unlike Zelda, she wasn't bitter about the two men risking the lives of everyone else in Sobibor to save their own necks. "I don't know what I would have done in their place," she said.

Like the other survivors I had interviewed, Esther had never really escaped from Sobibor. "When Zelda was alive," she told me, "we'd call each other every day and talk about it. I still think about it before I fall asleep, and then I dream."

"About what?" I asked.

"Mainly that I'm running, that the Gestapo is after me, that Wagner is after me, and that I can't run fast enough. Then I start screaming. I see children's heads smashed against wagons, people killed in front of me, people being tortured . . . It has left me so that I can never be happy, and I cannot help it."

Esther had clearly sorted out in her own mind the reasons she survived. At the top of her list is her cousin, Leon Feldhendler. She spoke of him with great pride. "He felt a responsibility toward others," she said. "Very few have that when their own lives are at stake. He never considered escaping to save his own skin. He felt responsible for us — like a father. You fought with almost anyone else at Sobibor, but not with Leon. You listened when he spoke. You felt good when he spoke. He helped a lot of us cope."

Esther also felt she survived because Gustav Wagner was not in the camp on October 14. "He would have sniffed the escape out like a dog," she told me. "He was the smartest Hitler could find. He even knew what you were *thinking*. Shrewd. That man was shrewd."

Esther paused to fish in her memory for a Wagner story. "Once, he gave me two pieces of candy," she recalled. A half-smile crossed her lips. "He probably had it on his conscience for the rest of his life, that he gave a Jew candy."

Esther's unwavering faith in God also saved her. Unlike Shlomo and Tom, she is still an Orthodox Jew. She and her husband own and run a kosher poultry-processing business. When she called my editor to agree to an interview, she added, "Tell him not to call on the Holy Days."

God was Esther's life vest. "I saw so many who didn't believe give up," she told me. "I always believed, but don't ask me why. It helped me. In such danger, you really need something to hang on to — hope. I think religion is hope."

"Others don't believe anymore," I said. "They can't understand how a God would allow all those innocent people to die. Doesn't that bother you?"

"If you're religious, you're not *supposed* to ask those kinds of questions," Esther said. "What did my father do wrong? What did my mother do wrong? What did all the children do wrong? — I really can't answer. And if you believe, you won't even try."

Esther loved talking about the uprising. And when she did, there was disbelief, almost awe, in her voice. "We felt we had no chance of getting out," she said. "But at least, we were doing something. We didn't go like lambs. Even if we killed one Gestapo, it was worth it. We were condemned people anyway. Why not try? If we had only known we'd close the camp down by escaping, it would have been a big thing for those of us who didn't make it."

I didn't feel any strong hatred or thirst for revenge coming through in Esther's voice, so I asked, "Did you hate the Nazis that much, that you'd risk your life to kill just one?"

"Yes. I had feelings of terrible hatred and revenge," she said. "I just couldn't figure out how any human being could do what they were doing. Didn't they think of their own wives and children when they killed us?"

The hatred was there now, in her face, in her eyes, in her strained voice. "What kind of human beings *were* they?" The question seemed wrung out of her, like water from a rock.

When she told me her personal escape story — her dream, her reunion with Idel, her survival in Stefan Marcyniuk's barn — Esther peppered her story with "luck" and "miracle" and "it was meant for us to live."

"I always feel that the dream helped me survive," she said, referring to the night before the escape, when she dreamed that her mother told her to go to the barn. "It was more luck than common sense."

If Esther still hated the Nazis, what she felt for the Poles was not love. "After we were liberated by the Russians," she said with bitterness, "we had to run constantly because the Poles were just as bad as the Germans."

Esther went back to Poland in 1977 to visit the Marcyniuks and to see Sobibor once again. Stefan had died, but Mrs. Marcyniuk was still alive and so were her children. Esther had remained close to them over the years and had helped them financially after they lost most of their wealth during the war. She dragged out a set of drawings of the farm that one of Stefan's sons had made for her. Among them were detailed sketches of the barn where Esther and Idel, Samuel and Avram had lived, including a scale drawing of their house inside the haystack.

"All of Stefan's children were well educated," Esther said, recalling how she had argued with them about the anti-Semitism of the Poles. " 'Why weren't the death camps in any other country but Poland? Why not in Germany — halfway between Holland and Poland?' . . . But they defended Poland."

Esther shook her head in disbelief. "They couldn't see it my way." She paused. "I hope you're not a Polack, are you?"

This time, she really laughed.

Esther said she didn't see Sobibor in 1977 because she became ill while visiting Maidanek, where the barbed-wire fences, watchtowers, and barracks brought back the old feelings of terror. "I got a hundred and two fever," she said. "Next time, I think I'll go to Sobibor first. That may be easier. I feel I should go back again, just as I went back to Poland — to Chelm — my birthplace. I was bitterly disappointed. I knew there was nothing left there for me, but I had to prove it to myself . . . If I see Sobibor, I will not want to go back again. As it is, I still feel there's something I should see."

We talked about the war crimes trials of the Sobibor Nazis. Esther was a witness at each. Hubert Gomerski was the first. He got life in 1948, but in 1978 he asked to be retried on a technicality.

"I saw him walking down the street before the 1978 retrial," Esther recalled. "The old fear came back. I didn't see him as Gomerski, the citizen . . . I saw him as Gomerski, the Gestapo. I was scared stiff. I looked behind me. I was afraid there was another one around to protect him . . . Then I felt anger. 'Look, he's walking down the street and nobody even cares.' "

Gomerski was being retried on yet another technicality in the fall of 1981, and Esther was asked to testify. This time she declined. "What's the use?" she said bitterly.

Erich Bauer was the second Sobibor Nazi to be tried. The German courts had already denazified him; that is, released him, even though they knew he was a Nazi officer, because they had found no evidence of his committing war crimes. The court apparently had not realized that Bauer was the

Badmeister of Sobibor. Samuel Lerer recognized him later on the street in Kreutzberg, West Germany, and turned him in. Samuel and Esther both testified against Bauer in his 1950 trial in Berlin.

"His wife and daughter said they didn't believe it," Esther recalled. "They said they had never heard about it. But I didn't believe them. I didn't *believe* them. All those suitcases filled with stuff from Sobibor that he brought home every time. They must have asked where he got it all from."

"How did you feel, testifying against Bauer?" I asked. He got life and subsequently died in prison.

"I still felt afraid of him," she said. "Yet I knew he was harmless. 'My God,' I thought to myself. 'This *nothing* had such power?' I also had a sense of revenge. I knew I was doing something against him. The world would know, and he would be punished."

Twelve more Sobibor Nazis were tried in Hagen, West Germany, in 1965 and 1966, among them Karl Frenzel, Kurt Bolander, Franz Wolf, and Karl Werner Dubois, who had played dead on October 14, 1943, after an escaping Jew had clubbed him. No one seems to know whether SS officers Groth and Poul — both of whom were transferred from Sobibor for raping Jewish women — survived the war or not.

Bolander hanged himself before his sentencing; Frenzel got life, but his sentence was later commuted and he is now free; Wolf got eight years; two Nazis got four years each; two more got three years each; and five others were acquitted for lack of evidence.

Esther was one of the witnesses who got Joseph (the Baker) Kliehr off the hook. She was not unhappy about that. "I don't even know why he was in Sobibor," she told me in defense of Kliehr. "Even the other Nazis picked on him."

She pulled another story from her memory and paused to dust it off. Kliehr was in charge of the barracks where the shoes of the murdered Jews were stored before being sent to Germany for resale, Esther said. He was a soft touch.

"I need some shoes," she told him one day.

"Sit down," he said, waiting on her as if she were his best customer.

"Do you want another pair?" he asked after he had fitted her.

Esther remembers the trial of Karl Frenzel the best. She still can't forget how he killed a baby. "That was the worst thing I saw," she told me. "It just won't leave me."

She described the murder to the court. How she had been working in the Merry Flea when she heard a new transport come in; how she had hidden behind a drape and watched out the window; how she'd seen Frenzel swing a baby by its feet against the boxcar and toss it into the miners' train, as if it were a dead rat.

"You've got to be a *beast!*" she shouted at Frenzel from the witness stand. "There's no word for someone who would do a thing like that."

Frenzel's defense attorney took full advantage of Esther's emotional state. Like a good lawyer, he began to stone her with questions to confuse her and to destroy her credibility. "When did you see it? On which day? At what time? Where did you see it? How far away was it? What color were the drapes? How many centimeters from the window?"

"Listen," Esther interrupted. "I don't have to answer you!"

"Why?" he egged her on.

"It's just one Nazi defending the other."

"How do you know I'm a Nazi?" he asked, hoping to prejudice her testimony.

"If I put an SS hat on you," she said (she was boiling now), "I'm sure I'd recognize that I'd seen you someplace."

Some German university students were observers in the courtroom while Esther sparred with Frenzel's attorney. When she returned to her hotel that evening, she found a card and a bouquet of roses from them. Would she be willing to answer questions in one of their classes?

"They were all so young," Esther recalled. "Afterward, a student came up to me and said, 'My father was a Nazi, but he didn't do anything wrong.'"

"I hate to tell you," she had answered, "but he did."

I didn't have to be very observant to notice how angry and upset Esther was, just talking about the Nazi trials. "Was justice done?" I asked her.

"Not at all," she said without a moment of reflection. "They just took advantage of us witnesses. We didn't keep records at Sobibor. It was our word against theirs. They just tried to confuse the witnesses. I had the feeling that they'd have loved to put *me* on trial.

"It was a joke! They showed no respect. If you met a younger judge, you could expect a little compassion and understanding. I always went by age. If the judge had been a student or judge before the war, I knew he was one of them."

Esther paused, taken aback by the strength of her own emotion. "Now," she said quietly, referring to Sobibor, "it's — nobody saw . . . nobody knew . . . nobody was there."

It would have been hard for me to accept what Esther had just said if I hadn't heard the same things from other survivors who had testified at the Nazi trials — the snickers, the laughter, the disrespect, the anti-Semitism clothed in judges' robes or hiding behind law degrees, the feeling of being on trial oneself, the disbelief at a system that hands out three-, four-, and seven-year sentences for killing Jews like deer out of season.

"I still have the note that came with the flowers," Esther said.

I had forgotten about it. I asked her to get it.

Because of the terrible afternoon [it said], you should have a little pleasure. These flowers are from us.

Chapter 41

The Partisans

J UST AS I was beginning to research *Escape From Sobibor,* I learned that Miriam Novitch, an Israeli, was in New York on business. She had interviewed most of the Sobibor partisans for her own book, *Sobibor: Martyrdom and Revolt,* a collection of short testimonies. I told Ms. Novitch I was writing a book and needed her help in finding and interviewing the Sobibor survivors now living in Israel. When I mentioned to her that I wasn't Jewish, she very nearly slammed down the phone.

"You'd never understand," she told me.

"That may be so," I said. I was getting hot myself and felt like telling her to forget it, that I didn't need her help. "But I'm writing it anyway."

"Why are Americans interested in Sobibor *now?*" she asked with bitterness. "Do they feel guilty?"

She finally agreed — with a certain amount of reluctance, it seemed to me — to help when I was ready to come to Israel. About six months later, Miriam called me from New York. Her attitude had changed completely. She was excited about the project. "When are you coming?" she asked. "How's the book going?"

In Tel Aviv I rented a car and drove straight north along the Mediterranean Sea to Kibbutz Lohamei Haghetaot (Ghetto Fighters), a few miles from the Israeli-Lebanese border. So that I wouldn't get lost trying to weave through Haifa at night, I picked up two Israeli soldiers with M-16s slung over their shoulders, hitchhiking home for the Sabbath.

When I arrived at the Ghetto Fighters' Kibbutz, founded by Holocaust survivors, resistance fighters, and partisans, Miriam had a cold supper and a bottle of Israeli wine waiting for me. A woman in her early sixties, with gray hair combed back into a bun, she collects Holocaust documents, films, and art for the three-story museum staffed by the kibbutz. She lives the Holocaust every waking moment.

Miriam, a White Russian by birth, had been studying in Paris to be a teacher, and when the war broke out she joined the French underground as a courier. "I used to dress like a pregnant woman," she recalled. "I'd have the documents in the pouch."

The Nazis caught her and sent her to a work camp in Vittel, France, where she met Yitzhak Katzenelson, a well-known poet whom the Jews smuggled out of the Warsaw ghetto with one of his sons just before the April 1943 uprising. Katzenelson's wife and two other sons had already been murdered in Treblinka.

During his ten months in Vittel, Katzenelson wrote a diary and his most famous poem, "The Song of the Murdered Jewish People." The Nazis eventually sent him and his son, Zvi, to the gas chambers in Auschwitz.

Miriam became the poet's courier. She cut her wrists to have an excuse to get inside the camp dispensary. While the medic was fetching bandages, she stole three empty jars, stuffed the manuscripts inside, and buried the jars. Later, a Frenchwoman who worked in the Vittel laundry smuggled the manuscripts out. After the Americans liberated Vittel, Miriam retrieved the poet's works, and the Ghetto Fighters' Kibbutz eventually published them.

Miriam has been unearthing art and documents ever since, traveling from old ghetto to old ghetto, embassy to embassy. She is driven by a determination, the likes of which I have never seen, not to let the world forget what happened to her and to her people.

Like other survivors, Miriam is a scarred woman. One day in Vittel, she was watching a group of sixty children playing in the camp yard. They had adapted to camp life, inventing new games and making toys out of sticks and boxes. Miriam left them for a few minutes. When she returned, they were gone — taken to the gas chambers in Auschwitz. She cannot erase that scene from her mind. "When I see children playing in the yard or in the street today," she told me, "I suddenly see *their* faces." Later, as she interpreted while I interviewed Sobibor survivors, she would begin to cry any time someone said "child" or "children."

One of Miriam's precious finds was eighteen pencil drawings of Sobibor by Joseph Richter. Miriam learned that the artist had left the sketches in Chelm during the war and had never returned to pick them up. She keeps the originals in the museum's basement vault to protect them from possible PLO attack.

I asked to see them. Joseph Richter made the drawings between 1942 and 1943 on old newspapers or on the backs of Nazi posters, then dated and signed them. Some appear to be quick gesture drawings; others were sketched with more attention to detail. Miriam has never been able to determine who Richter was. A Jew with false identity papers? Someone who escaped from Sobibor? (No one I talked to has ever heard of him.) A Pole? Whatever the case, the drawings are among the few Sobibor documents that still exist. I asked Miriam whether I could print some of them in *Escape From Sobibor*. She agreed, on condition that I not use them anywhere else nor give them to anyone else. "They could be used against us," she warned me.

A year earlier, I would have thought she was paranoid. "Why would anyone want to do that?" I would have asked in disbelief. But by the time I visited Israel, I knew better. Miriam seemed especially sensitive about one drawing, described on the back by Richter himself as follows: "At the station in Urusk, an old Jewish woman ran away; she had her right arm broken. German 'Grenzschutz' [Austrians] did not want to kill her. It was done by the Ukrainian police. One is digging a grave near the railway; another waits to shoot her. She begs: 'Only a little vodka.' "

I found the sketch very touching. To me, there was only one interpretation: the woman was begging for something to ease her pain, to help her face death, to numb the terrible waiting. But Miriam was afraid that anti-Semites would twist the picture to say: See these Jews? They are all drunks. All they can think about — even before death — is another belt of vodka. Good riddance.

*

We sat in Eda and Itzhak Lichtman's kitchen in Holon, close to Tel Aviv. After getting married, Eda and Itzhak had tried to pick up life where they had left it before the war. Itzhak opened a shoe shop in Israel after they emigrated in 1950; Eda continued to teach kindergarten. They are both retired now.

Eda looks like a sweet little grandma. Still watching over others, as she did in Sobibor, she kept offering Miriam and me coffee, tea, eggs, sweets.

I plugged in my tape recorder and, to the rattle of dishes, the munching of cookies, and Eda's voice phoning the other survivors to come over so that I could interview them, I began to question Itzhak. Miriam interpreted.

Itzhak was not well, and when I first saw him I thought to myself that he probably wouldn't remember much. I was wrong. His memory was excellent (Eda's was not), and a quiet fire still burned inside him. He pumped out a steady stream of facts, dialogue, details, and names.

When Itzhak began telling me how he had carried the pots of swill to the gate of Camp III and how the Ukrainian guard knocked him senseless with his rifle butt, Miriam turned to me and said, "Look at the poor man. I don't think he has fully recovered from that blow." She wasn't referring to the accuracy of his story, but to the vacant, almost haunted look in his face and eyes.

The West German government had invited Itzhak to testify at Gomerski's retrial, which was going on while I was in Israel. Itzhak was angry that he was too sick to go. After almost forty years, he still wanted to get "them," to punish "them" for what they had done to him, his wife and child, to his whole family.

While I was rounding off Itzhak's story, the other survivors began to arrive — Abraham, Aizik, Jacob, and Hella. The small apartment sounded like a shtetl on market day.

Abraham Margulies was an extremely articulate man, a printer with powerful hands and ink under his fingernails. Though he was sixty-one and his hair was streaked with gray, he seemed to have the vigor of a man in his forties. As he told me about his terrible experiences in unloading boxcars on the train brigade, his eyes frequently filled with tears: the beautifully dressed Austrian lady who had offered him a tip for helping her with her luggage; the transport of dead, decomposing Jews from another camp ("I cannot escape this. Until my last breath I'll remember"); the transport of the mentally sick, whom the Nazis tortured and taunted before gassing; the baby in the boxcar who had smiled so sweetly at him ("This I cannot forget. I didn't know I could cry anymore").

Aizik Rottenberg had been a construction worker at Sobibor. The Nazis caught him and his mother, two brothers, and a sister when they raided Wlodawa for the last time in May 1943. His father and another brother and sister had already been gassed at Sobibor.

Aizik had been hiding in a dugout behind a double wall of cement and stone while the SS and the Ukrainians were cleaning out the ghetto. A baby began to cry. "Someone wanted to smother it," Aizik recalled. "But the rest of us said no. A Ukrainian heard the baby and pulled us out."

Aizik and one of his brothers, who had been selected in Sobibor, knew about the escape well in advance. They stashed away extra clothes and hard sugar. After Sasha gave the escape signal on October 14, Aizik pounded a hole in the fence with a hammer. He waited a moment for his brother, saw him go down, and then ran.

Aizik told me how he and another Jew were treated by a German to whom they were betrayed after they had escaped from Sobibor. "He made us play dogs," he said, watching my face closely.

"Play dogs?" I wasn't sure what he meant.

"Yes." Aizik began to speak in a rapid-fire, excited voice. "We had to crawl on all fours and bark like dogs. We even stole food from the horses."

I tried to read Aizik's face and eyes. He seemed to be smiling, but I sensed it was out of deep humiliation. How does one survive treatment like that, I thought. How does one ever quiet the anger, find peace, still the memories? How can one ever look at a dog again and not remember?

Jacob Biskubicz, who had worked on the train brigade with Abraham, was one of the two boys Erich Bauer had commandeered on October 14 to unload his truck filled with vodka just minutes before the escape. When the Jews in Camp I let out a wild "Hurrah!" and stampeded toward the main gate, Jacob and David jumped from the truck. Bauer opened fire, killing David.

Jacob ran into the North Camp, where he hid until it was dark. Then he hacked through the fence with his knife and ran into the forest. He was the last Jew to escape from Sobibor. After wandering for several weeks, he met the partisans and fought alongside them until liberation.

Jacob spoke like a man still in a dream. Once he started his story, there was no way to stop him, even for a question. He almost shouted into my mike, and Miriam had a difficult time translating between his gulps for air. One memory was especially painful. Jacob's father, who was also in Sobibor, took sick one day. Jacob tried to cover for him, but when the man grew weaker, Wagner and Frenzel dragged him off to Camp III. Jacob tried to run after his father, but two prisoners held him down. The boy heard the final gunshot.

Hella Felenbaum-Weiss is a chain smoker who owns a café in Tel Aviv. Her light blond hair was swept back, her brown eyes seemed sad, and she spoke in a husky voice. She came to Eda's apartment with her husband, whom she had met while fighting with the Russians in Czechoslovakia. Like Esther, she still dreams of Sobibor. When she wakes up, she takes Valium to chase away the nightmares. But Hella is proud, even today, of the months she spent as a Russian partisan and the medals she won — a Red Star for bravery and five commendations.

Hella tended the cows of the farmer who had agreed to hide her because she looked so Polish. When the Germans attacked the farm village for sympathizing with the partisans, she fled to the forest, where she met some Russian POWs carrying toy rifles, which they used to frighten off the Poles or to back their demands for food. Eventually, she ended up in the Russian partisan regiment of Prokopyuk.

The Russians sent Hella to partisan school for six weeks to learn guerrilla warfare, weapons and explosives, and the principles of Communism. One day, Shlomo pranced into her camp on horseback, clutching his rifle. He had heard that there was a Jewish girl from Sobibor in the camp and had come to see for himself.

Hella started out as a medic, nursing wounded partisans, but soon she asked for active duty. "It broke my heart to see all the wounded," she told me.

Hella's commander assigned her to a partisan team that dynamited trains and bridges. "I feel good that I fought," she told me, adding that she was wounded once. "I didn't fight just for my own life, but for something bigger. Now, I couldn't kill a German. But then I could. The children I saw the Germans kill in Sobibor gave me the courage."

"Were there many women partisans?" I asked.

"Quite a few," she said. "Polish girls and Russian."

Hella went on to explain that the Russians had treated her and the other women with great respect. She recalled how her Russian commander had given her a pistol, saying, "If a Russian man tries to violate you, you have the right to shoot him."

"Did you kill any Germans?" I asked. It was hard for me to imagine Hella behind a gun. She was so short that the carpenter at Sobibor had built a stool for her to stand on when the SS came to her barracks so that she'd look taller and stronger.

"Oh, yes, I killed Germans," Hella said, telling me how she had fought in the battles of Michalowice and Tymen, Persow and Kosice, and Morawska-Ostrave. "For my brothers and my mother — "

Hella began to cry.

*

Outside Eda and Itzhak's apartment, I took some pictures of the partisans. Then Miriam and I left. On the way back to the kibbutz, Miriam was completely exhausted from the emotion and from the fatigue of translating. The survivors had stirred up her own memories of Vittel and the Holocaust years.

I was deeply disappointed that I couldn't arrange an interview with Yehuda Lerner, now an Israeli policeman in Jerusalem, because I especially wanted details about the assassination of the Nazis in Sobibor, the escape plan, and his activities with Chil's partisan unit in the Parczew Forest. At first, Lerner was reluctant to talk to me under any circumstances, but Miriam pressed until he consented. We agreed to meet in his home on the edge of Jerusalem. I drove from the kibbutz into the Holy City, only to find that he had been called out of town on police business. Miriam tried again, but Lerner was even more reluctant to talk. The best I could do was to get him to answer a dozen key questions by phone.

If Lerner was hesitant, Haim Lejst was eager. Miriam and I visited him and his wife in their beautiful Tel Aviv apartment. Haim had arrived in Sobibor in the spring of 1943, about the same time as Toivi. When he began to tell me how the Nazis had killed his mother, father, and five brothers with their wives and children, Miriam began to cry again.

Wagner selected Haim. "Gardeners?" the Nazi called up and down the line. "Gardeners?"

When Haim volunteered, Wagner led him to a strawberry patch in Camp II. "How would you take care of these?" he asked.

Haim explained.

"You passed," Wagner told him. "You'll work here."

Two incidents in particular stood out in Haim's mind. Once, when the Germans were burying mines around the camp, one exploded, killing a soldier. Haim had dared to smile, and a Ukrainian reported him to Frenzel.

"You think that's funny?" Frenzel demanded. "Maybe you'll think this is funny, too." He gave Haim seventy-five lashes, beating him almost to death.

Haim's other story was more grisly. Wagner used the miners' train to cart sacks of ashes from the crematorium in Camp III to the garden. "For fertilizer," he told Haim, who had to spread the ashes and bits of bone around the strawberries and vegetables. Wagner thought that using Jews to energize his food was funny. One day at roll call, he took a bite out of a large carrot. "There," he told the prisoners. "I just ate twenty Jews."

Haim's wife told me that her husband dreams about Sobibor every night and jumps out of bed screaming. In each dream, a Nazi is beating him. "All his faculties are affected," she told me. "He got so many beatings that there has been damage."

Haim was lucky after he broke out of Sobibor. A Polish farmer with ten children hid him. After resting and regaining his strength, Haim left, fearing that one of the children might let it slip that his father was helping a Jew. Haim found another heroic Pole who was already hiding six or seven Jews. He stayed with him until the end of the war.

Mordechai Goldfarb (the painter) was the last survivor I interviewed in Israel. His wife was reluctant to permit him to talk to me because he had a bad heart. She knew from past experience that when Mordechai talked about Sobibor, he couldn't calm down afterward. But as a favor to Miriam, she invited me to their Haifa home.

It was a warm evening. Mordechai was sitting in walking shorts in the small but tastefully decorated apartment in the hills of Haifa above the sea. He was tanned, young-looking, with brown hair, white sideburns, and hazel eyes. On the walls of the living room and kitchen hung dozens of his paintings. I thought I detected the Holocaust in them — elongated, tortured houses like flames hugging the cliffs, somber colors, sad faces, a haunting emptiness. "People used to tell me that I paint the Holocaust in everything I do," Mordechai told me. "But I don't anymore."

Mordechai was very articulate. Like a professional lecturer, he constantly watched my face as he spoke, to see how I reacted to his painful life story. When he talked about his brother, Avraham, to whom he had been tied when he arrived in Sobibor, his eyes misted.

"I didn't even know about the escape," Mordechai said, emphasizing the irony that he survived and his brother didn't. "My brother knew. He told me at noon, 'Today we're going to break out. It would be better if we don't go together. That way, maybe one of us will survive.' "

I noticed that whenever Mordechai mentioned his brother, he glanced at the wall to his right covered with paintings. One was an oil of a small boy, hands in his pockets, walking down an empty ghetto street. It was a haunting portrait.

"Is that your brother?" I asked.

"Yes, I painted it from an old photograph," Mordechai said. "Several people asked to buy it, but I won't sell. It's my favorite."

One day, Mordechai told me, he had heard that there was a Goldfarb in Israel with the same first name as his brother. Was Avraham still alive?

"I was so happy, I began to shout," Mordechai said. "Then, I met the man . . . It wasn't him."

*

After nine interviews in seven days, I was happy to leave Israel. My mind was numb from the tales of terror, brutality, and suffering I had heard. Unfortunately, there were still four survivors I hadn't talked to. Ber Freiberg, who had worked on the train brigade, was eager to see me, but he had guests and couldn't break away. Moshe Bahir and Ulla Stern (now Ilana Safran) were too sick to be interviewed, I was told. And I didn't have time to contact Fishel Bialowitz's brother Simha, who had worked in the pharmacy where Selma waited for Chaim on the afternoon of October 14.

On the plane back home, I opened Yitzhak Katzenelson's book, *The Song of the Murdered Jewish People,* which Miriam had given me as a parting gift. Inside, she had written, "To Richard — The Song of the Murdered Jewish People — And the Silence of the World."

I turned to the poem that so poignantly summarized what I had heard and felt in Israel. It began:

Sing! Take your light, hollow harp in hand,
Strike hard with heavy fingers, like pain-filled hearts
On its thin cords. Sing the last song.
Sing of the last Jews on Europe's soil . . .

How can I sing? How can I lift my head
With bleary eyes? A frozen tear
Clouds my eye . . . It struggles to break loose,
But, God, my God, it cannot fall! . . .

Come from Treblinka, Sobibor, Auschwitz,
Come from Belzec, Ponari, from all the other camps,
With wide-open eyes, frozen cries and soundless screams,
Come from marshes, deep sunken swamps, foul moss —

Come, you dried, ground, crushed Jewish bones.
Come, form a big circle around me, one great ring —
Grandfathers, grandmothers, fathers, mothers carrying babies.
Come, Jewish bones, out of powder and soup.

Emerge, reveal yourselves to me. Come, all of you, come.
I want to see you. I want to look at you. I want
Silently and mutely to behold my murdered people —
And I will sing . . . Yes . . . Hand me the harp . . . I will play!

Chapter 42

Selma and Chaim

I WROTE to Dr. Louis de Jong, director of the Netherlands State Institute for War Documentation, to find out whether any of the thirty-six thousand Dutch Jews sent to Sobibor had survived. Dr. de Jong had written an excellent article on Sobibor for *Encounter* magazine, and Sobibor was special to him. The Nazis had gassed his mother, father, and sister there.

Dr. de Jong wrote back to say that there were only two Dutch survivors — Ursula (Ulla) Stern, who lives in Israel and whom I had been unable to see, and Selma Wijnberg, who married Chaim Engel and now lives in Branford, Connecticut.

"I wouldn't talk to you if you were Jewish," Chaim Engel told me as we drove from his home to a shopping center for the Sunday *New York Times*. "You're the first non-Jew that has asked Selma and me for an interview. We're sick of being interviewed. But we think we owe it to you and to our grandchildren."

Chaim was a youthful sixty-six, with rosy cheeks and curly gray hair combed back as it was in Sobibor.

"We don't allow Sobibor to affect our lives," he said. "We don't talk about it much. It happened. We don't forget it. But we don't dredge it up."

I felt privileged to be with Selma and Chaim. Two people who have suffered so much had decided to trust me with their story — for their grandchildren. It was as if Selma and Chaim were about to write their will and had chosen me executor.

Selma Wijnberg-Engel had bagels and coffee waiting when we returned. She and Chaim live in a modern house surrounded by oaks, yellow poplars, and firs, not far from the Stony Creek harbor and New Haven. The plants that fill their front room were bathed in sun from the skylight cut into the slanted, cathedral ceiling. A white tablecloth with Hebrew characters was spread over the coffee table. "We aren't observant Jews," Selma explained, "but we feel very Jewish."

It was clear from the moment I met Chaim that he was not eager to talk about Sobibor, even though he had agreed to. "I don't know," he said, trying to squirm out of his promise after coffee. "I just can't get excited about talking. Let Selma go first. If there are still questions, you can ask me."

Chaim went into the garage to tack up insulation while Selma and I sat on the couch in the living room. I turned on my tape recorder.

Selma loves to talk, and when she does, her hands and eyes enter the conversation. She still sounds like a tomboy, and she has a friendly, trusting face, soft gray eyes that hint of mischief, and brown hair salted with gray. But when Selma began to tell me what happened to her and Chaim once they buried their son Emilchen at sea, a note of bitterness crept into her voice.

They got off the Dutch steamer in Marseilles and traveled by train to the Netherlands. "They quarantined us when we got there," she said. " 'More people?' they asked. 'We hardly have enough to eat ourselves. What are *you* doing here?' "

Selma forced a little laugh, as if to shrug off the hurt she still felt. "This was *my* Holland — the Holland I had dreamed about in Sobibor and in Adam and Stefka's barn," she said. "And I had told Chaim how beautiful it was. 'It was heaven,' I'd told him."

When Selma and Chaim reached Zwolle, they went to the Wijnberg family hotel. Selma knew that the Nazis had murdered her mother and two brothers somewhere in Poland — probably Auschwitz. But what about her third brother, who'd been in hiding when the Nazis nabbed her? Was he still alive? As she approached the hotel, Selma whistled a special tune. It was the signal the Wijnbergs had used during the war.

"My brother was sick that day," she recalled. "He thought he was going crazy when he heard the whistle. He looked out the window, and there I was."

335

Selma dug out a picture of her mother — a traditional black and white portrait of a woman in her forties with dark hair and lively eyes — and slipped it out of its frame.

"My mother must have thrown this out of the train on her way to Poland," Selma said. "Someone returned it to us after the war."

She read me the message on the back, written in pencil in a shaky script. It was signed by her mother. "Dear children — You heard about what happened. Who knows? With God's help, we'll see each other in better times. Be strong."

For once, I had run out of questions. What could I ask Selma? Her feelings were on her sleeve as she read the last words of her mother, who, even in death, had tried to comfort her children and hold the family together. Selma continued her story.

She and Chaim lived at the hotel with her brother and sister-in-law, had two children in a row, saved money, and waited until they could get permission from the Dutch government to open a clothing store. "Business licenses were controlled tightly," she explained. "Holland is very small."

During the five years that Selma and Chaim lived in Holland, they became more and more disillusioned. For the first year, no one would believe that the Nazis had run death camps and that they had escaped from one. And when the truth finally came out in magazines and newspapers, their friends didn't seem to care. That had hurt them both.

Besides, there was no Jewish community to speak of in Holland at that time, and Selma and Chaim felt like foreigners. They decided to emigrate. But where? Selma, who had been a Zionist ever since she turned sixteen, wanted to go to Israel; Chaim, who liked free enterprise and opportunity, wanted to live in America. Since they couldn't emigrate to the United States under the quota for Poles — Chaim was still a Polish citizen, and the waiting list for the United States was a lifetime long — they went to Israel.

"I loved it from the moment I got there," Selma said. "Chaim hated it. He was miserable on the kibbutz — just sick."

After nine months of community work and living, Chaim couldn't take the kibbutz anymore. He got a job as a waiter, rented a house, and saved his money. Eventually, his savings and a loan enabled him to buy a little vegetable store. Soon, he owned four stores in four villages.

"We stayed in Israel for seven years," Selma said. "I was never homesick again for Holland. Never a minute."

But Chaim still had his heart set on America, so in 1957 they emigrated again. "We had to keep it a secret," Selma explained. "In those days, it was like deserting Israel."

With just enough money to pay for legal fees, passage for themselves and their two children, a used car, and some furniture, they started all over again for the third time. There were jobs in factories, taking in ironing, an Arnold's Bread route franchise, a greeting card store, an ulcer, and finally a partnership in a jewelry store.

"For the first time in my life," said Selma, who is fifty-nine, "I feel really relaxed. Now I live."

Indifference about Sobibor still bothers her. "Who's going to read your book?" she asked me. "No one is interested."

She told me that none of her friends seemed to care that she and Chaim had escaped from Sobibor. Even the rabbi at the local temple didn't want to hear about the camp. Her daughter still refuses to listen to her mother's story, and her son only recently has become interested.

I began to question Selma about October 14, the day of the escape. The thing that seemed to impress her the most was that Chaim didn't desert her. "He was the only man who took his girl friend along," she said proudly. "He looked after me . . . He still does." She tossed her head back slightly and laughed in a delightful way, looking over to the door leading to the garage, where Chaim was still puttering.

I asked Selma how she felt now about Adam and Stefka. She admitted that while she and Chaim lived in the loft she thought that they were terrible people — mean and greedy.

"But now, when I look back," she said, "what they did was tremendous, even though we paid them. They risked their lives for us. They were heroes. We still send them packages and money. Whatever we can. They deserve it."

She paused for a moment, thinking of Adam. "I was good-looking in those days," she said. "And that saved our lives."

She talked about her pregnancy, her loneliness in Poland after the Russian liberation, the difficulties of her childbirth, and her poverty. "And we were *free*," she said, making sure I caught the irony. "Huh, we were free . . . But somehow we survived."

When I asked about the death of Emilchen and his burial at sea near the Isle of Naxos, Selma grew sad and quiet. Her eyes no longer twinkled in amusement over past hardships, and her face clouded. "There was no doctor," she said with a touch of bitterness. "No medicine. Just one more dead Jew. Who cared?"

337

The Dutch captain had cared. Selma reached into a box of old papers and photos and pulled out a piece of paper slightly yellowed at the edges. "This is a poem the captain wrote out for me, when the baby died," she said. "It's hard to translate."

"Try," I said.

"Mother, why do you cry? Why do you weep? I am an angel in the heavens . . ."

She stopped and folded the paper.

"Is the death of your baby a painful memory for you?" I asked.

"When I talk about it, yes," she said. "I have learned to block it out of my mind. You cannot live this way — remembering all the time. And all I want is to live." Then, as if to summarize her years in Poland, she added, "I came back to Holland with empty hands. No baby."

We went over her story from the day she arrived at Sobibor to the day of the escape. Small, sometimes almost irrelevant things leaped into her mind — vodka and pork fat on her birthday ("It was the first time I'd tasted pork, and I've loved it ever since"), hiding mushrooms in her bra and pants, jealousy over Chaim. Straining to remember and to be accurate, she became frustrated, because time, like acid, had corroded so many details. Besides, she had been delirious with typhus so long that she didn't remember much of what happened during her illness. "I should go under hypnosis," she said. "Then I'd remember everything."

After five hours of talking, Selma, Chaim, their fourteen-year-old dog Snoopy, and I took a walk to the Stony Creek harbor. As I strolled with Chaim, I tried to avoid talking about Sobibor; I didn't have my tape recorder, and I knew I would not be able to remember with accuracy the things he might tell me. But Chaim had SS Sergeant Hubert Gomerski on his mind. He and Selma were to leave soon for West Germany to testify at Gomerski's retrial. After all those years, Chaim explained, it was difficult to remember precisely which German did what. The defense attorneys were counting on that. But Chaim did remember Gomerski, the former boxer, quite clearly. One day, he said, he had overheard Gomerski telling Wagner that he had just killed a Jew in Camp III with eight lashes of his whip. It was as if Gomerski had broken some record for whipping.

When we got back to the house, Snoopy settled himself on the floor with great difficulty and went to sleep. Chaim and I sat in the living room and continued to talk.

"You'll hear my words," he said, as I turned on my recorder. "But you'll never understand."

"I can try," I said, weakly. And with that, we began to go over Chaim's story. I felt as relaxed with him as I had with Selma. He was a straightforward, gentle, meticulous man who studied languages for a hobby. He and Selma were planning a vacation in Italy, so at night he was working on his Italian.

I pressed Chaim to describe how he had helped assassinate SS Sergeant Beckmann in the Administration Building.

"I don't really like to talk about it," Chaim said. I had to pull the story out of him like a sliver from under a fingernail.

"Usually, I don't tell anyone about that part of the story," he admitted when we finished. "It was no act of heroism. I just did what I had to do. I'm not proud of it. I don't want you to use my name in that part of the story."

I was disappointed, but promised to use a pseudonym for him to protect his feelings.

"If I *didn't* do it, we were dead," Chaim continued, as if to excuse himself for an act he was ashamed of. "With a knife at your throat, you can do a lot of things."

"Were you scared?"

"I wasn't even thinking," he said. "I just wanted to help and to take revenge."

With pain in his voice, Chaim described how he, like Toivi, had had to cut the women's hair, how the Polish women would yell and scream, how the Dutch would sometimes plead, "What's going to happen to us?"

"I couldn't talk," Chaim said. "I couldn't tell them."

He recalled how the Belzec Jews resisted and were shot, and how a transport once arrived with 90 percent of the Jews already dead. Chaim didn't work in the train brigade, but when the Nazis needed extra help, he had to load the bodies onto the miners' train.

"It was unbelievable" was all he could say. "Unbelievable."

It was as if Sobibor were still a dream to Chaim, still incredible, something he would never believe, even though it had happened to *him*. He'd talk, shake his head in wonder as he dredged up the memories and examined them as if they had happened to someone else.

Chaim spoke shyly about how he fell in love with Selma. "I met her," he said, as if that explained everything. "We would go from one barracks to another. It was not really allowed, but they didn't care — " He shrugged, as if to say "One thing led to another."

"You tried to make your life normal at Sobibor," he continued. "Camp II had a routine. We did our work in sorting. Not under great pressure. We functioned normally. We needed someone. We tried never to think of tomorrow. Just to live for today. I always had some hope of getting out. I had no reason to believe it. But I did. It was a very false hope."

I asked Chaim why he thought he had survived when others had not.

"My attitude was to be not visible," he explained. "Not good, not bad. If the Germans didn't see you, you had a better chance to survive. If they knew you, you got caught. It was just plain luck. Smarter people there didn't make it. Whatever I decided, it just happened to be the right decision.

"I didn't do anything courageous. Any courageous act meant death. I think that the organizers of the escape were courageous. I was not the kind of person who would have been able to do it. Maybe I'm just too practical."

I couldn't help comparing Chaim to Tom and Shlomo, who were totally involved in Sobibor. Chaim seemed so calm, dispassionate.

"Why?" I asked him.

"Sure I'm bitter," he said. "Sometimes I think it was all a dream. I still can't conceive how people could do a thing like that." His voice rose slightly. I would have missed it, except that I was listening for it. And there was just a hint of passion and hurt. "I saw it. I lived it. I *have* to believe it. It was like that at Sobibor, too. I used to tell myself, 'No, that's a dream. It is not true.' "

"Do you think there ever could be another Holocaust?" I asked.

"Sure. Let me put it this way," he said. "If you take the lesson of the last one — the economy was bad, and they looked for a scapegoat. They could be looking for another scapegoat again. Intelligent people are saying today, 'It is not true. The Holocaust never happened!'

"They know it did, but they want to deny it because they want to bring up a new generation who *could* do it again. The roots are there. It all depends on how they grow. They may not, but you never know. If we really get into bad times — no oil — really bad times, and there's a war . . ." He paused. "If there's a lot of flammable stuff around and you throw one match, there can be a big fire. That's the reason it's so important to keep the memory alive, so that people know about it. Another ten or fifteen years, there won't be any witnesses."

Selma overheard our conversation about why Chaim survived. She deserted her cooking to join us. "I survived because I had Chaim," she said.

"She was a fighter," Chaim added proudly.

"Did you like that about her?" I asked.

Chaim looked shyly at Selma and laughed. "I guess so."

"Chaim and I are finished," I told Selma. "We made one deal."

She seemed surprised that Chaim would make a "deal" without consulting her first.

"He told me all about Beckmann," I explained. "But he doesn't want me to use his name."

"No? . . . Chaim, C-h-a-i-m." She sang his name. "Why not? He knows you're not proud of it. He'll write it the way it was."

She turned to me. "Is it important to use his name?" she asked, as if to get my support in assaulting Chaim's modesty.

"It would make the story more credible," I said. "And it would be difficult for me to tell about how you wiped off the blood and bandaged his hand and — "

"All right," Chaim said. "If you want to, I don't care."

After dinner, Selma brought out her photo album and the diary she had written in the barn after the escape. We looked at pictures of the family hotel in Zwolle; of her, Chaim, and Emilchen; and of Ulla Stern, her dear friend who lives in Israel.

Two pictures, both taken before the war and about the same time, struck me because of the great contrast. In one, Chaim stood next to his father. Both were dressed in black pants and long black coats. Chaim's father had an enormous beard. In the other, taken in Zwolle, Selma was posing with some of her female relatives or friends. The girls were in shorts, sandals, and blouses or halters.

For me, the two pictures beautifully illustrated the gulf between Holland and Poland, between Polish Jewish attitudes and Dutch Jewish attitudes, between assimilation and apartness. No wonder the Polish Jews didn't trust the Dutch Jews, I thought. They were centuries apart, and that gulf, despite common heritage and common fate, was too great for most Polish Jews to cross. Yet Chaim had crossed it and never regretted it.

Selma sat across the room from me under a lamp with her diary in her lap. Chaim was on the couch next to me, reading the *Times,* "his bible," as Selma calls it. Snoopy curled himself on the floor, and Kitty — Selma and Chaim's ancient cat — rested peacefully, tucked inside the dog's hind legs.

"It's been twenty or so years since I've looked at this," Selma said. The writing was tiny and so smudged with fingerprints and age that some of the entries were illegible.

I sat fascinated as she read aloud her personal thoughts written in Adam and Stefka's barn thirty-seven years before. From time to time, she'd chuckle in surprise at something she had long forgotten, or she'd toss a Dutch word at Chaim, asking for the equivalent in English, or she'd say, "Complain, complain! That's all I do in this is complain."

*

"My darling husband . . . I am still worried about the wounds in his arm . . . Our only determination is to survive this war. I hope luck will stay with us . . . God, let me die . . .

"April 23: I woke up this morning and I heard a bird singing. For a moment, I thought I was back in Zwolle. Then I remembered the reality. I am expecting a baby . . .

"Today, I spent my second birthday with Chaim, my darling husband . . . I hope the Russians come and we can live like humans. I believe I'm three months pregnant, but I feel good . . .

"Yesterday was very difficult. We were depressed. Stefka came and said she didn't believe we had given her all our money. She wanted the rest. She already had thousands. She is so greedy that she wants everything. We lie in the hay, and the world is filled with hatred against us . . .

"It is very hot. Even if you sit still, you perspire . . . Today we can hear the front. But for us Jews, the war is over. We lost . . . Yesterday, we got eight cherries and some noodles . . .

"July: For the first time this year, we could wash ourselves. We feel very clean. I hope we also washed ourselves clean of the scabies . . .

"July 10: I cannot stand it any longer. There are so many flies, and the heat! Will Stefka go to Chelm tomorrow and buy more medicine? We spent the whole day chasing flies away with handkerchiefs. And the itching! Life has no value anymore. Perhaps we will be able to go down tonight . . .

"Tonight, the whole night, I hear the front coming toward us. We hear a lot of Russian airplanes. As I write, I can see a lot of military cars moving away. Adam's brother visited and said everything along the Bug is burning. They told us, 'Everything is going well in the war' . . . The Germans would never believe it — but here we are, smoking a German cigarette . . .

"July 23: Tonight I hear shooting. Cars are moving all night. There is shooting from all sides and in the air . . .

"July 24: I can't believe it. I sit with Chaim in the grass and we are free . . .

"I can't write everything that has happened to me. I hope some of us will live to tell the world and bring shame upon every German . . ."

Chapter 43

Sasha

I KNEW I was in the Soviet Union when I reached Immigration. A dour matron, short, weary, and suspicious, sent my suitcase through the Phillips x-ray machine.

"Books?" she asked.

"Yes," I said. The immigration form I had signed on the airplane gave the Soviet Union the right to confiscate books, photos, tapes, and film.

"Open, please," she ordered.

I unlocked the bag and took out four books: *World War III, The Survivor, Confederacy of Dunces,* and *Of Blood and Hope.*

She pushed a button. A red light went on, and a floor supervisor came to the counter where I stood. He thumbed silently through each book, taking special care to examine the pictures of World War II and of the Holocaust. The Russian didn't say a word or even look at me. After about five minutes of browsing, he left. I closed my bags and walked into Russia.

The official Soviet tourist agency checked my name off its printout of tourists expected that day, and assigned a driver to take me to the Intourist Hotel, around the corner from the Kremlin and Red Square. The Soviets require that all hotel reservations be made in advance by a travel agent certified to deal with the Soviet Union.

The Intourist Hotel was hopping. There were French children with their teachers, Germans on vacation, Danes heading for Rostov by boat down the Volga and the Don. There were Cubans and Chinese.

343

The Intourist was well organized. It had a "floor lady" on each floor, sitting next to the elevator so that she could see everyone come and leave, to answer all questions. The front desk arranged tours, cabs, train and airline reservations. A doorman checked guest cards, requiring anyone without a card to sign the register. There were no stairs for guests in the twenty-story hotel.

Tom Blatt, who had agreed to be my guide in the Soviet Union and Poland, was not due to arrive for another twenty-four hours. I wandered around Red Square and walked through parks. There was no laughter. People seemed to shuffle from place to place. Few children played anywhere, even in the parks. The government-owned stores were filthy, with long lines of people waiting for bread or meat or milk. A fight erupted in front of one store over who was next in line, and the police came to settle it. Even though it was July, there was no fresh produce or fruit in the stores except for cabbage and some onions. The women wore ill-fitting, gaudy print dresses. There were no sidewalk cafés, theaters, bars, or music.

That night in the Intourist dining room, a young Russian woman and her boy friend confirmed my first impressions of Moscow. "I can't take much more of this," she said. "It's so depressing. Nobody works. All they do is drink vodka and sleep."

The next day, I waited for Tom and Dena to arrive from Warsaw, where they were vacationing. Since I wasn't sure whether they would be assigned to my hotel, I went to the central Intourist office. By this time, I knew the Russians watched their guests closely.

"I'm expecting a Mr. and Mrs. Blatt," I said. "Can you tell me whether they've arrived yet?"

The clerk checked her printout, then made a phone call.

"They have arrived," she said. "They were sent to the Cosmos Hotel by mistake. Wait, please."

She made another call. "Mr. and Mrs. Blatt have arrived at the Cosmos. The mistake has been corrected. They left the Cosmos five minutes ago by car. They will arrive at the Intourist within ten minutes."

Tom and Dena were registering when I walked into the lobby. I'd been worried when I learned that Dena was to come with Tom. How could I interview Sasha and Tom if she kept interrupting me? But my fears were groundless; Dena's attitude toward me had changed completely. She was eager to help.

Tom had a friend who worked in the Kremlin, and he wanted to invite her to the hotel for dinner. They met on the front steps, but she wouldn't come inside. She didn't want to risk signing the register lest she be reported, she said. The KGB would want to know why she was visiting three Americans. Tom found a side door that wasn't guarded, and we sneaked her into the dining room.

It all seemed a little melodramatic to me, until Tom couldn't find the packet of snapshots and papers he kept in a pocket of his shoulder bag. The next day, when he was looking for something else in the same pocket, he found his pictures and papers there. Tucked in the packet was the DO NOT DISTURB sign from his hotel room door.

"That shows you how stupid the KGB are," he said. "I'm going to keep this as a souvenir."

I had noticed something strange about my room, too, but hadn't given it much thought. Someone had hung the DO NOT DISTURB sign on the outside of my door after I left. It was hanging there when I got back.

Tom wasn't surprised that our rooms had been searched; he had lived in Communist Poland until 1957. It didn't take us long to figure out how the system worked. The hotel elevators went dead for about fifteen minutes every afternoon between one and two o'clock, the time when most tourists were eating lunch or sightseeing.

The atmosphere in Moscow was not conducive to honest interviewing. I assumed that my hotel room was bugged and wondered whether Sasha could afford to tell the whole truth. I felt, too, that my timing was off: Sasha, I was told, spent the summer in a *dacha* not far from Moscow, and I should have preferred to interview him in his home in Rostov-on-the-Don.

When I walked out of the summer downpour into the Intourist lobby, Alexander Pechersky was waiting. He stood up and walked slowly toward me, tall and straight, like a soldier. He was seventy-two, with a round face and stomach, ruddy cheeks, silver hair combed straight back, and soft eyes that crinkled when he laughed. I shook his hand; he bowed slightly. His arms were still strong.

Sasha and his wife, Olga, came to my room the next morning for the first of three days of interviews. Dena, Tom, and I hooked up our mikes. Tom, translating my questions into Russian, recorded them and Sasha's answers. I recorded Tom's English translation of Sasha's talk. Dena did the same, just in case my tapes were erased or confiscated before I had a chance to transcribe them. "These may be the last and most important interviews with Sasha," Tom had said. "We don't want to lose them."

Sasha too was aware of history in the making. I knew that he had been sick and that one of his lungs had been removed, so I didn't expect him to recall much detail. But I was mistaken. Sasha's memory was excellent; his mind sharp and forceful. Like Tom and Shlomo, he clearly distinguished between fact and fantasy, what he personally had seen and experienced, and what others had told him.

We systematically covered the planning of the escape, the Organization, and the details, clarifying, as we went along, misconceptions he had created in his own account, written in 1946 from the sketchy notes he had made in Sobibor. We filled in gaps and solved the contradictions that Yiddish and Russian writers had raised when they had sensationalized his story.

Sasha listened carefully to my questions, eyes on me as I spoke, leaning slightly toward Tom as he translated. If he was nervous with the mikes and tape recorders, Sasha didn't show it. He spoke in a rich, gentle voice that matched his delightful smile, setting his right elbow on the armrest and gesturing with his left hand. When he grew tired, his hand began to shake almost imperceptibly.

Olga was present at each session. Occasionally, she helped Tom find the right Russian word or make observations, or reminded Sasha to tell me something he had forgotten — an intimate detail, an anecdote. She was a cheerful woman. Open and warm, with sparkling eyes and a broad smile. She treated me to the first laughter I heard in Russia.

I asked Sasha when he had first decided to plan an escape. He had been working in the North Camp on the second or third day at Sobibor, he began. But before he could get further into his story, his face reddened and his eyes watered. He asked Olga, who was sitting close to the bathroom, for a glass of water. He sipped, tried to continue, but the tears began to roll down his gentle face, and his large frame began to shake. He covered his face with one hand for a moment without fighting back his tears. Then he continued.

He had been working close to the gas chambers in the woods, he said. He couldn't see Camp III because of all the pine trees, but he could hear screams, muffled like a chorus from far away. Then he heard a solo, clear and piercing: "Mama! Ma —— "

When the tears began again, Olga spoke up. "It reminded him of Ela," she said. "For a long time after Sobibor, Sasha screamed at night, calling out, 'Ela, Ela.' "

Sasha brushed away his tears. He had composed himself again, totally unashamed of his emotion.

"Do you still think or dream about Sobibor?" I asked.

"No," Sasha said. "I try not to think about it. When I do — as I'm doing here — I can see it all before my eyes. Just like a movie. I can still hear the children crying."

Sasha had been asked by the West German government to testify at the Sobibor war crimes trials in Hagen, West Germany, but the Soviet government would not allow him to go.

"Were you upset because you couldn't go?"

I could see that he was, and his answer made me aware once again that we were in the Soviet Union, where hotel rooms are bugged and where citizens who criticize the state are sent to prisons and asylums.

"No," he said. "I told them [the German prosecutors], 'I don't want to look on your faces when you won't give them [Nazis] the sentences they deserve. They deserve what they gave the Jews."

In Soviet war crimes trials in Kiev in 1963, Sasha had testified against eleven Ukrainian guards who had worked in Sobibor and who had survived the war. Ten were sentenced to death; one got fifteen years in prison. Sasha was proud that he had been able to nail them; he considered the death sentences to be just. He was angry that Nazis like Frenzel got life and then a parole, and that others, like Franz Wolf, got only seven years.

"Would you like to visit Sobibor again?" I asked.

"I would go back tomorrow."

I asked Sasha why he thought his plan had succeeded and that so many Jews had escaped.

"I thought we would kill a few Germans, and then someone would discover the bodies or become suspicious," he said. "But everything went according to plan, with the exception of the one German [Beckmann] killed in the Administration Building. It was simple, plain luck."

Two things prevented more Jews from escaping, Sasha emphasized. First, Frenzel didn't come to inspect the barracks in Camp I. "He probably had a premonition," he said. (It was Frenzel who had grabbed the machine gun, stopped the attack on the armory, and sprayed scores of escaping Jews.)

Second, the prisoners ran from Camp I to the main gate like a mob instead of in a column, as planned. If there had been an orderly column, Sasha said, they would have confused the guards and gained even more time before the guards opened fire.

Dena asked Sasha what his worst experience in Sobibor had been.

"All the days were the same," he said. "Except when the Organization met. Then, there was hope. You had to have hope. Otherwise, you'd never have made it."

347

Tom was surprised that nothing stood out in Sasha's mind as exceptionally cruel. Actually, Sasha had already answered the question when he cried over the child screaming "Mama!"

"For me," Tom said, "it was when Leon was beaten by 'Radio.'" Leon was the Polish Jew who had escaped from the Waldkommando and had been found wandering in the forest. Frenzel ordered Radio to whip him to death.

"It was the saddest, most brutal thing I ever saw," Tom said.

Tom and I had an agreement. If there were questions he wanted to ask Sasha, he could break in at any time. Because I knew Tom was eager to ask Sasha why he had deserted them in the forest, I created an opening.

"Tell me, step by step," I asked Sasha, "what you did after you left the others in the woods."

I could tell that my question embarrassed him. He shifted in his chair, avoided Tom's eyes, and his answer seemed to be inconsistent with what he had written in 1946.

"When we approached the village to find out where we were and to buy some food," he said, "some small boys told us the Germans were nearby, looking for us. 'You'd better run away,' the boys told us. 'The Germans will be back.' So we didn't go into the village. We kept walking and then got lost."

Tom didn't believe Sasha. "How could there be *boys* out there?" Tom asked in English. "It was four o'clock in the morning."

Sasha sensed Tom's hurt and skepticism. "We would have divided into small groups anyway," Sasha explained to me. "They were Polish and we were Russians. I gave them freedom. I got them out. The rest was up to them. We were *Russians.* We wanted to go back to Russia. The Polish Jews were already home."

Tom wouldn't leave it alone. He told Sasha that after liberation he learned that there were two Jewish partisan groups in that area with women and children. "Wouldn't it have been better if you had formed a partisan group with us?" he asked Sasha. "You would have been our leader."

Tom had told me in Santa Barbara that if Sasha had done that, he would have been an even greater hero.

"I am a Russian," Sasha said, with a note of finality. "I wanted to go back and fight for my country."

It was an honest and believable answer, even though it did not satisfy Tom. I changed the subject. Sasha had received a military decoration, but not for leading the escape from Sobibor.

"Were you disappointed that you didn't get a medal for Sobibor?" I asked.

Sasha evaded my question. He rolled up his pants leg and showed me the scar for which he received the Russian equivalent of the Purple Heart.

"Do you know that the escape from Sobibor was the biggest prisoner escape in all of World War II?" I pressed. "Either from a civilian camp or a POW camp?"

He nodded, but once again refused to criticize the Soviet government. "I believe that I did something very important. And good," he said, carefully picking his words. "But I was no hero. I just did my duty."

"Did the government refuse to decorate you because you were a Jew?" I asked.

Tom hesitated. "I won't ask him that. He won't answer it. He can't. I'm sure that's the reason."

I agreed not to put the Politruk on the spot. Anti-Semitism and the fear it engenders are still rampant in the Soviet Union. A friend of Sasha's had just published a novel in Yiddish based on the Sobibor story. We wanted to meet him, but the writer was afraid to visit us.

"Are you bitter about your suffering at the hands of the Germans?" I asked, changing the subject again.

"No," Sasha said. "People are people. Some are good. Some bad. During the war, I fought for the Russian people. After the war, I had no feelings of revenge."

I believed him. There was a gentleness about Sasha. He spoke with a touch of humility, and when he talked about Sobibor, he showed more sadness than anger or hatred. How unlike Tom and Shlomo, I thought. Sasha seemed calm and balanced; Tom and Shlomo, bitter and cynical. Could it be because Tom and Shlomo had been only adolescents at Sobibor, but Sasha, twice their age, had had loving and peaceful prewar experiences to build on, to remember, to give him strength, to balance the cruelty and hatred?

"I don't believe in people anymore," Tom interjected. "I mistrust them. People don't know themselves."

Sasha emphasized again that he had not lost his faith in people. Then, he smiled at Olga. "I believe in my *wife,*" he said. "Not in God. Children are supposed to have angel souls. How could God allow them to be murdered? They were just angel souls."

It was a good place to end the interview for the day. Sasha was getting tired, and I wanted to go over my tapes to prepare for the final session.

Sasha and Olga came to my room the next morning with a slab of Russian beer cheese and several large bottles of Russian beer. They said they were concerned about all the money I was spending on their lunches. I was moved, because not only didn't they have much money, but I knew that Olga must have waited in line for hours to buy the food.

I was disappointed, though not surprised, that Sasha had brought Olga for the last interview. I wanted to ask him about Luka, but I felt that I would not get a straight answer with Olga present.

Sasha sat in his chair next to the window, showing no signs of fatigue or impatience with my stream of questions. I had a lot of loose ends to clear up. When I finished, I simply said, "Tell me about Luka."

Barely had he begun to describe how he had asked Feldhendler for a woman who couldn't understand Russian to serve as a cover, when he started to cry for the second time. His emotion was intense. Several times he tried to finish the story, but couldn't. Olga tried to help him — completing sentences between his sobs.

"I regret to this day that I didn't trust her," Sasha said finally. "That I didn't tell her about the escape. I've never heard anything about her. I assume she didn't make it."

Olga chimed in again to say that for two years after Sobibor, Sasha would cry every time he said "Luka." With great pleasure, she explained how Sasha had carried Luka's shirt for the rest of the war. "It's in a museum now in Rostov," she said.

Sasha recovered his composure and, as if anticipating my next question, said, "There was nothing special between Luka and me."

Both Tom and I interpreted "special" as meaning that he had not slept with her. It was obvious to me — and to Olga, judging from her reaction — that any relationship (no matter how brief) that could evoke such emotion after almost thirty-eight years had been special indeed.

We talked briefly about the other Russians who had crossed the Bug with Sasha. Boris died of pneumonia in the Ukrainian farmer's home where Sasha had left him. Kalimali was killed during a mission. Arkady Vaispapir and five others survived the war. Sasha would not be specific about where they were now. When I mentioned Vaispapir's name in the hotel room, Sasha shook his head no, indicating that I should not mention Arkady in public. (Vaispapir and at least one other Sobibor Russian Jew work for the KGB.)

"Ask him whether he [Vaispapir] would be willing to be interviewed," I told Tom. "How can I find him?"

350

Tom refused. "Sasha could get in trouble, and he [Vaispapir] would never talk to you, anyway. It would be a waste of your time."

I was very disappointed, for my room was right around the corner from the Kremlin and the KGB, and I knew I'd never be back to the Soviet Union again — at least not on this book. But I respected Sasha's wish.

One of the seven Russians who had escaped from Sobibor and survived was Semyon Rozenfeld. When he and two other Jews lost Sasha after they crossed the field, they headed south for the Parczew Forest. In the woods near Janow, where Esther was buried under straw in Marcyniuk's barn, Rozenfeld found a hide-out that sheltered eight Jews — five from Sobibor and three from another camp.

Early in December, Polish partisans tracked the eleven Jews in the snow to their bunker, opened fire, and killed seven, wounding Rozenfeld in the leg. While the Poles were ripping apart the bunker beams to get inside, Rozenfeld strung three cartridges together and held a candle to them. The bullets exploded, and the Poles ran.

Rozenfeld and the other three Jews still alive hid out in farms and barns until July 1944, when the Red Army passed through. Although his leg wound was festering, Rozenfeld asked to be sent to the front. He was wounded in the hand and leg in western Poland. After a short rest in a hospital, he marched into Berlin with the Red Army.

The twenty-three-year-old Russian soldier, with hair as white as cotton, whom the Germans had captured near Baranowicze, carved a message on the Reichstag wall for all the Sobibor Jews:

BARANOWICZE — SOBIBOR — BERLIN

"Is there anything else you want to ask Sasha?" I said to Tom after I had finished my questions.

"Some more about leaving us in the woods," he said. "But what else can Sasha add?"

We walked to Red Square for pictures and good-bys. Olga invited me to stay in their Rostov home on my next trip to Russia. There were hugs and kisses all around.

Sasha smiled as I started to leave. His eyes crinkled and danced. "She doesn't even kiss her *husband* so much," he said.

Chapter 44

Sobibor

TOM AND I sat in the sidewalk café at the Europeska Hotel in Warsaw, waiting for David, a Sobibor survivor whom everyone had thought was dead.

Warsaw was a breath of fresh air, compared to Moscow. People laughed, even though the Communist Party Congress was meeting to decide the future of Poland, the threat of a Russian invasion hung over the ancient city like smog, and there were shortages of everything from meat to soap. There was music, sidewalk cafés, lovers in Jordache jeans, walking arm in arm, and children.

As we sipped soda and watched the changing of the guard across the square, I knew there was a struggle in Poland between Solidarity, the Polish Communist Party, and the Soviet Union. But judging from the atmosphere in the government-owned hotel, one would never know it. An entertainer sang love songs at the piano bar while prostitutes waited patiently for customers. In the dining room, guests dined on pork chops, ham, roast beef, and chicken. People around us in the café ate ice cream in tall silver dishes.

I wasn't sure that David would show up. Tom had called him five or six times. He made appointments and promises that he never kept. This was our last try. I was eager to interview him because he had worked in the train brigade at Sobibor.

David was on time. Short, squat, clearly once a powerful man, he had a dark complexion and gray hair — and he was one of the few thousand out of three million Jews still left in Poland. His co-workers had recently blackmailed him into an early retirement from his sensitive government job after they discovered he was a Jew. David's imprisonment in and escape from Sobibor were still a secret, and he agreed to talk to me on the condition that I use a pseudonym for him.

David was lonely. He had been forced to retire before he was sixty; his "friends" avoided him once they learned he was a Jew; there was no Jewish community he could turn to for support.

"Why don't you leave Poland?" Tom asked.

"It's too late," David said. "I'd never find work. I won't be a burden on anyone."

David was eager to help me put together the Sobibor story, but his memory was poor. Unlike many other survivors, he had never given testimony to the Yad Vashem Holocaust Archive in Jerusalem or to the Polish War Crimes Commission. He had never testified in Hagen or written a diary or been interviewed by the press. In fact, he had never before discussed his experiences in the camp.

David said that early in the day on October 14 he had sensed that something was going to happen in Sobibor. The camp was tense. There was an undercurrent of excitement. So when Sasha Pechersky made his speech and the mob rushed the main gate, David was not surprised.

David and another young Jew from the Bahnhofkommando, nicknamed Whitey because his hair was like snow, were swept into the crowd and through the fences close to the spot where Toivi had escaped. When David and Whitey reached the woods, they lost the main group and wandered until they stumbled onto the railroad tracks.

David chuckled. "We were so foolish, we just walked down the tracks to Chelm, my home town," he said.

David and Whitey hid outside the city until dawn; then, dressed like workmen in their blue train brigade overalls, they crossed the bridge spanning the Uherka River, a tributary of the Bug, and walked into Chelm.

"It was incredible." David chuckled again. "There were no Germans guarding the bridge. Maybe we made it into Chelm because the Germans never figured two Jews would be so dumb as to walk right down the tracks, over the bridge, and into town."

Once inside the city, David and Whitey easily passed as workers. They contacted friends, who hid them for several days, then led them to the partisans in the woods around Chelm. David fought with the guerrillas until the Russians liberated Poland, in July 1944. Whitey was killed on a raid.

"Which partisan group?" I asked.

David paused. "Leftist."

"Which leftist group?"

"Just left," David said. "Leave it at that."

David's fear of mentioning the name of the partisan group was another reminder that we were in a Communist-bloc country where fear was part of daily life. Like many Jews who had escaped the ghettos, the gas chambers, and the camps, David had joined Communist partisan groups. After the war, he moved up in the Communist government bureaucracy. It was a sad commentary, for the reason David (and other Jews) had joined the Communist Party before the war was that they saw it as the only alternative to a society under German or independent Polish rule that would not oppress Jews. Now, here David sat, nearly thirty-eight years later, an outsider in Communist Poland, hounded from his job by Polish Communist anti-Semites, friendless, and almost penniless. He had gambled on Communism and lost.

Before the war, David had been a mason by profession. The Nazis at Sobibor had selected him and a dozen other bricklayers to build the armory, some barracks in the North Camp, and the canteen, when they weren't unloading and cleaning the trains. David also helped build the Ukrainian brothels across the tracks behind the Sobibor station.

David said it would have been easy to escape while building the brothels because there were only two Ukrainian guards, and they were drunk most of the time. He seemed embarrassed. "But we never did it," he said.

We talked about his work on the Bahnhofkommando. He'd never forget one transport, he said. Not as long as he lived. "The whole train was loaded with decomposing dead people," he recalled. "I remember reaching into a car and grabbing an arm so that I could pull out the body. The arm came off in my hand."

David spoke in calm, matter-of-fact tones, like a man immune to shock or horror. After telling me all he could remember about the train brigade and how it worked, he apologized that he couldn't remember more.

*

Tom and I walked around the Old Town section of Warsaw, rebuilt after the Germans leveled the city to the ground in the fall of 1944, when the Home Army (AK) tried to stop the Germans who were fleeing west. Fewer than 10 percent of the forty thousand AK soldiers had guns. Those arms they did have they had captured from the Germans. The Red Army sat on a plain six miles east of Warsaw and waited until the Germans crushed the Home Army and razed the city. Only then did the Red tanks chase the Germans over the rubble.

It is a little-known fact that a thousand Jews fought alongside the Home Army, even though the AK hadn't lifted a gun to help the Warsaw Jews when they fought General Stroop's forces in the spring of 1943. Most of the Jews were members of Polish Communist partisan units; a few actually joined the Home Army, passing as Christians.

We sat in an outdoor café in the center of the Old Town cobblestone square. In one corner, artists hawked their paintings and carvings. In another, a blind veteran sat on the ground playing an accordion and singing Polish folk songs. Around his neck hung a sign, reading I WAS WOUNDED IN THE HOME ARMY FIGHTING FOR A FREE POLAND. Nearby, a Gypsy band played briskly while their leader, violin tucked under his arm, went from table to table asking for zlotys.

Tom and I had sour cream covered with chocolate sauce. I tossed another battery of questions at him, taking notes on a napkin. Tom's boyhood friend, Roman (the Catholic from Izbica who had hidden Tom after he was wounded), lived nearby. After our snack, Tom decided to drop in, unannounced, on Roman.

Roman didn't recognize Tom at first. Then his face lit up, and he kissed Tom on both cheeks. Roman's wife spread out the tablecloth and served sliced tomatoes, bread, a can of imported sardines, mineral water, and, of course, vodka. We chatted for several hours.

When Toivi came to Roman with a bullet in his jaw, Roman's father agreed to hide him for two weeks. Longer than that would endanger his whole family, he said. Toivi posed a problem. It was impossible to get medicine from the pharmacy without a prescription, and the local doctor would not prescribe without seeing his patient. Since Roman's father did not trust the doctor, he cleaned out his medicine cabinet for Toivi. Somehow, the disinfectant and gauze worked, and Toivi healed.

Toivi had told Roman and his father that he had been shot by Ukrainian partisans. The story was plausible, so they didn't question him further. Years later Tom told Roman that Bojarski was the one who had tried to kill him for his gold and diamonds.

Roman and Tom began to argue over their vodka.

"You should have told us it was Bojarski," Roman chided. "The Home Army would have punished him."

"Bojarski had relatives all over," Tom disagreed. "Somebody would have turned me in."

Roman nodded. "You're probably right. The Home Army wouldn't have done anything to Bojarski because you were a Jew."

Roman told us about an Izbica Catholic who was a pillar of the local church before the war. Once the Nazis decreed that it wasn't a crime to kill Jews, the devout Catholic murdered hundreds of Jews, including women and children. Even though the government-in-exile had ordered the death penalty for any Pole murdering, betraying, or blackmailing Jews, the Home Army never punished the man. "Because he never killed a *Pole,*" Roman explained.

Roman reminded Tom of how he had volunteered to work in exchange for food and shelter.

"What can you do?" Roman had asked Toivi.

"I can fix *anything!*" Toivi bragged.

"A clock?"

"Sure."

Roman suspected that Toivi didn't know a clock spring from a screwdriver, but he brought the old timepiece to the barn anyway. Toivi took it apart, but couldn't fix it.

In the Warsaw apartment Roman and Tom both laughed about the incident. "I hid the clock so that my father wouldn't find out and kick you out," Roman said. "Remember the gun?"

In order to keep Toivi in the barn past the two-week deadline his father had set, Roman brought Toivi an old, rusty rifle. Toivi took it apart but, once again, couldn't get it to work.

Like an actor, Roman played the dialogue.

"Can you fix guns?"

"Guns? Sure, sure!" Roman mimicked Toivi. "I can fix guns."

They both laughed, and we downed another shot of vodka.

The conversation drifted to Poland. Roman said that conditions in Izbica during the war were better than in Warsaw at the time we spoke. There was more and better food and fewer shortages.

"There's a Polish joke," he said. "A farmer was forced to send two tons of corn to Russia. By mistake, he left his jacket on the truck. Several months later, Russia announced she was going to give Poland a generous gift. She sent a truckload of corn across the border. And on the truck was the farmer's jacket!"

Roman became serious. His wife had spent her two-week vacation standing in lines. "She was so happy and proud," he said. "She got two big boxes of powdered soap."

He paused. "Poland is hopeless. There is nowhere to go. Nothing to do. I am like a vegetable. I'm happy I don't have young children. If I did, I would despair."

How fate had turned the tables, I thought. Almost thirty-eight years ago, Tom was hunted like a doe in open season. He walked on the brink of hopelessness; Roman was free. Now Tom is a successful businessman and free, but Roman is a prisoner in the country he loves, under a system he hates, walking on the same brink.

Before we said good-by, Tom gave Roman a precious gift. Ten packs of cigarettes.

*

On the way to Izbica, we stopped in Lublin. Tom's mother was born there; Tom had worked there in a bicycle shop after the Russians liberated the city; and Leon Feldhendler was murdered there by Polish nationalists.

We walked into a cobblestone courtyard of the old Jewish ghetto, once ringed by a German wall. Tom pointed to a second-story balcony hanging over a wall still pockmarked from machine-gun and rifle bullets.

"That's Feldhendler's apartment," Tom said, as if the Sobibor hero were still living there. I felt sad. As the spiritual leader of doomed and discouraged Jews, Feldhendler had brought some hope and unity to the camp. After it was all over — the fear, the pain, the planning, the escape, the forest, the Russian liberation — he had been shot to death in the middle of Lublin, in his own home, by Jew-hating Poles.

A woman watched me take pictures. "Are you from the Lublin newspaper?" she asked Tom. "No," Tom said, tongue-in-cheek; "from the Warsaw paper."

Tom became philosophical. He told me that in spite of everything that had happened to him — the murder of his brother, whom he loved so much, of his mother and father, of the Jews of Izbica — he still loved Poland. "I feel more comfortable here than I do in the United States."

I couldn't understand Tom. At that moment, as I stood under Feld-hendler's balcony, I hated Poland. I couldn't understand a people who killed and betrayed Jews, who plundered and robbed them. I found it difficult to make distinctions between good Poles and bad ones, between peacetime and wartime, between heroism and the desire to survive, even if that meant selling Jews to the Gestapo for sugar and security. I felt hatred even for that Polish woman living in what was once a Jewish ghetto. And the Polish Jews were not *my* people.

We walked out of the courtyard, past two sparrows who seemed to be playing in the dirt. We stopped and watched. They weren't playing. The larger bird was wounded, and the smaller one was savagely pecking it, its beak full of feathers.

"Just like life," Tom said. "The healthy picking on the weak. That's what everyone does. People look for weaknesses in each other, and then go after them."

We passed a Catholic church. "I don't know how people can believe those stories about God," Tom continued. "If there *was* a God, He would never allow those kinds of things to happen."

"What kinds of things?" I asked.

"Sobibor! I see everything from the perspective of Sobibor. Two birds fighting remind me of it. Passing a church, I think of Sobibor. Unconsciously, Sobibor has become my reference point."

We left Lublin and once again drove toward Izbica. Tom asked me whether I wanted to see Maidanek. "The Nazis didn't have time to blow up the camp before the Russians liberated Lublin," he explained. "What you'll see is the camp just as the Nazis left it. I know. I was there hours after the Germans fled. There were piles of bodies everywhere. Bodies were still burning in the ovens."

Maidanek stretched from the main highway for a mile over flat, open fields. If it hadn't been for the seven-foot-high, double-barbed-wire fence, Maidanek would have looked like a Boy Scout camp, with rows of neat wooden barracks, each identical with the other, and watchtowers spaced around the perimeter like little houses on stilts. In the background, across the field to the north, Lublin loomed up from the grass.

Tom became so tense that he was almost incoherent. "Are we going to stop now or on the way back to Warsaw?" I asked.

Tom didn't answer. He sped past Maidanek's front entrance, down the road parallel to the fence, and into a parking lot near the crematorium. He slammed on the brakes, backed up, and headed for the highway again.

"Aren't we going to stop?"

Tom didn't answer.

"Are those watchtowers and fences the same as Sobibor's?"

"Yes," he said finally. "It's the same. The same."

He slowed the car as we passed a watchtower so that I could get a better look. "I want to get out a minute to take some pictures," I said.

"Take them from the window."

"Come on, Tom. It's important. It'll only take a minute."

Tom stopped in the middle of the road. I snapped a few pictures, and before I could slam the door, Tom was driving off as if he were running, escaping again from Sobibor.

"If we're not coming back," I said, "I'd like to see the barracks, especially if they're the same."

"They're the same," he said.

We drove to the front entrance and parked. I was surprised when Tom walked through the gate and into the camp with me.

"Hurry," he said. "We don't have much time. We don't have much time."

The barracks were each two hundred feet long and seventy feet wide. Most were filled with huge photos — a horror gallery. One barracks had two-foot-wide cages stretching from the floor to the ceiling and running parallel to each wall. Piled inside the cages were thousands of pairs of shoes still tied together. Another barracks had cages filled with hats — bonnets, childrens' winter caps — and another cage was packed with prisoners' striped caps, yellow with age and smelling of mildew.

Tom walked through the barracks, checking the pictures, reading the captions, and searching for a reference to the escape from Sobibor. There was none. Another barracks had one of the original Maidanek ovens in the middle of the floor. "A product of the great German technology," Tom said.

After less than twenty minutes of running from barracks to barracks, we drove back to the main road. Tom had expressed no interest in visiting the crematorium at the far side of the camp. I didn't press him.

He was quiet for a long time as we drove toward Izbica. "You're in Sobibor, aren't you?" I asked finally.

"Yes," he answered.

The town of Izbica is a bowl with a highway and a railroad running through it. Before the war, the Jews lived in the center of the bowl; the Christians on the farms above them. We climbed up to the old Jewish cemetery on the northeastern lip of the bowl, from where we could see the rooftops below. On this hill, the Ukrainians guarding the ghetto had murdered hundreds of Jews. At the edge of the graveyard stood a twelve-foot stone monument, erected by a Catholic priest to commemorate the death of the shtetl. The priest, Jewish by birth, had been hidden during the war by Christians. After the war, he converted to Catholicism and now works as a priest in Jerusalem.

The cemetery was completely overgrown. Most of the Jewish gravestones — heavy, unpolished slabs — are gone now. The Christians of Izbica used them for building blocks. I saw several gravestones propping up a telephone pole near the cemetery.

After we climbed back down the hill, we drove through the back streets of the old shtetl. The houses had not changed since 1943, and the roads were mostly dirt, as they had been when Toivi lived there. Gone were the tannery, the blacksmith shop, the open market vibrant with buyers and sellers, the butcher shops, the synagogue, the library, the bakery, and the liquor store run by Toivi's father. There were horses and wagons in Izbica, just as there used to be, only now the wagons bounced on tires instead of on wooden wheels rimmed in steel.

I could feel Tom's sadness. Dena had told me the only time she saw Tom cry was during the movie *Fiddler on the Roof,* when the camera panned the Russian shtetl, with its tailors and coopers, farmers and musicians. "It reminded him of Izbica," she had said. "He had to get up and leave for a while."

Izbica was now dirty and lifeless, with hardly a sign of community or culture. We met two old men walking down the dirt street. Tom introduced himself, for everyone in Izbica used to know his father. They smiled and politely answered Tom's questions. When he gave them two cigarettes each, their faces lit up in pleasure.

"You see how they treat me now?" Tom said. "With respect. With smiles. If this were 1943, eight out of ten of these Christians in Izbica would betray me . . . and I'm being generous."

We parked around the corner from the house in which Toivi was born, behind a horse and wagon. An old, toothless man and woman lived there now, in the tiny row house with a wrought-iron balcony and shuttered windows. Tom and Dena had visited them the week before and paid three dollars and some cigarettes to go up to the bedroom so that they could see the attic where Tom, his brother, mother and father, and two hundred neighbors had hidden when the Nazis swept the ghetto for Jews to feed Sobibor and Belzec.

"Stay with him," Tom had heard the old lady tell her husband. "Maybe he's come back for the gold."

When Tom confronted her, she told him that she believed he returned to get the loot his father had hidden in the house before the Gestapo finally dragged the family off. She said that after the Germans had cleaned out the Jews, the Christians ripped apart most of the houses, looking for buried treasure.

The old man was glad to see Tom a second time, and invited him up to the attic again — for another three dollars.

Toivi's house was tiny by modern standards, with a small kitchen, dining room, and bedroom on the first floor. A set of steep steps led to the bedroom on the second floor that Toivi had shared with his brother. Toivi's father had cut a four-foot-high door into the wall under the sloping roof, creating an attic not visible from the street. Then he had placed a dresser in front of the door. I stepped inside the attic. It was hard to imagine that so small a room, now cluttered with junk, could have hidden so many people. "When we were here in the winter," Tom said, "steam would fill the bedroom after we opened the door."

We drove east, out of the old shtetl, down a wagon rut, and into the flat farmland. On our left was the beech and maple forest where Toivi, Wycen, and Kostman had hidden. I got out of the car, walked into the forest, and stood in the middle of the path that ran through it. It was so dark that the afternoon sun did not even penetrate. Two hundred yards away, across the road and over a ridge, was Bojarski's farm.

The apple orchard was still there, where the farmhouse used to be. The barn was also long gone. Bojarski went to jail several years ago, Tom said, but he could never find out exactly why. Bojarski's wife and daughter were still alive. The two men who tried to kill him were caught by the Polish militia after liberation and executed.

On the way back to the highway, we stopped at a barn hugging the hill that bordered the old shtetl. "I was hiding in the tannery during the roundup," Tom said, pointing to where the tannery had been. "I ran out the back when I saw the Gestapo coming. Then I saw Janek."

Janek was a Christian classmate and friend of Toivi's.

"I said to Janek, 'Please hide me,'" Tom continued. "'Go to the barn,' Janek said.

"As I was running into the barn, an old woman shouted, 'No, run! Run!' But I didn't run, because I knew Janek would hide me. He didn't. He walked up the hill with the Gestapo. I went to Sobibor."

*

The closer we drove to Sobibor, the more quiet and tense Tom became. We turned off the Chelm-to-Wlodawa highway onto a blacktop road surrounded by pine forests edged with young birch trees standing guard like white sentinels. Soon the railway tracks that carried two hundred and fifty thousand Jews to the gas chambers emerged from the trees on our left and ran parallel to the road.

Four miles into the woods, the road abruptly ended. On our left was a small train station that looked like a cottage. A white shingle with a single word hung from the roof over the door: SOBIBOR. A passenger train was chugging down the tracks toward Chelm, and a dozen villagers were standing on the platform with hand luggage. Behind the station stood a group of small houses — including the three that the Ukranians had used as brothels — resting on grassless, sandy soil.

The foresters' tower, as sturdy as it was in 1943, dominated the skyline on the right side of the road. It stood in an open field partly covered with piles of neatly stacked pine logs waiting for flatcars. In the shadow of the tower, and surrounded by shade trees, stood the two-story, green wooden house where Stangl and Reichleitner had once lived. With windows trimmed in white and protected by a wooden fence, the house looked like a forester's home. I expected to see children swinging on an old tire hanging from a tree branch.

After the war, the Polish government turned Sobibor into a memorial park and hired a caretaker, who lived in a frame house with a long, sloping roof. At some time within the last few years, however, the government fired the caretaker. Now, Sobibor looked like a vacant lot.

The caretaker's house, which rested close to where the Ukrainian barracks once stood, was being remodeled. Polish loggers said it was being converted into a pub. On the door, someone had painted in black letters "Don't piss here."

The small parking lot had grass and weeds growing between the flagstones and in what appeared to be flower beds. The rusting light poles reached toward the open sky like charred trees in a burned forest. Someone had stolen all the fixtures from them. On the flagstone square where the gas chambers had once stood was a twenty-foot-high stone sculpture of a half-charred woman looking to heaven. A burned child clutched her stone clothes. The woman's eyes were sunk deep into her skull, and there was anger, fear, and confusion in her face, as if she had been frozen in stone while singing "Eli, Eli." At her feet were bouquets of dead wildflowers, the only sign that someone had been there to visit her. Weeds were struggling to grow between the flagstones, and the large steel flowerpot was filled with brown weeds unable to survive the July sun.

Sixty yards away — just feet from where the bodies had been burned on beds of railroad tracks — was a round hill of ashes ringed by a three-foot-high stone wall. I poked the mound and found a bone the size of a bottle cap.

Tom was devastated. "You see now why I dream of coming back here to live?" he said. "buying some land . . . building a house for myself . . . taking care of the place . . . serving as a guide?"

A busload of forty or fifty children of all ages was visiting Sobibor that day. The children and their counselors were camping at a lake near the old fishery on the estate of Count Chelmicki, where Stangl and his family had briefly lived before the Kommandant of Sobibor was transferred to Treblinka. The lake was now a popular resort, and the fishery was gone.

The children were standing at a plaque riveted into a stone wall just feet from where the camouflaged, barbed-wire path led into Camp II and into the barracks where the Jews undressed. A young camp counselor in shorts, wearing sunglasses and a neatly trimmed beard and mustache, was explaining to the children what the plaque said. Behind him, in the shade of a half-dozen birch trees, were three picnic tables.

The plaque was a historical lie. It read: "Sobibor. In this place stood a Nazi death camp from May 1942 to October 1943. In it, they killed 250,000 Russian POWs, Jews, Poles, and Gypsies. On October 14, 1943, the prisoners revolted. After fighting with their Nazi guards, 400 escaped." The Polish War Crimes Commission had reported over thirty-five years ago that Sobibor was a death camp for Jews only.

"Excuse me, Richard," Tom said. "I have to listen to what he's telling them." Tom edged into the semicircle of children for a couple of minutes, then came back. "Wait," he said. "This is very important to me."

The counselor was explaining to the children — the future of Poland — that the Germans had gassed two hundred and fifty thousand people at Sobibor — civilians, women, children. But he didn't say a word about Jews.

Tom interrupted. "I was a prisoner here," he said. "I escaped."

The children gathered around Tom as if he were a friendly ghost. He told them the history of Sobibor, pointing to the spur where the boxcars once stood, filled with half-dead Jews; to an imaginary main gate; to barracks for Germans and Ukrainians; to watchtowers and fences and workshops. Then he took the children to a path leading toward the barracks where he had once shouted, "Hand luggage here," and to the shed where he had once cut women's hair. The cinder road cutting through the young pine trees the Germans had planted in October 1943 was slightly north of the original path. While Tom explained to those young children, eager and innocent, how Jews were gassed and their bodies buried, he fought back his tears.

The counselor interrupted. "Is what the plaque says true?" he asked.

"Absolutely not," Tom said. "We were *all* Jews."

The counselor invited Tom to the lakeside camp to talk to the rest of the three hundred children and their counselors. Tom was pleased and said he would come back later that week.

Tom watched the children walk down the cinder path to the charred woman and child in stone. "This trip was worthwhile," he told me. "The children must know the truth. Promise me you'll send me a set of your pictures of me with the children."

For the next hour, Tom walked me through Sobibor. He was very calm and quiet. His nervousness was gone; he walked slowly and didn't rush me. He seemed almost peaceful and distant, as if it all had happened to someone else, not to Toivi. But I could sense his sadness and inner turmoil.

We stood where the main gate used to be with its huge white sign, SS SONDERKOMMANDO, facing the pine forest into which Toivi and Shlomo, Sasha and Boris, Selma and Chaim had run while the mines exploded around them and the Ukrainians fired from the towers. We paused for pictures in front of Stangl's house, walked down the blacktop road Toivi had walked with his brother, mother, and father. "It was much nicer then," Tom said. "There was grass nicely cut and sunflowers along the road. The barracks looked like a Tyrolean village."

We paused at the spot where Toivi's incinerator shed used to be in Camp II — where he worked with Blind Karl and Wycen — then walked to Camp III. Tom pointed to the dried wildflowers at the feet of the stone woman and child.

"You think these are for the *Jews?*" he asked.

I didn't have to answer, for we both knew some Polish children had placed them there for their mythical forebears whom the Nazis had killed in Sobibor.

We strolled to the spot where the bodies were burned. Tom scraped between the long grass with his foot, then stooped to pick up a dozen bone fragments from the sand and ashes. In the palm of his hand, they looked like tiny beach pebbles rubbed clean and white by the sand.

"Why do you keep coming back?" I asked.

"I don't know."

"Will you come back again?"

"I don't know."

We both knew he'd be back next year or the year after, and that he'd keep coming back. I remembered that he had told me in Brazil that he never wanted to forget. He owed it to his mother and father and brother and the Jews of Izbica to remember. "It would be an insult to forget," he had said.

We cut into the pine trees and stood on the spot where Toivi had cut the women's hair, where he could hear the screams, where the plaintive melody wrenched from the hearts of a believing people who could not understand rose to the heavens, to a deaf God. Several years ago, Tom had found some of the barbed-wire fence still embedded in the old trees about ten feet from the ground. We looked for some, but couldn't find any.

"Do you notice how uneven the ground is back here?" he asked. The forest seemed to be covered with holes filled in with leaves and branches and erosion. "That's because the Poles came here after the war to dig."

"Dig?"

"For buried treasure," Tom said. "For about ten years, they kept coming with shovels, until the government stopped them."

Tom told me that one summer as he was walking through the camp, he overheard a Polish Catholic priest explaining Sobibor to a younger priest and a woman.

"He was calling the Jews 'kikes' and other such names," Tom said. "I interrupted. 'They are not "kikes," I told the priest. 'They are Jews. You may be wearing the garb of a Christian, but you do not have the soul of a Christian.' "

God hung over Sobibor like a gigantic unspoken question. He was all-powerful, yet seemed helpless in the face of a human hatred that knew no bounds. All-knowing, yet strangely indifferent. All-present, yet distant and aloof. All-loving, but deaf to the cries of His people. All-innocent, but guilty of neglect. All-pure, but covered with ashes.

It was fitting, I thought, that we leave Sobibor shrouded in the mystery of how men could be so cruel, and their God so deaf.

*

Disregarding the DANGER — STAY OFF sign, I climbed to the top of the foresters' tower. There was no one to stop me. The forest of the owls stretched in all directions as far as my eyes could see. If there were farms carved out of it, if villages and towns grew in it, I couldn't tell. It was still and peaceful. The pine logs stacked below me looked like wooden bridges spanning an open field. At my back, somewhere in the woods, the Bug River flowed north to join the Vistula and then to meet the Baltic Sea at Gdansk. Along the east bank of the Bug stood watchtowers manned by Russian soldiers who kept the Ukrainians inside the Soviet Union. On the west bank (the Polish side), there were no towers; there were few Poles who wanted to swim to Russia.

It was difficult for me to believe that more than two hundred and fifty thousand men, women, and children had been murdered below me in the fields and in the woods where the young pines fought with the underbrush and with each other to survive another summer.

I tried to imagine what Sobibor had looked like to the Ukrainians who once had stood inside huts on stilts, as I was doing. But I couldn't.

I closed my eyes and tried to hear the screams, the Jews singing *"Es War Ein Edelweiss"* as they marched from Camp I to Camp II, the gunshots, the cracks of the whips, Wagner bellowing. But I couldn't.

The late afternoon sun silently bathed the treetops, and the air hung motionless. Not even the pines whispered the way the poems say they do. I faced the gas chambers and strained to hear "Eli, Eli." But I couldn't.

It was presumptuous of me even to try. For I could not understand Sobibor. I couldn't begin to fathom the hopelessness, the terror, the pain, the wrenching cry of a people who believed in a God Who didn't seem to believe in them. I was an outsider standing in a tower looking down at the footprints of history — pines that were thirty-eight years old, empty fields, train tracks, and a lone sign that said SOBIBOR.

I remembered that Tom had told me in Santa Barbara that he wanted a book on Sobibor so that the world would not forget. I had dismissed his concern. How *could* the world forget? If there was one thing I was certain of then, it was that we would always remember.

Now, as I stood in the foresters' tower, I knew how easy it was to forget. The weeds and tall grass that were slowly strangling Sobibor told me that. The "Don't piss here" sign, the historical marker that lied, the dried wild-flowers offered to the "Polish Christian" woman and child in stone, the mound of ashes blown by the wind and covered with marmot holes, the pits in the woods left by the treasure-hunters, the children who would never be told that Jews were murdered in Sobibor because of hatred and indifference and greed — all those told me how easy it is to forget.

I remembered the conversation I had with a Jew on my flight to the Soviet Union to visit Sasha.

"What do you do?" the man had asked me.

"Write," I said.

"What?"

"Books." I explained the Sobibor project.

"Why do you want to write about *that?* Who's going to read it? Who cares about three hundred Jews, anyway?"

His questions had rumbled in my mind for days. I remembered how Tom had argued in Brazil that there would be another Holocaust. I didn't believe him then. But as I stood in Sobibor — like a researcher, high above the reality — I was no longer so certain.

Afterword

O N A SUNDAY NIGHT in April 1987, approximately 31.6 million people watched Alan Arkin as Leon Feldhendler, Rutger Hauer as Sasha, and Joanna Pakula as Luka in *Escape from Sobibor.* Millions more have seen the three-hour CBS movie on HBO, in reruns, or on video since then. The film played in so many countries around the world and in so many languages, it became impossible to keep track. CBS made it part of its "Television Reading Program," which introduced the movie, book, and teleplay (written by Reginald Rose) to thousands of school children across the country. Letters poured in to Toivi, Esther, and Selma and Chaim, and they were invited to speak in classrooms and auditoriums. They learned firsthand that children care deeply about them and what they and their families suffered. It was as if a whole new generation was discovering the Holocaust through these personal stories of hope and survival.

To the credit of the Polish government, the movie aired in Poland as well. The impact was immediate and concrete. The government removed the old, inaccurate plaque at the entrance to the camp and replaced it with one that said in several languages, including Hebrew, that the Nazis killed 250,000 Jews in a death camp there. The Polish government paved the road and parking lot and repaired the sculpture of the half-charred woman looking to heaven as she clutches a burned child. It built a fence around the spot where the gas chambers once stood and converted one of the houses that had served as SS living quarters into a small museum. It planted grass and flowers. It lit an eternal flame, which leaps high into the air, at the feet of the woman and child. Now, when Polish school children come to visit Sobibor, they leave flowers at the monument for the *Jews* whose bones lay buried in the mound of soft ashes nearby.

If that wasn't vindication enough, on October 14, 1993, the fiftieth anniversary of the escape from Sobibor, the Polish government sponsored a televised memorial at the camp. To the music of a military band and before representatives of each country that had sent Jews to Sobibor as well as 1,500 Poles, Esther and Toivi carried a banner that said, "In memory of the 250,000 who perished here." They placed it where the gas chambers had once stood, and a Rabbi offered a memorial service in accordance with Jewish law. That night, Esther and Toivi lit 250 candles in glass jars, one for each 1,000 Jews who did not escape from Sobibor, and placed them in a circle around the mound of ashes. "You couldn't believe it," Esther said after she returned. "It was wonderful. You didn't know you were in Poland."

Escape from Sobibor had its impact in this country as well. The U.S. Holocaust Memorial Museum in Washington, D.C., included interviews with Toivi, Esther, and Selma and Chaim in its continuous videotape of survivors. And the uprising and escape from Sobibor receives prominent mention in the museum's displays.

Unfortunately, not everyone was happy with *Escape from Sobibor*. A chapter of the Ukrainian Congress Committee sued CBS and the Chrysler Corporation, which sponsored the movie, alleging they "misused the presentation as a vehicle to launch an unprecedented, prejudicial and misleading attack" against Ukrainians in this country. In particular, they objected to the movie's portrayal of *all* Sobibor guards as Ukrainian and as "Nazi mercenaries," while failing to state that millions of Ukrainians fought against the Germans. The court dismissed the suit on technical grounds, but not before Chrysler backed away from the sequel, "Escape from Sobibor: The Aftermath," already scripted. The sequel was to begin in the woods after the escape and end with a gathering of survivors at Leon Feldhendler's funeral in Lublin.

*

In retrospect, *Escape from Sobibor* played a small but important role in raising the consciousness of Jews, especially American Jews. Time and again, younger Jews who privately nursed feelings of shame over the alleged passivity of Holocaust victims suddenly showed an angry interest. "How come I never heard about any of this?" they would demand in almost disbelief. Since the publication of the book in 1982, other writers, researchers, and filmmakers have begun to explore the resistance theme, and teachers of social history have become increasingly hungry for more stories about the Jews who fought back and the Christians who helped them.

The renewed interest in Jewish resistance has caused me to rethink the contribution of the book to the history of World War II. It has become clear that most, but not all, Holocaust historians have trapped themselves in a catch-22 of their own making. On the one hand, they take pride in basing their writings and critical analyses on official records. And the Nazis were very obliging. They left behind millions of documents and reports and thousands of films and photographs. On the other hand, these papers, films, and pictures do *not* document and scarcely mention Jewish resistance to the Nazi machine. Add to this critical omission that the vast majority of resisters were killed without witnesses and one has what can only be called a cruel historical hoax.

I voiced my concern about the distorted "passive Jew" theory to a highly respected Holocaust historian whom I met at an international conference. Why, I asked, did he relegate the escape from Sobibor to a brief footnote in his thousand-page book? Because, he said, the escape was an interesting aberration and a footnote was all it deserved. How could he be so certain that resistance was a mere aberration, I asked? Because, he said, there are no documents. What about the survivors, I asked? They are too emotional, he said, and their memories are not to be trusted. Documents are frequently inaccurate, I countered. They often distort. By way of example, I pointed out three factual errors in his own footnote about Sobibor. The historian dismissed me like a student and, in subsequent reprints of his classic, repeated the same three errors in the same skimpy footnote.

Over the years, I have encountered similar closed-mindedness and intellectual snobbery among other Holocaust historians who build on each other's writings. Unfortunately, their writings are based on the same flawed premise: If the Nazis didn't write about it, it didn't happen; and if they did write about it but did not give it much significance, it wasn't significant. More unfortunately, in portraying Jews as a flock of sheep on the road to slaughter, these historians have committed the unpardonable sin of distorting history. By so doing, they have caused intense suffering and irreparable damage to the Jewish people.

Escape from Sobibor challenges those historians and their false logic. Like other "impossible" events in history, the escape has become an important *symbol*. It represents the buried stories of hundreds of thousands who fought and died in ghettos no one ever heard of; who tried to escape on the way to camps but never made it; who fought back inside camps but were killed anyway; who managed to escape only to be recaptured and executed; who formed or joined partisan groups from the woods of Vilna to the forest of the owls and who never saw liberation as Toivi, Shlomo, Leon, and Esther did.

In some small way, I hope that the republication of *Escape from Sobibor* will encourage historians and other researchers, writers, and artists to take a second critical look at that painful period we call the Holocaust and unearth even more stories of Jewish resistance and Christian heroism. Perhaps the sheer number and weight of these stories will be enough to balance the scales of "history" and finally give to the Jewish people and those who helped them their rightful recognition.

Acknowledgments, Sources, Notes

Acknowledgments

I wish to thank: Miriam Gilbert, Mary Ann Larkin, Maya Latynski, and Krystyna Smith for translation services; Feiga Zylberminc of the Hebraic Section of the Library of Congress for help in finding research materials; Sandra Vadney for copy-editing and typing the first draft of this manuscript; Aviva Kempner and Esther Raab for critically reviewing the manuscript; Miriam Novitch for her help in finding and interviewing survivors in Israel, and for her hospitality.

Finally, I wish to thank my editor, Frances Tenenbaum, for her patience with a long-overdue manuscript, and my wife, Paula Kaufmann, for her support and understanding.

Sources

In researching this book, I interviewed the following Sobibor survivors, as well as two others who requested not to be identified: Thomas Blatt, Chaim Engel and his wife, Selma Wijnberg-Engel, Jacob Biskubicz, Mordechai Goldfarb, Chaim Korenfeld (through Thomas Blatt), Haim Lejst, Yehuda Lerner (by telephone), Itzhak Lichtman and his wife, Eda Lichtman, Abraham Margulies, Esther Raab, Aizik Rottenberg, Alexander Pechersky, Stanislaw Szmajzner, and Hella Felenbaum-Weiss.

Besides general books and articles on the Holocaust, I used the following sources, among others, which deal specifically with Sobibor:

Ainzstein, Reuben. "The Sobibor Uprising," *Jewish Resistance in Nazi-Occupied Eastern Europe.* London: Paul Elek, 1974. (English) A highly documented, fifty-page account of the Sobibor revolt and escape. Unfortunately, the author relies on Tomin and Sinilnikow (see next page) as a major source, and their book is totally unreliable. Furthermore, the author relies on the names and dates Pechersky used in his own brief account (see below). The names and dates are incorrect. The author's footnotes, however, are quite valuable.

Blatt, Thomas. "No Time for Tears," *Santa Barbara News & Review,* December 1977. (English) A survivor's account of his escape from Sobibor, based on a diary. The article is rich in detail and very well written.

Blatt, Thomas. "Blood and Ashes," *Jewish Currents,* December 1978. (English) A survivor's brief summary of the revolt, based on what he saw and heard.

Bower, Tom. "Gustav Wagner: Angel of Death," *Listener,* June 21, 1979. (English) A short article on Wagner, his escape, capture, and suicide. Skimpy, but an accurate summary.

de Jong, Louis. "Sobibor," *Encounter,* December 1978. (English) Background article on the camp, emphasizing details about the 34,000 Dutch Jews who were sent to Sobibor, and describing the camp's death system. De Jong is the director of the Netherlands State Institute for War Documentation, founded in 1945. His article is very accurate.

Judgment Against Erich Bauer, November 11, 1950. (German) A ten-page summary of the war crimes trial against the former SS man in charge of the Sobibor gas chambers. A valuable document, because it describes the death system at Sobibor from arrival to burial. It also contains good eyewitness testimony against Bauer.

Lukaszkiewcz, Zdzislaw, "Sobibor Extermination Camp," *German Crimes in Poland,* ed., Central Commission for War Crimes. Warsaw: 1946–1947, vol. II. (English) The author was the judge of the court at Siedlce, where the Sobibor investigations were held after the war. The article, a summary of those investigations, contains a basic description of the camp and how it worked. Thin, but basic for historical reasons.

Novitch, Miriam. *Sobibor: Martyrdom and Revolt.* New York: Holocaust Library, 1980. (English) The English edition of this work is a basic fact book in the form of a collection of short testimonies from thirty survivors or their spouses. Its excellent introduction presents an overview of Sobibor and Operation Reinhard. The Hebrew edition contains the brief testimony of Leon Feldhendler, based on a few pages he wrote before he was murdered. That testimony is apparently the only eyewitness account the Sobibor leader left.

Pechersky, Alexander. *The Sobibor Revolt.* Moscow: Emes, 1946. (Yiddish) Written in diary form from sketchy notes taken in Sobibor, this thirty-five-page pamphlet describes events leading up to the revolt, the revolt itself, and the author's subsequent escape back to the Soviet Union. Because Pechersky led the revolt with Leon Feldhendler, his pamphlet carries great weight and is accurate to a point. But it has three flaws: the dates and times are unreliable, most of the names are incorrect, and the work smacks slightly of Communist propaganda. The pamphlet has been translated into English and appears in Novitch's book and in *They Fought Back: The Story of Jewish Resistance in Nazi Europe,* ed., Yuri Suhl. New York: Schocken Books, 1967.

Rueckerl, Adalbert. *Nazi Death Camps in the Light of the German Criminal Process.* Munich: Deutscher Taschenbuch Verlag GmbH, 1977. (German) A highly accurate description of Sobibor as a camp — Germans, guards, physical details, the system — based on the testimony of Jews and Germans at the Sobibor war crimes trials. Rueckerl was the head of the division of the German Justice Department that prosecuted the Sobibor Nazis. The book is a unique contribution, for Rueckerl had access to those trial records and transcripts that are not open to the public. Many of the details in the book, which also deals with Belzec and Treblinka, come from the Germans themselves. An excellent background book.

Rutkowski, Adam. "Resistance at the Death Camp of Sobibor," *Bulletin of the Jewish Historical Commission,* nos. 65–66, 1968. (Polish) This highly documented, sixty-page article is based exclusively on the testimonies of Sobibor survivors and other eyewitnesses found in the archives of the Historical Commission and in Yad Vashem in Jerusalem. Its strength is its organization, scholarly research, and footnotes. Its weakness is its lack of critical evaluation of the survivors' accounts.

Sereny, Gitta. *Into That Darkness: From Mercy Killing to Mass Murder.* London: André Deutsch, 1976. (English) The author was the last writer to interview Franz Stangl, one of Sobibor's Kommandants. The book contains a richness of detail on Stangl, his feelings, his family, and his first weeks at Sobibor. The book also has some excellent background on Gustav Wagner and Hermann Michel, Hitler's euthanasia program, and the Nazi Vatican escape route.

Szmajzner, Stanislaw. *Hell in Sobibor: A Tragedy of a Young Jew.* Rio de Janiero: Edições Bloch, 1968. (Portuguese) The most thorough account of the history and the development of Sobibor by a survivor who was in the camp from the very beginning up to the uprising. It is also one of the few accounts written by a key member of the Organization. Half of the book deals with the author's life before Sobibor; the other half concerns the camp, the uprising, and the escape. The book is very accurate when the author writes about the events he saw; it is not completely reliable about the events to which the author was not an eyewitness.

Tomin, V., and A. Sinilnikow. *Return Undesirable: A Documentary Story.* Moscow: Molodaya Guardia, 1964. (Russian) The book is totally unreliable; it is a nonfiction novel. It is impossible to tell from the book what is fact and what is fiction. Many of the details in the book dealing with the revolt and escape have been refuted by Szmajzner, Blatt, and Pechersky as pure fiction. Unfortunately, the book has been used uncritically as a source by other authors.

Yizkor Book in Memory of Wlodawa and the Region of Sobibor. Published by the Association of Immigrants of Wlodawa and surrounding area in Israel, ed.,

Shoman Kanc. Tel Aviv, 1974. (English) An anthology of articles and personal testimony about Wlodawa and Sobibor. An excellent resource book, but it is difficult to determine whether the authors of articles were survivors or not, and if they were not, where they got their information.

Notes

Preface

Most accounts say approximately thirty Sobibor Jews survived the war. That number is a serious miscount. The following list (46) was compiled with the help of the survivors still alive: Philip Bialowitz, his brother, Simha, and his wife, Lea Reisner-Bialowitz; Moshe Bahir; Jacob Biskubicz; Thomas Blatt; Leon Cymiel; Josef Dunietz; Chaim Engel and his wife, Selma Wijnberg-Engel; Ber Freiberg; Mordechai Goldfarb; Salomea Hannel; Moshe Hochman; Zyndel Hoenigman; Avram Kohn; Chaim Korenfeld; Haim Lejst; Samuel Lerer; Yehuda Lerner; Itzhak Lichtman and his wife, Eda; Yefim Litvinovskiy; Abraham Margulies; Yehezkiel Menche; Zelda Metz; Alexander Pechersky; Naum Platnitskiy; Shlomo Podchlebnik; Haim Powroznik; Esther Terner-Raab; Aizik Rottenberg; Semyon Rozenfeld; Ilana Stern-Safran; Stanislaw Szmajzner; Boris Tabarinskiy; Kurt Thomas; Haim Tregor; Arkady Vaispapir; Hella Felenbaum-Weiss; Aleksei Wycen; Riva Feldman-Zelinska; Meir Ziss; Hershel Zukerman and his son Joseph; and one Polish survivor who requested to remain anonymous.

Besides these survivors, there is one who lives in Canada. His name could not be verified. Both Leon Feldhendler and Josef Kopf survived until the Soviets liberated Poland, but were killed by Poles before the war was over.

No one knows how many Jews were killed in Sobibor. The figure of 250,000 is based on the report of the Polish Central Commission for War Crimes. The commission arrived at its figure (which it admits is an undercount) by extrapolating, since the Germans did not keep records of the number of transports and the number of Jews per transport. The commission reasoned as follows:

> Assuming that the exterminatory action at its highest peak lasted approximately four months (June–October 1942) and that the average monthly transports in that period were no more than twenty, we would have a total of eighty transports. For the sake of precaution, we accept the number of sixty transports, i.e., the figure given in the statement of the witness Parkila (the Polish stationmaster of Sobibor), whose evidence is the most objective and detailed. The number of persons in one transport was estimated by witnesses to have varied from 2000 to 4000 persons. Taking 3000 as the average, 180,000 people were brought in sixty transports. Since it is beyond any doubt that the exterminatory action continued until the uprising, we may without any risk of exaggeration assume that in the period between October 1942 and October 1943 the number

374

of transports averaged not less than two per month, which gives twenty-four transports for the entire period — some 72,000 victims.

Thus the total number of victims brought in by train was about 250,000, not including all those people who reached the Sobibor camp on foot, in motor cars, and in carts. Their number was by no means insignificant, since one of the witnesses (by the name of Fajenbaum) was driven to the camp in a group of some 4000 persons.

Thomas Blatt interviewed the stationmaster of Sobibor after the war. The stationmaster recalled Karl Frenzel sending a telegraphed message to Lublin shortly after the revolt, describing the escape and asking for help. The stationmaster did not recall the exact time of the telegram, but he did remember that the reason Frenzel sent it was that the telephone wires had been cut. The telegram has never been found.

The October 14, 1943, report, entitled "Report of the Order Police in the District of Lublin," can be found in Novitch and in *Documents of Destruction,* ed., Raul Hilberg, Chicago: Quadrangle, 1971. There is a longer and more complete report, written on March 17, 1944, by the commander of the Security Police and the SD for the District of Lublin, Border Commissariat of Chelm. The latter report erroneously fixes the date of the uprising as October 15 instead of October 14. I quote the report in full from Novitch's appendix, which has the original German and an English translation:

REPORT

Re: Struggle against bands.
Event: Commander's Order No. 11 of March 11 1944, Abs. 105.
Enclosure: None.

In the afternoon hours of October 15, 1944, about 300 prisoners of the Special Lager Sobibor undertook — after having disarmed a part of the guards and killed an SS Führer (officer) and 10 Unterführer (noncoms) — an escape which partly succeeded.

From the Border Police Post Chelm an Einsatzkommando was dispatched including the following SS men:

SS Untersturmführer	Benda, Adalbert,
SS Hauptscharführer	Pruckner, Ludwig,
SS Hauptscharführer	Benzler, Hermann,
SS Oberscharführer	Scholz, Erich,
SS Oberscharführer	Theimer, Rudolf,
SS Oberscharführer	Schloegl, Konard, and
SS Rottenführer	Reinert, Adolf.

In addition to this were also alerted the Wehrmacht and the police. In view of the nature of the Special Lager and its prisoners, the Wehrmacht was ordered to organize an immediate posse after the fugitives, and the Police to secure the safety of the Lager outside its fences.

The Einsatzkommando sent from the Border Police Commissariat in Chelm conducted the mopping-up of the inner camps of the Lager. Our men were fired at many times by the prisoners caught in the camp, in the night of October 15, 1943, and in the early hours of October 16, 1943. During the mopping-up of the camp itself, our men had to use arms because the prisoners resisted arrest. A great number of prisoners were shot; 159 prisoners were treated according to order.

All the men of the Einsatzkommando were equal to their task.

Evidence: Report to the Commandant of the Sipo/Security Police and the SD for the District of Lublin, of October 16, 1943. — Greko Chelm — B. No. 285/43.

— Signed: Benda, SS Untersturmführer For accuracy.— [signature illegible], SS Hauptsturmführer and Crim. Pol. Comm. L.S.

The Polish Central Commission for War Crimes simply reported that after the revolt, all the equipment was removed from Sobibor, the buildings were blown up, the rubbish carried away, and pine trees planted. Novitch gives the date for the end of Operation Reinhard as follows: "Operation Reinhard was officially ended on October 19, 1943, as was mentioned in a letter from Globocnik to Himmler. Following Globocnik's advice, farms were built on the site of the three death camps and farmers were paid to take care of them." I have not seen the letter to which Novitch refers. Novitch also describes the cleanup of the camp as follows: "The cleaning-up operations of Sobibor were carried out by thirty Jewish prisoners who were sent there from another camp. In November, they were murdered near a woods in groups of five and their bodies incinerated. Among them were women. The SS men Juehrs and Zierke, who were present at the executions, testified at the Hagen trials."

Some writers have stated that 400 Jews escaped from Sobibor. The Germans reported that 300 escaped and that 159 were "treated according to order." If there were 600 Jews in Camp I at the time of the revolt and if we use the German figures, which are about as reliable as one can find, we realize that approximately 140 Jews were killed during the revolt and break-out by machine guns, rifles, and land mines.

Chapters One to Five

Most of Chapters One to Five are based on Stanislaw (Shlomo) Szmajzner's book and on my extensive interviews with him in Goiania, Brazil, in April 1981.

Page 10: My description of the Sobibor barracks and watchtowers is based on those still standing in Maidanek, which I visited in the summer of 1981 with Thomas Blatt. Mr. Blatt told me that the Maidanek barracks and watchtowers are identical with those which once stood in Sobibor.

Page 10: According to former death camp Nazi Franz Suchomel, German officers and noncoms carried Walther or Nagan pistols, and used Czech Mausers model 24 and Finnish submachine guns for emergencies. See Sereny, p. 123. From what I can gather, the Ukrainian guards also used Mausers.

Page 12: The description of Franz Stangl is based on Szmajzner and Sereny. Stangl succeeded Richard Thomalla, who was Sobibor Kommandant during the construction phase of the camp. He was not Kommandant when the gassings began there. No one is quite sure what has happened to Thomalla.

Page 20: One of the problems I had in researching this book was getting a balanced picture of how the Jews stood up to the human degradation and terror to which they were subjected. Most of the survivors whom I interviewed did not want to discuss the action of some Jews, which, if taken out of context, could be considered by some as immoral. They meant such things as Jews killing each other to survive or blackmailing each other or collaborating with the Germans. Szmajzner was an exception. He told me that he decided to tell the truth even if it hurt someone. Thus, his brief description of the activities of the Jewish ghetto police and the Judenrat is of great importance for this book. For an excellent and balanced analysis of the Judenrat, see Isaiah Trunk, *Judenrat: The Jewish Councils in Eastern Europe Under Nazi Occupation,* New York: Stein and Day, 1977.

Page 29: I have been unable to determine the first name of the Ukrainian Klat or Klatte. Because I'm not sure which spelling is correct, I chose "Klat" and have used it consistently. Nor have I been able to determine the first name of SS Oberscharführer Poul. Technically speaking, Oberscharführer is a technical sergeant and Scharführer is a staff sergeant. I usually refer to both as "sergeant."

Page 33: Szmajzner calls Avi "Abrão" in his Portuguese book. In Yiddish, his name was Avraham (formal) or Avi (a nickname). I quote Avi's letter to Shlomo directly from Szmajzner's book, with his permission and in translation. Szmajzner no longer has the original letter, so what he printed in his book was a reconstruction from memory.

Chapter Six

The material about Itzhak is based on my interview with Itzhak Lichtman in Holon, Israel, in November 1981 and on his testimony in Novitch.

Page 41: The names of the towns and villages listed in this chapter and in other chapters come from a chart in Rueckerl. The chart, based on war crimes trial testimony, tries to reconstruct which transports arrived in Sobibor, when, and how many people they carried. The list is incomplete but accurate.

Page 41: The material on Himmler's first visit to Sobibor is based on the eyewitness accounts of Szmajzner, Itzhak Lichtman, and Moshe Bahir. Lichtman's and Bahir's testimony can be found in Novitch.

Chapter Seven

The material on the development of the SS is based on: Heinz Hoehne, *The Order of the Death's Head: The Story of Hitler's SS,* trans., Richard Barry, New

York: Coward-McCann, 1970; and Eugene Kogan, *Theory and Practice of Hell*, trans., Heinz Norden, New York: Berkley, 1980.

Page 45: The initiative for setting up Chelmno apparently came from SS Gruppenführer Arthur Greiser. As early as the autumn of 1941, he asked Heydrich to send trained executioners to help him get rid of the 100,000 Jews still in the Wartheland. Himmler and Heydrich sent Hauptsturmführer Lange. Adolf Eichmann, the Gestapo expert on the Jewish question, also visited Chelmno and saw the gas vans and burial.

Eichmann described what he saw as follows:

I followed the van and then came the most horrifying sight I've ever seen in my life. The van drew up alongside of a long pit, the doors were opened and the bodies thrown out; the limbs were still supple, as if they were still alive. They were thrown into the pit. I saw a civilian pulling teeth with a pair of pliers and then I took off. I rushed to my car and departed and said no more. I was through. I had had it. A white-coated doctor said I ought to look through the peephole and see what went on inside the vans. I refused. I couldn't. I couldn't speak. I had to get away. Frightful, I tell you. An inferno. Can't do it. I can't do it.

(See Hoehne, pp. 373 et seq.)

Pages 46–47: The best source of information about Stangl and Wirth, the euthanasia program, and its relationship to the three death camps is Gitta Sereny. Much of her research on Stangl and the euthanasia program is original.

Page 47: The description of the Sobibor gas chambers and the test gassing came from Rueckerl, whose book was based on verifiable trial testimony. Rueckerl was not certain whether the diesel motor came from a truck or from a tank. According to most sources, it was a tank motor.

Page 47: For the complete text of Himmler's July 19, 1942, order to make the General Government Judenrein by the end of the year, see Hoehne, p. 378.

Page 47: Gerstein did not receive his orders directly from Himmler, but orally from SS officer Guenther of the Central Security Office. See Saul Friedlaender, *Kurt Gerstein: The Ambiguity of Good*, trans., Charles Fullman, New York: Knopf, 1969.

Pages 47–50: The account of Gerstein's visit to General Globocnik's office, his orders, his visits to Belzec and Treblinka, and his conversations with Christian Wirth are all based on Gerstein's own account of the incidents, written in French. See Friedlaender. Von Otter has confirmed meeting with Gerstein in the train from Warsaw to Berlin and submitting a report to Sweden. The Swedish government sent the British Foreign Office a summary of the von Otter report in August 1945, three years after von Otter met Gerstein. By that time, of course, the Russians had already occupied eastern Poland, and all the camps had long since disappeared. Friedlaender gives the full text of the Swedish report to the Foreign Office. Gerstein was caught by the French after the war and committed suicide before his case could be settled. His account has stood the test of time.

Page 48: According to the report of Aloïs Berezow, the Polish stationmaster at Belzec, the camp opened in mid-March 1942 and ran continuously (except during May and June) until October 1942. It was phased out between October and December 1942. From March until October, one to three transports arrived in Belzec daily, averaging forty cars per transport and 100 persons per car. From October to December, the transports were cut to two per week. The commission estimated that not fewer than 600,000 persons were gassed in Belzec, including 1000 to 1500 non-Jewish Poles. The report gives a schematic diagram of the gas chambers. See Eugene Szrojt, "The Belzec Extermination Camp," *German Crimes in Poland*, ed., Central Commission for War Crimes. Warsaw: 1946–1947, vol. II.

Chapter Eight

Sobibor was constantly expanding. Even on the day of the revolt itself, new buildings were under construction. Thus, it is impossible to come up with one composite description of the camp that would be valid for any given month. My description is based on Rueckerl and on the testimony of SS Sergeant Erich Bauer.

Pages 56–57: The story of Kapo Franz comes from Szmajzner. It is impossible to determine whether the Jews in Camp III actually tried to escape or whether the Germans just killed them because the transports had stopped temporarily or because the Jews were worn out and needed to be replaced. Furthermore, Itzhak Lichtman recalls the Ukrainian bragging about the massacre, but he is not absolutely certain that the Ukrainian was Klat. It could have been someone else, though that is unlikely.

Chapter Nine

My description of the Sobibor system is based on Rueckerl, Novitch, Szmajzner, Blatt, and many other survivors.

Page 60: Statistics about the flight of the Jews to the Parczew and other forests come from Shmuel Krakowski, *The War of the Doomed: Jewish Armed Resistance in Poland, 1942–1944*, trans. from the Yiddish by Orah Blaustein. I have read the book in manuscript form. The Michael Knopfmaker story comes from Novitch. Knopfmaker fought with the Russian partisans and survived the war.

Pages 61–63: The stories of resistance by Polish Jews come from my interviews with Abraham Margulies and other train brigade workers, as well as from Novitch and Rutkowski.

Page 62: The dog Barry was eventually transferred to Treblinka. The personality of the mongrel has been analyzed by the Max Planck Institute for Behavioral Research in Seeviesen, Upper Bavaria, at the request of the Court of Assizes. The institute verified that Barry, psychologically speaking, could have acted the way survivors described. For a summary of the institute's findings, see *The Death Camp Treblinka*, ed., Alexander Donat, New York: Holocaust Library, 1979, pp. 312–

315. The book also quotes the testimony of surgeons, stating that a man will not necessarily die if his genitals have been bitten off.

Page 63: Abraham Margulies and other train brigade survivors have told me about the Jew who escaped in the boxcar full of clothes. Thomas Blatt, who was not at Sobibor at the time, does not believe that the escape was possible, because Frenzel would have noticed during roll call that the man was missing, and he would have punished the train brigade, probably with death. Blatt argues that under those circumstances, the train brigade would never have helped the man. Those who defend the story argue that there was no roll call in the early fall of 1942, since the number of worker Jews was still small.

Chapter Ten

The Josel and Mordechai Goldfarb material is based exclusively on my interviews with them.

Chapter Eleven

The Karski material in this chapter is primarily based on my interviews with the former courier, who teaches political science at Georgetown University in Washington, D.C., and on his book, *The Story of a Secret State,* Boston: Houghton Mifflin, 1944. The last five chapters of Karski's book deal with his conversations with the two Jewish leaders in Warsaw, his visits to the ghetto and to Belzec, and his reports to the world. I also used Walter Laqueur, *The Terrible Secret,* Boston: Little, Brown, 1980. Laqueur's appendix deals with Karski and goes beyond the courier's 1944 book.

Page 72: The identity of the Zionist leader is not known with certainty. Laqueur believes he was either Menahem Kirschenbaum or Adolf Berman and leans toward Berman. This is the only reason I identify him as Berman in this book.

Page 74: Berman and Feiner did not tell Karski that Jews were being gassed at the death camps. It is not clear why they omitted that important fact. It is hard to believe that they did not know about the gassings by September 1942, when most of the Jews in the eastern ghettos seem to have known. Perhaps they did not want to frighten Karski; perhaps they weren't sure; perhaps they didn't want to prejudice him.

Page 77: There were other demands as well. Principally, that both Jewish and non-Jewish civic leaders send money to bribe the Gestapo, to buy false Aryan identity papers, and to feed and clothe the starving; that Jewish leaders in London — Bundist Szmul Zygielbojm and Zionist Dr. Ignace Szarcbard — make sure that the Polish government fully communicate all the demands to the Allied Council; and that Jan Karski do his utmost to arouse public opinion in behalf of the helpless Jews.

Page 81: There are no records that explain why the Jews were sent out of Belzec instead of being gassed there, or where the Germans actually sent them once they left the camp. My explanation is that the gas chambers were not working on that day. That the Jews were sent to Sobibor is an assumption based on the following reasoning:

According to the Polish Central Commission for War Crimes, Belzec was accepting, on the average, only one transport per week in the fall of 1942, because the camp was being phased out. The gas chambers there had been known to malfunction, as Gerstein found out when he visited the camp six weeks before Karski did. And Belzec was an unpredictable and poorly managed camp. SS Captain Gottlieb Hering, Belzec's Kommandant in the fall of 1942, was a disciplinary case. He was tried but exonerated before an SS court in 1944. (See *Documents of Destruction*, p. 204.) Furthermore, if the Jews could not be killed at Belzec, it would be logical for the Germans to send them to Sobibor, which was nearby and which could easily handle a transport that size. Sobibor presented the simplest solution, and therefore I present it.

The train brigade Jews at Sobibor recall many transports coming from other camps. They do not recall, however, a transport from Belzec in the fall of 1942. That does not refute my explanation, since the transport Karski saw leaving Belzec may have been identified (if it was identified) by the ghetto from which the Jews had originally come.

Finally, most of the Jews recall at least one transport of decomposing bodies, the worst of which arrived in the spring or summer of 1943.

Chapter Twelve

This chapter is primarily based on my interviews with Karski; his book; Walter Laqueur; Gitta Sereny; and Martin Gilbert, *Auschwitz and the Allies,* New York: Holt, Rinehart & Winston, 1981.

Page 83: Karski does not have a summary of the report the Polish government-in-exile sent to the Foreign Office detailing his observations. I quote the summary from Gilbert, pp. 93–95. Gilbert quotes from the Foreign Office papers. The Polish government embellished Karski's story by adding that Jews were being gassed.

Page 84: The Bund report, entitled "Report of the Bund Regarding the Persecution of the Jews," can be found in *Midstream,* April 1968. The report does not speak of gassing at Treblinka, Belzec, and Sobibor, but does give details of the gassing at Chelmno. The Polish government-in-exile information bulletin that spoke of gassings in the death camps of eastern Poland was published in the *Fortnightly Review,* during the first week of July 1942 and is quoted in Gilbert, p. 47.

Page 84: The Gerhard Riegner cable is discussed in most books that deal with the question of what the west knew and when, especially in Laqueur and Gilbert.

Pages 85–86: The material on the Richard Lichtheim letter and report comes from Laqueur. The summary of the meeting with Leland Harrison in Berne is based on Gilbert.

Page 86: The source for the Foreign Office cable is Gilbert, p. 101. The source for the Wells-Wise discussion is Arthur D. Morse, *While Six Million Died,* New York: Hart, 1967, p. 23. The source for the quote on "Wailing Jews" is Laqueur, p. 83.

Page 87: For the discussion of the reprisal bombings and the rejection of the demand, see Gilbert, p. 106.

Pages 87–89: The discussion about the acceptance of Jewish refugees into Palestine and England is summarized, for the most part, from Gilbert, in particular pp. 77, 119, and 132.

Page 89: The decree calling for sanction against Poles who killed or blackmailed Jews is quoted from Stefan Korbonski, *The Polish Underground State,* New York, Columbia University Press, 1978, p. 126. Korbonski was a member of the Polish underground and chief of civilian resistance. He gives the names of the eleven Poles who were executed.

Pages 89–90: For the discussion of ransoming Jews, see Gilbert, pp. 119 and 135 in particular. Karski told me about his interview with Lord Selborne. Besides briefing Anthony Eden and Lord Selborne in London, Karski met with, among others: Arthur Greenwood, Labour Party; Lord Cranborne, Conservative Party; Hugh Dalton, president of the Board of Trade; Miss Ellen Wilkinson, Labour member of Parliament; William Henderson, Labour Party leader; Owen O'Malley, British ambassador to the Polish government; Anthony D. Biddle, American ambassador to the Polish government; Sir Cecil Hurst, chairman of the United Nations War Crimes Commission; and writers and editors H. G. Wells, Arthur Koestler, Victor Gollancz, Allen Lane, Kingsley Martin, Ronald Hyde, Gerard Berry. See *Congressional Record,* December 15, 1981, E5847.

Page 90: Berman and Feiner had told Karski to deliver the demand about excommunication of Catholics who collaborated in the Final Solution only to the president of Poland himself. The two Jews were sensitive to the fact that if others knew about the demand, they could try to embarrass or manipulate the Pope, and that could possibly militate against his intervening. Carlo Falconi argues in his book, *The Silence of Pius XII,* Boston: Little, Brown, 1970, that Karski visited Pius XII himself. Falconi's source is a close friend of Karski's. I asked Karski whether he ever had an audience with Pius XII about the Jewish demands. He told me he did not and that the Pope was informed of his message to the world through the president of Poland and through the Catholic leaders he had met in the United States.

Page 90: The note of the Polish ambassador to the Vatican can be found in Sereny, p. 331. The letter of the president of Poland to the Pope is quoted in full in Falconi, p. 218.

Pages 90–91: The specific examples of what the Vatican knew and when are drawn from a variety of sources: Sereny, Falconi, Morse, Laqueur, and Gilbert. The source for the quotation from the Vatican report submitted to the State Department is Morse, p. 22.

Chapter Thirteen

This chapter is based on Szmajzner's and Novitch's books and on my interviews with Szmajzner, Esther Raab, and Eda and Itzhak Lichtman.

Page 93: I have not been able to identify the German whom the Jews called "the Red Dumpling."

Chapter Fourteen

Pages 101–103: The Nazi games and the plan to poison the Germans, which I describe in this chapter, are based on the eyewitness accounts given in Novitch and in Rutkowski.

Page 103: Szmajzner told me that he could recall about ten suicides in Sobibor in the winter of 1942–1943.

Page 104: The official SS report I refer to is the Korherr report, quoted in full by Laqueur and others. Himmler commissioned the SS statistician on January 18, 1943, to provide an interim report on the Final Solution, which he submitted on March 23, 1943.

Page 104: For the U.S. delay in accepting the Allied Joint Declaration and the refusal of Pius XII to endorse it, see Laqueur, pp. 225–227; Morse, p. 29; and Gilbert, pp. 103–105.

Page 105: The account of Himmler's second visit to Sobibor is based on Szmajzner, Rueckerl, and Moshe Bahir's account in Novitch.

Pages 106–107: The material on the sick and the dispensary is based on my interviews with Josel.

Chapter Fifteen

This chapter is based almost exclusively on my interviews with Selma and Chaim Engel.

Page 108: For statistics about the Dutch whom the Nazis sent to Sobibor, see Louis de Jong. The Germans must have kept records of the nineteen trains that left Westerbork for Sobibor, since de Jong and others have listed the dates of all transports and the number of Jews on them.

Page 112: The details on how the Germans disposed of the goods they took from the Jews is taken from Léon Poliakov, *Harvest of Hate*, New York: Holocaust Library, 1979, pp. 77–82. See also Sereny, and Lucy Dawidowicz, *The War Against the Jews, 1933–1945*, New York: Holt, Rinehart & Winston, 1975. Thomas Blatt told me that the goods were taken from Sobibor and stored in Lublin. I assume they were either sold there or shipped elsewhere.

Page 116: Some Polish Jews are sensitive today about their mistrust of the Dutch Jews. Thomas Blatt, for example, seems to think that I have depicted the distrust too strongly. But others, like Szmajzner, Selma and Chaim Engel, and Esther Raab, have indicated that the distrust was strong for the reasons I have given in this chapter and elsewhere in this book.

Chapter Sixteen

The Toivi material in this chapter is based exclusively on my interviews with Thomas Blatt.

Page 122: On August 16, 1942, the SS Central Office for Economic Affairs and Administration issued the following order:

The Head of the SS Central Office for Economic Affairs and Administration, SS Group Leader Pohl, has ordered that care is to be taken to make use of the human hair collected in all concentration camps. This human hair is threaded on bobbins and converted into industrial felt. After being combed and cut, the women's hair can be manufactured into slippers for U-boat crews and felt stockings for the Reichsbahn.

(See Léon Poliakov and Josef Wulf, *The Third Reich and the Jews,* Paris: Gallimard, 1959, p. 67.)

Page 124: The escape attempt and the laying of the mines is based on my interviews with Szmajzner, Blatt, and Josel, as well as on Szmajzner's book and Rutkowski's article.

Chapter Seventeen

Page 126: The facts on the Warsaw ghetto uprising are principally taken from Poliakov, *Harvest of Hate,* pp. 229–242. The last message from the Jews of Warsaw is quoted from Gilbert, p. 131.

Page 127: Besides those listed in this chapter, Karski saw the following American writers and editors, among others: Mrs. Ogden Reid, publisher of the *New York Herald Tribune;* Walter L. Lippmann; George Sokolsky; Leon Denned, editor of the *American Mercury;* Eugene Lyons; Dorothy Thompson; William Prescott, of the *New York Times;* and Frederick Kuhl of the *Chicago Sun. Congressional Record,* December 15, 1981, E5847.

Pages 127–129: The account of Karski's visit to General Donovan is based exclusively on my interview with Karski. The account of his visit with Frankfurter is based on my interview with Karski, on his book, and on Laqueur. The account of Karski's visit to President Roosevelt is based on my interview with Karski, on his book, and on the published diary of Ambassador Jan Ciechenowski, *Defeat in Victory,* New York: Doubleday, 1947.

Page 129: For details on the Sweden plan, see Sereny, pp. 215–217. For details on the Bermuda Conference, see Laqueur, pp. 133–134; Gilbert, pp. 131–137; and Henry L. Reingold, *The Politics of Rescue,* New York: Holocaust Library, 1970, pp. 167–208.

Pages 130–131: The account of Karski's visit to Zygielbojm (whose wartime code name was Artur) is based on my interview with Karski, on his book, and on Laqueur. For background material on Zygielbojm, see Aviva Ravel, *Faithful Unto Death: The Story of Arthur Zygielbojm*, Montreal, published by Arthur Zygielbojm Branch of the Workman's Circle (undated). Zygielbojm's last letters are quoted from Ravel, pp. 178–180.

Chapter Eighteen

The Toivi material in this chapter is based exclusively on my interviews with Thomas Blatt.

Page 133: The full text of the Pohl-to-Himmler letter, dated July 15, 1943, is: "Following your order that the transit camp of Sobibor in the district of Lublin should be transformed into a concentration camp, I had a talk on the subject with SS Gruppenführer Globocnik. Your aim to install in Sobibor a depot for arms taken from the enemy can be achieved without transformation. We prefer that everything stays as before. Please let me know your answer, which is important for General Globocnik and myself." Quoted in Novitch, p. 30. If Himmler wrote an answer, the letter has not been found to date.

Pages 138–140: The Maidanek story is based on Szmajzner's book.

Chapter Nineteen

Page 143: I have reconstructed the thinking and character of Leon Feldhendler from my interviews with survivors, most of whom remember the son of the rabbi. According to Ainzstein, Feldhendler was writing his memoirs when the Poles murdered him in Lublin, in the summer of 1944. I have read three pages of Feldhendler's recollections, published in the Hebrew edition of Novitch, but the material was not very helpful.

Page 143: Szmajzner and Blatt do not believe that Feldhendler knew about the uprising in Treblinka because *they* didn't know about it. Rutkowski also argues that no one in Sobibor knew about Treblinka. But Pechersky insists that both he and Feldhendler knew. In a letter to Ainzstein, Pechersky said, "We knew about it, but we did not know the details."

There will always be some difference of opinion as to whether the Treblinka revolt or the Sobibor revolt was bigger and more successful. I do not wish to enter the debate. In Treblinka, the Jews got into the armory by making a key from a wax impression. They smuggled out hand grenades. On the day of the escape, they cut the electricity (the fences were electrified) and the telephone wires, and they burned down most of the camp. About 200 broke out, and about sixty survived the war. Very few Germans and guards were killed in the revolt. For years, the only basic account of the Treblinka escape was Jean-François Steiner, *Treblinka*, New York: Simon & Schuster, 1967. Historians now consider the book to be more of a novel than a nonfiction book. The best book on the topic is an anthology of eyewitness testimonies, *The Death Camp Treblinka,* ed., Alexander Donat, Holocaust Library, 1979.

Page 144: Most of the survivors I interviewed remembered vividly the killing of the Belzec Jews and the notes in their pockets. The texts of the notes, as recalled by survivors, can be found in Novitch.

Pages 144–145: The details of the three escape plans are based on Rutkowski, Blatt, Szmajzner, and Novitch.

Page 145: The story of the Chil partisan group's attempt to blow up the railroad to Sobibor comes from A. Shenko, "In a Jewish Division," *Yitzkor Memorial,* pp. 21–22. Shenko was an eyewitness. Blatt and others recall another incident when the weather was still cold. The Germans woke up the Jews in the middle of the night and made them stand in the yard. Blatt said that he learned later that a Russian partisan group had wandered close to the camp by accident and had set off a land mine. He recalls hearing the mine explode.

Page 147: Five Jews escaped from the Waldkommando and survived until the Russian liberation in July 1944 — Shlomo Podchlebnik, Josef Kopf, Zyndel Hoenigman, Simha Bialowitz, and Chaim Korenfeld. Kopf was murdered by Poles as he traveled by bike (he borrowed the bike from Blatt) to his village to reclaim his family's property.

Szmajzner makes several errors in his account of the escape. Podchlebnik and Kopf went to a village well for water, not to a stream in the woods. They offered the Ukrainian not diamonds, but a gold watch. And the other Jews did not know of the escape plan in advance. My basic source for the account of the escape itself comes from Chaim Korenfeld, whom Blatt interviewed for me in São Paulo, Brazil, and from Blatt, who had interviewed Podchlebnik and Kopf.

Page 148: The details about the murder of the Polish Jews in retaliation comes from my interviews with survivors, all of whom were eyewitnesses, and from Szmajzner's book and Moshe Bahir's account in Novitch. There is some disagreement as to whether Karl Frenzel or Johann Niemann gave the coup de grâce.

Page 148: The story of the whipping to death of Leon Blatt comes exclusively from my interview with Thomas Blatt (no relation to Leon).

Page 149: The Kapo escape plan is based on my interviews with Blatt and Josel, and on Szmajzner's book.

Chapters Twenty to Twenty-Three

These chapters are based primarily on my interviews with Alexander Pechersky and his own account, translated into Yiddish and published in 1946. I have checked most of his dates and names as carefully as I could and corrected those which needed changing.

Page 153: For more information on the Minsk ghetto as a center of resistance, see Lucien Steinberg, *Not As a Lamb: Jews Against Hitler,* trans., Marion Hunter, New York: Atheneum, 1974, Chap. 29.

Page 160: I am not positive that it was Drescher who saw Pechersky taking notes for his diary. But I assume it was the boy, because he was Feldhendler's courier.

Pages 161–164: Blatt and others treat with skepticism Pechersky's stories about his pouring out his soup after Zukerman's beating and his standing up to Frenzel. I was not able to verify Pechersky's accounts through other eyewitness accounts. However, I do not doubt that the stories are true.

Page 172: The Shlomo material is based on my interview with Szmajzner and on his book.

Page 176: No one is certain how many times the Organization met, or where, and who was present at each meeting. Here and in the rest of this section, I have pieced together the details of each meeting as best I could. I suspect there were more short conferences than I have described.

Chapter Twenty-Four

The Berliner incident is based on my interviews with Blatt, Josel, and Szmajzner, as well as on Szmajzner's book. After I had completed this manuscript, I found out that Philip (Fishel) Bialowitz is still alive and lives in New York. Although I spoke to him briefly on the phone, I did not interview him on the Berliner assassination.

Page 181: The song *"Es War Ein Edelweiss"* was one of the most popular marching songs in Sobibor. I found the text in an old Nazi songbook.

Chapters Twenty-Five to Thirty

These chapters are based primarily on my interviews with Alexander Pechersky and his own account of his days in Sobibor. I have changed names and dates when necessary.

Page 192: Esther Raab and Itzhak Lichtman recall Feldhendler leading the Yom Kippur prayers in a barracks. Several survivors told me that the Organization used the prayer service as a cover for another meeting. Esther could not recall that. Since I could not verify to my satisfaction that there was a meeting at the same time and in the same barracks, I did not include the account in the text.

Pages 199–200: The material about Selma's typhus and the sick prisoners comes from interviews with Selma and Chaim Engel and Josel.

Page 200: There is another version of Goetzinger's death, i.e., that he was killed accidentally in the North Camp when he picked up a Russian-made hand grenade, which exploded in his hand. My version comes from Esther Raab, who has good recall. Besides, Zelda Metz (who worked in the North Camp) would have told Esther about a grenade accident had there been one. She didn't.

Pages 207–208: How the various prisoners learned about the escape plan is based on my interviews with Esther Raab, Chaim Engel, Szmajzner, and on Szmajzner's book.

Pages 211–230: The Josel, Shlomo, Selma, and Chaim material is based on my interviews with these survivors.

Page 212: Pechersky wrote that he sent Boris, not Kalimali, to Camp II. But Blatt, who bunked in the same barracks as Kalimali, insisted he saw Kalimali come to Camp II. I trust Blatt's memory more than Pechersky's on this point.

Pages 215–216: The Toivi material and the account of the Joseph Wolf assassination is based on my interviews with Blatt and on his articles. I have found no eyewitnesses to the assassination itself.

Page 217: The account of the cutting of the telephone wires is based on my interviews with Josel.

Pages 219–223: The assassination of Niemann is based on my telephone interview with Yehuda Lerner (an eyewitness) and on Szmajzner's book; the Fallaster assassination is based on my interview with Itzhak Lichtman (an eyewitness) and on Pechersky's and Szmajzner's writings. I am not positive that it was Boris and Grisha who killed Fallaster; no one seems to be completely certain about who killed the Nazi. The assassinations of Greischutz and Klat I have pieced together from a variety of sources. I am reasonably certain that the two Russians who killed the German and the Ukrainian were Vaispapir and Rozenfeld. I was unable to contact Vaispapir when I was in the Soviet Union. Finally, I cannot verify the exact spelling of SS Sergeant Friedrich Gaulstich's name.

The Germans reported, on March 11, 1944, that eleven Germans were killed. I have verified six: Beckmann and Joseph Wolf (Camp II), and Niemann, Fallaster, Greischutz, and Gaulstich (Camp I). I have not been able to pin down with any degree of certainty the names of the other five or where they were killed. It is possible that some, if not all, were killed during the break-out itself. I decline to even list the names of the Germans who *may* have been killed lest that confuse an already confusing issue.

Page 223: There appears to be an inconsistency between Szmajzner's story about the ammunition and Pechersky's. When Pechersky searched the barracks, he found no bullets. Szmajzner did. I don't doubt either story. Szmajzner had more time inside the barracks. Perhaps he searched where Pechersky did not.

Pages 224–225: The Beckmann assassination account is based on my interview with Chaim Engel. I am certain that other Germans besides Beckmann and Wolf were killed in Camp II, but I was unable to verify my suspicion through eyewitness accounts.

Page 226: I am not certain who cut the electricity. Blatt and others believe it was Josef Dunietz. Some writers have stated that the Sobibor fences — if not all, then at least some — were electrified. I have not been able to verify that fact to my own satisfaction. Therefore, I have omitted it from the basic story.

Chapter Thirty-One

This chapter is based on the eyewitness accounts of Szmajzner, Pechersky, Blatt, Raab, Josel, Engel, and Lichtman, as well as on the writings of Szmajzner, Blatt, Pechersky, and Novitch.

Page 229: Several survivors, including Pechersky himself, recall Pechersky giving a last-minute speech. The quotation comes from Blatt.

Page 229: The Jacob incident in Camp II is based on my interview with Jacob Biskubicz.

Page 230: There is another version of the last words of the Ukrainian Albert Kaiser. According to some survivors, he was shouting, "Who took the guns?" or some such sentence. (See Novitch.) Those words do not seem logical to me.

The German report dated October 14, 1943, mentions that two guards were killed. The report could be referring to Klat and Kaiser. However, the document says they were *shot* to death. Klat and Kaiser were chopped or stabbed to death. I have seen estimates that as many as thirty Ukrainians were killed during the uprising and escape. The only two I can verify are the two I mention.

Page 230: According to another version, the Waldkommando was late in returning from the North Camp or from their work outside the camp; the revolt started while they were still in Camp II; the Waldkommando attacked the armory. That version does not seem consistent with the rest of the facts.

The attack on the armory is confusing. The Germans say in the October 15, 1943, report that the Jews "overpowered the guards, seized the armory, and, after an exchange of shots with the camp garrison, fled in unknown directions." Did the Jews actually seize the armory, as the German documents suggest? If they did, why didn't they use the machine guns stored inside? I suspect that they attacked the armory, but before they could enter, Frenzel opened fire with a machine gun and the Jews scattered. Perhaps the German report exaggerated to save face. Whatever the case, no one — Pechersky included — can verify that any Jew actually got inside the armory.

Chapters Thirty-Two to Thirty-Five

The Sasha chapter is based on my interviews with Pechersky and on his pamphlet. The Toivi chapter is based on my interviews with Blatt and on his articles. The Esther chapter is based on my interview with Esther Raab. The Shlomo chapter is based on my interviews with Szmajzner and on his book.

Page 238: Ainzstein is the source for the fact that it was Feldhendler who wanted to carry Leitman rather than let him shoot himself. I removed the word "Poles" from the original quote and replaced it with "Feldhendler" to avoid long explanations.

Chapter Thirty-Six

The material on Mietek's and Chil's partisans comes from my interviews with Samuel Gruber, who manages a hotel in New York; from his book as told to Gertrude Hirschler, *I Chose Life,* New York: Shengold, 1978; from the *Yizkor Book in Memory of Wlodawa and the Region of Sobibor;* and from Shmuel Krakowski, *The War of the Doomed,* trans. from the Yiddish by Orah Blaustein (in manuscript form).

Page 275: The Home Army was not a static or homogeneous organization. It was a growing coalition of underground organizations or military units affiliated with the various pre–World War II political parties. One by one, between 1939 and 1944, these organizations were incorporated into the Union for Armed Struggle, later called the Home Army. Among them were: the Peasant Battalions, the Peasant Party, the National Military Organization, the Socialist Fighting Organization, the Camp of Fighting Poland, the units founded by Komorowski and Rudnicki, the Secret Polish Army, Unia, the Union for Military Action, Raclawice, the Polish Military Organization, the Freedom and People Union, the Armed Confederacy, the Association of Reserve Noncommissioned Officers, the Secret Military Organization, and some units of the National Armed Forces (NSZ). These NSZ units were bitterly anti-Semitic.

Several organizations refused to join the Home Army: the Polish People's Army, the Communist People's Army, and the rest of the NSZ units, which were also violently anti-Semitic.

When the Jews report killings by Polish partisans, therefore, it is frequently difficult to determine whether the assassins were members of the Home Army (AK) or of the independent NSZ.

Page 276: Order #116, issued by AK Commander Bor-Komorowski on September 15, 1943, states:

> Well-armed groups ramble endlessly in cities and villages, attack estates, banks, commercial and industrial companies, houses, and large farms. The plunder is often accompanied by acts of murder, which are carried out by Soviet partisan units hiding in the forests or ordinary gangs of robbers. Men and women, especially Jewish women, participate in the assaults . . . I have issued an order to the region and area commanders to go out with arms, when necessary, against these plunderers or revolutionary robbers.

Quoted from Krakowski, who argues convincingly that AK units took this order as an excuse to kill Jewish partisans.

Page 277 and following: According to some reports, which I was unable to verify, Greenshpan was a hero with warts. He allegedly refused to accept all the Jews who came to him, allegedly keeping some away by firing at them or threatening to kill them. Because I could not verify these reports, I did not include them in the text itself.

Greenshpan is still alive, living in Brazil, reports to the contrary notwithstanding. Gruber told me he still corresponds with his old friend. Unfortunately, I learned

of Greenshpan's whereabouts after I had returned from Brazil. I have made no attempt to interview him.

Pages 277–279: I have tried to piece together from interviews and other written accounts (Novitch, Gruber, Karakowski) who escaped with whom from Sobibor and who joined Greenshpan with whom. If I have erred, it is not in the case of who found the partisans, but which of their companions did not. Gruber speaks of a Dutch Jew from Sobibor in the Mietek-Chil group by the name of Ruth. According to Gruber, she died before liberation. I have not been able to trace her identity.

Most of the Sobibor survivors I interviewed were reluctant to talk about their activity with the partisans, which is why material about them in this chapter is slim.

Chapters Thirty-Seven to Forty-Three

Page 280: The Selma and Chaim chapter is based exclusively on my interviews with Selma and Chaim Engel.

Page 312: The Stangl escape story is based on Stangl's own account to Sereny.

Page 351: The Rozenfeld material comes from Yuri Suhl, *They Fought Back*, pp. 45–46. Suhl took the material from a 1963 issue of *Sovietisch Heimland*.